Windows® 2000 Routing and Remote Access Service

New Riders

Other Books by New Riders Publishing

Windows NT Power Toolkit
Stu Sjouwerman and Ed Tittel,
0-7357-0922-X

Planning for Windows 2000
Eric Cone, Jon Boggs, and Sergio Perez,
0-7357-0048-6

Windows NT DNS
Michael Masterson, Herman Kneif, Scott
Vinick, and Eric Roul, 1-56205-943-2

Windows NT Network Management:
Reducing Total Cost of Ownership
Anil Desai, 1-56205-946-7

Windows NT Performance
Monitoring, Benchmarking and Tuning
Mark Edmead and Paul Hinsburg,
1-56205-942-4

Windows NT Registry: A Settings
Reference
Sandra Osborne, 1-56205-941-6

Windows NT TCP/IP
Karanjit Siyan, 1-56205-887-8

Windows NT Terminal Server & Citrix
MetaFrame
Ted Harwood, 1-56205-944-0

Cisco Router Configuration &
Troubleshooting
Mark Tripod, 0-7357-0024-9

Exchange System Administration
Janice Rice Howd, 0-7357-0081-8

Implementing Exchange Server
Doug Hauger, Marywynne Leon, and
William C. Wade III, 1-56205-931-9

Network Intrusion Detection:
An Analyst's Handbook
Stephen Northcutt, 0-7357-0868-1

Understanding Data Communications,
Sixth Ed.
Gilbert Held, 0-7357-0036-2

SQL Server System Administration
Sean Baird, Chris Miller, et al.,
1-56205-955-6

Domino System Administration
Rob Kirkland, 1-56205-948-3

Understanding Directory Services
Beth & Doug Sheresh, 0-7357-0910-6

Understanding the Network:
A Practical Guide to Internetworking
Michael Martin, 0-7357-0977-7

Internet Information Services
Administration
Kelli Adam, 0-7357-0022-2

Inside Windows 2000 Server
William Boswell, 1-56205-929-7

Windows 2000 Active Directory
Edgar Brovick, Doug Hauger,
William C. Wade III, 0-7357-0870-3

SMS 2 Administration
Michael Lubanski and Darshan Doshi,
0-7357-0082-6

Windows® 2000 Routing and Remote Access Service

New
Riders

201 West 103rd Street,
Indianapolis, Indiana 46290

Kackie Charles

Windows® 2000 Routing and Remote Access Service

Copyright © 2000 by New Riders Publishing

FIRST EDITION: *May 2000*

All rights reserved. No part of this book may be reproduced or transmitted in any form or by any means, electronic or mechanical, including photocopying, recording, or by any information storage and retrieval system, without written permission from the publisher, except for the inclusion of brief quotations in a review.

International Standard Book Number: 0-7357-0951-3

Library of Congress Catalog Card Number: 00-100405

04 03 02 01 00   7 6 5 4 3 2 1

Interpretation of the printing code: The rightmost double-digit number is the year of the book's printing; the rightmost single-digit number is the number of the book's printing. For example, the printing code 00-1 shows that the first printing of the book occurred in 2000.

Composed in Quark and MCPdigital by New Riders Publishing

Printed in the United States of America

Trademarks

All terms mentioned in this book that are known to be trademarks or service marks have been appropriately capitalized. New Riders Publishing cannot attest to the accuracy of this information. Use of a term in this book should not be regarded as affecting the validity of any trademark or service mark. Windows is a registered trademark of Microsoft Corporation.

Warning and Disclaimer

Every effort has been made to make this book as complete and as accurate as possible, but no warranty or fitness is implied.

The information is provided on an as-is basis. The authors and New Riders Publishing shall have neither liability nor responsibility to any person or entity with respect to any loss or damages arising from the information contained in this book or from the use of the discs or programs that may accompany it.

Publisher
David Dwyer

Associate Publisher
Brad Koch

Executive Editor
Al Valvano

Managing Editor
Gina Brown

Product Marketing Manager
Stephanie Layton

Acquisitions Editor
Theresa Gheen

Development Editor
Katherine Pendergast

Project Editor
Elise Walter

Copy Editor
Lunaea Hougland

Indexer
Tim Wright

Manufacturing Coordinators
Chris Moos
Jim Conway

Book Designer
Louisa Klucznik

Cover Designer
Aren Howell

Proofreader
Debbie Williams

Composition
Amy Parker

Contents

I Installation and Configuration   1

1 Overview, Features, and Benefits   3
Remote Access Components   4
Routing Components   6
Other Features   8
Summary   9

2 Remote Access Server   11
RAS Overview   12
Authentication and Authorization   21
User Access Configuration   39
Summary   46
References   46

3 Dial-Up Networking   47
Dial-Up Networking Overview   47
Hardware Installation   53
Configure Dialing Parameters   56
Configuring a Dial-Up Connection   59
Incoming Connections   64
Summary   66
References   66

4 Routing Protocols   67
Routing Concepts   69
Unicast Routing   73
Multicasting   74
IP Routing   78
Other Routing Protocols   109
Demand-Dial Routing   113
Summary   118
References   119

5   Configuring the Windows 2000 Router   121
Configuration Basics   121
IP Routing   125
IPX Routing   139
Demand–Dial Routing   143
AppleTalk Routing   153
Filtering   154
Conclusion   156

II   Advanced Administration   157

6   Routing Tools   159
Netsh   159
mrinfo   166
pathping   167
Scheduling Tools   169

7   Virtual Private Networks   173
VPN Defined   174
New Features of Windows 2000 VPNs   175
Anatomy of a VPN Connection   176
Types of VPNs   178
VPN Tunneling Protocols   180
VPN Routing   185
VPNs and Firewalls   189
VPN Configuration   191
References   212

8   Windows 2000 Connection Services   213
Connection Point Services   214
Connection Manager   219
References   228

9   Internet Authentication Service   229
Overview of IAS   229
Planning Your IAS Deployment   233
Installation and Configuration   236

IAS Scenarios   242
References   243

III   RRAS Planning   245

10   Bandwidth and Telecommunications   247
Bandwidth and Usage Statistics   248
Telecommunication Services   254
References   259

11   Shared Internet Connectivity   261
Network Address Translation Protocol   262
Internet Connection Sharing   270
References   273

12   Network Design   275
Small Office/Home Office Networks   276
Medium-sized Networks   279
Large Networks   282
References   284

IV   Appendixes   287

A   Technical Overview of RAS Communications   289
Windows 2000 Security   290
Internet Protocol Security   297
References   312

B   Troubleshooting   313
Remote Access Server and Dial-Up Networking   314
Virtual Private Networks (VPNs)   317
Routing Problems   319
Demand-Dial Routing   323

C   Glossary   327

Index   341

About the Author

Kackie Charles, MCSE, MCT, has been working with Windows NT since 1995, and has been Microsoft certified since 1996. Kackie was the principal instructor at New Horizons Computer Learning Center from 1995 to 1998, and joined Unisys Corporation as a network design engineer in 1998, where she was an enterprise architect for the Navy Standard Personnel System program. Kackie was recognized for her work on NSIPS by the Naval Reserve Information Systems Office and was presented with the Unisys Award for Excellence. In 1999, Kackie started Kackie Charles Systems Engineering, through which she actively supported the NSIPS program as part of the Systems Engineering/Deployment group. As part of this team, she supported the implementation of NSIPS software on over 400 servers and over 4000 workstations worldwide. In March 2000, Kackie joined Woosh! in Palo Alto, CA, as an IT Specialist.

Kackie is the technical editor of *The Complete Idiot's Guide to Networking* and *Teach Yourself Windows Networking in 24 Hours, Second Edition*.

About the Technical Reviewers

These reviewers contributed their considerable hands-on expertise to the entire development process for *Windows 2000 Routing and Remote Access Service*. As the book was being written, these dedicated professionals reviewed all the material for technical content, organization, and flow. Their feedback was critical to ensuring that *Windows 2000 Routing and Remote Access Service* fits our reader's need for the highest quality technical information.

Chris Lowe is a Senior Technical Consultant with Aspect Computing Pty. Ltd. (http://www.aspect.com.au). With over 10 years of industry experience, he specializes in Windows NT 4.0 Server and Workstation, Internetworking technologies, and integration with NetWare environments. Chris holds a B.A. in computing, an associate's degree in applied computing, and is also a Microsoft Certified Systems Engineer. Chris lives in Canberra, Australia, and can be contacted via email at chris.lowe@aspect.com.au.

John McCabe is an MCSE and Senior Consultant for DeCarlo Schmitt Associates, part of the DSA Group. He specializes in Windows NT and Windows 2000, SMS, and Internet technologies, primarily focusing on the financial industry. He has been an active Microsoft Consultant for 4 years, working with Windows 2000 beta releases since the summer of 1998.

Mary McLaughlin, MCSE+1, MCT, ASE, ACT, lives in the Boston area with her beloved daughter, Margaret. She started as a systems administrator 10 years ago and she has worked consistently on small- to medium-sized LANs and WANs for profit and non-profit organizations. In the past five years, her focus has been training individuals in Windows 2000, Windows NT, and Compaq Technologies. Currently, she is involved in security solutions, such as firewall, Virtual Private Network (VPN) and public key infrastructure (PKI) technologies. Mary has a B.A. in economics, summa cum laude.

This book is dedicated to six very special people:
Greg—You are the center of my universe.

Melissa—Here's to another 18 great years.

Mom and Dad—Thanks for everything. I wouldn't be here
without your love and support.

Grammie and Bumpaw—I love you and miss you.
Thanks for rooting for me!

Acknowledgments

This book would not have been possible without the help of some really great people. Thanks to everyone at New Riders—especially Al Valvano, Katie Pendergast, Theresa Gheen, Elise Walter, Lunaea Hougland, and Lisa Thibault for keeping my panic attacks at bay and my rambling thoughts in order. Thanks also goes to technical editors Chris Lowe, Mary McLaughlin, and John McCabe, for their advice, encouragement, and for keeping this book in the realm of non-fiction.

Hats off to the entire NSIPS Team, particularly the Deployment Group. Special thanks to Mike Stankewicz, Billie Jo Free, and Jim Welborn for picking up my slack while I was working on this book, Rob Tillman for letting me pester him with hundreds of security questions, Al Hughey for hiring me (Go Hogs!), and Tony Barnes for letting me stick around. It was a pleasure working with the entire team and I wish you all the best. Thanks to Tim Boots for teaching me everything I know (and for his extraordinary patience). No one could have a better mentor! Gary Winker gave me a great job and a fantastic opportunity—Thanks so much. Melissa Izor was the hostess of some fabulous work parties and I thank her for that (and everything else). I have two words for you: Costa Rica! Hugs and kisses to Mom and Dad for hosting Command Central for a while. Thanks to Angie, Cory, Tim, and Dillon for special help on Chapter Five. Cory and Turbo get special kudos for keeping me company all hours of the day and night. Buckets of thanks to Harriette and Gary for cheering me on. Thanks to The Group (Andrew, Katie, Jack, Michele, Patrick, and Cindy) for the moral support—see you in Park City! Note to Warren Knight—I thought when this was over we could get back on track with Telecom Group, but it looks like we will have to move things west. Thanks for all your advice, ideas, and encouragement! To my neighbors on Berclair—thanks and I miss you already!

Saving the best for last, I would like to express my eternal love and gratitude to my husband/hero Greg who took such good care of me while I was engrossed in this enormous project. Without his love, support, motivational speeches, countless trips to PJ's, fabulous cooking, and patience while I counted out my drawers, I would not have survived the last 9 months (or the 5 fantastic years preceding that). I can honestly say he worked as hard as I did. Thanks for PM5 and moving to Silicon Valley.

Tell Us What You Think

As the reader of this book, you are the most important critic and commentator. We value your opinion and want to know what we're doing right, what we could do better, what areas you'd like to see us publish in, and any other words of wisdom you're willing to pass our way.

As the Executive Editor for the Networking team at New Riders Publishing/MTP, I welcome your comments. You can fax, email, or write me directly to let me know what you did or didn't like about this book—as well as what we can do to make our books stronger.

Please note that I cannot help you with technical problems related to the topic of this book, and that due to the high volume of mail I receive, I might not be able to reply to every message.

When you write, please be sure to include this book's title and author as well as your name and phone or fax number. I will carefully review your comments and share them with the author and editors who worked on the book.

Fax: 317-581-4663

Email: nrfeedback@newriders.com

Mail: Al Valvano
Executive Editor
New Riders Publishing
201 West 103rd Street
Indianapolis, IN 46290 USA

Introduction

Welcome to *Windows 2000 Routing and Remote Access Service*. This book was written to help you use Windows 2000 to connect your networks and users in a variety of ways. The Routing and Remote Access Service (RRAS) has many exciting new features that can be easily integrated into new or existing networks. After you have discovered what those features are and what they do, this book will guide you in the implementation of those features.

Who This Book Is For

Windows 2000 Routing and Remote Access Service is for the experienced administrator. The reader is assumed to have some knowledge of TCP/IP, Windows NT domains, and the Active Directory. Administrators of all sizes of networks will find the information presented in this book to be helpful in the planning and implementation of RRAS. Readers with experience in large routed networks or at Internet Service Providers (ISPs) will find this book particularly informative.

What's in This Book

Windows 2000 Routing and Remote Access Service is divided into three sections. The first section covers the setup of routing, remote access, and dial-up networking. The second section covers advanced administration tools and other features that complement RRAS including Virtual Private Networks (VPNs) and Internet Authentication Service (IAS), as well as bandwidth, telecommunications and design issues. The final section includes information about security, troubleshooting, and a glossary.

Part I: Installation and Configuration

This section includes the necessary information to install and configure remote access service, dial-up networking, and routing. Chapter 1, "Overview, Features, and Benefits," provides a broad look at the new features and benefits of using Windows 2000 Routing and Remote Access Service. The remote access components and routing components are covered independently in this section. Chapter 2, "Remote Access Server," delves into the remote access service, its setup, and the authentication methods available with Windows 2000. Chapter 3, "Dial-Up Networking," provides coverage of dial-up networking—the client end of the remote access service. Modem installation and connection configuration are discussed here. Chapter 4, "Routing Protocols," is a discussion of routing protocols included with Windows 2000; and Chapter 5, "Configuring the Windows 2000 Router," demonstrates how to configure the Windows 2000 router.

Part II: Advanced Administration

The second section discusses other administrative tools and features of Windows 2000 RRAS and wraps up with a look at some RRAS design scenarios. Chapter 6, "Routing Tools," provides information on command-line administration of RRAS and various other management utilities included with Windows 2000. Virtual Private Networking is covered in Chapter 7, "Virtual Private Newtorking." This chapter provides general information about VPNs as well as information specific to Windows 2000 VPNs. Chapter 8, "Windows 2000 Connection Services," shows you how to create, manage and distribute phonebooks to remote users. The Internet Authentication Service is discussed in Chapter 9, "Internet Authentication Service." IAS is the Microsoft RFC-compliant RADIUS server. Bandwidth and telecommunications are covered in Chapter 10, "Bandwidth and Telecommunications." This chapter shows you how Windows 2000 can help you make the most of your available bandwidth. A variety of telecommunications services are discussed as well. Chapter 11, "Shared Internet Connectivity," focuses on connecting your network to the Internet using Windows 2000. The section wraps up with Chapter 12, "Network Design," a look at various RRAS design options for networks of various sizes.

Part III: Appendixes

Section three is composed of three appendixes. Appendix A, "Technical Overview of RAS Communications," presents some of the security features in Windows 2000 and provides instructions for the configuration of (IPSec) Internet Protocol Security. Appendix B, "Troubleshooting," is a troubleshooting guide that will help you solve common RRAS problems. And finally, Appendix C, "Glossary," is a glossary of terms related to RRAS.

How to Use This Book

Administrators with less experience with routing and remote access will find it helpful to read the first section from start to finish. More experienced administrators might prefer to use the table of contents and index to target the specific topics that interest them. The second section will be of interest to all administrators. This section is a guide to what other things can be done with RRAS. A good approach to this section is to scan the chapters to get an overview of what each of the features does and then go back over the chapters of interest for more of a detailed look. The final section is designed as a reference tool. You can flip back and forth to it to look up the definition of terms or acronyms, or scan through the troubleshooting and security appendices for topics of interest.

The author welcomes any comments you have regarding the book. She can be reached at author@kcse.net.

I

Installation and Configuration

1 Overview, Features, Benefits

2 Remote Access Server

3 Dial-Up Networking

4 Routing Protocols

5 Configuring the Windows 2000 Router

1

Overview, Features, and Benefits

WITH THE ADVENT OF WINDOWS 2000, Microsoft is introducing its most feature-rich version of the Routing and Remote Access Service (RRAS) to date. It combines the functionality of past versions of the multiprotocol router and the remote access service (RAS) included with past versions of Windows NT. It also adds a number of enhancements, including wizards to assist with the configuration process and new security features. The rationale for combining the multiprotocol router with the remote access service into a single service is the Point-to-Point Protocol (PPP). PPP is used to negotiate and establish the point-to-point dial-up connections used with RAS, and the demand-dial routing capabilities included with Windows 2000. Microsoft determined that it made perfect sense to join these two services on that basis—and indeed it does. The Routing and Remote Access Service provides the administrator with a unified tool that can be used in any size network, from a two-computer small office/home office (SOHO) network to a network containing thousands of workstations in several different locations.

More and more companies have workers who telecommute. In addition, there is a huge movement toward the creation of extranets, in which companies allow their partners and customers to have access to or join their resources with the corporate resources of the primary company. These types of business arrangements are becoming more and more common. Many solutions that have been implemented to allow remote access or join different networks utilize tools from several different vendors.

With Windows 2000 Routing and Remote Access Service, administrators will only need one tool to fufill all their routing, remote access, and Virtual Private Network (VPN) needs.

This chapter is intended as a high-level overview of the features of the Routing and Remote Access Service. The following chapters will present detailed information about various components as well as configuration of the service. Pointers throughout this chapter will direct you to other chapters where you can find additional information about a particular topic. Because the remote access service component is the feature with which most administrators are familiar, we will start there. We will work our way through the routing component next, and wrap up the chapter with a look at some of the other features of Windows 2000 that further enhance the Routing and Remote Access Service.

Remote Access Components

Windows 2000 remote access is a dream to implement. It can be used with a variety of connectivity options, from standard dial-up and ISDN lines to high-speed connections, such as frame relay. Chapter 2, "Remote Access Server," will cover the specifics of the server side of remote access. Chapter 3, "Dial-Up Networking," will cover the client side. This section will walk you through the remote access features in Windows 2000, including:

- Demand-dial routing
- A comprehensive suite of authentication protocols
- Data encryption
- Point-to-point tunneling, including VPN capability
- Efficient bandwidth utilization
- Wizard-based configuration
- Security and policies
- Authentication, authorization, and accounting
- Internet Connection Sharing

Demand-Dial Routing

Using demand-dial routing can help reduce the cost of wide area network (WAN)-based network communication. If a particular WAN circuit in your network is used frequently, but not constantly, you might want to implement demand-dial routing over that link. When the router on one side of the circuit receives a packet destined for the remote network on the other side of the circuit, it will dial the other router and transmit the data. Because the WAN link is used only on an as-needed basis, and can be configured to disconnect after a predefined period of inactivity, usage costs associated with a dedicated circuit can be reduced.

Authentication Protocols

Windows 2000 supports a wide range of authentication protocols, enabling you to extend your remote access service to a variety of client types. Included protocols are:

- Password Authentication Protocol (PAP)
- Shiva-PAP (SPAP)
- Challenge Handshake Authentication Protocol (CHAP)
- Microsoft Challenge Handshake Authentication Protocol (MS-CHAP), versions 1 and 2
- Extensible Authentication Protocol (EAP), including EAP-TLS and EAP-MD5
- Remote Authentication Dial-In User Service (RADIUS)

Data Encryption

The Routing and Remote Access Service provides strong link encryption methods suitable for use in North America and countries not on the US embargo list, as well as methods that meet encryption export restrictions.

Point-to-Point Tunneling

Windows 2000 supports tunneling using Point-to-Point Tunneling Protocol (PPTP) and Layer 2 Tunneling Protocol (L2TP). Both of these tunneling methods can be used as VPN solutions on a client/server or server/server basis (see Chapter 7, "Virtual Private Networking," for more information). This is a definite benefit over other commercially available VPN solutions that only support client/server tunnels.

Efficient Bandwidth Utilization

In addition to demand-dial routing, the Routing and Remote Access Service supports these other bandwidth-saving features: Multilink with Bandwidth Allocation Protocol (BAP), and RAS Idle Disconnect. Multilink is an RFC-compliant method of bundling multiple WAN links to create a larger-bandwidth virtual channel. BAP builds on the Multilink capability by dynamically adding or dropping additional lines as needed. RAS Idle Disconnect can be used to free up WAN links when utilization falls below an administratively set level based on idle time or amount of bandwidth used (see Chapter 10, "Bandwidth and Telecommunication," for more information).

Wizards

The Routing and Remote Access Service uses a series of wizards to make it easy to configure various components of the service, including remote access. Although it is possible to configure the components directly, the wizards are a tremendous help when initially configuring the service, providing tips and hints on usage and configuration parameters.

Security and Policies

The security features of the Routing and Remote Access Service include the capability to use smart cards for remote client access. Access also can be controlled by policies, which prohibit or grant access based on parameters, such as Windows 2000 group membership or time of day. (See Chapter 2 for details on enabling smart card support and creating remote access policies.)

Authentication, Authorization, and Accounting

Authentication refers to the process of validating a user's identification. Authorization refers to the process of determining whether a user has access permission. Accounting refers to the process of tracking usage of a particular service, such as a remote access server. There are two authentication and authorization providers available for remote access users: the Windows 2000 accounts database or a RADIUS server, such as the Internet Authentication Service (IAS), included in Windows 2000. (Chapter 2 provides a discussion on authentication versus authorization. For more information on RADIUS and IAS, see Chapter 9, "Internet Authentication Service"). IAS can be used to provide accounting services as well.

Internet Connection Sharing

Through dial-up networking, users can share a single connection to the Internet with other computers in the network. This is an ideal way to grant Internet access to several computers in a SOHO network (see Chapter 11, "Shared Internet Connectivity," for more information).

Routing Components

The Windows 2000 router is a fully functional multiprotocol router. It provides a cost-effective alternative to other routing products available on the market today. Windows 2000 is compatible with a wide range of local area network (LAN) and WAN adapters, meaning that your current Windows infrastructure will most likely be supported. It is an open and extensible platform—third-party software or hardware vendors can write their own custom solutions to integrate in the Routing and Remote Access Service. In addition to these features, a wide array of routing protocols is supported, including:

- RIP for IP, versions 1 and 2
- OSPF
- DHCP relay agent
- IP multicast routing

- RIP and SAP for IPX
- AppleTalk routing
- Network Address Translation

This section will present a brief overview of these protocols. You will find more information on these subjects in Chapter 4, "Routing Protocols," and Chapter 5, "Configuring the Windows 2000 Router."

RIP for IP, Versions 1 and 2

Routing Information Protocol (RIP) is a routing protocol that's ideal for use in small-to medium-sized networks. RIP is a distance vector routing protocol. Distance vector routing uses the Bellman-Ford algorithm. Each router keeps a routing table with one entry for every possible destination in the system. RIP routers share their route information in RIP-routed environments by means of announcements. Windows 2000 RIP is easily configured and is interoperable with other vendors' routers running RIP. Because of the manner in which routing information is announced throughout a RIP environment, however, it is unsuitable for use in large routed networks.

Open Shortest Path First

Windows 2000 Open Shortest Path First (OSPF) is an RFC-compliant link-state IP routing protocol. It was developed in concert between Microsoft and Bay Networks. OSPF is more efficient than RIP in large routed networks because it uses Dijkstra's algorithm to compute the best route to a destination. This algorithm analyzes the network topology as recorded in the link-state database in each router to determine the least-cost route. OSPF also eliminates the problems of loops that can occur in RIP-routed networks.

DHCP Relay Agent

The DHCP (Dynamic Host Configuration Protocol) relay agent enables a single DHCP server to service networks to which it is not directly connected. DHCP traffic is not typically passed over routers, which means a DHCP client must be on the same network as a DHCP server to take advantage of the dynamic addressing capability of DHCP. The agent listens for DHCP client traffic and forwards this traffic to the DHCP server.

IP Multicasting

The Windows 2000 router supports multicast forwarding and a limited version of multicast routing. In IP multicasting, hosts use the Internet Group Management Protocol (IGMP) to indicate to IP routers they are listening for IP multicast traffic on a specific IP multicast address. A multicast router forwards multicast traffic to those networks where hosts have indicated they are listening for such traffic. All Windows 2000 computers are IP multicast-capable and can both send and receive IP multicast traffic.

RIP and SAP for IPX

Novell NetWare networks typically use Internetwork Packet Exchange (IPX) as their primary LAN protocol. The Routing and Remote Access Service enables you to successfully implement a Windows 2000 router in such an environment. RIP for IPX is used to broadcast IPX network routes to other routers. The Service Advertising Protocol (SAP) enables hosts that provide services to other hosts (file and print servers, for example) to advertise their addresses and the services they are providing.

AppleTalk Routing

It is possible to integrate a Windows 2000 router into an AppleTalk network. The Routing and Remote Access Service supports AppleTalk seed routing, and enables Macintosh networks to be connected to each other without requiring additional client software.

Other Features

There are several other Windows 2000 features that enhance the Routing and Remote Access Service, including:

- Internet Authentication Service, an RFC-compliant RADIUS server
- Virtual Private Networking
- Connection Manager Administration Kit

Internet Authentication Service

Internet Authentication Service (IAS) provides central administration of authentication, authorization, and accounting of users. It can be used to effectively manage remote user access from a central database, rather than from several separate servers. One IAS strategy you can implement uses IAS in conjunction with outsourcing remote user dial-up access to other providers, such as an ISP. Chapter 9 explains how this strategy can free you from having to maintain banks of modems and expensive dial-up lines.

Virtual Private Networking

A Virtual Private Network (VPN) enables remote users or an entire remote network to access the corporate intranet. The VPN connection is a tunneled and encrypted means of securely sending private data over a public network such as the Internet. A VPN also can be used over a private network to provide an extra level of security to data traveling within the corporate intranet. Windows 2000 supports PPTP using Microsoft Point-to-Point Encryption (MPPE) and L2TP using Internet Protocol Security (IPSec). See Chapter 7 for details on the function and configuration of VPNs.

Connection Manager Services

Connection Manager is an application that performs client dialing and connection services. Two components included in Windows 2000 enable you to effectively deploy the Connection Manager to your remote users. The first, Connection Manager Administration Kit (CMAK), enables you to give your remote users a custom dial-up networking phone book within the Connection Manager. The customized Connection Manager dialer can include various Point of Presence (POP) access numbers. The dialer can automatically launch specific applications before or after dialing a remote access connection. A second component of the Connection Manager service is the Connection Point Service. This service runs on a Windows 2000 server and provides updated phone book information to remote clients that have been configured for this service. See Chapter 8, "Windows 2000 Connection Services," for more details on these great features.

Summary

As you can see, the Windows 2000 Routing and Remote Access Service is a powerful product. The number of ways in which this service can be integrated into existing networks, as well as its use as a building block for creating new networks, is virtually unlimited. RRAS takes advantage of current connectivity methods and is extensible as well—new solutions for new technologies can easily be developed and implemented. Additionally, it can take the place of several third-party products you might have been considering implementing in your network, resulting in potentially substantial cost savings. As you go through the rest of this book, you will see how the Windows 2000 Routing and Remote Access Service is easy to configure and consequently easy to implement in a network of any size and/or configuration.

2

Remote Access Server

Windows 2000 offers a feature-rich remote access server (RAS) that gives remote clients the capability to connect to a private network, intranet, or the Internet. Windows 2000 RAS is an open and extensible remote access platform based on industry standards, such as PPP, TCP/IP, and IPX. APIs are available for developers to create management tools or snap-ins to support other protocols that RAS doesn't support out of the box.

The RAS client and server software is fully integrated into the Windows 2000 operating system so you can easily set up a remote access system for your users. You have the choice of allowing users connecting to the remote access server to access resources only on that server or resources in the rest of the network as well. RAS server-only access is called *point-to-point remote access connectivity*, and access to the entire remote network is called *point-to-LAN remote access connectivity*. Users can access resources as if they were a node on the LAN to which they are connecting.

RAS Overview

The Windows 2000 RAS provides three different types of remote access connectivity for clients:

- Dial-up networking (DUN)
- Virtual Private Network (VPN)
- Direct serial or infrared connections

Chapter 3, "Dial-Up Networking," will cover the client side of DUN in detail, and Chapter 7, "Virtual Private Networking," will cover both the client and server sides of VPN. This chapter focuses on the server implementation of RAS—the remote access components, their functions, and how to install and configure them.

A computer running Windows 2000 Professional can accept up to three incoming calls, but no more than one of each of the types listed. On a Windows 2000 server, the number of inbound calls is limited only by the hardware configuration of the computer. This is an improvement on previous versions of Windows NT, which limited simultaneous inbound connections to 256 on the server and one on the workstation.

Remote Access Is Not Remote Control

Before we talk about what RAS is and does, let's talk about what RAS is not. Remote access services are not the same thing as, and should not be confused with, remote control software, such as pcANYWHERE. RAS is a software connection solution that provides connecting users with access to resources on remote networks. A multiprotocol router forwards the inbound traffic from the server that accepts the incoming call to resources on the remote network.

Remote control software, on the other hand, is designed to allow remote users to run applications and use the server's CPU, keyboard, mouse, and so on over a remote connection. Remote control software is a great way to remotely troubleshoot a computer because it provides the illusion that you are actually sitting in front of the remote computer. If you want to provide a means for remote users to access resources on the corporate network while they are out on the road, however, RAS may be a better choice for several reasons.

- First, it is included with Windows 2000, so you don't have to buy another piece of software.
- Second, it is designed to handle communications for multiple users better than remote control solutions.
- Finally, it enables your users to access needed resources remotely while protecting the network with Windows 2000 security.

Remote Access Server Architecture

We will begin our examination of the Windows 2000 RAS with a look at the technical architecture of the service. Figure 2.1 is a diagram of the components of a RAS. An explanation of each of the components follows the diagram.

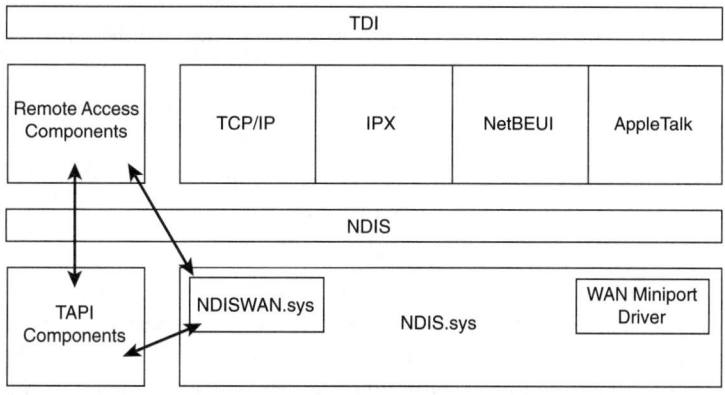

Figure 2.1   Remote access server architecture.

- **LAN protocols.**   TCP/IP, IPX, NetBEUI, and AppleTalk are supported by the Windows RAS.

- **Remote access components.**   These RAS APIs provide the interface for RAS applications, link control protocols, authentication protocols, network control protocols, and remote access protocols. The remote access components provide these services by communicating with either NDISWAN.sys or TAPI (Telephone API), as shown in the diagram.

- **TAPI components.**   These APIs provide call-control for all TAPI-aware applications. TAPI components communicate with the NDISWAN driver to provide connection management.

- **NDIS.sys.**   This interface provides a Network Driver Interface Specification (NDIS) wrapper interface to supported network protocols.

- **NDISWAN.sys.**   This interface provides both an IEEE 802.3 miniport interface to LAN protocol drivers and a LAN protocol interface to WAN miniport drivers. Remote access connections get packet framing, compression, and encryption from this driver.

- **WAN miniport driver.**   There is one WAN miniport driver for each physical dial-up device.

A single adapter called the *RAS server interface* represents all inbound connections to the RAS. A separate interface is created for each outbound connection initiated by the remote access server.

Certain events occur to establish a session between the remote client and the RAS server:

1. The client requests a connection from the server. This request is received by the RAS components, which pass the call connection information to the TAPI components.

2. TAPI sends connection information to the telephony devices, such as modems or ISDN adapters.

3. RAS components negotiate the PPP connection directly with NDISWAN.sys. The RAS components determine which link, authentication, and network control protocols are to be used for this connection.

After the connection is established, NDISWAN.sys can receive requests from the LAN protocol drivers. The job of NDISWAN.sys is to decide the appropriate device and port to be used for this connection. It then compresses and encrypts data and forwards the complete PPP frame to the WAN miniport driver. The WAN miniport driver forwards the frame to the dial-up adapter.

Now that the remote access connection is established and functional, the remote client can access resources on the RAS or on hosts beyond the RAS on a remote network. If the latter scenario is the case, the RAS acts as a multiprotocol router to forward the traffic to the appropriate destination. A Windows 2000 RAS can route IP, IPX, and AppleTalk protocols. Point-to-LAN routing is an option that is configurable by the administrator. For security reasons, you might want to turn this feature off, to prevent remote access clients from reaching the rest of your network.

To support remote clients that use NetBEUI, Windows 2000 includes a NetBIOS gateway. The *NetBIOS gateway* allows a remote user to access any NetBIOS-based network resource that is reachable from the remote access server over NetBEUI, TCP/IP, or IPX. Keep in mind that sockets-based resources will not be available to NetBEUI dial-up clients.

At the time the NetBEUI remote access client makes a connection, the client passes its NetBIOS name to the NetBIOS gateway. The gateway is responsible for ensuring the client's NetBIOS name is added to the NetBIOS name table on the server. The NetBEUI traffic from a remote client is then also passed to the NetBIOS gateway and sent over the appropriate protocol to a NetBIOS resource on the network. The reverse is also true: When the remote access server receives a packet from a host on the network, it checks the packet for the NetBIOS name of the client. If the remote client is indeed the destination, the data is sent on to the client using NetBEUI, and the gateway handles any required protocol translation.

Enabling Routing and Remote Access Service

To enable the Routing and Remote Access Service (RRAS), perform the following steps:

1. Install and configure all appropriate hardware.

2. Open the Routing and Remote Access console. Click Start, Programs, Administrative Tools. Select Routing and Remote Access from the menu.

3. By default, the local computer is displayed. If it is not listed, or you want to add another server, right-click Server Status, then click Add Server.

4. In the Add Server dialog box, select the option that is applicable for the server you want to add, then click OK.

5. Right-click the server you want to enable as a remote access server and click "Configure and Enable Routing and Remote Access."

6. The Routing and Remote Access Wizard appears. Follow the onscreen instructions. When the wizard is finished, you are prompted to start the Routing and Remote Access Service.

After the service has been enabled, you can edit the remote access server's properties directly, as shown in Figure 2.2 below.

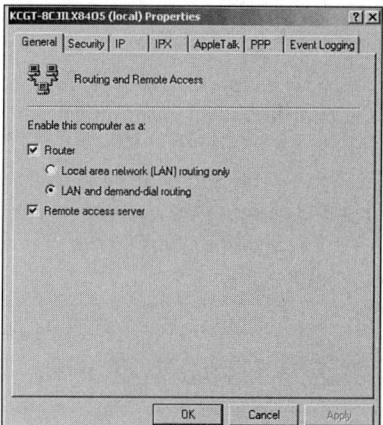

Figure 2.2   A Routing and Remote Access Server's properties sheet.

Right-click the server you want to modify and select Properties from the menu. The properties sheet contains the following configuration information:

- Whether this server acts as a router and/or a remote access server.
- The authentication methods and providers to be used. Configuration options will be covered in the "Authentication and Authorization" section of this chapter.
- Whether a remote user will be allowed to access only this server or the entire network. Each protocol tab on the Properties sheet will ask this question in a slightly different manner.
- How IP and/or IPX addresses are assigned to connecting clients.
- PPP configuration options for multilink, LCP extensions, and software compression. These topics will be covered in Chapter 10, "Bandwidth and Telecommunications."
- Event logging preferences.

This information is requested by the Routing and Remote Access Wizard when RRAS is initially enabled on the server. The wizard also requests information about how specific devices installed on the server are to be configured. You can configure devices individually or as a group. After the wizard has been completed, the configuration can be changed by opening the Ports properties sheet for the appropriate server.

LAN Protocols Supported by RAS

Windows 2000 remote access server supports TCP/IP, IPX, NetBEUI, and AppleTalk protocols through PPP connections. This offers administrators the capability to easily incorporate a computer running Windows 2000 Server in an existing network using these protocols. Because Windows 2000 Server automatically uses whatever supported protocols are already installed and running on a server, configuring an existing server as a remote access server is relatively simple. This section discusses the LAN protocols and protocol-specific configuration options.

TCP/IP

TCP/IP is the most widely used protocol in the world. Because of its scalability and flexibility, it is used on networks of all sizes, from those containing only a couple of workstations to those with thousands of computers in many locations connected with various types of LAN, metropolitan area networks (MAN), and WAN links. Configuring a TCP/IP RAS server requires that you specify how remote clients will be assigned an IP address. Name resolution is also an important configuration option. These parameters are configured on a server-by-server basis. Let's begin by examining IP address assignment.

Assigning IP Addresses

When a remote client connects to a remote access server, it is assigned an IP address in one of three ways:

- From a DHCP server
- From a pool of static IP addresses
- From a static IP address assigned on the dial-in properties page of the user's account

If you have a DHCP server on your network, you can take advantage of it when configuring your remote access server. Using the Routing and Remote Access Wizard or the remote access server properties sheet, select the Use DHCP to Assign Remote IP Addresses option. When using DHCP, the RAS retrieves ten IP addresses from a DHCP server. The RAS uses the first IP address in the group retrieved. The remaining addresses are assigned to remote access clients. When clients disconnect, those IP addresses are returned to the pool of available IP addresses. When all ten IP addresses are in use, the remote access server obtains ten more.

If the DHCP server isn't available when the Routing and Remote Access Service is started, the Windows 2000 remote access server compensates for this by assigning AutoNet addresses. This is service is called Automatic Private IP Addressing (APIPA). These addresses come from a pool of private network IP addresses, ranging from 169.254.0.1 to 169.254.255.254. The remote access server obtains these IP addresses in blocks of ten, just as it does from a DHCP server. Private network addresses provide remote access client connectivity to the entire remote network, however, only if the remote network also is using AutoNet addresses. If the local network does not use reserved network addresses, remote access clients will only be able to access resources on the remote access server. Additionally, APIPA only hands out IP addresses, not gateways or name servers. This means that APIPA clients will have very limited ability to communicate with other network hosts.

When a DHCP server becomes available, the remote access server will use it the next time it needs to retrieve a group of IP addresses. Those addresses will be assigned to remote access clients that connected *after* the DHCP addresses were obtained.

By the way, if you stop the Routing and Remote Access Service, all remote client DHCP-obtained IP addresses are released. Keep this in mind if you are troubleshooting by starting and stopping services.

Tip

You can change the number of number of IP addresses retrieved from a DHCP server at one time by changing the value of HKEY_LOCAL_MACHINE\System\CurrentControlSet\Services\RemoteAccess \Parameters\Ip\ InitialAddressPoolSize. Ten is the default, but you might find it beneficial to increase this number on a highly utilized remote access server.

If you don't have a DHCP server, or choose not to use it for remote access clients, you can specify a pool of static IP addresses to be assigned to remote clients. Unlike previous versions of Windows NT, the pool of IP addresses is not entered as a range with certain exceptions. Instead, you enter the range as an IP address and a mask. Windows 2000 calculates the number and range of available addresses based on the IP address and subnet mask. Windows 2000 supports Variable Length Subnet Masking (VLSM).

Your remote access server uses the first IP address in the static pool of IP addresses. Don't forget about this when entering the IP address range to identify the range. When entering your IP address range, you specify the first IP address in the range and either the last address in the range or the number of IP addresses that are required. Windows 2000 will automatically calculate the subnet mask.

You can choose to use a static pool that is or is not part of the remote access server's LAN. There are things to keep in mind whichever way you decide to go. If your remote access server does use a static range pulled from the LAN network segment, be sure that any DHCP servers on that network are not assigning addresses from the same range. It is an easy thing to overlook, but a pain in the neck to try to figure out what is causing a seemingly random duplicate IP address error. On the other hand, if you use a separate subnet for your remote access clients, you must enable routing on the server or use static routes to the remote clients on all routers in your network. If you don't, traffic from the LAN won't be able to get back to the remote clients. If you are using the OSPF routing protocol on a remote access server, you must configure it as an autonomous system boundary router (ASBR) that will accept routes to the static IP address pool used by your remote clients. OSPF is a routing protocol commonly used in very large networks. For more information, see Chapter 4, "Routing Protocols."

You can assign individual users specific IP addresses. This is assigned through the dial-in properties sheet of the users' accounts. More specific information on client configuration can be found in Chapter 3. A remote access policy also must be configured to allow a user to request a specific IP address. Policies will be covered in the section "Remote Access Polices" later in this chapter.

Name Resolution

Remote access clients can use all the same name resolution methods that you would expect in a normal network client, including WINS, LMHOSTS, DNS, and HOSTS. LMHOSTS and HOSTS files are placed on the remote client. One benefit of using these files is that name resolution requests are not sent over a slow link. Windows 2000 Routing and Remote Access Service does not provide a method for central management of these files, however, so use them only when the resources they refer to do not change IP addresses or names often.

The name servers that are assigned to the server's LAN interface (which are attached to the remote access clients) are assigned to the dial-up client. If there is a single LAN interface, that interface's name server addresses are assigned to all remote clients. If there are multiple LAN interfaces, the one used for name server assignment is selected at random.

A new feature of RRAS is that Windows 2000 and Windows 98 clients can be assigned a DNS and WINS server IP address from an available DHCP server on the remote network. Note that the DHCP server does not actually assign the remote client an IP address. The client uses the `DHCPINFORM` message to request specific DHCP options. In order for this to work, you must configure the remote access server to act as a DHCP relay agent (see Chapter 4 for more information). These addresses will overwrite those addresses assigned initially during the connection process, as described in the previous paragraph.

If you would like to mandate a specific WINS and DNS server for use by all remote access clients, you can change the value of the following keys to the IP address of the name servers:

- HKEY_LOCAL_MACHINE\System\CurrentControlSet\Services\ RemoteAccess\Parameters\Ip\DNSNameServers

- HKEY_LOCAL_MACHINE\System\CurrentControlSet\Services\ RemoteAccess\Parameters\Ip\WINSNameServers

On the other hand, there might be specific instances when you do not want the remote access server to assign any DNS and WINS server. If this is the case, change the value of these keys to 1:

- HKEY_LOCAL_MACHINE\System\CurrentControlSet\Services\ RemoteAccess\Parameters\Ip\SuppressDNSNameServers

- HKEY_LOCAL_MACHINE\System\CurrentControlSet\Services\ RemoteAccess\Parameters\Ip\SuppressWINSNameServers

IPX

A Windows 2000 remote access server running the NWLink IPX/SPX/NetBIOS Compatible Protocol can support remote access clients running IPX. The remote access server acts as an IPX router and forwards Routing Information Protocol for IPX (RIP for IPX), Service Advertising Protocol for IPX (SAP for IPX), and NetBIOS over IPX traffic from the remote access client to the remote network.

Remote access servers also assign IPX addresses to remote access clients. The remote access server can automatically generate this address. Alternatively, it can be assigned from a static pool of IPX addresses. The administrator configures the static pool of addresses in much the same way as a static pool of IP addresses.

AppleTalk

Routing and Remote Access Service also supports remote Macintosh clients running AppleTalk. The remote access server must be running AppleTalk protocol. Note that the Windows 2000 remote access server does not support Windows 2000 clients running AppleTalk.

NetBEUI

Windows 2000 supports NetBEUI dial-up clients with the NetBIOS gateway described in the overview of this chapter. Remote clients that run Windows NT 3.1, LAN Manager, MS-DOS, and Windows for Workgroups require NetBEUI over a remote access connection.

Remote Access Protocols

Windows 2000 Server supplies two remote access protocols: Point-to-Point Protocol (PPP) and Microsoft RAS protocol. Windows 2000 also supplies a Serial Line Internet Protocol (SLIP) client component, but does not support a SLIP server component.

PPP

The Windows 2000 remote access server supports PPP. PPP creates, maintains, and ends a logical link between a remote client and server. It also provides several other functions, including multiprotocol data link layer encapsulation, and framing and protocol configuration. This is a very useful remote access protocol: Any protocol-compliant PPP client can dial in to a Windows 2000 remote access server and access resources using any of the preceding LAN protocols. This means UNIX, Linux, Macintosh, as well as Windows 9x and Windows NT 3.5 and later clients can dial in to your RAS server. And because Windows 2000 supports the PPP client, the Windows 2000 remote access client can access any PPP-compliant dial-up server as well.

PPP connection negotiation has four parts or phases:

1. **PPP configuration.** During this phase, Link Control Protocol (LCP) is used to negotiate options for the connection, including authentication methods to use, compression, and multilink options.

2. **Authentication.** The authentication method chosen in phase one is used to verify the identity of remote clients.

3. **Callback.** If callback options have been configured, the server will disconnect the connection and call back the client at a preconfigured number.

4. **Protocol configuration.** LAN protocol negotiation occurs during this phase. The client and server decide which protocol will be used for this connection.

A PPP connection can be terminated at any time by either party or by a hardware or line failure.

Microsoft RAS Protocol

Microsoft RAS protocol, or MS-RAS, is a proprietary remote access protocol that supports NetBIOS clients that do not use PPP, including Windows NT 3.1, Windows for Workgroups, MS-DOS, and LAN Manager clients. MS-RAS allows these NetBEUI-based clients to dial in to a Windows 2000 server and access remote resources through the NetBIOS gateway.

Authentication and Authorization

Authentication is verification of the identity of the user attempting to connect to a remote access server. The client sends credentials to the server in the form of a password, digital signature, or other means as required by the authentication protocol in use. *Authorization*, on the other hand, is verification that the connection attempt is allowed. Authorization happens after a user has been authenticated. Every attempt to connect to a remote access server has to be authenticated and authorized if the connection is to succeed.

An example of this two-step process is making a withdrawal from an ATM. First you swipe your card and enter a PIN to certify your identity. Just possessing an ATM card and a matching PIN, however, doesn't mean you'll be permitted to withdraw cash from an ATM. When you enter a request to withdraw $100, the ATM checks to be sure you have that balance available before it spits out a stack of twenties. If you don't, the ATM ends the transaction. Windows 2000 RAS works the same way. A user can have all the right certificates or passwords, but the server's policy might not permit that user to access the server. If this is the case, the connection attempt is denied.

Windows 2000 has taken authentication to new levels, far and away better than Windows NT 4.0. It is now possible to authenticate both users and computers. Smart cards and user credentials are used to validate identity of the user, while machine certificates are used to verify that an attacker's computer is not spoofing a computer's identity. In this section, we will discuss credentials used to authenticate a user attempting to connect to a remote access server. Note that the terms user and client are interchangeable.

When the identity of a remote access user is authenticated, the authorization process begins. The remote access policy of that remote access server and/or the dial-in property of the user's account must grant access to the user. If the user is authorized to make a remote access connection, then the user now has access to the remote network. Keep in mind that the user has access based on the user credentials supplied during logon, but that same user can also supply additional credentials to access other resources by filling in the pop-up dialog box requesting username and password. This can make it very difficult to audit usage or access of network resources, and is a very good reason to be positively dictatorial about password confidentiality.

An authentication protocol is selected during the first phase of PPP connection establishment. During the second phase, the selected protocol is used to authenticate the client. Windows 2000 supports several authentication protocols, and also allows unauthenticated users access to your network if you so choose. In this section, traditional credentials-based authentication methods—EAP, MS-CHAP, MS-CHAP version 2, CHAP, SPAP, and PAP—are covered, as well as unauthenticated access. When we have finished with the authentication methods, we will examine the choices for authentication providers on a remote access server.

We will explore these PPP authentication methods in order of strength, highest to lowest, beginning with EAP. By the way, Windows 2000 applies multiple authentication methods in that order, too, highest to lowest, until a common authentication method is found between client and server.

EAP

Extensible Application Protocol (EAP), is a PPP authentication protocol. It is a flexible protocol that allows the specific authentication mechanism to be swapped in and out to provide a custom authentication solution for any given implementation. EAP authentication mechanisms include MD5-CHAP, smart cards, and token cards. EAP has another added plus: because the EAP architecture supports plug-in modules, new authentication methods can be created for future security needs.

Unlike other PPP authentication protocols that specify the authentication mechanism during link establishment, during LCP, PPP peers agree only that they will use EAP. The LCP packets exchanged between the computers include an option byte indicating that the sending host wants to use authentication protocol 0xC2-27. EAP messages continue to use this ID for the rest of the EAP negotiation process. The specific method to be used for authentication, called the *EAP type*, is selected by the dial-up client and the remote access server during the connection authentication phase. Windows 2000 supports EAP-MD5 and EAP-TLS EAP types right out of the box. The same EAP type must be installed on both the authenticator and the remote access client in order for successful authentication to occur.

The EAP protocol is actually just a series of messages sent in a specific order. These messages are requests for authentication information and responses to the requests. The content of these "conversations" is where the flexibility of the EAP protocol becomes evident. The length and type of requests differ based on the EAP type. Because the content of the messages is not set in stone, third-party developers can create new authentication mechanisms. Further, EAP types can allow a layered approach to security. This is possible by querying each component of an authentication method separately, with each method indicating a level of authentication.

The classic example of layered authentication is the use of token cards. The authenticating server makes a query for each parameter required by the token card, such as a username, a PIN, or password, and the token generated by the card. If the client answers all the queries correctly, he or she is authenticated and cleared to access the network based on any authorization parameters that might be in place.

Now let's take a look at the EAP types supported by Windows 2000.

EAP-MD5

EAP-MD5 combines EAP with the *Challenge Handshake Authentication Protocol* (CHAP). CHAP authenticates users based on username and password. MD5 authentication is normally performed during link establishment, but when it is used with EAP, the client and server perform authentication during the connection authentication phase. At that time, CHAP challenges and responses are performed according to the following process:

1. The remote access server sends a request to the client. This is called an EAP-Request message, and its function is to request the identity of the client.

2. The remote access client sends an EAP-Response message to the authenticator. The response contains the user's ID.

3. An EAP-Request message is sent from the server to the client. It contains the MD5 challenge string.

4. The client replies with an EAP-Response message containing the MD5-based hash of its user ID and password.

5. If the client response was correct, the client is authenticated, and a Success message is sent from the authenticator to the client.

EAP-TLS

EAP also supports *Transport Layer Security* (TLS) for use with security certificates. EAP-TLS is based on *Secure Sockets Layer* (SSL) and is required if you want to use smart cards for authentication. It also provides mutual authentication, data integrity, and confidentiality between PPP peers by offering:

- Symmetric and asymmetric encryption for client-only or mutual authentication
- Encryption algorithm negotiation
- Private keys for message encryption
- Secure encryption key exchange
- Message integrity and user authentication employing a message authentication code (MAC)

EAP-TLS mutual authentication is done through the exchange and verification of certificates. The remote access client sends a user certificate to the server, and the authenticator sends a machine certificate to the client. EAP-TLS can support registry-based certificates, but Microsoft recommends that if you use EAP-TLS, you do so only in conjunction with smart cards.

If you plan to use EAP-TLS for remote access authentication, your remote access server must be a member of a Windows 2000 mixed-mode or native-mode domain. Windows 2000 remote access servers configured as standalone servers do not support EAP-TLS.

Smart Cards

Smart cards can be used in conjunction with the Windows 2000 logon process and are one of the strongest forms of user authentication in Windows 2000. You also can use them to authenticate the identification of remote access clients. The process for setting up smart card remote access authentication includes the following steps:

1. Install a computer certificate on the remote access server.

2. Enable a domain-wide smart card logon process.

3. Configure smart card authentication on the remote access server.

4. Configure smart card authentication on the dial-up or VPN remote access client.

Each of the steps necessary to configure smart card authentication on the remote access server will be covered in this section. The last step, client setup, will be covered in Chapter 3.

Install a Computer Certificate on the Remote Access Server

To install a computer certificate on the remote access server, you have to have a certificate authority (CA) available to issue certificates. After a CA is online, you can install a certificate on the remote access server computer by configuring automatic certificate allocation from an enterprise CA or by using Certificate Manager to obtain a computer certificate. Only one of these methods needs to be used. If you would like more information about certificates and public key infrastructure (PKI), refer to the Windows 2000 Server Resource Kit.

To configure a certificate authority and install the computer certificate:

1. If you have not already done so, install the Windows 2000 Certificate Services component as an enterprise root certificate authority. To do this:

    1. Ensure that the computer that will be a CA is a domain controller (DC). If it is not, promote it by running dcpromo at a command prompt. Follow the instructions in the Active Directory Wizard that pops up.

2. Install the Windows 2000 Certificate Services component as an enterprise root CA. Go to Start, Programs, Administrative Tools, Configure Your Server. Click Advanced, then Optional Components. Start the Windows Components Wizard. (Alternatively, you can go to Control Panel, Add/Remove Programs, and select Add/Remove Windows Components). Select Certificate Services as shown in Figure 2.3 below and follow the directions in the Windows Components Wizard.

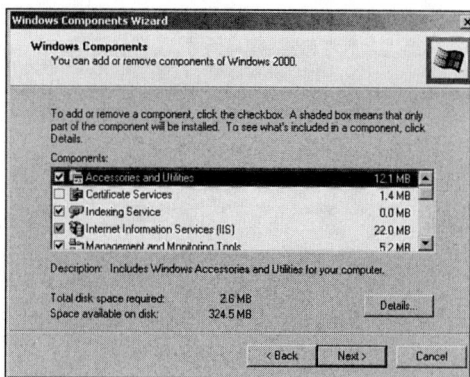

Figure 2.3   The Windows Components Wizard.

2. Specify the manner in which the remote access server will receive its certificate:

- If you want to allow auto-enrollment of machine certificates, configure Group Policy to configure automatic certificate allocation from an enterprise CA. After you have done that, make sure the remote access server has received a certificate. Do this by restarting the computer or by running `secedit /refreshpolicy_machine_policy` at command prompt.

- If you want to enroll machine certificates manually, you can use the Certificate Request Wizard in the Certificates snap-in in the MMC.

Enable a Domain-Wide Smart Card Logon Process

Enabling a domain-wide smart card logon process involves three steps:

1. Configure the CA to issue smart card logon certificates through Group Policy.

2. Prepare a smart card certificate enrollment station by installing a smart card reader and installing an Enrollment Agent certificate through the Certificates snap-in in the MMC.

3. Set up a smart card for user logon by requesting a certificate through the enrollment station you created in the last step.

Configure Smart Card Authentication on the Remote Access Server

To configure the remote access server running Windows 2000 for smart card remote access:

1. In the Routing and Remote Access console tree, right-click the name of the remote access server, then click Properties.

2. Click the Security tab, select the "Extensible Authentication Protocol (EAP)" check box as shown in Figure 2.4, then click OK.

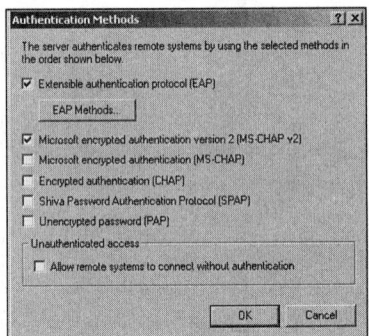

Figure 2.4   Enabling EAP on a remote access server.

3. In the console tree, double-click the name of the remote access server, then click Remote Access Policies.

4. Right-click the policy smart card remote access clients will use, click Properties, then click Edit Profile.

5. Click the Authentication tab, and put a check in the Extensible Authentication Protocol check box. Click "Smart card or other certificate (TLS)," then click Configure.

6. In the Smart Card or Other Certificate (TLS) Properties dialog box, select the appropriate machine certificate, then click OK.

7. Click OK to save the changes to the profile. Click OK again to save the changes to the policy.

CHAP, MS-CHAP, and MS-CHAP v2

Windows 2000 supports three types of challenge-response protocols:

- CHAP
- MS-CHAP
- MS-CHAP v2

CHAP is an industry standard method of remote access authentication. Microsoft's versions of CHAP use different encryption methods and offer certain features that CHAP does not. In this section, we will look at each implementation of CHAP and explore their features and differences. In a slight twist on the highest-to-lowest-security theme, we will look at the three versions of CHAP from lowest to highest levels of security. The reason for this is you need to understand the less secure methods of CHAP to appreciate the more secure methods.

CHAP

Although it is the least strong of the three CHAP methods we will look at, CHAP offers better security than authentication protocols like PAP and SPAP (both will be covered later in this section). These other protocols use less secure means to transmit passwords. CHAP uses a challenge-response mechanism to authenticate remote access clients. Its inner workings are fully described in RFC 1994. CHAP is one of the most widely used remote access authentication mechanisms, and is supported by many vendors. Using CHAP on a Windows 2000 remote access server allows authentication of non-Windows clients that also support CHAP.

How It Works

The development of CHAP was due to security concerns for passwords being passed between client and server in clear text format. CHAP addresses this problem by encrypting passwords with an MD5 hashing scheme. The way it works is as follows:

1. The remote access server issues a CHAP Challenge message containing a session ID and a challenge string. A unique challenge is generated for each client connection attempt, preventing the reuse of CHAP responses in a replay attack.

2. The remote access user sends back a CHAP Response message. The response contains the user's name, the challenge string, session ID, and the client's password. The user's name is sent in clear text, but the rest of the information is first encrypted using MD5 and then sent as a one-way hash.

3. The remote access server also hashes the challenge string, session ID, and client's password. The server compares the hash it generates to the hash the remote client sends to the server. If the hashes match, a CHAP Success message is sent to the client. Hashes that do not match result in the sending of a CHAP Failure message.

Note that the password is hashed before it is sent. This eliminates the concern of sending a clear text password over the Internet because the hashed password and challenge information can't be decrypted. Both the server and the client must know the password, however, and it must be available to each in a clear text format. Obviously, storing clear text passwords on a computer would a big security hole—the first thing an attacker would go for is the passwords list. Windows 2000 prevents this possible backdoor by allowing the passwords to be stored in a reversibly encrypted format.

Concerns

There are a few caveats to consider when implementing CHAP. It is disabled by default, and unless a remote client requires it, it is recommended that you use MS-CHAP or MS-CHAP v2 (the Microsoft-preferred method) instead. If you must use it, keep these things in mind:

- CHAP passwords can't be changed during the authentication process. Users will have to log on to the LAN or to the remote access server with an alternate authentication method to change a password that has expired or that must be changed at next logon.

- The CHAP algorithm is very well known, making it vulnerable to a brute force or dictionary attack. Develop a strong password policy. Require passwords to use a minimum of 8 characters and a mix of upper- and lowercase letters, numbers, and punctuation.

- The challenge method prevents replay attacks, but it does not prevent attacks involving remote server impersonation, because CHAP only provides one-way authentication.

Implementation

To enable CHAP authentication, follow these instructions:

1. Enable CHAP on the remote access server. In the Routing and Remote Access console, right-click the server on which you want to enable CHAP, then click Properties. Click the Security tab, then click the Authentication Methods button. Put a check mark in the box next to "Encrypted authentication (CHAP)."

2. Enable CHAP in the remote access policy. Specific details for creating and modifying policies will be covered later in this chapter.

3. Enable storage of a reversibly encrypted form of the user's password. This can be done by user account or for an entire domain. This option can be enabled through the Windows, Security, Account Policies, Passwords section of the Group Policy console for a domain member, or the Local Computer Policy console for a standalone server.

4. Force the users to change their passwords. This must be done to ensure that all remote access passwords are stored in a reversibly encrypted form. If they are not reversibly encrypted, Windows 2000 can't authenticate remote clients using CHAP. Existing passwords are not automatically converted to this format when the option to do so is enabled. To do this, you can reset user passwords or set user passwords to be changed the next time each user logs on.

5. Enable CHAP on the remote access client. This will be covered in Chapter 3.

MS-CHAP

Microsoft has attempted to address some of the vulnerabilities of CHAP by creating Microsoft CHAP. In addition to support in Windows 2000, many Network Access Server (NAS) vendors support MS-CHAP in their software. One of the primary features of MS-CHAP (or MS-CHAP v1, as it is also called) is that it doesn't require plain text passwords on the server that performs authentication. Recall from the last section that CHAP requires plain text passwords to create the identification verification hash. A workaround to storing clear text passwords on a CHAP-authenticating server is to enable reversibly encrypted passwords. MS-CHAP stores a reversibly encrypted MD4 hash of the password to validate a challenge response.

Another feature of MS-CHAP is its support for changing passwords during the authentication process. Both MS-CHAP and MS-CHAP v2 support this and are the only authentication protocols supplied with Windows 2000 to do so.

Additionally, Microsoft Point-to-Point Encryption (MPPE) can be used in conjunction with MS-CHAP to encrypt data sent over the remote access connection. And finally, MS-CHAP supports LAN Manager authentication for older Microsoft operating systems such as Windows NT 3.5x and Windows 95. MS-CHAP also allows clients to log on to a Windows domain over a dial-up link.

How It Works

The MS-CHAP authentication process is as follows:

1. The remote access server sends an MS-CHAP Challenge message. This message contains the session ID and the randomly generated challenge string. This challenge string is unique to each new connection attempt and prevents reuse of packets in a replay attack.

2. The remote access client sends back an MS-CHAP Response message. This message contains the username and the challenge string, session ID, and password. The username is sent in clear text, and the challenge string, session ID, and the previously hashed password are sent as an MD4 hash.

3. The remote access server duplicates the hash and compares it to the hash in the MS-CHAP Response. If the hashes are the same, the remote access server sends back a CHAP Success message. If the hashes are different, a CHAP Failure message is sent.

Concerns

Although MS-CHAP offers some benefit over CHAP, it is important to consider some of its negatives before implementing it. MS-CHAP only offers one-way authentication of the client, not the server. It doesn't protect remote access clients from an attacker using a computer that impersonates your remote access server.

Speaking strictly from a cryptographic point of view, LAN Manager authentication is very weak. Further, MS-CHAP only uses 40-bit encryption and uses the same cryptographic key for every connection attempt with the same password.

Implementation

To implement MS-CHAP authentication, you must do the following:

1. Enable MS-CHAP on the remote access server. In the Routing and Remote Access console, right-click the server on which you want to enable MS-CHAP, then click Properties. Click the Security tab, then click the Authentication Methods button. Put a check mark in the box next to "Microsoft encrypted authentication (MS-CHAP)."

2. Enable MS-CHAP in the remote access policy. Specific details for creating and modifying policies will be covered later in this chapter.

3. Enable MS-CHAP on the remote access client. This will be covered in Chapter 3.

LAN Manager support for MS-CHAP is not enabled by default. To use it to authenticate older Microsoft operating systems, you must edit the registry on the remote access server.

1. Open the registry editor of your choice by typing `Regedt32` or `Regedit` at a command prompt.

2. Navigate to this key: HKEY_LOCAL_MACHINE\System\CurrentControlSet \Services\RemoteAccess\Policy\Allow LM Authentication.

3. Change the value of this key to 1.

MS-CHAP v2

MS-CHAP v2 is the strongest of the CHAP methods supported by Windows 2000, but it is less secure than EAP. MS-CHAP v2 solves some of the concerns with the first version of MS-CHAP. It allows mutual authentication of clients and servers. The cryptographic key used for challenge response is based on the user's password *and* the random challenge string generated for each connection attempt. In other words, each time a connection is attempted with the same password, a different cryptographic key is used. Different crypto keys are created for transmitted and received data, and stronger initial data encryption keys are generated as well. MS-CHAP v2 still supports password change during the authentication process, and remote clients can still use MS-CHAP v2 to log on to a Windows domain over a dial-up link.

Another change is that MS-CHAP v2 no longer supports LAN Manager challenge responses and password changes. To use Windows 95 clients with MS-CHAP v2, you will need to install the Windows Dial-Up Networking 1.3 Performance and Security Upgrade. Keep in mind that this upgrade provides MS-CHAP v2 support only for virtual private network (VPN) connections, not dial-up connections.

How It Works

MS-Chap authentication proceeds as follows:

1. The remote access server sends a challenge containing a session ID and a randomly generated challenge string.

2. The remote access client sends a response containing the username, a randomly generated peer challenge string, and a one-way MD4 hash of the received challenge string.

3. The server examines the response from the client. If it matches the hash on the server, it sends a success message. Otherwise, authentication fails.

4. In addition to the success message, the server also sends an authentication response to the client, intended to prove the server's identity. This message is based on the initial challenge string, the peer challenge string, the encrypted response of the client, and the user's password.

5. The client verifies the authentication response. If the response is correct, the remote client will use the connection. However, the client will terminate the connection if it is not able to authenticate the server's identity.

Implementation

MS-CHAP v2 is enabled by default on Windows 2000. That means that all you have to do is configure the remote client to do MS-CHAP v2. That will be covered in Chapter 3.

SPAP

Shiva Password Authentication Protocol (SPAP) is a two-way reversible encryption authentication method used by Shiva clients and servers. SPAP allows Windows 2000 clients computer running Windows 2000 to make a connection to a Shiva LAN Rover NAS, as well as enabling a Shiva client to make a connection to a remote access server running Windows 2000. It is more secure than sending clear text passwords over the line, but less secure than any previously discussed authentication methods.

How It Works

SPAP authentication uses the following message exchange process:

1. The remote access client sends an SPAP Authenticate-Request message. The message contains the username and encrypted password.

2. When the remote access server receives the message, it decrypts the password, and verifies that the username and password are correct. If the credentials match the credentials stored on the server, it returns a SPAP Authenticate-Ack message to the client. If the credentials are not correct, the server returns a SPAP Authenticate-Nak message to the remote access client along with the reason why the user's credentials were not correct (incorrect password, no such username found, and so on).

Concerns

Consider these factors carefully before implementing SPAP in your network. SPAP is vulnerable to replay attacks because it reuses the encrypted password for each connection attempt. Further, SPAP does not authenticate the server to the client, which leaves the client open to a server impersonation attack. Unless SPAP is absolutely required, its use is not recommended, particularly in VPN implementations. Finally, SPAP does not allow password changes during the authentication process.

Implementation

To enable SPAP, do the following:

1. Enable SPAP on the remote access server. In the Routing and Remote Access console, right-click the server on which you want to enable SPAP, then click Properties. Click the Security tab, then click the Authentication Methods button. Put a check mark in the box next to "Shiva Password Authentication Protocol (SPAP)."

2. Enable SPAP in the remote access policy. Specific details for creating and modifying policies will be covered later in this chapter.

3. Enable SPAP on the remote access client. This will be covered in Chapter 3.

PAP

Password Authentication Protocol (PAP) uses clear text passwords for authentication. It offers the least security of all the previously mentioned authentication protocols. It is basically the protocol of last resort, meaning if the client and server are unable to negotiate any stronger form of authentication, they can always fall back on this if both computers have been configured to allow it.

How It Works

PAP uses a simple message exchange process to authenticate users:

1. The remote access client sends an **PAP Authenticate-Request** message. The message contains the username and encrypted password.

2. When the remote access server receives the message, it decrypts the password, and verifies that the username and password are correct. If the credentials match the credentials stored on the server, it returns a **PAP Authenticate-Ack** message to the client. If the credentials are not correct, the server returns a PAP Authenticate-Nak message to the remote access client.

Implementation

To enable PAP-based authentication, you must do the following:

1. Enable PAP on the remote access server. In the Routing and Remote Access console, right-click the server on which you want to enable PAP, then click Properties. Click the Security tab, then click the Authentication Methods button. Put a check mark in the box next to "Unencrypted password (PAP)."

2. Enable PAP in your remote access policy. Specific details for creating and modifying policies will be covered later in this chapter.

3. Enable PAP on the remote access client. This will be covered in Chapter 3.

Concerns

Because PAP offers relatively little security, take note of these issues before you implement it:

- PAP sends user passwords in clear text. Anyone with a sniffer can grab PAP packets and pull the users' passwords from them.

- PAP offers no client or server authentication, and leaves the server open to replay attacks.

- PAP does not allow users to change passwords during authentication process. This can be a problem if a user's password expires.

Unauthenticated Access

There are circumstances where user authentication is not needed. Perhaps you have a remote access server that is host to applications and data that must be accessible to business partners, clients, or remote employees who do not have access to the Internet. If this data is not sensitive, and the number of user accounts that must be created to support the remote clients is large, you might find it acceptable to allow unauthenticated user access with a guest account or by the use of a protocol that uses the caller's phone number as credentials. Windows 2000 supports DNIS authorization, ANI/CLI authentication, and guest authentication. We will cover each of these unauthenticated access methods in this section.

DNIS

DNIS, which stands for *Dialed Number Identification Service*, authorizes connections by the telephone number the user calls. Note that this is not the user's phone number, but rather the number the user dials. DNIS sends the dialed number to the receiving hardware. This is the same technology that allows a single phone number to use multiple voice mailboxes.

To set up DNIS on your remote access server, follow these instructions:

1. Allow unauthenticated access on the remote access server. In the RRAS console, right-click the appropriate server, then click Properties. Click the Authentication Method button, then select the Security tab. Put a check in the box for "Allow remote systems to connect without authentication."

2. Create a remote access policy on the remote access server that allows DNIS-based authorization. Set the Called-Station-Id condition to the connection device's phone number. Policy creation will be covered in more detail later in this chapter in the section "Remote Access Policies."

Most phone companies provide DNIS, but you need to check that your hardware supports it as well. If your phone company or hardware doesn't support DNIS, you can manually configure the port with its phone number. In the RRAS console, right-click Ports, then click Properties. Click the appropriate device, then click Configure. Type the phone number of the port in the "Phone number for this device" field, then click OK. (If your hardware and phone company support this service, your phone number will automatically appear in the configuration dialog box.)

ANI/CLI

Automatic Number Identification/Calling Line Identification (ANI/CLI) authentication uses the phone number of the caller for user credentials. ANI/CLI is similar to the caller ID service offered by the phone company, but don't confuse it with caller ID authentication. (For more information on caller ID authentication, see Chapter 3.) Caller ID authorization requires users to send a username and password. ANI/CLI authentication does not send a username and password to the remote server.

To allow ANI/CLI connections, follow these procedures:

1. Allow unauthenticated access on the remote access server. In the RRAS console, right-click the appropriate server, then click Properties. Click the Authentication Method button, then select the Security tab. Put a check in the box for "Allow remote systems to connect without authentication."

2. Create a remote access policy on the remote access server that allows ANI/CLI authentication. Set the Called-Station-Id condition to the connection device's phone number. Policy creation will be covered in more detail later in this chapter in the section "Remote Access Policies."

3. Create user accounts for every phone number that will dial up to be authenticated by ANI/CLI. Set the user account name to the phone number the remote user will be calling from.

4. Edit the registry to tell the server that the calling number is the user ID. Change the value of the key HKEY_LOCAL_MACHINE\System\CurrentControlSet\Services\RasMan\ppp\ControlProtocols\BuiltIn\User Identity Attribute to 31. This value is used only if no other username is sent by a remote client.

You can specify that the calling number will always be used instead of a username by setting the value of the key HKEY_LOCAL_MACHINE\System\CurrentControlSet\Services\ RemoteAccess\Policy\Override User-Name to 1. Be aware of the ramifications of simultaneously setting both of the keys mentioned here—the Override User-Name to 1 and the User Identity Attribute to 31. If this is done, the remote access server will allow only ANI/CLI authentication. *All* other methods of authentication will be suppressed, preventing users from accessing the remote network as they normally do.

Guest Account

Windows 2000 has a built-in guest account that is disabled by default. This account, when enabled, can be used to allow a user without an account in a domain to access the resources on a remote network. The user does not send specific user account credentials when he or she attempts a remote connection. Instead, the guest account is used as the credentials of the dial-up user. This is perfect for situations where you don't know what phone number a client will use to dial up your server, or you do not want to create hundreds of user accounts to match the identity of the remote user. Be cautious when using this method, though. Any user who dials up your server will be allowed into the remote network with whatever permissions you have given the guest account. Also, there is no way to distinguish between unauthenticated clients using the guest account after they are in your network, which can make it difficult to pinpoint security problems or track resource usage.

To enable guest account access, complete the following steps:

1. Allow unauthenticated access on the remote access server. In the RRAS console, right-click the appropriate server, then click Properties. Click the Authentication Method button, then select the Security tab. Put a check in the box for "Allow remote systems to connect without authentication."

2. Enable unauthenticated access on the appropriate remote access policy. Specific details on this topic will be covered later in this chapter.

3. Enable the guest account. On the Dial-up tab of the user account properties sheet, select Allow access or Control access through Remote Access Policy as appropriate for your security policy.

If, for security reasons, you do not want to use the built-in guest account, you can create another user account as a substitute:

1. Create a user account. On the Dial-in tab of the user account properties sheet, select Allow access or Control access through Remote Access Policy as appropriate for your security policy.

2. Edit the registry to change the key HKEY_LOCAL_MACHINE\System\ CurrentControlSet\Services\RasMan\ppp\ControlProtocols\BuiltIn\Default User Identity to equal the name of the account created in step 1.

Keep in mind that using a separate user account for unauthenticated remote access users is only marginally more secure than the guest account. By not using the guest account, you make it difficult for attackers to guess at account credentials. If a hacker knows the username of an account, such as Guest, all he or she has to do is crack the password with brute force. Therefore, use the guest account with discretion, and consider not displaying the name of the last user who logged in the logon screen. This can be set in the Group Policy console.

Authentication Providers

Remote access authentication can be provided by two sources:

- A Windows 2000 server
- A server that provides Remote Authentication Dial-Up Service (RADIUS)

A log of connection requests and sessions will be maintained by these sources. The system event log also stores information about RAS connection attempts that can assist with troubleshooting. This section will look at how Windows 2000 authentication works in different Windows environments, and then wrap up with a brief look at how RADIUS is used. For more information about RADIUS, refer to Chapter 9, "Internet Authentication Service."

Windows 2000 Authentication

There are a few basic ways a remote access server can be configured in terms of how it applies permissions and which user accounts databases are used for authentication:

- Windows 2000 standalone server
- Windows 2000 member server in a Windows NT 4 domain
- Windows 2000 member server in a mixed-mode or native-mode Windows 2000 domain
- Windows 2000 remote access server providing cross-forest authentication
- Windows NT 4 Server in a Windows 2000 domain
- Windows NT 4 Server running Service Pack 3 and earlier

This section will cover these options and point out some important things to be aware of when implementing a remote access server in these environments.

You set authentication and logging on a remote access server in the Routing and Remote Access console. Right-click the desired server, then click Properties. Click the Security tab, then select an authentication and logging method from the drop-down lists.

Standalone Server Running Windows 2000

A standalone Windows 2000 remote access server uses the local user accounts database to authenticate remote clients, and all dial-in user properties on the user account property sheet will be available.

Member Server in a Windows NT 4 Domain

A Windows 2000 remote access server that is a member of a Windows NT 4 domain can use the local accounts database or 4 domain accounts database. Only the options applicable to Windows NT 4 dial-in permissions will be available for configuration.

Member Server in a Mixed-Mode or Native-Mode Windows 2000 Domain

A Windows 2000 remote access server that is a member of a mixed-mode or native-mode Windows 2000 domain has the same options to authenticate remote access clients as a member server in a Windows NT 4 domain—the local accounts database and the Windows NT 4 domain accounts database—plus the Windows 2000 domain accounts database. Keep in mind that a mixed-mode domain controller must be compatible with Windows NT 4. This requirement limits the dial-in user properties on the Windows 2000 domain controller to those found on a Windows NT 4 controller.

Upgrading a Windows 2000 Server's Role

When you upgrade a Windows 2000 server from a standalone server to a domain controller, it is configured for a mixed-mode domain by default. (You can switch from mixed-mode to native-mode in the Active Directory Users and Computers console. Moving from native-mode to mixed-mode cannot be done.) A mixed-mode domain controller limits the dial-in user properties on the Windows 2000 domain controller to those found on a Windows NT 4 controller. How does this affect the dial-in properties configured on this server?

When you move from standalone to mixed-mode, the values of all previously set permissions are preserved, even if the option that it applies to is now unavailable.

When a mixed-mode domain controller becomes a native-mode domain controller, all dial-in properties configured while the remote access server was still a standalone will be available again.

For example, the Assign a static IP Address property for a user account on a standalone server is set to 10.0.1.1. When this server is upgraded to a domain controller, this property becomes unavailable, but the value is preserved in case the domain is ever promoted to native-mode. When the domain is upgraded from mixed-mode to native-mode, this property is once again available and remains configured with the IP address of 10.0.1.1.

When you install and enable Routing and Remote Access on a server, it is automatically added to the RAS and IAS Servers security group. To access user accounts in other domains, you need to add the computer account to the domain RAS and IAS Servers group through the Active Directory Computers and Users console.

Cross-forest Authentication

To allow cross-forest remote access authentication, you must loosen the security of the Active Directory of the remote forest to allow the remote access server to access user account properties in that forest. Active Directory security normally uses Kerberos to authenticate users, but cross-forest authentication doesn't use Kerberos, it uses NTLM (NT LAN Manager) security. NTLM doesn't provide the level of authentication that Kerberos provides. By default, the security of the Active Directory requires Kerberos authentication, so it must be loosened to allow NTLM. This must be done for cross-forest authentication of remote access users whether the "home" domain of the RAS server is a Windows 2000 or Windows NT 4 domain. You can loosen Active Directory security at the time you promote a domain controller in a remote domain, or you can run the command `netsh ras set domainaccess legacy` at a command prompt on a domain controller in the remote domain. NTLM supports up to 128-bitencryption for challenge/response authentication. However, methods for attacking NTLM networks are widely published. If you cannot avoid using cross-forest authentication, keep in mind that NTLM is a security risk for all involved forests in your enterprise.

Windows NT 4 Remote Access Server in a Windows 2000 Domain

A Windows NT 4.0 Service Pack 4 (and later) member of a Windows 2000 domain can access its local accounts database. It must also access user account properties in a Windows 2000 domain, but this capability is disabled by default. To enable a Windows 4 server to access user account properties of a remote Windows 2000 domain controller, loosen the Active Directory security at the time you promote a domain controller. Alternatively, you can run the command `netsh ras set domainaccess legacy` at a command prompt on a domain controller.

Windows NT 4 Service Pack 3 and Earlier

When using a remote access server running Windows NT 4.0 Service Pack 3 or earlier, you must enable it to authenticate against a remote Windows 2000 domain controller. To enable this behavior, configure the Active Directory to allow the Everyone object read access on all properties on all user objects. In the Active Directory Users and Computers console, grant list contents, read all properties, and read permissions to the root and all subobjects of the domain. For security reasons, the method is not recommended. Microsoft has stated that the Microsoft-supported direction for Windows NT 4 is to upgrade to SP 4.0 or later, with the preferred method upgrading the server to a Windows 2000 member server in a Windows 2000 mixed-mode or native-mode domain.

RADIUS

A Windows 2000 remote access server can use a RADIUS server for authentication. Microsoft offers a RADIUS product for Windows 2000 called Internet Authentication Service (IAS), which will be covered in detail in Chapter 9. If RADIUS is the selected authentication method, the credentials of the user attempting to connect are passed to the RADIUS server. RADIUS provides authentication and authorization services, both of which must be successful for a connection attempt to be successful. The RADIUS server indicates success by returning an accept message to the remote access server. A reject message indicates that the connection attempt was not authenticated and/or authorized, and the connection attempt is refused.

User Access Configuration

After a user has been authenticated, he or she must then be authorized. Authorization simply means that a user has been given permission to establish and use a connection with a remote access server. There are two parts to controlling client access: the user account and the remote access policy. We will explore each method in this section.

User Account Configuration

Dial-in permissions can be granted to a user account through the Active Directory or Local Users and Groups console, depending on the configuration of the remote access server. After you have opened the Properties sheet for a user, click the Dial-in tab. This is where all user account configuration for remote access takes place. The configurable options are explained in the following section.

Remote Access Permission (Dial-In or VPN)

The options for remote access permission specify whether a user is allowed remote access to the dial-up server. The settings are:

- **Allow access.**   Explicitly allows a user remote access to a remote server. Windows NT 4 user accounts upgraded to Windows 2000 that were previously configured with dial-in permission enabled are set to Allow access by default.

- **Deny access.**   Explicitly denies a user remote access to a remote access server.

- **Control access through Remote Access Policy.**   Access to the remote access server is governed by the specific settings of a remote access policy. This option is only available on standalone Windows 2000 Server and members servers of Windows 2000 native-mode domains. Windows NT 4 user accounts upgraded to Windows 2000 that were previously configured with dial-in permission disabled are set to Control access through Remote Access Policy by default.

Verify Caller ID

By configuring this option, you are requiring that this user always call from the number you enter here. Using the caller ID functionality of the modem and the phone connection, Windows 2000 verifies that the caller's number matches the entry in the user's profile. If it does, the connection is accepted. If the number does not match, the connection is denied. This option is not available on remote access servers in a Windows NT 4 or Windows 2000 mixed-mode domain.

Callback Options

These options specify whether the server is to call back the remote client. The choices you have are:

- **No Callback.**   Callback is not enabled.
- **Set by Caller.**   The caller will specify a number the server will call back. This is helpful for remote users who must call long distance.
- **Always Callback to.**   Requires that the server will always call back the number specified here. This gives you a little bit of security—if an attacker attempts to dial in to your network and guesses a user's name and password, configuring callback will disconnect the call and call back to the number specified.

A Windows 2000 remote access server that is a member of a Windows 2000 native-mode domain can use up to 128 characters in the callback number. Any other configuration can only use up to 48 characters.

Assign a Static IP Address

This feature allows you to assign a specific IP address to a user when a connection is made. If you have a large number of remote access clients, you can use specific IP addresses for remote users to track bandwidth usage on the network. This option is not available on remote access servers in a Windows NT 4 or Windows 2000 mixed-mode domain.

Apply Static Routes

Although you can use this setting to define a specific route for a user, it is actually designed to be used for demand-dial routing. Each demand-dial router uses a user account to dial in to a remote access server to join two networks. Each router is associated with a user account. For more information on demand-dial routing, see Chapter 4. This option is not available on remote access servers in a Windows NT 4 or Windows 2000 mixed-mode domain.

Tip

If your hardware or your inbound line does not support caller ID, don't configure this setting. If you do, remote access connections will always be denied, no matter what number the user calls from.

Remote Access Policies

Remote access policies give you the capability to approach remote access security granularly. You can set rules to allow or reject connection attempts based on membership in groups, by time or day of week. You can also specify the limits on the connection concerning bandwidth or encryption usage. In this section, we will look at how to set up a policy and how the policies are enforced.

Remote access policies are stored on the remote access server they are intended for. If you want to manage all policies for all RAS servers from a single place, you will need to use the Windows 2000 IAS as a RADIUS server. IAS installation and configuration will be covered in Chapter 9. Keep in mind that centralized management of remote access policies is an all or nothing approach. You can manage all policies for a given RAS server locally or you can manage all policies centrally. Windows 2000 does not support simultaneous use of policies stored locally and remotely.

How Policies Are Applied

When using remote access policies, remote connections are authorized only if the remote client's configuration matches at least one of the remote access policies. If the remote client does not match at least one policy, the connection will be refused, even if the remote user's account properties allow remote access. This means you have to have at least one policy configured to control connection attempts, otherwise, all connection attempts will be rejected.

When a user dials in to the remote access server, the remote access server decides to accept or reject an incoming request according to the following process:

1. The remote access server checks the policy list. If there are no policies, the connection attempt is rejected. If policies exist, the first policy in the list is checked for compliance with the user's settings.

2. If the remote user does not match *all* of the conditions of the policy, the next policy in the list is checked for compliance. This process continues until a matching policy is found or until there are no more policies. If no matching policy is found, the connection attempt is rejected.

3. If a connection attempt meets all the requirements of the policy, the remote access permissions for the user attempting the connection are examined. If Deny access is set for the account, the remote access server rejects the connection attempt.

4. If Allow access is set for the account, the remote access server compares the remote user's configuration to the user account properties and the matching profile properties. If the connection attempt does not match both the settings of the user account properties and the profile properties of any of the policies in the list, the connection attempt is rejected.

5. If the connection attempt matches the configuration of the user account properties and the profile properties, the connection attempt is accepted.

6. If the remote access permission is set to Control access through Remote Access Policy, the remote access sever checks the remote access permission setting of the policy. If the policy states Deny remote access permission, the connection attempt is rejected. If Grant remote access permission is selected, the remote access server compares the user account properties and profile properties. If the connection attempt does not match the settings of both the user account properties and profile properties, the connection attempt is rejected.

This is a long and involved process. It gives the administrator the flexibility, however, to set very specific criteria for accepting or rejecting a connection attempt. It is a good idea to familiarize yourself with this process to make troubleshooting remote access problems easier. You might find that administration and troubleshooting are easier in the long run when you design policies based on group membership, rather than creating different policies for different users.

How to Create a Policy

A remote policy is really just a rule that states the conditions that must be met in order for a remote user to connect to the remote access server. To create a remote access policy, use the Remote Access Policy Wizard. The wizard can be launched from the Routing and Remote Access console. Click the server on which you want to configure a policy, then right-click Remote Access Policies, then click New Remote Access Policy. You then specify the policy name, the policy conditions, whether permission is granted or denied based on this policy, and the specific user profiles that must be met to complete the connection. We will discuss the specific policy conditions and profile settings in this section, beginning with the default policy.

The default policy is automatically configured to deny access to users dialing in at any time, any day of the week. If you want to allow anyone with dial-in permissions on their user account to access this server, all you have to do is change the permission on this policy to Grant remote access permission, and you are in business. Any user with dial-in permission can access this server 24 hours a day, seven days a week. You can create much more elaborate policies, however, and that is what we are going to talk about now.

Conditions

Conditions are the elements of a policy that define the circumstances under which a connection attempt will be allowed. You can set multiple conditions, which serves to narrow the field of potential connections. Remember, a user must meet *all* the connection conditions before a connection is permitted. The following table shows the conditional parameters you can set for your policy:

- NAS IP Address
- Service Type
- Framed Protocol
- Called Station ID
- Calling Station ID
- NAS Port Type
- Day and Time Restrictions
- Client IP Address
- Client Vendor
- Client Friendly Name
- Windows Groups

Most of these options are obvious in what they require of the remote user, but a few of them need a little explanation. Client IP Address, Client Vendor, and Client Friendly Name are used by RADIUS clients connecting to a server running Internet Authentication Service (IAS and RADIUS will be covered in Chapter 9).

Many of the options allow you to use pattern matching in place of specific characters. You can require that all callers originate their calls from a specific area code, for example, but not from a specific phone number. Simply substitute wildcards for the optional characters—for example, 101-★★★-★★★★ will filter in or out all callers from the 101 area code, depending on your permission setting. (Don't forget that to use caller ID functions on your RAS server, your hardware and telephone service must also support it.)

Remote Access Permission

After you configure the appropriate conditions for a policy, you then specify whether these conditions are to allow or deny a connection. Choosing the option Grant remote access permission allows the remote users meeting the conditions to proceed to the next step in granting remote access permissions. On the other hand, choosing Deny remote access will prohibit all users who meet those conditions.

Remote access permission can be granted or denied at the user account level, as mentioned previously in this section. The user's account remote access permission overrides the remote access permission on a policy. If you choose the Control access through Remote Access Policy option, however, the remote access permission policy will determine whether the user is granted access.

Controlling access through policies can provide a convenient method of managing large numbers of remote users. Let's say you want to allow all the accountants who work in the satellite offices across the country to have remote access to the network all the time. You can create a set of conditions that allows the Accountants Group to have access 24 hours a day, seven days a week. Then you set the remote access permission to Grant access permission. Now let's say you want to limit the hours accountants can use these resources. Instead of having to configure logon hours on the accountants' user accounts individually, you can change the hours on the conditions of the policy. Or, to temporarily prevent remote access by the Accountants Group, you can simply change the grant access permissions for that policy to Deny remote access permission. When you are ready to allow access again, just change the permission back to Grant access permission.

Profile

After a remote user has cleared the conditions and permissions access hurdles, they come to the next block: a remote access policy profile. A *profile* is a method of requiring a specific remote client configuration, and it is made up of five options: Dial-in Constraints, IP, Multilink, Authentication, Encryption, and Advanced properties. The profile is reached by clicking the Edit profile button on the policy property sheet, or through the Remote Access Policy Wizard during the initial policy configuration. The profile properties sheet is shown in Figure 2.5 below.

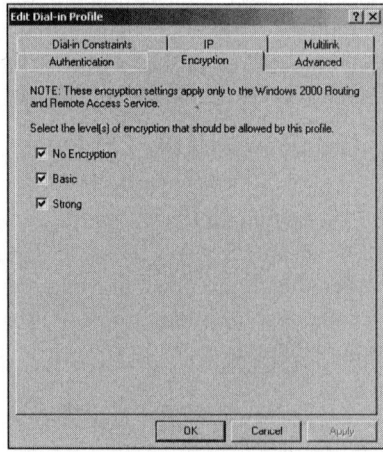

Figure 2.5   The remote access policy profile properties sheet.

There are quite a few limitations you can put on a remote client connection attempt:

- **Idle disconnect time.** This parameter lets you specify how long a connection can be idle before the connection is closed. This is especially useful when your remote access users connect by long-distance, or if you have a limited number of dial-in ports.

- **Maximum session length.** You can also specify a maximum length of time for any connection. You might want to set this for remote users who are inappropriately using your remote access server as a free ISP at night and on weekends. By forcing a session to close after a specific length of time, you can free up dial-in for other users who might need the connection for something besides access to CNN or eBay.

- **Day and time limits.** Here is another place to set the day and time of a connection attempt. Just as an FYI, a connection that is already in session when the time or date limits are reached will not be disconnected. In other words, if you set a profile for no access after 5 p.m., and a user connects at 4:59 p.m., he or she will not be disconnected at 5:00. However, the user will not be able to connect to new resources after the set time has been reached.

- **Dial-in number.** This is helpful for remote access servers that have multiple inbound phone lines. You might want to restrict users or groups of users to a specific dial-in number.

- **Dial-in media.** You can also restrict a connection to specific media or connection types. For instance, you might only want to allow ISDN connections or VPN connections on a specific remote access server. VPNs will be covered in Chapter 7.

The IP properties of a connection profile can allow a client to request a specific IP address if the client is configured to do so. This property can also be used to set filters for the types of traffic permitted to and from remote clients. The filter is set on an exception basis—either all traffic is allowed or only specific types of traffic will be allowed. In addition to defining traffic types, you can set source or destination addresses for permitted traffic.

If you have enabled multilink and *Bandwidth Allocation Protocol* (BAP) on your server, you can control the usage of the lines here. Setting multilink options will limit the number of ports a remote user can use. BAP settings enable you to set the usage parameters to be used in a connection that uses BAP (multilink and BAP will be covered in Chapter 10).

By setting the authentication types for a profile, you are requiring that certain authentication protocols must be used for that connection. You might want all weekend dial-in users to authenticate with smart cards, for example, instead of another authentication method. In this case, you would set the authentication type to EAP and specify Smart Card or other Certificate. (See the "Authentication and

Authorization" section earlier in this chapter for more information on how to set up smart card authentication on a RAS server.) The remote access server must be configured to accept the authentication protocol specified in the profile.

Setting encryption for a remote connection is especially important for VPN connections, although it can be set for PPP connections. This allows the flexibility of setting custom policies for different groups of users that might require no, moderate, or very strong encryption.

If RADIUS clients will be connecting to your remote access server, you can set additional options that will be passed to the client by the IAS server. The only options that apply to non-RADIUS dial-in clients are: Account-Interim-Interval, Framed-Protocol (set to PPP by default), Framed-MTU, Reply-Message, and Service-Type (set to Framed by default).

Summary

That wraps up our look at the remote access server, how it works, and how to configure it. Windows 2000 offers great new security features that are incorporated into many components of the OS, including RAS. As you saw in this chapter, a user must be authenticated and authorized before connecting to the remote access server. Authentication, which verifies the identity of the remote user, can use clear text passwords or it can require smart cards. Authentication is the process of granting permission for a remote user to establish a connection. It can be as simple as giving a single user the ability to dial in, or it can be very complex with multiple policies governing the who, when, and how of the connection. For more information on these topics, refer to the Windows 2000 Resource Kit.

References

Following is a listing of several RFCs covering topics in this chapter. You might want to refer to the RFCs for additional clarification. RFCs are Internet Standards that have been compiled by the Internet Engineering Task Force (IETF). They are found in several locations on the Internet, including `http://www.cis.ohio-state.edu/hypertext/information/rfc.html`

RFC 1055: A Nonstandard for Transmission of IP Datagrams Over Serial Lines: SLIP.
RFC 1661: The Point-to-Point Protocol (PPP)
RFC 1994: PPP Challenge Handshake Authentication Protocol (CHAP)
RFC 2716: PPP EAP TLS Authentication Protocol.

3

Dial-Up Networking

Configuring a computer running Windows 2000 Server or Windows 2000 Professional to act as a dial-up client is a fairly simple two-stage process:

- Installing and configuring the hardware
- Installing and configuring the software

In this chapter, we will examine how to perform both of these tasks to allow a client to successfully dial up a remote server. Let's begin with an overview of dial-up networking.

Dial-Up Networking Overview

A dial-up connection can allow remote users to access a single computer, a remote LAN, or the Internet. Common usage scenarios for dial-up connections are:

- Allow a single remote user to connect to his or her office computer while on the road
- Join many users in multiple locations to a remote LAN to allow them to use corporate resources
- Access an Internet point of presence (POP) server

Windows 2000 provides many security features in its remote access client software. Domain logon, smart card authentication, encryption, and callback are just a sample of the features supported on the remote client. The use of these features is dependent on what is supported by the remote access server, however. For instance, you might not be able to use the callback feature with your ISP, but you can log on to a Windows 2000 domain over the same connection. This apparent drawback does have a positive side: The ISP you choose does not have to use a special configuration or special infrastructure. If a remote user can connect to the Internet in some way, then he or she can connect to the corporate network over that connection.

An example of a large number of users connecting to a corporate network over an ISP is the Navy Standard Integrated Personnel System (NSIPS). I worked on this project as a systems engineer, first designing the enterprise architecture and later working on the actual deployment of the project (more on the deployment aspect later in the section called Hardware Installation later in this chapter). NSIPS is a personnel and pay system that replaced 10 legacy systems. It is deployed worldwide to ship and shore sites, with every site offering varying levels of network connectivity. When I say varying, I mean everything from fiber to the desktop to 10BaseT to sneakernet, and from satellite uplinks to high-speed WAN links to dial-up Internet access. Because NSIPS was not an infrastructure project, the goal was to use existing connectivity to join all sites. In hundreds of places, the only option was to use a dial-up ISP to connect to the central data stores. Using dial-up networking and a third-party VPN solution, remote sites are able to securely process transactions in a distributed Oracle database with a PeopleSoft front end. The dial-up connection is transparent to the applications running over this link. Because NSIPS does not rely on a bank of modems to accept incoming connections, remote clients never have to wait for a free modem to process their transactions, and there are no huge bills for long distance or 800-number access to the modem banks.

Shop Around for Special ISP Features

It is a good idea to shop around for an ISP before choosing one. A growing number of ISPs are increasing their service offerings to corporate customers. Many now offer end-to-end protection of dial-up connections through VPNs or other security features. If you have a very large remote user base accessing your network through a dial-up connection to an ISP, you might find it easier or more cost-effective to allow the ISP to provide the security you need, especially if your administrative staff is small. However, your network is only as secure as the ISP's network, and you don't have the same control over configuration as you would in your own network. Be sure you are thoroughly informed about the level of security of the ISP's network and how it in turn could affect your network's security.

Another relatively new service offered by ISPs is "roaming." This service allows partner ISPs to share their POPs with each other. This sharing service enables traveling users to connect to the Internet through a local number, rather than a long distance or 800-number call to the home POP.

Connectivity Components

Windows 2000 supports a variety of protocols, hardware, and media types used to create a connection between two computers. This section will examine the connection protocols, access methods, and LAN protocols used for a dial-up session.

Connection Protocols

Windows 2000 supports two connection protocols:

- Point-to-Point Protocol (PPP)
- Serial Line Internet Protocol (SLIP)

PPP is provided for both the Windows 2000 remote access server and remote client, while SLIP is only provided for the Windows 2000 remote access client.

PPP

PPP is a standard protocol set that allows remote clients and servers to establish a point-to-point connection. Because PPP is an industry standard, it offers interoperability between remote access clients using software from different vendors. PPP is a much more flexible connection protocol than SLIP. With PPP, remote clients and servers can negotiate for authentication and encryption methods, including newer authentication methods such as smart cards. PPP also offers a choice of LAN protocols to be used over the link. Most ISPs use PPP as the connection protocol of choice.

SLIP

SLIP is an older connection protocol. Although not commonly used today, it is provided as connection choice for Windows 2000 dial-up clients. Some corporations and government agencies still use SLIP on their UNIX remote access servers, so you might need to configure a remote client to use SLIP in that environment. SLIP connections are not as feature-rich as PPP connections. For example, you don't have a choice of LAN protocols—TCP/IP is the only supported protocol. Additionally, you have to log in through a terminal window, which can be difficult for remote users, especially when the connection is slow and the window does not respond to keyboard entries quickly. You can automate the logon with a script to ease this process for the remote user, but this can be difficult too. SLIP doesn't support authentication as part of the protocol, unlike PPP, which offers the wide array of authentication protocols discussed in Chapter 2, "Remote Access Server." Further, SLIP does not support encryption, which means that all text based data (like user name and password) transmitted over the link during session establishment are sent in the clear.

Access Methods

Windows 2000 supports analog telephone connections, ISDN, X.25, serial, and parallel connections.

Analog Phone Connections

The typical remote connection happens over an analog phone line, also known as POTS (plain old telephone service) or PSTN (public switched telephone network). The only equipment you need for this type of connection (besides the phone line) is a modem supported by Windows 2000.

The typical maximum speed for a POTS line is 56Kbps; however, Federal Communications Commission regulations limit analog service to 53Kbps in the United States. Bandwidth on a POTS line can vary greatly from place to place and connection to connection. You may dial up an ISP and get a connection as low as 19.2Kbps this time, and connect at 46.4Kbps the next time. In other words, the bandwidth of an analog line is not guaranteed. If you need a guaranteed high-speed connection, you might want to consider a digital line. Another option is to use multilink. Multilink allows you to bundle bandwidth from separate phone lines with separate modems into a single channel, increasing throughput. Multilink will be covered in Chapter 10, "Bandwidth and Telecommunications."

ISDN

Integrated Services Digital Network (ISDN) lines offer guaranteed bandwidth from 64 to 128Kbps. This service is available in many areas, but you will need to check with your telephone company to verify it is available in your area. ISDN is often given other names by the marketing departments of telephone companies, so check carefully that what you are ordering is actually ISDN service. With the faster ISDN speeds come higher prices—ISDN adapters and lines usually cost more than POTS modems and phone lines. However, the higher bandwidth may increase availability of resources and user productivity, consequently decreasing the total cost of ownership of ISDN.

ISDN is broken into three channels: two 64Kbps B channels used for data and one 16Kbps D channel used for signaling. It is possible to join two B channels with Multilink, effectively doubling bandwidth. Using Bandwidth Allocation Protocol (BAP), you can introduce another level of efficiency in your ISDN connections. BAP adds available links to a connection when extra bandwidth is required, and it will remove those extra links when they are no longer needed. BAP can save money by dropping unneeded connections over long distance links. BAP can also increase the usage of these long-distance links, and, hence, increase the total cost of a dial-up link. Be sure that you evaluate the potential cost of lines added with BAP. You could get a nasty surprise when the first phone bill comes in, if that link uses more bandwidth than had been anticipated.

Cable Modems

In areas where the cable television provider is also in the ISP business, you may choose to use a cable modem to connect your network to the Internet. A cable modem provides broadband Internet access at speeds of 10 to 30Mbps. Cable service providers in some areas can also provide connectivity between sites via metropolitan area networks. Contact the cable provider in your area to find out if this service is available.

X.25

X.25 uses a packet-switched network to send data from source to destination. Its use is more common in other countries than in the United States. X.25 connections provide speeds up to 56Kbps in the US, and up to 64K in Europe. Microsoft recommends ISDN over X.25 where it is available, because it offers higher speeds and increased reliability. Other services offering higher speeds than x.25 might be available in your area.

Direct Access

You can directly access another computer by using serial or parallel connections. Reasons you would set up a direct connection include joining a computer on one network to another computer on a physically separate network, or connecting a Windows CE device to a network computer.

Security is something you should consider before implementing such a connection. Remember from Chapter 2 that a remote connection attempt is authenticated to verify the identity of the user, and then authorization is used to control access to the network resources. Because direct connections are not always authenticated (depending on the connected device), you should make sure that you have secured sensitive information and resources to prevent unauthorized access.

Serial connections use a serial cable (RS-232, null modem) and COM ports at each end of the connection to join two computers or Windows CE devices. Infrared serial access is also frequently used with laptops or palm/hand held computing devices. The infrared port is configured to emulate a serial port, which is treated as a serial connection to another computer. Infrared connections can attain speeds up to 4Mbps.

Infrared and radio-based wireless access is another option for connecting laptops and other devices. Infrared, or IrDA, uses line of sight infrared transmission of data at speeds from 4Mbps to 16Mbps. Bluetooth is a proposed specification for short-range, point-to-multipoint voice and data transfer via radio waves. Bluetooth can transmit through solid objects from distances up to 10 m, and at speeds of up to 1Mbps. While IrDA offers greater speeds, Bluetooth offers greater flexibility of use and configuration.

Windows 2000 uses the DirectParallel driver to join two computers with ECP parallel ports. To create this type of connection, use Parallel Technologies' Basic or Fast parallel cables. These cables can attain speeds of up to 1mbps. For more information this product, see the Parallel Technologies Web site: http://www.paralleltechnologies.com.

LAN Protocols

Windows 2000 supports TCP/IP, IPX, NetBEUI, and AppleTalk LAN protocols over a dial-up link.

TCP/IP is the most widely used network protocol. It is routable and offers administrators flexibility in address assignment and name resolution. However, because it is a routable protocol, it has a higher overhead than other LAN protocols, such as IPX and NetBEUI. It is also complex to configure, compared to these other protocols. Clients can request a specific IP address, or they can be assigned an IP address by the remote access server to which they connect. Additionally, remote clients can take advantage of all regular TCP/IP name resolution methods:

- Broadcasting
- WINS
- DNS
- LMHOSTS files
- HOSTS files

WINS and DNS servers can be assigned by the remote access server, or the remote client can use locally assigned WINS and DNS servers.

IPX is typically used in networks where Novell servers are located. IPX addresses are provided to dial-up clients by a remote access server. A dial-up client running Client Service for NetWare can access resources on a Novell server on a remote network. IPX may be a better choice for a small- to medium-sized network than TCP/IP. It doesn't require extensive configuration and has less overhead than TCP/IP.

NetBEUI is a non-routable protocol that is ideal for use in small networks. It is easily configured on the client (all that is required is the computer name) and is supported by Windows 9x, Windows NT 3.x and later, Windows for Workgroups, LAN Manager, and Windows 2000 clients. It has very little overhead and is extremely fast. Although there is an inexorable migration toward using TCP/IP in every network, TCP/IP carries a lot of overhead, both on the cable and in terms of administration and configuration issues. NetBEUI is a great choice for use in a very small network that doesn't connect to any other network.

AppleTalk is the primary network protocol of Apple Macintosh networks. Windows 2000 dial-up clients can use AppleTalk to access a Macintosh remote access server. However, Windows 2000 dial-up clients cannot use AppleTalk to access a Windows 2000 remote access server.

Hardware Installation

One of the best new features of Windows 2000 (at least in my opinion) is the support for Plug and Play. Hardware installation was one of the biggest problems on the personnel and pay project I worked on with the US Navy. This project deployed 800 Windows NT 4.0 Servers and 4,000 Windows NT 4.0 Workstations worldwide. The hardware for the project came from different vendors, had different configurations even within the same vendor's model, and was to be configured at the site by local personnel who might or might not have been computer literate. An ideal solution would have been to create a scripted installation. However, as we did not know specifically what hardware was where and Windows NT 4.0 does not support Plug and Play, this was not an option. Manual installation of Windows NT was required in most cases, and one of the most difficult things to configure, as it turned out, was the modem.

Modem vendors don't always put a sticker or other identification on their hardware to indicate manufacturer, model, chipset, and so on. If a user misplaced (or never received) the original driver disk or other documentation, it was virtually impossible to know exactly what type of modem was installed. Plug and Play would have been a dream come true for this project! Hopefully, these types of deployment nightmares will be eliminated with the advent of Windows 2000 Server and Professional.

Another feature in Windows 2000 is USB (Universal Serial Bus) support. USB devices require little or no configuration. Just plug in the device and you are ready to go. The USB device firmware contains all the information about the device, which eliminates the need for further manual configuration. USB devices include printers, scanners, external storage media, and modems.

Modem Installation

The first step is to physically install the modem. The next time you power up the computer, Windows 2000 will most likely detect and install your hardware for you. If you are installing a PC card modem, you don't have to power off the computer to install—just pop it in. In either case, however, if it is not detected, or if an incorrect modem is detected, just follow these procedures to complete the install.

1. In Control Panel, open Phone and Modem Options. Click the Modems tab, as shown in Figure 3.1.

2. Click the Add button. The Install New Modem Wizard will start. You can click Next to allow Windows 2000 to try to detect your modem, but chances are, if it didn't detect it on boot-up, it won't detect it now either. If this is the case, click Next and the wizard will ask you to select the modem from a list. You can save yourself a couple of minutes by selecting "Don't detect my modem; I will select it from a list," and then clicking Next.

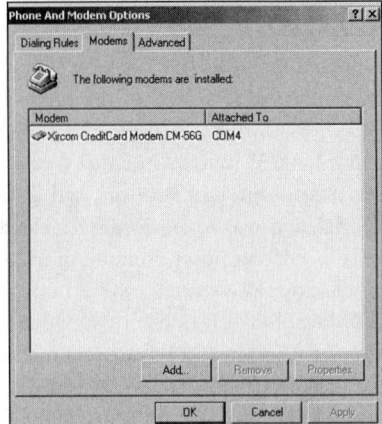

Figure 3.1   Install modems through Phone and Modem Options.

3. Select your modem from the list that appears. If your modem does not appear or you want to use a different driver, click Have Disk… and specify the location of the driver you want to use. Click Next.

4. Select the port or ports on which you want to install the modem, then click Next. Windows 2000 will install the selected modem on the selected port or ports.

5. When Windows 2000 has completed the installation, click Finish. You are now ready to configure the dialing properties of the modem.

If you don't see your modem in the list and you don't have a Windows 2000 driver, you have two options. One is to try the Windows NT 4.0 or Windows 9x driver for that modem. The other option is to choose Standard Modem Types from the Manufacturers list, and select one with the appropriate speed.

Always Shop from the Hardware Compatibility List!
I said earlier that installing the modem is the first step, but selecting the right modem should really come first. I can tell you from experience there are few things more frustrating than troubleshooting a flaky modem problem. Not all modems are created equal, and modems that are not on the HCL can cause problems with other seemingly unrelated things, such as name resolution on the local LAN or domain logons. Sure, the modem may work correctly now, but what about after you install the newest version of AOL or add/remove a protocol? The cheap modem you picked up on sale may not seem like such a bargain after you spend an entire weekend trying to figure out why the senior vice president of marketing gets a bluescreen every time he launches Internet Explorer on his laptop.

Here are a few helpful hints for installing modems:

- If you installed the modem before installing Windows 2000, but the installation hangs or takes an inordinately long time, try this: Remove the modem, install Windows 2000, and install the modem after you have completed the Windows 2000 install.

- If you are installing the same modem on multiple ports, you can speed up the process by duplicating the modem to other ports. Right-click the modem you want to duplicate, then select Duplicate from the pop-up menu. Click All ports or Selected ports as appropriate.

- You can copy the properties of one modem to another modem too. Right-click the modem with the properties you want to copy, then select Copy Properties. Right-click the modem with the properties you want to overwrite and select Apply Properties.

ISDN Adapter Installation

To install an ISDN adapter, follow these instructions:

1. Power off your computer and physically install the ISDN adapter.

2. Power up the computer and install the driver as prompted by Windows 2000. If Windows 2000 does not detect your adapter, use the Add/Remove Hardware tool in Control Panel.

3. Although not required, it is a good idea to restart your computer at this point, especially if you have installed multiple adapters.

When the process is finished, you will need to configure the ISDN adapter for use with your phone service. This configuration can be done from Device Manager. To reach the Device Manager, click Start, Settings, Control Panel. Double-click System to launch that applet. When the System applet has opened, click the Hardware tab, then click the Device Manager button. Depending on the type of ISDN adapter, you may find it listed as a network adapter card or as a modem. Right-click the adapter and click Properties. In the window that opens, you will configure the SPID (Service Profile Identifier)/phone number for your ISDN line, the local telephone company switch type, and line-type negotiation, if required for your adapter. You will need to get all this information from your telephone company.

X.25 Card Installation

You can use X.25 packet assemblers/disassemblers (PADs), X.25 cards, or a modem with a dial-up X.25 carrier. (To allow inbound X.25 connections on a computer running Windows 2000 Professional or Windows 2000 Server, however, you must use an X.25 card.)

To install an X.25 device, power off the computer, physically install the device, restart the computer, then consult the manufacturer's documentation for further details.

Configure Dialing Parameters

Now that you have installed your remote access hardware and drivers, you need to set up the dialing instructions. These instructions are not the specific phonebook entries to dial an ISP, but instead are the prefixes, calling card numbers, and so forth that are used to actually dial the modem. These settings are configured on the Dialing Rules tab of the Phone and Modem Options in Control Panel.

Dialing rules are the equivalent of the dialing locations in Windows NT 4.0. Simply stated, they are the configuration governing how a connection is to be dialed when you are in a specific location. After they are configured, you select the one that applies to your location, as shown in Figure 3.2.

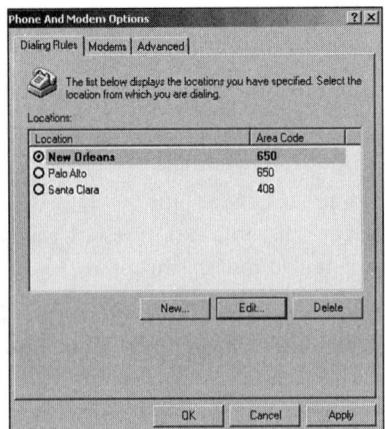

Figure 3.2   A list of configured dialing rules.

The dialing rules you configure will be available to all modems you install, and can be selected at the time a dial-up connection is initiated. To configure a new rule, click New on the Dialing Rules tab. You must configure general, area code, and calling card information. Each of these topics corresponds to a tab on the Location properties sheet, as shown in Figure 3.3.

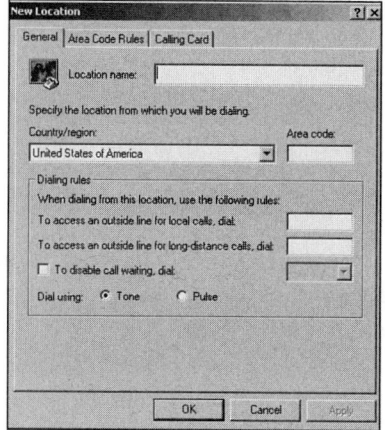

Figure 3.3   Dialing Rules properties sheet.

General

This tab is where you configure the name of the rule and any special dialing instructions for accessing an outside line or local or long distance calls, disabling call waiting, and whether to use tone or pulse dialing.

Area Code Rules

Area code rules stipulate how to dial a specific area code and the prefixes in that area code. To create a new area code rule:

1. Click the New button on the Area Code Rules tab.

2. Enter the area (or city) code to which this rule will apply. Area code rules work by exclusion, meaning that a rule applies to all prefixes in an area code or only those prefixes designated. For instance, you might have a rule that includes only the 555 prefix in the 505 area code. Select "Include all the prefixes within this area code" or "Include only the prefixes in the list below" as appropriate. If you selected the latter option, enter the desired prefixes and click Add when done.

3. If special numbers must be dialed before the phone number, such as 1, 0, or the area code, check the appropriate box.

Not all prefixes in an area code use the same dialing instructions, however. Here is a possible scenario you encounter. Let's say that your area code covers the city you live in and several outlying areas. Calls within the city do not require the area code when dialing. When you want to call the outlying areas, you must dial 1 + area code + the number. If your users will be accessing dial-up numbers in local and outlying areas, you should create two rules for the area code, as illustrated in Figure 3.4.

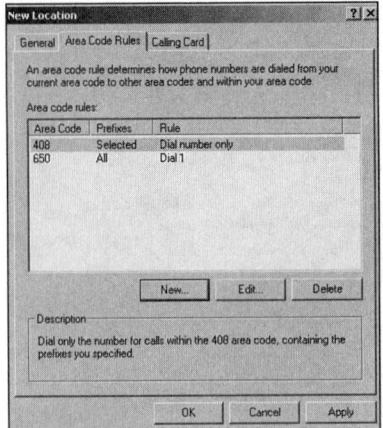

Figure 3.4   Multiple area code rules for a single area code.

Area code rules can also be helpful if your users frequently make international calls that involve complicated prefix combinations.

Calling Card

If you are using a calling card to charge a long distance dial-up connection, you can enter that information here. Note that the calling card account and PIN numbers do not display after they have been configured, and they are stored in an encrypted form.

Smart Card Installation

Windows 2000 supports smart card authentication over a dial-up link. This section will detail the installation of a smart card reader. Configuration of smart card authentication will be covered later in this chapter.

To install a smart card reader:

1. Power off the computer and physically install the device.

2. Restart the computer. Windows 2000 should detect the device and install the driver automatically. If it does not, use the Add/Remove Hardware tool in Control Panel to install the device driver.

3. Refer to your manufacturer's documentation for specific configuration instructions.

Configuring a Dial-Up Connection

After the hardware is installed and the phone line to be used is working, you can begin setting up a dial-up connection. In this section, we will explore the options for configuring Windows 2000 to act as a dial-up client. Dial-up connections are now made through Network and Dial-Up Connections. A wizard helps you setup the initial connection, which can be modified at any time.

Connection Properties

We will run through the configurable properties of a dial-up connection. To launch the wizard:

1. Click Start, Settings, Network and Dial-Up Connections, Make New Connection.

2. Normally, you would answer all the questions by the wizard with an appropriate response. However, for the sake of discussion in this instance, accept all the defaults by clicking Next, until prompted to click Finish.

3. When you have completed this, right-click the dial-up connection you have just created and select properties. The Dial-up Connection Properties sheet should be displayed. If you wish to connect to this new connection you may do so at this time. Otherwise, click Cancel.

There are five tabs on the Dial-Up Connection Properties sheet, but we will only examine four of them in this section. Internet connection sharing will be covered in Chapter 11, "Shared Internet Connectivity." The General, Options, Security, and Networking tabs allow you to set various options for outgoing connections. If you want to accept incoming dial-up connections on a Windows 2000 server that is not a domain controller, or on Windows 2000 Professional, you will configure this through the Users and Networking tabs. Incoming connections will be covered at the end of this chapter in the section "Incoming Connections."

General

This tab is where you specify the basic things used to create a connection. These include the modem/modems or other device to be used to create the connection, and the phone number/numbers each device is to dial. In other words, you can use multiple devices to make a connection, and you can configure a different phone number for each device to call. If you would like to monitor the status of a connection from the taskbar, configure that from the General tab as well. Just put a check mark in the box for "Show icon in taskbar when connected."

You can make connection-specific configuration changes for each modem you select by clicking the Configure button. The Modem Configuration dialog box, shown in Figure 3.5, allows you to set various options, including maximum connection speeds and modem protocols. If you are going to use a script or need to open a terminal window before dialing into a remote server, you will configure those options here too.

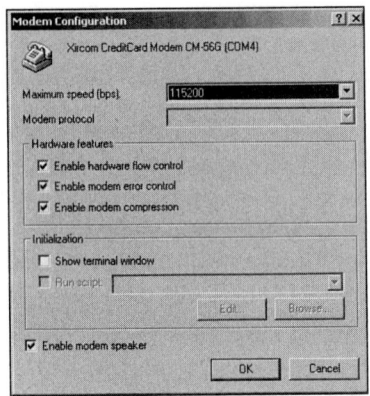

Figure 3.5   Configuring connection-specific options.

Options

The Options tab is where you can choose to view connection attempts while in progress, to be prompted to supply password or certificate information and domain logon information. You can also configure the connection attempt to bring up the phone number to be dialed, to be verified and modified if needed. This can be especially helpful if you would rather use a single dial-up connection from multiple locations. For instance, you might dial up your ISP's POP from home, where you do not need to dial any special numbers, but at the office you might need to dial 9 to get an outside line. Personally, I prefer this method to using multiple connections. You might find that some of your users will prefer to do this rather than remembering which connection they use from home or the office.

Another great thing you can configure from here are redial attempts. Let's say your remote users need to dial in to a remote access server at your office. The server can only allow 25 users to connect simultaneously. While most of the time this is not a problem, you may have a peak time when the server is always busy. You can set your client connections to keep redialing a set number of times, with a predetermined pause between each attempt. For example, you could configure a connection to redial 10 times, with a 10-second pause between each attempt. This way, users are not forced to manually attempt the connection again and again. It is also possible to configure a connection to disconnect itself after a period of inactivity—a great thing for clients of a server with a limited number of inbound lines.

You can configure multiple devices to dial out of this computer as well, provided you have installed and configured multiple devices. Your choices for using multiple devices are:

- Dial only first available device

- Dial all devices

- Dial devices only as needed

These options will only appear if your computer is configured with multiple dial-up devices.

Automatic dialing governs the time and usage minimums for the automatic dialing of another line. Automatic hangup governs the duration and usage levels that will cause Windows 2000 to automatically end the connection on the additional device. If you have decided to let Windows 2000 to dynamically add and hang up devices, the last connected device will disregard the Automatic hangup settings. The remaining device will instead automatically disconnect after 20 minutes of inactivity.

X.25 connection configuration is handled on this tab as well. Clicking the X.25 button brings up the X.25 connection dialog box. Here you will provide the name of the X.25 network to which you want to connect as well as the x.121 address, the X.25 equivalent of a phone number.

Security

From this tab, you will configure authentication and data security options required for this connection. The option to require secured password, allow unsecured password, or use smart card authentication is configured from the drop-down box.

To configure advanced security options, click the Settings button. The Advanced Security Settings dialog box, shown in Figure 3.6, is where data encryption is configured as required or optional. Further security options for authentication are configured on this tab. Only configure these advanced settings if you know your remote server supports them. (For a complete discussion of these protocols, see Chapter 2.)

Only One User Number Is Stored

Because a remote access server that requires callback only stores a single user number, only one device can be called back on a dial-up client computer, eliminating multilink capabilities. If both incoming lines on a dial-up client use the same phone number, such as a dual-channel ISDN, this is not a problem.

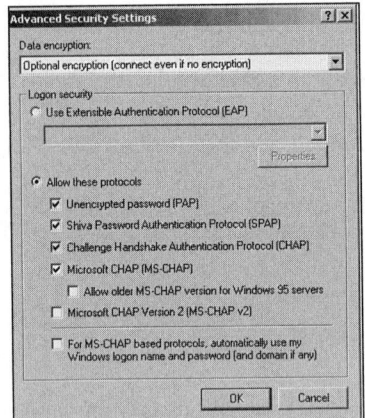

Figure 3.6 Advanced dial-up security settings.

Networking

On this tab you can select the variety of server (PPP or SLIP) to which you wish to connect. By clicking the Settings button, you can set various PPP options. The default settings should be adequate, unless your ISP or other provider has instructed you otherwise. You can also choose which networking components you would like to be available to a connection. Keep in mind that networking options are not connection-specific, however. Changes you make to one connection will affect all other connections. This means that if you specify that TCP/IP is to be used, then all dial-up connections will use TCP/IP.

Advanced Configuration

You can adjust additional parameters in the Network and Dial-up Connections folder by clicking Advanced on the menu bar, as illustrated in Figure 3.7.

This section will discuss the configuration options covered in the Advanced menu.

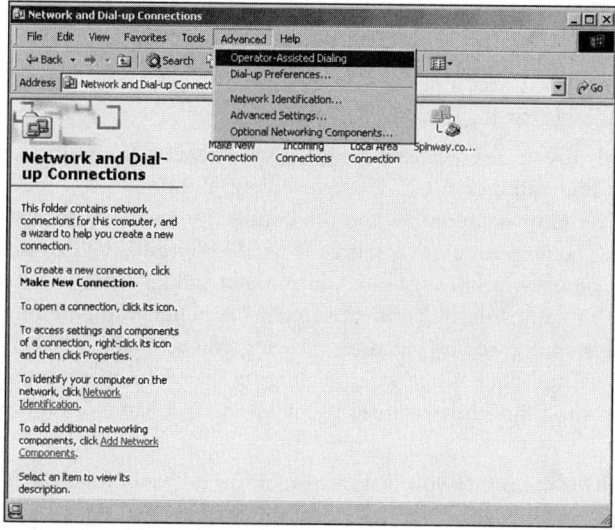

Figure 3.7   Advanced connection configuration.

Operator Assisted Dialing

If you require an operator's assistance when dialing a phone number, selecting this option will enable you or the operator to manually dial the number before initiating the modem. To use this feature:

1. Click the menu option Operator Assisted Dialing.

2. Open the dial-up connection you want to use. At this time you can call the operator through a telephone connected to the same line the modem will use.

3. When the operator has connected your call, click Dial on the dial-up connection. You can hang up the phone after the modem has taken control of the line. A good indication of the modem controlling the line is hearing the modem negotiation/handshake squeal or being prompted for a username and password.

Dial-Up Preferences

The Dial-Up Preferences menu option opens a dialog box with three tabs:

- **Connections.** Allows or prevents users from creating or modifying dial-up connections. If only an administrator can make a change to an dial-up connection, this can increase the workload of the administrator if the connections change frequently. On the other hand, if you know that these connections will rarely, if ever, change, this can cut down on administrative support time. Users will not be able to "accidentally break" a dial-up connection, reducing the time needed to troubleshoot and reconfigure user-modified dial-up connections. Another option available here is the ability to create or modify a dial-up networking connection before the Windows logon takes place. This is helpful in situations where domain logon takes place over a dial-up connection. This allows you to modify a dial-up entry without first logging on to Windows.

- **Autodial.** If you or your users frequently access data from a remote network, you may find autodial to be most convenient. Windows 2000 will remember the location of network resources and the connection used when that resource was accessed. The next time the resource is needed, autodial will automatically dial the connection without user intervention, not unlike setting up Internet Explorer to automatically connect to your ISP when you type in a URL. Autodial is configured by location, allowing you to enable it when dialing up from home, and disabling it when dialing up from the office (locations correspond to the dialing rules you set up in Phone and Modem Options in Control Panel).

- **Callback.** If the server you dial in to requires callback, you will configure it here. You can also specify the phone numbers that are assigned to the installed devices on your computer.

Advanced Settings

The Advanced Settings menu option will allow you to boost performance of your network connections by changing the order of your bindings. By moving more frequently used protocols to the top of the list, you are telling Windows 2000 to use those protocols first when communicating with remote hosts, which speeds up the connection time.

Copying a Dial-Up Connection

After you have set up a dial-up connection, you can save yourself some time in setting up other connections on the same computer by copying an existing connection and modifying it to suit the needs of the new connection. To copy a dial-up connection, right-click the desired connection, then click Create Copy.

Incoming Connections

If you manage a small network, you might not need to set up a full-blown remote access server. A computer running Windows 2000 Professional or Windows 2000 Server (as a standalone) can be configured to allow inbound connections as well (Windows 2000 Server running as a member server or a domain controller will run Routing and Remote Access Service). Windows 2000 Professional will allow one each of the following connections:

- Dial-up
- VPN
- Direct connections

Hardware capability is the only limit on the number of incoming connections to Windows 2000 Server. Windows 2000 inbound connections can support these client types:

- Windows NT 3.1, 3.5, 3.51, and 4.0 clients
- Windows 98 clients
- Windows 95 clients
- Macintosh clients
- Windows for Workgroups, MS-DOS, and LAN Manager clients
- PPP clients

To set up Windows 2000 to allow incoming connections, launch the Make New Network Connection Wizard. To get there, click Start, Settings, Network and Dial-up Connections. Provide the following information when requested by the wizard:

- **Accept incoming connections.** Select this option. Click Next.
- **Devices for Incoming Connections.** Select the device (or devices) that will be used for incoming connections. If you select multiple devices, you can use multilink. Click Next.
- **Incoming Virtual Private Connection.** The default is to allow VPN connections to this computer. The only requirement for this option is that your computer must have an FQDN or IP address that is reachable from the Internet (see Chapter 7, "Virtual Private Networks," for more information). Click Next.
- **Allowed Users.** Specify which users you would like to have remote access to this computer. Click Next.
- **Networking Components.** Select and configure the LAN protocols you would like to be used with this connections. Click Next.
- **Connection Name.** What would you like to call this connection? Click Finish.

After you have configured the connection through the wizard, you can go back and edit it later though its properties sheet. To do this, just right-click the connection in the Network and Dial-up Connections folder. There are a couple of other options that might be of interest to you on the Incoming Connections properties sheet. Both of those are found on the Users tab. Here, you can choose to require remote access users to encrypt data and passwords. By setting this, clients that connect must also be configured to require encryption. The other option gives directly connected devices, such as a Palm Pilot with an IR port or a laptop with a parallel connection, the capability to connect without providing a password. This might be a convenience for your users, but you might find that the threat of "unauthorized synching" is not worth the convenience.

Summary

To summarize this chapter, Windows 2000 dial-up networking is an easily configurable remote access client. It can be used to create VPN connections, dial-up connections, and can even be used to accept incoming connections on computers that are not running the full blown Routing and Remote Access Service. That offers a nice remote access solution for small or home offices looking for easy configuration and ease of management. Chapter 11 will introduce you to a set of tools that will ease client configuration issues. These tools can be a great help when using dial-up networking in an environment where there are numerous remote users. From here however, we will move into Chapter 4, which will focus on routing traffic with Windows 2000.

References

You can find more information on dial-up networking in the following sources:

- *Benefits for Mobile Users,* Windows 2000 Product Facts, Microsoft TechNet.
- *In a Windows NT 4.0 Environment,* Windows 2000 Product Facts, Microsoft TechNet.

4

Routing Protocols

Routing and Remote Access Service for Windows 2000 offers a feature-rich software router. Small, medium, and large businesses can use the Windows 2000 router for local or wide area network (LAN or WAN) or Virtual Private Network (VPN) connections. RRAS is integrated in the Windows 2000 Server operating system, offering the administrator a cost-effective routing tool. Not only is upgrading expensive routing hardware not required, but the Windows 2000 router works with literally hundreds of network adapters found on the Windows 2000 Hardware Compatibility List. This means that you can probably use your existing hardware to implement Windows 2000 routing or to provide the mobile workers at your company with a VPN connection to the corporate network. RRAS was designed to be an extensible platform as well. In addition to supporting a range of industry standard protocols, a set of Application Programming Interfaces (APIs) is available to third parties. Vendors can use these APIs to port existing routing protocols not provided by Windows 2000, or possibly to create new routing protocols, giving these vendors new revenue opportunities in the open networking industry.

There are many new and exciting features in RRAS, which complement and enhance routing and remote access functionality found in previous versions of Windows NT Server. However, before we look at all the features of Windows 2000, let's start with a quick look at the history of routing in Windows NT.

Windows NT 3.x provided for simple IP routing through a static router. Beginning with Windows NT 3.51 Service Pack 2, Routing Information Protocol for IP version 1 (RIP for IP v1) was supported. Later, with the advent of Routing and Remote Access Service (Windows NT 4.0 post-Service Pack 3), available routing services expanded to include RIP v1 and v2, Open Shortest Path First (OSPF), IP packet filtering, and demand-dial routing. Today, Windows 2000 offers the most full-featured suite of RRAS features to date, including:

- A GUI tool—the Microsoft Management Console (MMC)—for administration of the Windows 2000 router. (The Routing and Remote Access console is covered in detail in Chapter 2, "Remote Access Server" and Chapter 5, "Configuring the Windows 2000 Router.")

- A command-line interface for scripting and remote administration of the Windows 2000 router. (`Netsh.exe` and `routemon` will be covered in detail in Chapter 6, "Routing Tools.")

- Routing for Internet Protocol (IP), Internetwork Packet Exchange (IPX), and AppleTalk.

- IP unicast routing protocols and services: Open Shortest Path First (OSPF) by Bay Networks and Routing Information Protocol (RIP) versions 1 and 2.

- IPX routing protocols and services: Routing Information Protocol (RIP) for IPX and Service Advertising Protocol (SAP) for IPX.

- IP multicast services: Internet Group Management Protocol (IGMP) version 2 router and proxy to enable the forwarding of IP multicast traffic.

- Industry standard support for Dynamic Host Configuration Protocol (DHCP) Relay Agent and Internet Control Message Protocol (ICMP) router discovery.

- IP network address translation (NAT) services to simplify connecting small office/home office (SOHO) networks to the Internet.

- Demand-dial routing over dial-up WAN links.

- VPN support with PPTPL2TP over Internet Protocol security (IPSec).

- Tunneling support using IP-in-IP tunnels.

- IP and IPX packet filtering for performance and security.

- Support for Windows 2000 power management capabilities.

- Simple Network Management Protocol (SNMP) management capabilities with support for popular management information bases (MIBs).

- Extensive support for networking media, including 10 or 100Mbps ethernet, token ring, Fiber Distributed Data Interface (FDDI), ATM, ISDN, T-Carrier, frame relay, DSL, X.25, and analog modems.

In this chapter, we will take a look at important routing concepts and various unicast and multicast routing protocols and services, with a primary focus on IP routing as implemented in Windows 2000, particularly RIP and OSPF protocols. Features, benefits, and possible uses will be examined here. Installation and configuration of these protocols and services will be covered in Chapter 5, "Configuring the Windows 2000 Router."

Those of you who have used other routing products and tools will discover how Windows 2000 implements industry standard protocols, and where, in certain cases, it does not implement particular features of an RFC-based protocol. For those of you who have limited exposure to routing, this chapter will be a helpful introduction to routing protocols.

Routing Concepts

Routing is the mechanism for sending data from a source to a destination, either on a local network or between networks. There are two basic types of routing: host routing and router routing.

Host routing occurs when the source host forwards data to the destination host. The sending host must use the destination address to determine whether the destination host is on its own network or a remote network. If the destination is on the source network, the packet is sent directly to the destination host. If the destination is a remote network, the packet is forwarded to the gateway or router.

Router routing happens when a router receives a packet that is to be forwarded. When the router receives the packet, it determines if it is to be sent to a host on the local network or if it needs to be sent on to another network. If another network is indeed the destination, the router forwards the packet to the next router. This process is repeated until the destination network is reached and the destination host receives the data. The decision to send the packet to a specific router is based on data contained in routing tables.

Routing Tables

The routing table is a database of routes from the local network to remote networks. The routing table is not exclusive to a router. IP hosts also have a routing table that is used to decide the best router for the packet to be forwarded.

Each router between the source and destination makes its routing decision based on its local routing table. If the routing table of the source, destination host, or routers is incorrect, whether because of an incorrect configuration or because of a change in network status, routing problems can result. Troubleshooting routing problems can involve attempting to route data from different computers to narrow down the fault area, verifying configuration information, or it can even require that network sniffer traces be run to collect source and destination routing information from different points on the network. For more troubleshooting information, see Appendix B, "Troubleshooting."

Several types of routes can be present in a routing table, including:

- **Network route.** A route to a specific network ID.

- **Host route.** A route to a specific host address. The routing decision is made by examining both the network ID and host ID. These types of routes are often used to build custom routes for specific types of network traffic. Specifying a particular route to a network printer used for very large print jobs, for example, can ease congestion in a network by routing the print jobs through less crowded segments. (Although the ideal situation would be to isolate that printer on its own network, "political" circumstances occasionally prevent such a move. If this has happened to you, you know exactly what I am talking about.)

- **Default route.** A route that is used when no other routes for the destination are found in the routing table. For example, let's say you need to download the latest driver for your NIC from the manufacturer's Web site. The route to `http://www.NICmanufacturer.com` is probably not in the routing table of either your computer or your network's routers. The default route is used in this case to forward traffic to another more knowledgeable router, perhaps belonging to your ISP. A sample routing table is depicted in Figure 4.1. The headings of each column in the table are explained below.

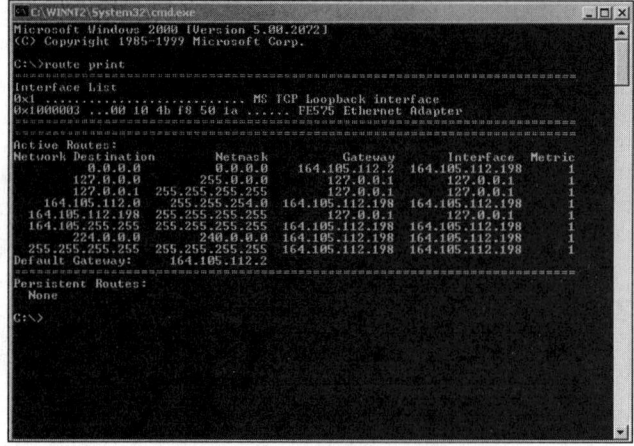

Figure 4.1 A routing table.

- *Network destination* is the destination. This column can contain a host address, a subnet address, a network address, or a default gateway.

- The *netmask* is used to distinguish the network ID portion of the destination IP address from the host ID.

- *Gateway address* is where the packet needs to be sent to leave this network. This can be the local network card or a local gateway (router).

- *Interface* is the address of the NIC over which the packet should be sent out of the local network.

- *Metric* is the number of hops to the destination. Each hop is a router that must be crossed to get to the destination. The metric is used to determine the best route.

Static and Dynamic Routers

Now that we have talked about routing tables and how routers decide to route traffic between networks, we need to talk about how that information actually gets into the routing table. There are two basic ways to populate a routing table: statically and dynamically. Each method has its benefits.

Static Routing

On a static router, the routing tables are manually configured. The network administrator builds and constantly updates the routing table, entering all routes in the routing table. Static routers work well for small networks, but are not the best choice for large or frequently changing networks due to the amount of manual administration involved. Static routers do not detect changes in network topology or link outages, nor do the routes in the routing tables have an expiration date. Every time you add a new router or a router goes down, you have to run around to all the static routers in a network and change the routing tables. In a small network, this isn't that big of a deal. In a large network with 10 or 12 routers, this could be a headache you don't need.

Figure 4.2 is an example of an ideal location for a static router. A computer training company has two distinct parts to its business: the operations side and the classroom side. The administrator would like to set up an easily maintained network that will isolate each network's traffic from the other. The only requirement is that the classroom side must be able to reach the server that stores all the classroom software and also acts as the print server for the operations side. The simplest solution involves two NIC cards in the server. Each NIC is configured as an interface for its network and forwards data to the appropriate network. Only one static route is needed for each network.

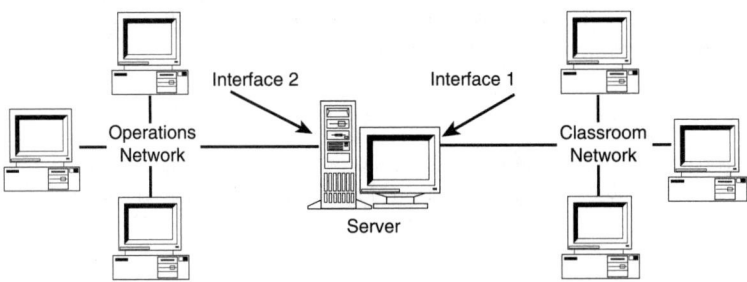

Figure 4.2   A simple network using static routing.

Dynamic Routing

A dynamic router has routing tables that are created and updated automatically through continuous communication between routers. Routing information is exchanged between routers either at a predetermined interval or on request. When installed and configured, dynamic routers require little administrative maintenance. The information that dynamic routers learn from other routers expires after a specific amount of time. At the end of a route's life, the router queries other routers to determine if the links in the expired route are still good. If a router has gone down, this change is noted and is propagated to other routers on the network. Routing protocols enable this information exchange and allow dynamic routers to overcome faults and changes in topology very easily. Dynamic routing is a great choice for medium-sized to very large networks.

Let's revisit the training company we talked about in the last section. This company has grown large enough that it now requires three separate networks and two servers to accommodate the needs of the users. A simple solution would be to install two network cards on each server, connect two networks to each server and to run RIP or OSPF routing protocols to route the traffic to the right network. One of the networks, in this case the new network, will be connected to both servers, as shown in Figure 4.3.

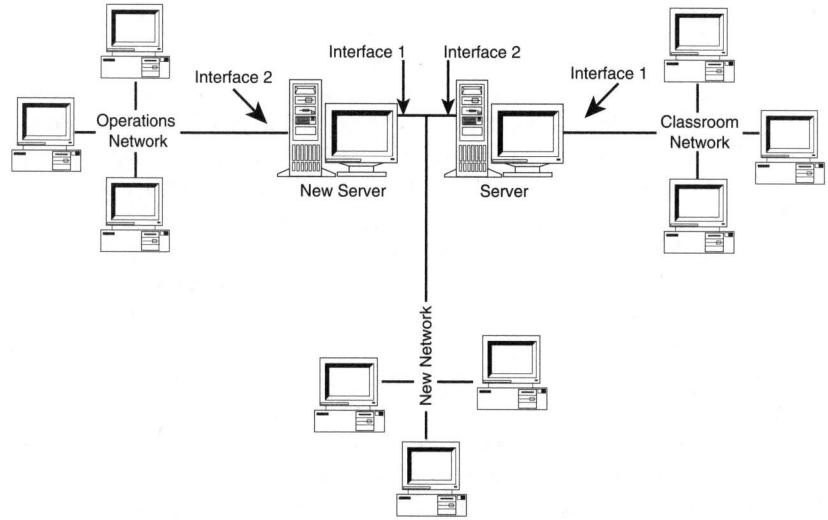

Figure 4.3   A more complex network using dynamic routing.

Unicast Routing

Unicast routing is defined as traffic that is forwarded over multiple networks and is destined for a single host. This is also known as point-to-point delivery. Windows 2000 supports IP, IPX, and AppleTalk unicast routing with a veritable plethora of protocols. Table 4.1 shows the unicast routing protocols Windows 2000 supports out of the box.

Table 4.1   **Windows 2000 Supported Unicast Routing Protocols**

IP Protocols	IPX Protocols	AppleTalk Protocols
RIP for IP	RIP for IPX	Routing Table Maintenance Protocol (RTMP)
OSPF	SAP for IPX	
DHCP Relay Agent		
NAT		
IP Packet Filtering		
ICMP Router Discovery		

Multicasting

Delivering data to multiple destinations on an internetwork is called point-to-multipoint delivery. There are three point-to-multipoint delivery methods: unicasting, broadcasting, and multicasting. Each one sends data to a different destination address and has various features and drawbacks. Multicasting is one technique of delivering this data without tying up unnecessary amounts of bandwidth. In this section, we will look at various methods of point-to-multipoint data delivery, multicast routing protocols, and how Windows 2000 supports multicasting.

A host sending a unicast message addresses the data packet with the IP address of the destination host. This is a great way to send data to a single host or a small amount of data to a small list of recipients. However, the message is duplicated for each recipient. As the number of recipients and amount of the data to be sent increase, the added network overhead also increases. If you are sending the same data to 25 computers, you are going to clutter up the network with 25 copies of the same data. The more data pumped over the network, the slower the data will travel. Not exactly an ideal situation if you are doing over-the-network software upgrades in a large network!

Another method of delivering data to multiple recipients is by broadcasting. This method doesn't send duplicate copies of the same message over the network nor does it require a list of recipients to be maintained. It works by sending the data to the broadcast address of the subnet. However, broadcasting has drawbacks. Every node on the network processes every broadcast message to determine if the packet is destined for that node, adding additional strain on those devices. Furthermore, broadcast packets are not forwarded by routers. This means that while everyone on a subnet gets the broadcast, not everyone on the internetwork gets it. Remember NetBEUI? It is a great protocol for very small networks—it's fast, incredibly easy to set up, and doesn't add a lot of network overhead. However, because NetBEUI is broadcast-based, you can't route it. This means users on one side of a router can't access resources on the other side. The same thing is true of broadcast messages—only one side of a router will receive the message.

Finally, there is multicasting. Multicasting sends messages to a multicast address. One copy of the data is sent, only those nodes that have been configured to listen for it are disturbed, and multicast routers can forward this message to other subnets. Multicasting can be best compared to a television broadcast. Imagine your local PBS station. It broadcasts one copy of its programming on a certain frequency that can be picked up by any device tuned to that channel. And, just as television broadcasts are limited by distance, multicast messages are also limited by boundaries. These boundaries are based on a scope of IP addresses, called a multicast scope, or by limiting the time-to-live (TTL) value in the IP header. If the TTL is exceeded, the packet is silently discarded. It is important to remember that multicast datagrams only offer best-effort delivery. There is no guarantee that packets will be delivered or will arrive in a specific order. Multicasting uses Class D IP addresses (224.0.0.0 to 239.255.255.255).

Multicasting Uses

Much of what network users do on a network involves point-to-point delivery: printing, email, or accessing files on a server. However, multicasting offers an alternative to unicast- or broadcast-based traffic for some applications. An investment firm might run real-time stock quotes on the desktops of all its brokers. If the ticker was run as a unicast application, it would eat up a serious chunk of bandwidth between the opening and closing bells on whatever markets it tracks. Using broadcast technology would utilize processing resources on every computer on that subnet, not just the brokers' boxes. However, using multicasting, the stock quotes get to the right users with a minimum of network overhead. There are many applications for this type of data transmission, including audio or video multicasts and whiteboard applications that let a group of users have a virtual meeting over the Internet or intranet.

There is an international IP multicast network called the Internet Multicast Backbone, also known as the MBONE. It looks something like a chain of islands joined by tunnels and overlays the worldwide Internet. The MBONE was built as a test-bed for multicast applications. It started with 40 subnets in four countries in 1992. By 1996, the MBONE had grown to more than 2,800 subnets in 25 countries and continues to grow today. Although the MBONE and the Internet share long-haul links in many places, they use different routers in most areas because the MBONE requires multicast capable routers. Multicast routers are joined by virtual point-to-point connections called tunnels. These tunnels hide encapsulated multicast traffic from Internet routers installed between MBONE routers.

Multicast Groups and IGMP

Multicast groups are a collection of hosts that want to receive multicast information. Membership is voluntary, and clients can leave or join at any time. A host can belong to multiple groups simultaneously and does not have to belong to a group just to send messages to group members. There is no maximum number of hosts that can belong to a group, nor are there restrictions on the physical location of members. In order for a host to join a group, it must first announce its intention to do so by registering the IP multicast address from which it wants to receive traffic. Internet Group Membership Protocol is used by routers to collect and maintain a list of group members on locally attached networks.

Routing Protocols

Routing protocols are used to determine paths over which multicast data can be forwarded to destination networks. Distance Vector Multicast Routing Protocol (DVMRP), Multicast OSPF (MOSPF), Protocol Independent Multicast-Dense Mode (PIM-DM), and Protocol Independent Multicast-Sparse Mode (DIM-SM) are common multicast routing protocols. However, Windows 2000 does not provide any multicast routing protocols. There is an option for single router networks or single networks attached to the MBONE. The IGMP router and IGMP proxy can be used to provide multicast forwarding in those types of networks. It is possible to set up the IGMP router and proxy components to forward traffic on a network with multiple routers, but Microsoft doesn't support or recommend this. Instead, it offers a set of APIs that can be used to port existing or create new multicast routing protocols to be used in these larger environments.

Multicast Addressing

A collection of hosts defined as a group are assigned a multicast address. This address is used as the destination IP address for any packet to be received by the entire group. This address is a Class D address, which ranges from 224.0.0.0 to 239.255.255.255. Out of this group of addresses, 224.0.0.255 is reserved for use by routing or other function protocols. There are certain other well-known groups and uses that have been assigned addresses from this range by IANA (Internet Assigned Numbers Authority), such as 224.0.13.000 to 224.0.13.255 for Net News. For more information on these reserved addresses, see RFC 1700, "Assigned Numbers," at `ftp://ftp.internic.net/rfc/rfc1700.txt`.

Windows 2000 Multicasting

Windows 2000 supports both multicast forwarding and routing. Multicast forwarding is defined as the intelligent forwarding of multicast traffic, and multicast routing is the propagation of multicast group membership information.

Multicast Forwarding

Multicast forwarding involves a router sending multicast traffic to or in the direction of networks where hosts are listening. This keeps multicast traffic from being forwarded to networks where there aren't any hosts listening for multicasts. Hosts and routers have to be multicast-capable or forwarding will not work properly.

Multicast-capable hosts must be able to send and receive multicast packets and register the multicast addresses the host is listening to with the local router. This information allows the router to forward the multicast data to the host that is listening for it. Windows 2000 Server and Professional are ready for IP multicasting: they are IP multicast-capable and can send and receive IP multicast traffic.

Multicast-capable routers have to be able to use multicast routing protocols to propagate group listening information to other multicast routers. These routers listen for IGMP Membership Report packets, track multicast addresses, and listen for multicast traffic on all attached networks. When multicast traffic is received, the router must forward the multicast packet to local networks where hosts or other routers have nodes that are listening. The Windows 2000 TCP/IP protocol stack provides the capability to listen for and forward traffic.

Multicast Routing

Multicast routers propagate group membership information to other multicast routers. Intelligent multicast forwarding decisions are made based on the routing information provided to routers across the network. Routing protocols are used to announce multicast group information to other routers. As previously mentioned, Windows 2000 Server doesn't include any multicast routing protocols, although the Windows 2000 platform is open and extensible, allowing developers to create new or port existing protocols.

IGMP Router

The IGMP router listens for IGMP Membership Report packets and tracks group membership. Remember to enable the IGMP router on all router interfaces where multicast hosts are listening for multicast traffic. If this isn't done, only those networks where the IGMP router was enabled will receive multicast traffic.

IGMP Proxy

The IGMP proxy acts as a proxy multicast host. It receives IGMP Membership Report packets on all configured interfaces, and forwards this information over one interface to the upstream router. The upstream router then adds that multicast data to its own multicast tables. Through these tables, the upstream router knows to forward packets to the network of the IGMP proxy for the multicast groups registered by the router running the IGMP proxy. All appropriate multicast traffic received on IGMP proxy interfaces is forwarded to the upstream router as well. The Windows 2000 IGMP proxy is designated for use only in a single router network or a single network Intranet connected to the MBONE.

Upstream and Downstream
Upstream refers to routers in the direction data is received, while downstream refers to routers in the direction information is sent.

IP Routing

IP routing protocols will be the first stop on our trip through the world of routing protocols. Windows 2000 provides IP routing protocols that serve a variety of purposes. We'll take a look at RIP first.

RIP for IP

Routing Information Protocol for IP is a distance-vector protocol used widely in small and medium-sized networks. RIP is an Interior Gateway Protocol (IGP) used to route data within autonomous networks. An autonomous network is defined as a network that has finite boundaries or falls under a single administrative authority. It could be a corporate intranet or a private network segment within a larger network.

Windows 2000 supports RIP for IP version 1 (v1) and version 2(v2). RIP is defined in RFCs 1058 and 1723. RFC 1058 covers the initial version of RIP. RFC 1723 updates the specifications in RFC 1058. The common features of both versions of RIP for IP, such as the basic routing-update process, metrics, and convergence, will be discussed in this section, then we will move on to the distinct features of each version.

Routing Updates

RIP routers send messages called advertisements to other routers at regular intervals and when the network topology changes. By default, a router announces its current, unchanged routes to all attached networks every 30 seconds. When a RIP router receives a change, it revises its routing table to include the new information. The router then begins the process of advertising the changes to other routers. Routing change advertisements are sent separately from the regularly scheduled advertisements.

RIP v1 announcements are sent through IP subnet and MAC-level broadcasts. You can configure RIP v2 routers to use multicasting for RIP announcements (for more information, see Chapter 5). Broadcasting RIP routing table announcements contributes a great deal of overhead in large networks. If you use RIP over WAN links, a significant portion of the (expensive) bandwidth could be devoted to sending RIP traffic instead of users' data. For these reasons, RIP is better suited for use in small and medium-sized networks, and is not recommended for use in WAN implementations.

Metrics

RIP routers use distance-vector-based routing to advertise the routes in their routing tables. The announcement contains the metric (hop count), known as the distance, and the direction the route is located, known as the vector. Routing information exchanged between RIP routers is unsynchronized.

RIP uses hop count to measure the distance between the source and destination networks. Each hop in a route from source to destination is assigned a value, usually 1. When an advertisement containing new or updated information is received by a router, the metric in the update is increased by one and the destination network is entered in the routing table. The next hop is the sender's IP address.

Routing Tables

The RIP standard allows multiple entries in the routing table for the same destination network if multiple paths are available. The routing process picks the best route based on the lowest metric or "cost." The metric used in RIP is hop count, so the route with the fewest hops is selected as the best route. However, Windows 2000 and other RIP router products store only the single lowest metric route for any network. If several lowest metric routes are received by the router, the first lowest hop count route received is stored in the routing table. This method reduces the potential strain on network resources that could be caused by propagating all possible routes. A RIP router storing a complete list of every network and every possible way to reach every network can have hundreds of entries in its routing table. In a large network with multiple routes to each segment, there could potentially be thousands of entries in the routing tables. Only 25 routes can be sent in a single RIP packet, so large routing tables must be split apart and sent as multiple RIP packets.

Hop Counts

Hop count is the metric used for a route entry in a RIP for IP routing table. The hop count refers to the number of routers a packet must cross to reach the destination network. RIP has a maximum hop count of 15. In other words, between any two hosts there can be no more than 15 routers. Networks that are 16 or more routers or hops away are unreachable. An administrator could modify routing table metrics so that slow links appear to the router to have higher hop counts than a faster link. For example, a network printer could be reached by crossing 2 routers joined by very slow network segments. The same printer could also be reached by crossing 3 routers joined by relatively speedy network segments. The RIP router would by default choose the slowest path in this case because the hop count is lower.

However, the administrator can modify the route metric for the slower links to make the shorter path have a higher and therefore less optimal hop count. The router would then discard the slower link in favor of the faster route because it now has the lowest metric.

Keep in mind that total hop count between any two networks can't exceed 15 or attempts to reach that network will result in Destination Unreachable–Network Unreachable messages from the RIP router. Another thing to remember is that when a Windows 2000 router announces a non-RIP learned route (such as a static route), it advertises it with a hop count of two, even if it is directly connected to that network.

How RIP for IP Works

There are three phases of operation for RIP for IP routing.

- **Initialization.** During the initialization phase, the router announces itself and receives routes from neighboring routers.
- **Timers.** The second phase is the periodic advertisement process.
- **Administrative router shutdown.** The third and final phase is the advertisement of unreachable routes when a router is brought down by the administrator.

Initialization

When a RIP router starts up, it advertises the networks it is attached to on all its interfaces. The adjacent routers receive the RIP announcement and update their routing tables with the new network information.

The initializing RIP router also sends a request for all routes from other routers. The General RIP Request is sent over all locally attached networks. When neighboring routers receive the General RIP Request, they reply to the router with the routing information. The initializing router builds its routing table with the data it receives.

Timers

RIP routers announce routes on all interfaces every 30 seconds. The type of announcements the RIP router makes is dependent on the configuration of the router. If it is configured to perform split horizon announcement, for instance, it only advertises in one direction. Split horizon is covered in its own section a little later in this chapter.

Administrative Router Shutdown

If a router needs to be taken offline for maintenance or for some other reason, an administrative shutdown is performed. This action causes a triggered update to be sent to all locally attached networks. The triggered update advertises that the networks available through the router have a hop count of 16. This effectively says that all networks accessed through this router are now unreachable. This change is cascaded through the network by other RIP routers using triggered updates.

Failed Links and Routers

RIP for IP routers will also react to changes in topology due to links and routers that fail for non-administrative reasons.

Link failures can be quickly detected and propagated through the network if supporting hardware is in place. If a LAN or WAN link on a router's interface fails and the interface hardware supports media fault detection, this change in status is made known to the router by the interface. The router then sends a triggered update to other routers.

Router failures can take as long as three minutes before the change is noted by neighboring routers. If a router fails, possibly due to a power outage or hardware fault, it can't inform the neighboring routers that the networks to which it provides a gateway have become unavailable. To prevent unreachable networks from staying in routing tables forever, each dynamically learned route has a default lifetime of three minutes. If the entry is not announced again within three minutes, the route's hop count is changed to 16 and triggered updates will propagate the change through the network. The entry will ultimately be removed from the routing table if it is not replaced by a route with a lower hop count. Networks sometimes "lose" packets, and it is possible that an announcement might not make it to the destination on the first try. Therefore, a reasonable response time of three minutes was established to keep routing table entries from timing out too soon.

Convergence

When all the routing tables in all routers in a network contain the most up-to-date routes, a condition known as *convergence* is said to have been reached. Because RIP announces its routes in an unsynchronized and unacknowledged manner, convergence problems can result. Certain configuration options in Windows 2000 can assist in the reduction of common problems. This section will examine the primary convergence problem of distance-vector routing networks: the count-to-infinity problem, and a secondary problem, looping.

RIP routing's asynchronous announcement scheme causes the count-to-infinity problem. RIP routers add routes to their tables gathered from the advertisements of other routers. As previously described, the RIP standard allows multiple entries in the routing table for the same destination network if multiple paths are available. The routing process picks the best route based on the lowest metric. However, Windows 2000 routers store only the single lowest metric route for any network. If several lowest metric routes are received by the router, the first lowest hop count route received is stored in the routing table. A lower cost route will only be replaced with a higher cost route if it is being advertised by the same source as the lowest cost route currently in the routing table. In certain situations, this can cause the count-to-infinity problem. Let's see how the training company used in the previous examples is impacted by this problem. The topology of the network is illustrated in Figure 4.4.

Unexpectedly, the link from Router 2 to Network C goes down. Router 2 detects this and, as shown in Figure 4.5, Router 2 changes the hop count for the route to Network C to infinity. A hop count of infinity indicates a network is an unreachable distance away. Sixteen is used as the generic infinity number because it is the lowest number in infinity. It is important to have a reasonably low infinity number because the hop count on a RIP router will increment until infinity is reached.

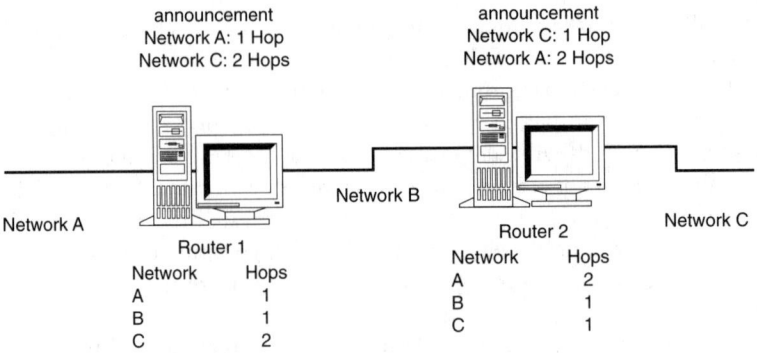

Figure 4.4 A converged network.

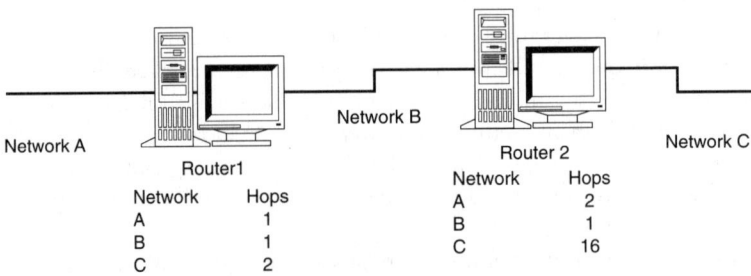

Figure 4.5 Router 2 updates its route to Network C.

Before Router 2 is able to announce the new hop count to Network C in a regularly scheduled announcement, it receives an announcement from Router 1. Router 1 has announced a route to Network C which is 2 hops away. Because a 2-hop route is better than a 16-hop route, Router 2 updates its routing table entry for Network C, discarding the 16-hop (unreachable) route shown in Figure 4.6.

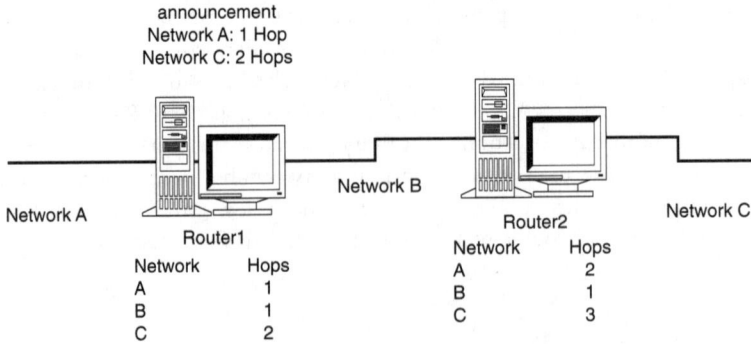

Figure 4.6 Router 2 incorrectly updates its learned route to Network C.

Router 2 now advertises its new routes. Router 1 learns that a 3-hop route is available to Network C through Router 2. The route to Network C in Router 1's routing table was originally learned from Router 2, so Router 1 updates its route to Network C to 4 hops. (See Figure 4.7.)

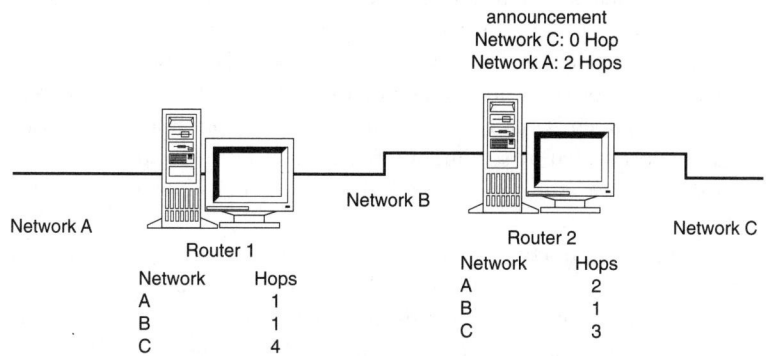

announcement
Network C: 0 Hop
Network A: 2 Hops

Network A

Network B

Network C

Router 1

Network	Hops
A	1
B	1
C	4

Router 2

Network	Hops
A	2
B	1
C	3

Figure 4.7   Router 1 updates its route to Network C.

It is now Router 1's turn to announce its new routes. From Router 1, Router 2 discovers that Network C can be reached in 4 hops through Router 1. Because the route to Network C on Router 2 was originally learned from Router 1, Router 2 updates its route to Network C to 5 hops.

The two routers continue to announce routes to Network C until infinity (16) is reached. Network C is then considered unreachable, and the route to Network C is eventually timed out of the routing table. This is one of the reasons why the maximum hop count for RIP for IP is set to 15. If infinity was set higher, it would take longer for convergence to be attained.

Looping is another problem in RIP routing. It occurs when the route to one network goes through another network, which then loops back to the first network and will continue until infinity is reached. In the previous example, the route from Router 1 to Network C is through Router 2. The route from Router 2 to Network C is through Router 1. A loop sits between Router 1 and Router 2 for Network C for the term of the count-to-infinity problem.

In real life, routers and links fail and come back up fairly frequently. How do you avoid the count-to-infinity and looping problems just described? There are three configuration options you can use to help reduce the occurrence of these problems: split horizon, split horizon with poisoned reverse, and triggered updates.

Split Horizon

The lack of truly reliable information is partly the cause of routing problems. Being careful about which routers are told of updates is one way to alleviate some of the problem. It is not smart for a router to claim that it can reach a network through the neighbor(s) from which the route was learned. Most people have had this experience: You tell "Bob" a joke. Two days later, Bob tells you the exact same joke, completely forgetting you were the source. If you were to go back to Bob and repeat the joke again because you forgot you told him and that he told you, that would be akin to the looping problem between Router 1 and Router 2 above. Split horizon is a way to get around problems caused by sending routing updates to the router from which they were learned. It leaves out routes learned from one neighbor in updates sent to that neighbor.

Split horizon gets rid of count-to-infinity problems and routing loops during convergence in single-path networks, and reduces the chances of count-to-infinity in multipath networks. Split horizon also aids in reducing convergence time by not allowing routers to advertise in the direction from which those networks were learned. The only information sent is destined for those networks that are beyond the adjacent router in the opposite direction. Networks learned from the neighboring router are not included. It can be thought of almost as a one-way announcement. Remember that old party game where you whisper something to the person next to you, and that person then whispers it to the next person and so on? You only whisper in one direction, and split horizon only announces in one direction.

Split Horizon with Poisoned Reverse

Split horizon with poisoned reverse is more dependable than simple split horizon. Let's say routers are advertising routes traveling through each other. A loop can form between these two routers, as we have seen in the case of the training company. The loop continues until infinity is reached, at which time the loop is broken. If the routers are configured to announce routes in a given direction with a metric of 16, the loop will break instantly. Without the poisoned reverse, the reverse routes are simply not advertised and the unreachable routes will be removed by waiting for a timeout. The poisoned reverse eliminates the timeout waiting period. The disadvantage of poisoned reverse is that it increases the size of the routing messages because it is announcing all the networks it is possible to reach. All a given router needs to know from any other router are the local networks that interface through that router. It is the administrator's job to determine whether it is better to have slightly slower convergence times instead of lesser routing overhead or vice versa.

Triggered Updates

Split horizon with poisoned reverse will prohibit loops in single path networks. Loops are still possible in multipath networks where the routers might still mislead each other with incorrect routes. For example, Router A might believe it has a route through

Router B, Router B through Router C, and Router C through Router A. Split horizon is not capable of stopping this type of loop. It will only be eliminated when the hop count reaches infinity and the network involved is then known to be unreachable. Triggered updates are a method of speeding up convergence in these situations. Triggered updates are rules that require a router to send almost immediate update messages whenever it changes the hop count for a route even if it is not yet time for its regular every-30-second advertisement. This triggered update cascades through the network until it reaches areas that are not impacted by the update. Triggered updates are not foolproof, however. While triggered updates are being sent, regular updates might be simultaneously occurring. Routers that haven't gotten the triggered update will send outdated information on the changed route. It is conceivable that after the triggered update has been received by a router it could receive a normal update from a router that doesn't know of the new route information. This could reintroduce an orphaned piece of the bad route. If triggered updates occur quickly enough, the likelihood of this happening is slim. However, the count-to-infinity problem is still possible.

Windows 2000 RIP Features

Windows 2000 implementation of RIP for IP offers many features, including

- Full RFC 1058 and 1723 compliance.
- Split horizon, split horizon with poisoned reverse, and triggered update convergence mechanisms.
- Configurable announcement interval (default is 30 seconds).
- Configurable routing table entry timeout value (default is three minutes).
- Capability to act as a silent RIP host. A silent RIP host listens for, but does not send, announcements.
- Peer filtering, which lets a router accept or discard updates of announcements from specific routers identified by IP address.
- Route filtering, which enables a router to accept or discard updates of specific network IDs or from specific routers.
- RIP Neighbors, which gives routers the capability to unicast RIP announcements to specific routers to support non-broadcast networks such as frame relay.
- Capability to announce or accept default routes or host routes.

RIP for IP Version 1

RIP version 1 (v1) is defined in RFC 1058 and is widely deployed in small -to medium-sized networks. Up to now, we've been discussing the common features of RIP v1 and v2. In this section, the focus will be on the unique features of RIP v1. Following this section, we will address RIP v2.

Message Format

RIP messages are encapsulated in User Datagram Protocol (UDP) packets. The messages leave the source router with the IP address of the sending router interface, and are destined for the subnet broadcast IP address. UDP port 520 is used for sending and receiving RIP messages. The message itself is made up of a 4-byte RIP header and the data payload of RIP routes. The entire RIP message can have a maximum size of 504 bytes, but the number of routes that can be carried in a single message is limited to 25. If there are more routes, they are split into multiple messages for transmission. If you count the 8-byte UDP header, the maximum size of the message is 512-bytes. Figure 4.8 illustrates the RIP v1 message format.

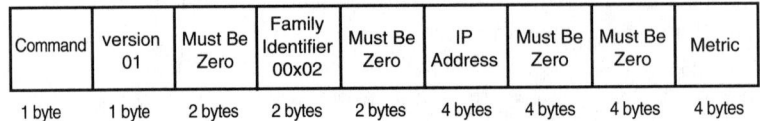

Command	version 01	Must Be Zero	Family Identifier 00x02	Must Be Zero	IP Address	Must Be Zero	Must Be Zero	Metric
1 byte	1 byte	2 bytes	2 bytes	2 bytes	4 bytes	4 bytes	4 bytes	4 bytes

Figure 4.8   RIP v1 message format.

Each one of the fields in the message has a specific purpose, explained below:

- **Command.** This field indicates whether a specific message is a request or a response. It is a 1-byte field that contains 0x01 or 0x02. 0x01 represents a request for routes, such as a General RIP Request. The entry 0x02 indicates a response containing all or part of a neighboring router's routing table. A RIP response can be a result of a RIP request or as the result of a periodic or triggered update message.

- **Version.** A 1-byte field that represents the version of RIP. RIP v1 is indicated by 0x01.

- **Family Identifier.** A 2-byte field that identifies the protocol family.

- **IP Address.** A 4-byte field that indicates the IP network ID. The network ID can be one of the following: a class-based network ID, a subnet ID, an IP address, or 0.0.0.0 (for the default route). A General RIP Request uses 0.0.0.0.

- **Metric.** A 4-byte field that displays the number of hops to the destination network. The metric is set to 16 for a General RIP Request or to indicate that the network is unreachable.

- **Must Be Zero.** These fields allow for future development of the protocol.

RIP v1 Shortcomings

RIP v1 was developed in 1988 to serve the routing needs of LAN-based IP networks. Ethernet networks support MAC-level broadcasting. This broadcast method allows a single packet to be received and processed by multiple network nodes. This is not a desirable characteristic in today's networks because all nodes must process all MAC-level broadcasts. Another one of RIP v1's downsides is that it does not support sending a subnet address with the route announcement. At the time RIP v1 was originally designed, there were plenty of IP addresses to go around. Today, however, administrators are using Classless Inter-domain Routing (CIDR) and variable length subnetting to conserve scarce IP addresses. For these reasons, and a few others described in the following list, RIP v1 is not as useful as RIP v2.

- **Broadcast announcements.** RIP v1 route advertisements are addressed to the IP subnet and MAC-level broadcast. Non-RIP hosts may also receive RIP announcements. This can contribute a substantial amount of broadcast traffic on each subnet. One upside to this is that the broadcast nature of RIP v1 also permits the use of silent RIP. A silent RIP host listens for RIP announcements, but does not advertise its own routes. Silent RIP can be enabled on non-router hosts (such as Windows 2000 Professional) to create a routing table with as much detail as a router's. The more detailed routing information a host has, the better routing decisions a host can make.

- **Broadcasting uses significant amounts of bandwidth.** By default, a RIP router broadcasts lists of networks it can reach every 30 seconds. This can use up quite a bit of bandwidth, causing sluggish network response times. The amount of overhead required by these broadcasts is dependent on the size of the network and the number of routes that must be advertised.

- **Subnet mask not advertised with route.** RIP v1 was designed for IP networks where the network ID can be learned from the initial three bits of the IP address in the route. The router has to figure out the network ID from a very small amount of information. For each route in a RIP v1 message, the router follows the procedures in Figure 4.9.

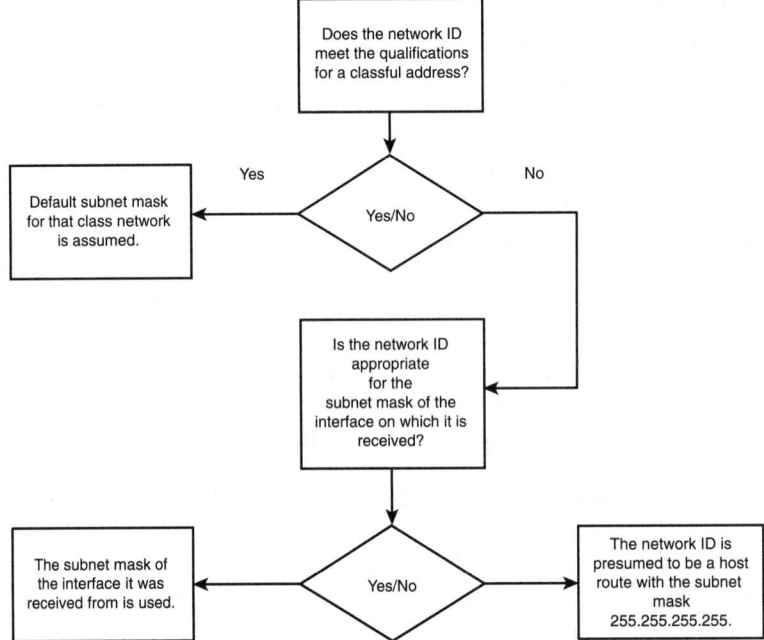

Figure 4.9   RIP v1 route interpretation process.

This means that RIP v1 can be used in subnetted networks in limited situations. Supernetted routes might be perceived as being all on a single network ID, instead of the range of network IDs they are intended to include. It is also possible for subnet routes to be seen as host routes if they are announced outside the subnetted network ID.

Supernetting

Supernetting refers to the practice of aggregating consecutive same-class network addresses into a single network to increase the number of hosts a network address can support. For more information on supernetting—also known as Classless Inter-Domain Routing (CIDR)—see RFC 1518, "An Architecture for IP Address Allocation with 1519 Classless Inter-Domain Routing (CIDR): An Address Assignment and Aggregation Strategy."

RIP routers advertise the class-based network ID only outside the subnetted environment, so subnets must be contiguous in order for subnet announcements to be forwarded appropriately. If subnets of an IP network ID are disjointed, the network ID will be announced by other RIP routers as a class-based advertisement. This can result in IP traffic being forwarded to the wrong network.

- **No defense from rogue RIP routers.** RIP v1 does not provide a defense mechanism from a RIP router advertising false or erroneous routes. All RIP v1 advertisements are accepted and processed the same way, no matter what their source. A hacker could use this lack of protection to launch a denial-of-service attack by overwhelming RIP routers with hundreds or thousands of false or inaccurate routes.

- **Difficulty in troubleshooting.** RIP can be difficult to troubleshoot because the source of the problem could be distributed over many different routers. In general, most problems in RIP routing stem from incorrect configuration and propagation of bad routes.

RIP for IP Version 2

When the second version of RIP was proposed, it was hotly contested. By that time, OSPF had been implemented in the field, and it addressed many of the problems inherent in RIP v1. However, many people felt that RIP had not been made obsolete for a few reasons: RIP uses very little bandwidth in smaller networks, administrative upkeep and implementation of RIP are low when compared to other protocols like OSPF, and RIP was more widely implemented than OSPF. Because it was evident that RIP would be around for some time to come, it made sense to expand the feature-set of RIP. RIP version 2 is outlined in RFC 1723.

RIP v2 Message Format

To ensure backward compatibility, RIP v2 leaves the structure of the RIP message format intact. It differentiates itself from RIP v1 by using fields that were defined in RIP v1 as Must Be Zero, and by setting the Version field to 0x02 to denote a RIP v2 message. The Command, Family Identifier, IP Address, and Metric fields are the same as RIP v1. Figure 4.10 illustrates the RIP v2 message format.

- **Route Tag.** The Route Tag field is used for tagging specific routes for administrative purposes. Originally it was intended as a way to differentiate RIP-based routes from non-RIP routes, particularly internal network routes from external network routes. Multiprotocol routers should offer the capability to allow the route tag to be configured for routes that have different sources. Windows 2000 supports the configuration of the route tag for RIP v2 interfaces.

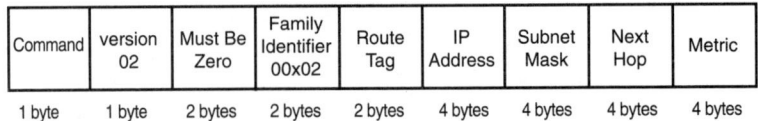

Command	version 02	Must Be Zero	Family Identifier 00x02	Route Tag	IP Address	Subnet Mask	Next Hop	Metric
1 byte	1 byte	2 bytes	2 bytes	2 bytes	4 bytes	4 bytes	4 bytes	4 bytes

Figure 4.10   RIP v2 message format.

- **Subnet Mask.** The 4-byte Subnet Mask field contains the subnet mask of the network ID of the IP address listed in the IP Address field. If this field entry is zero, no subnet mask has been included for this route. In mixed environments where RIP-1 routers may hear and use the information a RIP-2 router provides, the following regulations apply:
  - Information internal to one network can't be advertised into another network.
  - If information about a subnet might cause a RIP v1 router to think an IP address is a host route, it can't be advertised where a RIP v1 router could misunderstand it.
  - Supernetted routes can't be advertised where they could be misinterpreted by RIP-1 routers.

- **Next Hop.** This shows the next hop IP address to which data should be forwarded. If the value 0.0.0.0 is present, it indicates the route must be made through the interface over which the announcement is made.

  Specifying the next hop allows optimal routing decisions to be made. Let's say a packet is destined for a computer on the local subnet. Designating the host as the next hop will save the packet one hop. How does it do this? By stating that the next hop sends the packet directly to the destination host, rather than to the router that announced this route. Of course, the next hop must be directly reachable on the logical subnet on which the advertisement is made. If it is not, the next hop is treated as 0.0.0.0, the default route.

RIP v2 Authentication

The simple password authentication offered by RIP v2 hampers the placement of unauthorized RIP routers on the network. A simple password is not a perfect solution, though, because passwords are sent in clear text. Any network sniffing tool can be used to capture the password as it moves through the network.

Two fields are used to specify that a RIP message contains authentication information, as shown in Figure 4.11. First the Family Identifier field is set to 0xFF-FF. The Authentication Type field is usually the Route Tag field, but in this instance it indicates the type of authentication being used. Simple password authentication uses a value of

0x00–01. The first 16 bytes after the Authentication Type are used to store the authentication value, which in this case is a password. Because the authentication data is stored in the area where a route would normally be stored, RIP v2 announcements using authentication can only carry a total of 24 routes. RIP v1 routers will ignore these entries because the Family Type is unknown. All subsequent routes will be recognized, however.

Command	version 02	Must Be Zero	Family Identifier FFFF	Authentication Type 00x01	Simple Password	Simple Password	Simple Password	Simple Password
1 byte	1 byte	2 bytes	2 bytes	2 bytes	4 bytes	4 bytes	4 bytes	4 bytes

Figure 4.11   RIP v2 authentication message format.

Mixed RIP v1 and RIP v2 Environments

RIP v2 routers and RIP v1 routers can coexist, but this should be done vigilantly. As previously mentioned, RIP v1 routers do not use the Subnet Mask field in the route. Therefore, RIP v2 routers can't advertise routes that can be misunderstood by a RIP v1 router. Neither Variable Length Subnet Masks (VLSM) nor disjointed subnets can be used successfully in mixed RIP environments.

Announcement addressing is another issue to be considered. RIP v2 announcements are multicasted, and RIP v1 routers only use broadcast announcements. This means RIP v2 routers on the same network as RIP v1 routers must be configured to broadcast announcements.

Features of RIP v2

Several features were added to RIP to help limit broadcast traffic, accommodate the use of variable length subnetting, and provide a level of security against malicious routers.

- **Multicasted RIP announcements.** RIP v2 can send multicast announcements to the IP multicast address 224.0.0.9 with a TTL of 1 instead of broadcasting announcements, so you don't need Internet Group Membership Protocol (IGMP) to register host group membership.

- **Subnetting.** RIP v2 advertisements send the subnet mask with the network ID, allowing it to be used in subnetted, supernetted, and VLSM environments. Disjointed subnets are also supported.

- **Authentication.** RIP v2 allows authentication to substantiate the source of incoming announcements. RFC 1723 supports various types of authentication methods, but Windows 2000 only supports simple password authentication.

- **RIP v1 compatibility with RIP v2.** RIP v1 was designed to accommodate future extensibility. If a RIP v1 router receives a message that is not specifically identified as RIP v1, it won't discard the RIP announcement. It just uses the RIP v1 defined fields. RIP v2 is backward compatible as well. RIP v2 routers will send a RIP v1 response to a RIP v1 request unless they have been configured not to do so.

OSPF

Open Shortest Path First (OSPF) is an IP routing protocol. OSPF is defined in RFC 158. In the mid-1980s, it was becoming evident that RIP would be inappropriate in large, heterogeneous networks. OSPF is a link state routing protocol that uses link state advertisements (LSAs) to propagate information to other routers within the same area. The LSA includes information about various routing variables, including interfaces, gateways, and metrics. OSPF routers collect link state information into a link state database (LSDB) that is synchronized between neighboring routers. Based on the LSDB, each router calculates the shortest path to other routers using a Shortest Path First (SPF) algorithm. In this section, we will focus on the OSPF packet structure and how OSPF works, and look at various ways of organizing networks that use OSPF.

OSPF requires more processing power than RIP and offers more control over various aspects of the routing process. OSPF's many features make it a better choice for larger networks than RIP, including:

- Faster detection and proliferation of topology changes than RIP. One of the benefits of faster propagation of network data is that the count-to-infinity problem doesn't happen with OSPF.

- OSPF routes are always loop-free.

- Large networks can be broken down into contiguous groups of networks. These groups are called areas. Routing table entries can be minimized by a technique call summarizing, first described in RFC 1247. Using these summary routes also allows the creation of default routes for routes outside an area or autonomous system (AS). If you use RIP for IP, you can't subdivide your network and you don't get the benefit of route summarization.

- OSPF advertises the subnet mask with the network, which gives support for VLSM, disjointed subnets, and supernetting.

- Route exchanges between OSPF routers can be authenticated. Windows 2000 OSPF supports simple password authentication.

- External routes (routes outside of the AS—see "Organizing the OSPF Network" later in this chapter) can be advertised internally so OSPF routers can calculate least-cost routes to external networks.

An additional OSPF feature is the *type-of-service* (TOS) request. TOS routing supports upper-layer protocols that stipulate particular types of service. Applications such as a real-time video conferencing, for example, could flag certain data as urgent. If high-priority links are available, they can be used to transmit the urgent data. Type of Service (TOS) routing is not supported by Windows 2000, nor is load balancing for equal cost routes as outlined by RFC 1583.

OSPF Packet Format

Figure 4.12 illustrates the OSPF packet structure.

Version Number	Type	Packet length	Router ID	Area ID	Checksum	Authentication type	Authentication
1 byte	1 byte	2 bytes	4 bytes	4 bytes	2 bytes	2 bytes	8 bytes

Figure 4.12   The OSPF packet structure.

The functions of the headers are as follows:

- **Version Number.** Version of OSPF.
- **Type.** OSPF packet type can be one of the following types: Hello, Database Description, Link state Request, Link state Update, or Link state Acknowledgment.
- **Packet Length.** Specifies the packet length, including OSPF header.
- **Router ID.** Packet source.
- **Area ID.** The area where the packet is a member (for a definition of the term area, see "Organizing the OSPF Network" later in this chapter).
- **Checksum.** Checks the packet contents for errors.
- **Authentication Type.** Specifies the type of authentication.
- **Authentication.** Contains authentication information such as password.
- **Data.** Payload.

Operation

There are three main phases of OSPF operation. First, the LSDB is put together from neighboring routers, then the shortest path to each node is calculated, and finally the router creates routing table entries that contain all the pertinent information about routes.

Collecting LSDB Data Through Link State Advertisements (LSAs)

OSPF routers regularly exchange link state advertisements with each other. Each OSPF router must gather an LSA from every other router in the AS. The LSDB is a compilation of these LSAs. A copy of the LSDB is stored on each router in an area. The process works like this: When a router initializes, it sends out an LSA that contains only its own configuration. As time goes by, it gets LSAs from other routers and includes these routes in its own LSA. Eventually, it propagates those LSAs to its neighbor routers through a mechanism called flooding. An LSA from every router will be flooded across the AS so every router has every other router's LSA. At first glance, this might seem to generate a vast amount of traffic, especially in large networks. However, OSPF is very efficient in how it spreads LSA information. OSPF floods LSAs between specific routers it has formed an adjacency with. The details of the synchronization of the LSDB between neighboring routers will be discussed in the "Synchronization and Adjacencies" section. Figure 4.13 is a sample network of OSPF routers flooding information across an AS.

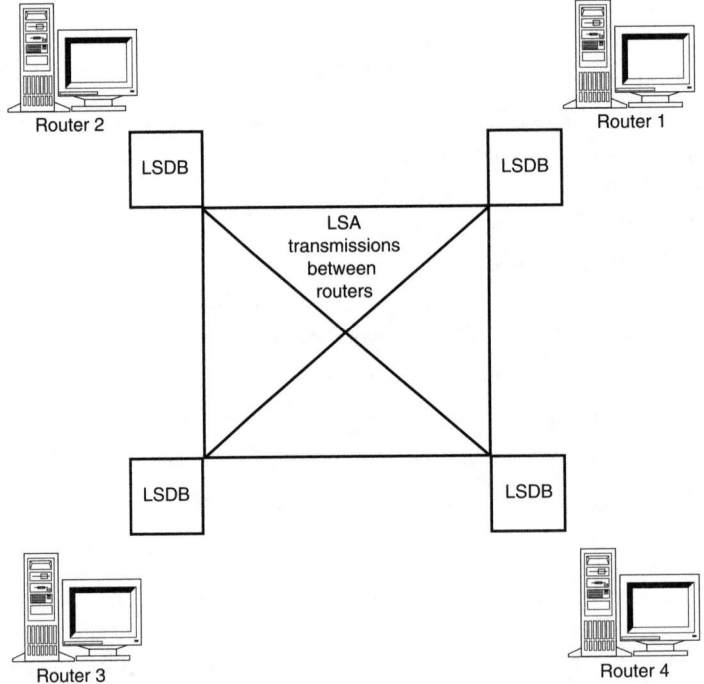

Figure 4.13   Forming an OSPF link state database (LSDB).

Each router has a router ID identifying it in each of the LSAs that make up the LSDB. It is a unique 32-bit dotted decimal number that might also be the IP address of one of the interfaces of the router. However, the router ID is not used as a destination address for the router. It is only used to identify the router in the AS. A common practice is to use the highest or lowest IP address assigned to the router as the router ID. This ensures that every router ID will be unique.

Each routing interface is assigned a cost by the administrator. The cost can represent available bandwidth, speed, reliability of a link, or other variable. This is a unitless measurement, meaning it doesn't imply anything specific except that a cost of 3 is more expensive than a cost of 2, but less expensive than a cost of 4. Let's say you have a network that has two paths to a server. One route travels through a crowded, slow network segment. The other route goes over a relatively unused segment. You can assign a lower cost to the interface using the less crowded network to indicate that it is the preferred path to the server.

Calculating the SPF Tree

After the LSDB is compiled, each router determines the least-cost path to the destination using the Dijkstra algorithm. The router reviews the LSDB and calculates the shortest, least-cost path to all the other routers and networks from that router. The resulting data structure is called the SPF tree. The SPF tree will be different for each router in the network, because the routes are calculated based on each router as the root of the tree. The cost of a path is derived from the cost assigned to each interface by the administrator, as discussed in the previous section. Dijkstra's algorithm is part of the branch of mathematics called graph theory. It was developed to determine the least-cost path between a single vertex and all other vertices in a graph. If you are interested in the mathematical computation involved in Dijkstra's algorithm, check out `http://n100.is.tokushima-u.ac.jp/%7Eikeda/suuri/dijkstra/Dijkstra.html`

Create Routing Table Entries

After the SPF tree is calculated, it is used to create the routing table. An entry for each network in the AS is constructed from the data in the tree. The resulting routing table entry contains the network ID and subnet mask, the IP address of the appropriate neighboring router over which traffic can be forwarded, the interface over which the neighboring router is reachable, and the OSPF-calculated cost to the network. The metric unit for the routing table entry is the calculated cost, rather than the hop count used in RIP routing.

Synchronization and Adjacencies

In order for the LSDB to be kept current, this information has to be synchronized between routers. One way to synchronize data is to have every router exchange data with every other router on the network. Doing so would eat up a lot of precious bandwidth. An alternative method is to exchange this information only between neighboring routers. Routers, just like people, need to know who their neighbors are. Neighboring routers are introduced to each other by forming adjacencies. Not forming adjacencies properly will result in convergence problems. Not surprisingly, this is one of the most common configuration problems in OSPF routed networks.

Forming an Adjacency

The first task of a router upon initialization is to send out an announcement in the form of a Hello packet. This packet holds all the important information about that router's configuration. The Hello packet is sent upon initialization and as a periodic update as long as the router remains online. The default Hello packet interval is 10 seconds. A Hello packet can also contain a list of neighboring routers that have announced themselves, if the packet comes from a router that has been online for some time. However, when a router initializes, this information is still unknown.

After the initial Hello packet is sent, the router listens for the Hello packets of other routers. It creates a list of routers to include in subsequent Hello packets. From the incoming Hello packets, the initializing router can find out the specific router or routers with which an adjacency is to be established. These specified routers are known as the designated router (DR) and the backup designated router (BDR).

The routers that form an adjacency describe the contents of their LSDBs with a series of Database Description Packets. During this process, called the Database Exchange Process, a master/slave relationship is formed between the two routers. Each router compares its own LSAs with the LSAs of its neighbor. There might be LSAs that need to be requested from the neighbor to completely synchronize the LSDB. These LSAs are requested with Link State Request packets. The response is sent in Link State Update packets. When each router's requests have been filled, the LSDBs of the neighboring routers can be considered synchronized and an adjacency formed.

Now that the all-important adjacency has been established, the router can begin sending out its periodic Hello packets to let neighboring routers know it is still operating on the network. If a neighboring router does not receive a Hello packet for a specified period of time (40 seconds by default), the router whose packets are missing is presumed to be out-of-service. This is known as the Dead Interval (RFC 1583 refers to this as the RouterDeadInterval). The router that detects this updates its LSDB and then sends Link State Update packets to its neighbors to let them know of the change in the LSDB.

In the event of changes, such as a downed link or router or the addition of a new network that alters the LSDB of one router, the LSDB of adjacent routers are no longer synchronized. The router whose LSDB has changed sends Link State Update packets to its adjacent neighbors. Receipt of the Link State Update packets is acknowledged by the receiving routers. After this exchange is completed, the LSDBs of the adjacent routers are once again synchronized. The same update process is used when a new router's Hello packet is received by an existing router. The existing router updates its LSDB and alerts its neighbors of the change, thereby keeping the database in synch.

There are certain configuration parameters that must match in order for adjacencies to form properly. As previously mentioned, incorrectly formed adjacencies are a very common OSPF problem. If the following parameters do not match, adjacencies will not be established and synchronization will fail:

- **Authentication type.** If the routers are using simple password authentication, neighboring routers must use the same password.
- **Hello Interval.** The Windows 2000 default is 10 seconds.
- **Dead Interval.** The Windows 2000 default is 40 seconds, or four times the Hello Interval.
- **Area ID.** The area in which this router belongs.
- **Stub area membership.** If this router is a member of a stub area, that is indicated here. (Area IDs and stub areas will be explained in the upcoming section called "Organizing the OSPF Network.")

Remember the router IDs we talked about earlier? They are the one configuration parameter that absolutely must not match. The router ID is a unique identifier for each router in an AS.

Network Types

Each interface of an OSPF router must be configured for the appropriate network type, and the OSPF message address is set for the network type specified for the interface. Three network types are supported by OSPF:

- **Broadcast.** Two or more routers connect this type of network, and broadcast traffic is passed. Examples of broadcast networks are ethernet and FDDI.
- **Non-broadcast multiple access (NBMA).** Two or more routers connect this type of network, but broadcast traffic is not passed. OSPF must be configured to use IP unicasting instead of multicasting. Examples of NBMA networks are ATM and frame relay.
- **Point-to-point.** As the name implies, only two routers can connect this type of network. Examples of point-to-point networks are WAN links such as DSL or ISDN. It is important to remember that OSPF over nonpermanent, dial-up links isn't supported by Windows 2000. This means you can't configure a demand-dial connection to use OSPF.

Designated Routers

In any given OSPF routed network, adjacencies must be formed to control the amount of synchronization traffic flooded across a network. In a point-to-point network, the only adjacency possible is between the routers at each end of the link. The amount of convergence traffic is self-limiting. Broadcast and NBMA networks, on the other hand, have many possible adjacency combinations. A network can form a total of $n \star (n-1)/2$ adjacencies, where n represents the total number of routers. Let's look at an example network.

Rushmore High School, depicted in Figure 4.14, has an ethernet network with an OSPF router joining each of the four buildings on campus. Without regulating adjacency formation, every router could form an adjacency with every other router. This creates a total of six adjacency relationships, and unnecessary flooding occurs as each router synchronizes with every other router. As the network grows in size, the number of possible adjacencies that can be created grows with it. This process is called scaling. In a network with eight routers, 28 adjacencies are possible!

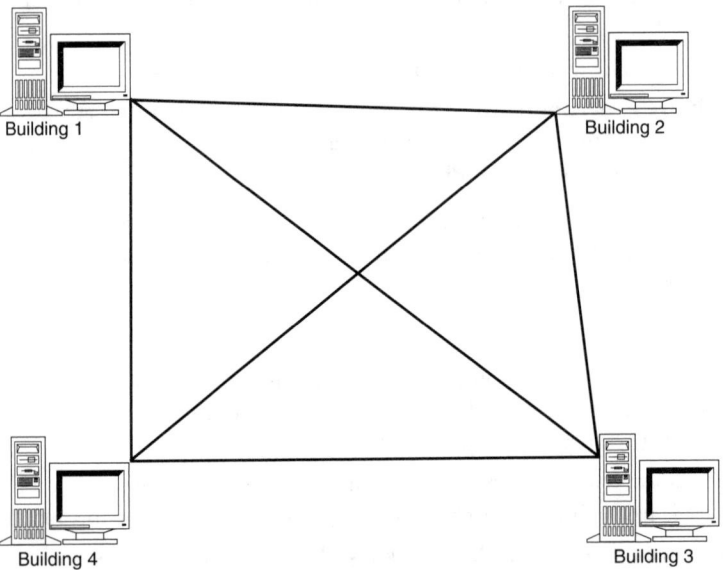

Figure 4.14   Uncontrolled adjacencies.

To avoid the network overhead that would be created by scaling, broadcast and NBMA networks elect a designated router (DR). The DR acts as a hub and forms adjacencies with the remaining routers on the network. By using DRs, only (*n*-1) adjacencies have to be established. The election of a DR is based on the router priority value and is similar (although not identical) to the election of a browse master. The router with the highest priority is elected the DR. The default value is 1. If a router is configured with a value of 0, it will never become the DR. A router that is slow or unreliable can be configured this way to prevent it from ever becoming the DR. Take care to avoid setting all routers to a priority of 0, though. If that happens, no router will act as DR, and no adjacencies will form. Translated, this means that the LSDBs of the routers will never synchronize and traffic cannot be sent across the network. You can also use router priority to ensure that proper communications occur on a network. For example, NBMA networks often use a star configuration. (See Figure 4.15.)

In such a case, the DR has to be the hub router because it is the only router that can reach all other routers. You should set its router priority to 1, and the remaining routers' priorities to 0 to prevent one of them from becoming the DR.

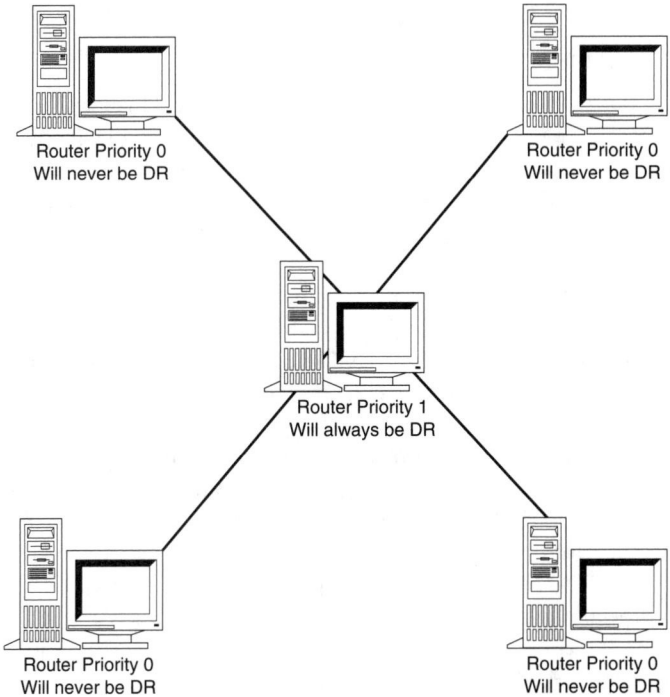

Figure 4.15   Star configuration with DR.

The Hello packet is used to elect and announce the DR for a network. If a DR has previously been elected, it is included in the packet. Otherwise, the sending router's router priority is included. If several routers tie for the highest router priority, the router with the highest router ID is elected the DR. If a DR has already been elected, a new or initializing router on the network will not automatically become the DR just because it has a higher router priority than the current DR.

Designated routers offer a fault-tolerant feature. If a DR goes down, a new DR must be put into place and the appropriate adjacencies formed with it. If this isn't done quickly, a loss of connectivity can result. A backup designated router (BDR) is the solution to this problem. The BDR forms adjacencies with all routers on the network at the time it is elected and will immediately become the DR when the original DR fails. When this happens, it sends LSAs to its adjacent routers announcing that it is now the DR. There could be a short time period where connectivity is lost while adjacent routers are notified of the change in DRs. The BDR is elected by the exchange of Hello packets between routers. Each Hello packet has a field identifying the BDR. If a BDR isn't designated, the router with the highest router priority that is not currently the DR will become the BDR. If several routers have the same highest router priority, the router with the highest router ID will be elected to be the BDR.

Organizing the OSPF Network

OSPF lets you build a network with a hierarchical structure. There are various benefits of doing so, not the least of which is reducing the size of routing tables by creating segments that don't need to know everything about every router in every other segment. At the top of this hierarchy is the autonomous system (AS). This is a group of networks that is controlled by a single administrative authority. Let's consider the fictitious company of MoonShot.

MoonShot is a large software company with headquarters in—where else? Silicon Valley. There are also satellite offices in Seattle and Austin, joined to each other and the headquarters in Redwood City, California, by WAN links. The collection of networks is called the AS and is represented on the Internet by the domain name moonshot.com. The term "domain" can be used in place of AS, although domain registration is not a requirement for an AS. It is just a convenient means of marking the borders of an autonomous network. OSPF is used within the AS, but may receive routes from and send routes to other ASs. Because OSPF is designed to serve within the AS, it belongs to the group of protocols called interior gateway routing protocols. Protocols that are responsible for routing traffic between ASs are called exterior gateway routing protocols.

The AS is broken down into segments called areas. Each area is a group of contiguous networks. In the case of MoonShot, the areas are Redwood City, Seattle, and Austin. These areas are known on the Internet as redwoodcity.moonshot.com, seattle.moonshot.com, and austin.moonshot.com, respectively. Routers that have more than one interface can participate in more than one area, and if they do so, they are called area border routers (ABRs). These routers keep a separate topological database for each area. The topological database is made up of all the LSAs from the routers in an area, and it can't be seen by routers outside the area. This means that the internal area topologies of Redwood City, Seattle, and Austin are invisible to each other. Isolating network topologies from each other is called partitioning and helps keep down the amount of OSPF traffic on the network. Isolating networks with containing sensitive data can also provide an additional level of security.

After an area is established, routing decisions must be made for packets based on source and destination addresses. Intra-area routing happens if both the source and destination addresses are in the same area. Inter-area routing happens when the source and destination are in different areas. The backbone is responsible for passing routing information between areas. The backbone is made up of all area border routers, any networks that are not completely included in one area, and any other routers attached to the backbone, as shown in Figure 4.16.

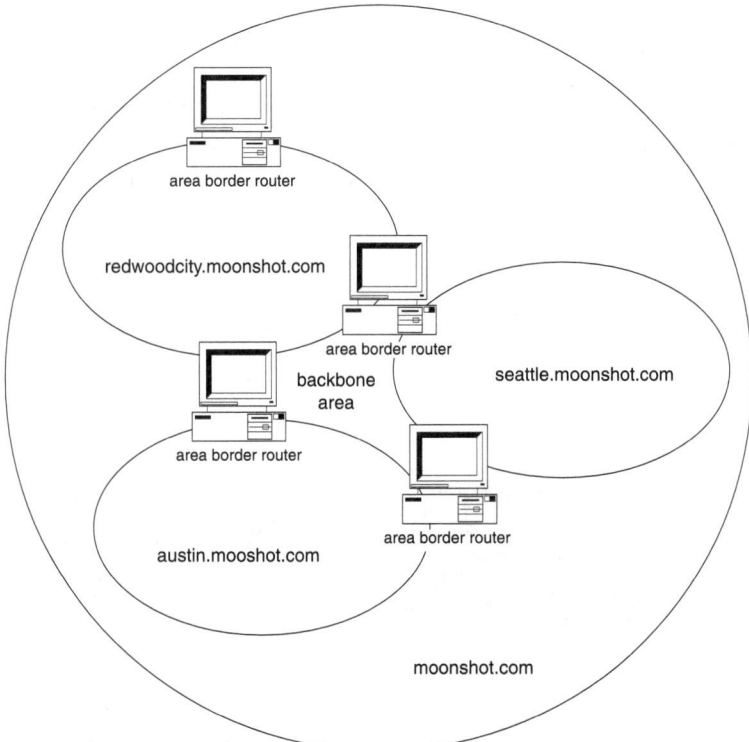

Figure 4.16   The hierarchy of the MoonShot network.

OSPF Router Types

To divide an AS into areas, you place routers in certain locations to join or divide segments. The duties of a router are determined by their location or role in the AS. These roles are as follows:

- **Internal router.** All interfaces on a router are connected to the same area. An internal router contains a single LSDB because it is only connected to one area.

- **Area border router (ABR).** If the interfaces on a router are connected to different areas, it is known as an ABR. This type of router has one LSDB for each area it is connected to.

- **Backbone router.** A router that has an interface on the backbone area. ABRs and internal routers on the backbone area are considered backbone routers.

- **AS boundary router (ASBR).** Any router that exchanges routes with sources outside of the AS. ASBRs announce external routes throughout the AS.

Virtual Links

Figure 4.16 shows MoonShot's domain structure. All areas are connected to the backbone. It is possible to design an architecture that leaves an area without a direct connection to the backbone. Let's imagine that MoonShot opens another office in San Francisco. This office is placed in its own area called `sanfrancisco.moonshot.com`, and is connected only to `redwoodcity.moonshot.com`, as shown in Figure 4.17.

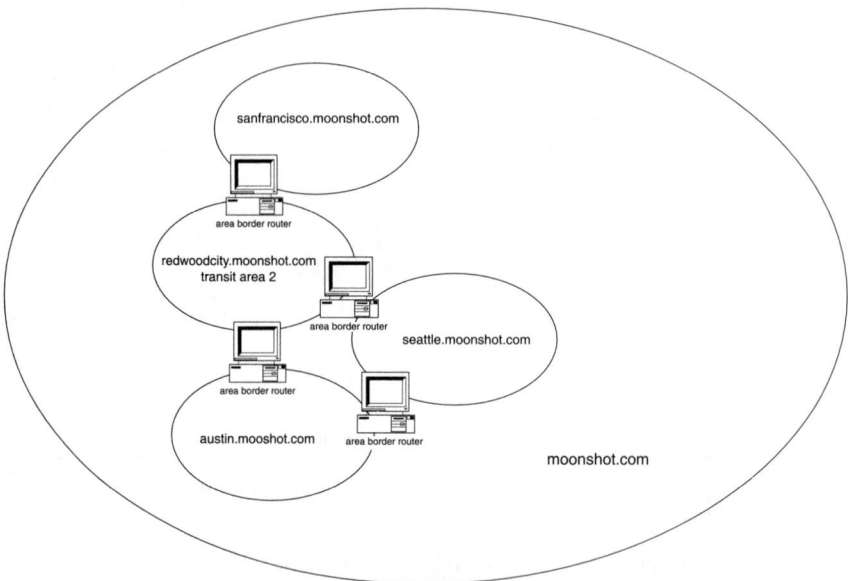

Figure 4.17   An area without a direct connection to the backbone.

In order for the San Francisco area to communicate with Seattle and Austin, a link to the backbone must be created. A virtual link is used to join two routers that interface with the same non-backbone area, such as between San Francisco and Redwood City. The common area is called the transit area. Every transit area must have one ABR that is connected to the backbone because virtual links cannot cross multiple transit areas. In other words, you can't route a virtual link across two areas before you get to the backbone. Figure 4.18 illustrates this no-no.

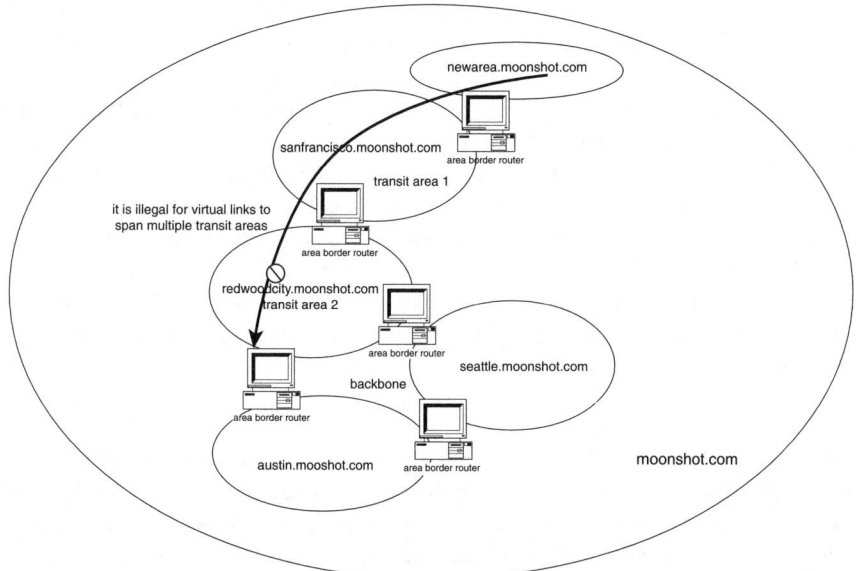

Figure 4.18   A virtual link cannot cross multiple transit areas.

A virtual link is exactly what it sounds like: a logical rather than physical link to a backbone ABR. Each virtual link neighbor router is configured with the transit area's area ID and the router ID of its virtual link partner. OSPF calculates and uses the least-cost path between the ABR of the area not connected to the backbone and the ABR that connects the backbone to the transit area. Virtual links behave like physical OSPF links in every other respect. Adjacencies must be established between routers, LSAs must be exchanged, and all adjacency configuration parameters (announcement intervals, authentication, and so on) must match.

External Routes

OSPF routers can learn routes from other routing protocols, interfaces that don't use OSPF, or static routes. These types of routes are called external routes. The AS border router propagates this information through the AS in the same manner OPF routes are propagated.

The ASBR will advertise all external routes to its neighbors. This announcement includes the default gateway for the router making the announcement. The default gateway is the exit point for traffic destined for networks outside the AS, and it must be valid for every OSPF router in the AS. A valid default route has a next-hop gateway address outside the AS. If an ASBR default gateway points to another router within the AS, traffic can't exit the AS through the default gateway. This route is only configured on the router that can reach the external network directly: the AS border router. One way to avoid a bad gateway situation is by not using a default gateway on the ASBR.

If the default route is not valid for all OSPF routers, it should not be advertised. By default, ASBRs will import and advertise all external routes. To keep incorrect routing information from being advertised, external route filters can be configured. These filters screen out improper or even malicious routing information. Windows 2000 allows ASBRs to filter external routes according to the route source or by the individual route. This means the ASBR can be configured to accept or reject the routes of specific external sources, like certain routing protocols, static routes, or SNMP. Specific route filters are based on network ID and subnet mask pairs configured on that ASBR. External route filtering is also an acceptable method for avoiding bad gateway problems. The ASBR is configured to reject routes from network ID 0.0.0.0 and mask 0.0.0.0. All other routes will be accepted, and the router will not advertise its own default gateway.

Stub Areas

It's possible for an AS to have lots of external route information, which will be flooded throughout the AS. Advertisement of this information can make up most of the topological database of an area's routers. To minimize the database size and the amount of network overhead used by these announcements, as well as the memory and processing requirements for any given area's internal routers, OSPF provides for the configuration of certain areas as stub areas. External advertisements aren't flooded into stub areas. Instead, external routing in stub areas is based on a default route.

Stub areas work by converting all external routes into one default route. This means that routing tables of routers in the stub areas hold intra-area routes, inter-area routes, and a default route. Another technique for minimizing the routing table entries in a stub area is compacting all inter-area and external routes into single default route. This is called a totally stubby area and is the logical equivalent of saying "all destinations out of this area use this route." The routing tables in a totally stubby area list only intra-area routes and a default route.

Here is an analogy that might help you understand stub areas. Think of your house as an area, your neighbors' houses as other areas, and your neighborhood as an AS. You are sitting in the living room watching TV when you decide you would like a cookie. You walk from the living room to the kitchen using a mental map of your house (your routing table). When you have completed this intra-area transit, you discover that you don't have any cookies, so you decide to go next door to see if the neighbor has some. Using your mental map again, you walk to the front door and leave the house. You make a decision at that time how you will walk over to their house, depending on weather conditions and obstacles in your path. Alternatively, you could have decided to go to the store to buy cookies. You always take the same route to the store, regardless of the possible conditions on the path to the store. Think of this as a static route, which is an external route. The same conditions apply to the trip to the store as the trip to the neighbor's house. You walk to the front door and out of the house before you make any decisions about how to get to a destination. This means that your front door is the default route to any destination outside of your house.

Every router in, and interface on, a stub area must be configured to indicate membership in a stub area. A special option bit, the E-bit, in the OSPF Hello packet declares that a router has membership in a stub area. If the E-bit equals 1, the router can accept and flood AS external routes. When the E-bit is 0, the router may not accept and flood AS external routes. Before an adjacency is established, routers verify that the E-bit received in the Hello packet matches their configuration. If it doesn't match, an adjacency can't be formed. There are a couple of other restrictions on stub areas too: Stub areas can't be transit areas for virtual links, nor can ASBRs be placed in a stub area.

Network Address Translation (NAT)

If you want to connect to the Internet, you have to use unique—and valid—IP addresses. Valid means that they were assigned by InterNIC. In some cases, the owner of a very large network, such as Microsoft, is assigned a range of addresses by InterNIC. Typically, though, a network is allocated these IP addresses by its ISP. Each computer that wants to communicate on the Internet has to have its own public address. This has significantly reduced the pool of available public addresses.

This shortage of available IP addresses is a big problem facing the administrators of private networks and ISPs. In certain circumstances, Network Address Translation (NAT) is a possible solution to these problems, at least until the next generation of IP addressing and supporting hardware is made available. NAT is an IETF (Internet Engineering Task Force) standard that defines a method for using a private addressing scheme internally on a LAN and a public addressing scheme on the Internet for external traffic. A network address translator sits between the Internet and the private network to convert addresses between private and public addresses.

NAT can be used in small offices or home offices very easily, although there are some downsides to NAT. We will cover those later, in the "Drawbacks of NAT" section. In any given LAN, only a small number of hosts are communicating outside of the LAN at any given time. As a result, only a few of the IP addresses ever need to be globally unique. NAT can be thought of as a unique-IP-address-on-demand service. It translates private addresses to globally unique addresses only when hosts need to communicate with the outside world.

InterNIC

InterNIC is a collaborative group of corporations, including AT&T and Network Solutions, Inc., that acted as a central network information center for Internet-related services, such as domain name registration services and directory and database services. Recently, domain name registration has been privatized and falls under the umbrella of another group called the Internet Corporation for Assigned Names and Numbers (ICANN). For more information on InterNIC and ICANN, refer to http://www.internic.net.

Because NAT is an address reuse solution, it is necessary to segment IP address space into two parts for proper functionality. The reusable addresses used internally are also called local addresses. The globally unique addresses are also called global addresses. An address can be a local address or a global address but not both. If an address acts as both, routers in any given LAN might not be able to distinguish the global address from its own local address if they are identical. Another caveat for the same reason: A router running NAT shouldn't advertise internal networks on the Internet. However, global information that NAT receives from the Internet can be advertised on the LAN.

NAT Operation

NAT boxes are positioned at the border between LANs and the Internet. Each NAT has a table that holds local IP address and globally unique address pairs. The IP addresses inside the LAN are not globally unique, meaning they are reused in other LANs. The globally unique IP addresses are allocated according to current address allocation schemes. InterNIC has also reserved network IDs for use in private networks. The private network IDs include:

- **A Class A address.** 10.0.0.0 with the subnet mask 255.0.0.0
- **A Class B address.** 172.16.0.0 with the subnet mask 255.240.0.0
- **A Class C address.** 192.168.0.0 with the subnet mask 255.255.0.0

Besides these reserved addresses, Microsoft has reserved the network ID 169.254.0.0 with the subnet mask of 255.255.0.0. This network is to be used in Windows 2000 private networks and in Windows 98 when it is unable to obtain an IP address from any other source.

The addresses inside a LAN can be reused by any other LAN. However, if two LANs must communicate with each other, the IP addresses in each LAN must be unique or at least perceived as unique by the other LAN. At each exit point between two LANs, or a LAN and the Internet, a NAT box is installed. Multiple NATS can be installed on a single LAN, but each NAT has to have the same translation table.

Here is an example of a LAN using NAT to communicate over the network. Figure 4.19 is a diagram of the communication path.

Mary's Pie Shop is using the 192.168.0.0 network for its LAN and the public address of a.a.a.a. The NAT translates all private addresses to the public address. Mary sits at a computer with the address of 192.168.0.15 and uses Internet Explorer 5.0 to connect to a Web site at b.b.b.b. IP packets are sent with the destination IP of b.b.b.b and the source IP of 192.168.0.15.

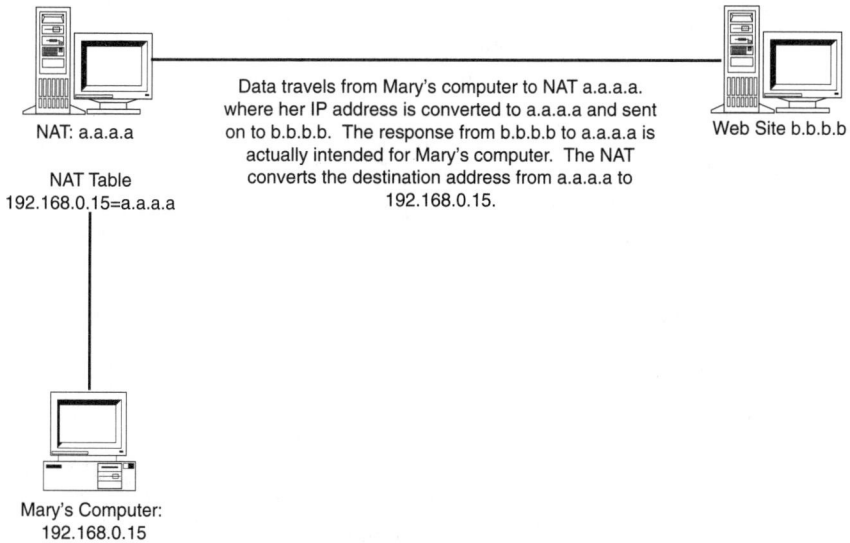

Data travels from Mary's computer to NAT a.a.a.a.
where her IP address is converted to a.a.a.a and sent
on to b.b.b.b. The response from b.b.b.b to a.a.a.a is
actually intended for Mary's computer. The NAT
converts the destination address from a.a.a.a to
192.168.0.15.

NAT: a.a.a.a

NAT Table
192.168.0.15=a.a.a.a

Web Site b.b.b.b

Mary's Computer:
192.168.0.15

Figure 4.19   NAT operation.

These IP packets are forwarded to the default gateway by Mary's computer, and from there they travel through NAT. NAT leaves the destination IP intact, but changes the source address to 192.168.a.a. NAT keeps track of the changed source address and a source port number in a table. The translated IP packets are sent to the destination. When the response packets are received by the NAT, the packets contain the destination address of 192.168.a.a and the source address of b.b.b.b.

NAT looks up the mapping of 192.168.a.a to 192.168.0.15 by its port number in its translation table. It then re-addresses the packet with the destination IP and forwards it to the computer at 192.168.0.15. The forwarded packet contains the destination address of 192.168.0.15 and the source address of b.b.b.b.

Dynamically selected TCP and UDP ports are used to differentiate one LAN host from another in the event that multiple private addresses are converted to a single public address.

NAT Editors

NAT translates IP addresses in the IP header, TCP port numbers in the TCP header, and UDP port numbers in the UDP header. Conversion of any other addressing information requires additional translation, which is performed by a NAT editor. A NAT editor makes additional modifications to the IP packet and payload as necessary to include the correct address and port information. Hypertext Transfer Protocol (HTTP) traffic doesn't need a NAT editor because HTTP only uses an IP address in the IP header and the TCP port in the TCP header. However, other applications require NAT editors to completely translate source, destination addresses and ports as appropriate for communication. Any application where the IP address, TCP port, or UDP port is stored in the payload will require a NAT editor. An example of this is FTP. FTP includes IP addresses in the FTP header for the FTP PORT command. NAT has to correctly convert all IP address in the FTP header and data stream or connectivity problems may occur. Windows 2000 includes NAT editors for FTP, ICMP, and PPTP. NAT editors for other applications can be created, but IPSec and H.323 traffic can't be translated even with a NAT editor.

Drawbacks of NAT

While NAT seems like an ideal solution for address reuse, it does have certain drawbacks. One of these is limited options for security. Because of the way NAT does address translation, you can't encrypt anything that carries an IP address or is derived from an IP address. It also makes tracking the source of an intruder or hacker difficult, because the source IP is stripped away during translation. Further, NAT is not suitable for large networks where many hosts are communicating on the Internet simultaneously. The size of the mapping tables in this environment can cause performance problems. Also, any application that locates a resource based on IP address rather than host name will require a NAT editor to ensure that proper communication is established. You should consider these things carefully before you implement NAT in a production environment.

ICMP Router Discovery

Internet Control Message Protocol (ICMP) is a maintenance protocol. It is used to create and maintain routing tables and troubleshoot problems with the ping and tracert utilities. ICMP also supports router discovery and advertisements to hosts on a network. When a computer starts up, it will probably only have a few entries in its routing table. When that host sends data to a specific network, it first checks its routing table to see if there is an entry that matches the IP address of the destination. If a match is not found, the packet is sent to the default gateway. When the default gateway receives this packet, it checks to see if it has a matching route. Routers propagate routing information to each other, so the default gateway might know a route to the destination. If the default gateway does know a route, it forwards the packet appropriately, and performs the extra service of delivering an ICMP redirect message to the sending host to alert it to the better route. Another function of ICMP is notifying hosts on a network that a router is still active. Periodic announcements are made to hosts with this information.

Windows 2000 TCP/IP supports ICMP router solicitations, and the Windows 2000 router supports ICMP router advertisements.

DHCP Relay Agent

Dynamic Host Configuration Protocol (DHCP) uses broadcasts to request and assign IP addresses. Because routers don't normally pass broadcast traffic between networks, you must have some mechanism for DHCP broadcasts to reach every network where you want to have automatic IP address assignment. One way is to set up a DHCP server on each network. Alternatively, a router or a computer can be configured to act as a DHCP relay agent. It is the DHCP relay agent's job to listen for DHCP broadcasts and direct them to a specific DHCP server or servers. The DHCP relay agent also steers DHCP server responses to DHCP clients. Windows 2000 Server can be configured as a DHCP server or a DHCP relay agent.

Other Routing Protocols

Windows 2000 supports routing protocols for non-IP networks. This section will begin with a look at IPX routing, specifically RIP and SAP for IPX. It will conclude with AppleTalk routing, where it will cover AppleTalk nodes, routers, and zones.

IPX Routing Protocols

Windows 2000 Server offers a feature-rich Internetwork Packet Exchange (IPX) router. It blends an IPX routing agent and a Service Advertising Protocol agent into a single routing tool. Windows 2000 supports RIP for IPX, the routing protocol of choice in IPX networks. While this is the only IPX routing protocol provided by Microsoft, Windows 2000 Server is an open and extensible routing platform. Third-party vendors can provide additional IPX routing protocols for use in mixed Windows 2000-Novell networks. Other highlights of the Windows 2000 IPX router include:

- Independent configuration of each interface to filter inbound and outbound routes, announcements, and packets. This filtering is based on exceptions—you can allow all routes, announcements, or packets except those you specify. Alternatively, you can reject all routes, announcements, or packets except those you specify.
- Advertisement of static IPX routes with RIP for IPX.
- Support for SAP, including advertisement of static SAP service names and filtering of SAP service names and announcements.
- Static NetBIOS names can be forwarded through IPX broadcasts over both LAN and demand-dial interfaces.

In this section, we will briefly look at some of these features as well as the functions and operations of RIP and SAP for IPX.

RIP for IPX

RIP for IPX is very similar to RIP for IP, but it uses an extra field that tracks the tick count. The tick count is an attempt to predict how long it will take a packet to arrive at its destination network. RIP for IPX routers broadcast their routing tables using split horizon propagation. The default interval for announcements is 60 seconds. RIP for IPX is also capable of making a triggered update announcement to notify other routers about a change in network topology.

IPX Routing Tables

RIP is responsible for building and maintaining IPX routing tables. IPX routing table entries contain this information:

- **Network number.** The IPX network number that identifies a destination network.
- **Forwarding MAC address.** The MAC address given to an IPX packet when it is forwarded to the next hop.
- **Tick count.** How many ticks it takes to reach the destination network.
- **Hop count.** The number of hops (routers that must be crossed) to reach the IPX network number.
- **Interface.** May also be called the port. This defines which interface is to be used when forwarding IPX traffic with this route.

It is possible for multiple routes to a network to exist. If this is the case, the IPX router will pick the route with the fewest ticks. If two or more routes have the same number of ticks, the router will choose the route with the least number of hops.

RIP for IPX Operation

Upon initialization, the IPX router announces the network numbers directly attached to it. Neighboring IPX routers add these entries to their routing tables. The new router builds its routing table by requesting routing information from its neighboring routers. Every 60 seconds by default, a router advertises its routing table to neighboring networks. When adjacent routers receive these periodic announcements, they check their routing tables and make any necessary changes.

How Many Ticks Does it Take to Get to the Center of an IPX Network?

One tick equals about .056 seconds, but it is strictly a best-guess estimate. The router arrives at the tick count after considering other RIP messages' relative delivery rates and the speed of network segments. Usually a LAN link equals one tick. WAN links have longer delivery times; generally they are somewhere in the neighborhood of six or seven ticks.

Occasionally, the administrator might need to take the router offline. When a router is downed gracefully, it sends an announcement to all locally attached networks. This announcement declares that all routes previously available through it now have a hop count of 16. Neighboring routers update their routing tables and then advertise the changes through a triggered update. If a router unexpectedly fails due to a hardware or software problem, a power outage, or other problem, it can't announce that any routes formerly reachable through it are now unavailable. The neighboring routers simply do not receive any further announcements from this router. However, if after a specific period of time the routes received from the downed router are not refreshed, the routes will time out. At that point, the hop count for routes through this router will be updated to 16 and this information will be propagated through the network. Eventually a route that has timed out will be removed from the routing table. The default timeout value is three minutes.

If your hardware is capable of detecting media faults, RIP for IPX will announce a failed link by marking all routes through the faulty area as unreachable.

SAP for IPX

SAP allows computers that provide services on a Novell network to advertise service names, types, and IPX network addresses. These service hosts could be servers providing file, print, or application services. IPX routers gather the service and IPX network address information and store it in a database called a SAP table. The SAP table is used to provide service name resolution for clients. When a client computer refers to a service by name, the SAP table matches the service name to an address on an IPX internetwork.

In order for clients throughout the internetwork to locate and use services, the SAP table is advertised and propagated by IPX routers. The manner in which this is done is very similar to the way IPX routes are announced. Periodically, new services are announced and propagated, and when their service advertisements are no longer received, they will time out of the SAP. SAP uses split horizon and triggered updates to propagate SAP tables; router and link failures are handled in the same manner as RIP for IPX.

AppleTalk

AppleTalk was established as the protocol of choice in the early days of networking Apple computers. Nowadays, the preferred protocol in Macintosh networks is TCP/IP, but many older networks still use AppleTalk. Windows 2000 Server lets you continue using the older AppleTalk protocol without necessitating a client change, or you can replace AppleTalk with Apple File Protocol over TCP/IP.

To identify each node and network, AppleTalk uses unique addresses. The addressing scheme is made up of a network number and a node ID. (Actually, three values are assigned: network number, node ID, and socket number. The socket number is rarely referred to by the user, so an AppleTalk address is written as a two-part address.) The network number identifies a subnet, while the node ID identifies a specific host on that network. These network numbers are two-byte values that provide more than 65,000 network numbers. AppleTalk supports 253 nodes per network number assigned to a subnet. This means you can assign multiple network numbers to a single subnet to support the number of nodes residing on that subnet. If there are 25 nodes on one subnet, that subnet needs only one network number. If there are 300 nodes on a subnet, you assign the subnet two network numbers. The group of network numbers assigned to a subnet is called a range. A subnet can have multiple network numbers, but it can have only one network range.

Nodes

In order for computers on an AppleTalk network to communicate with other, each node has to obtain a valid network number and node ID. The subnet network range must also be known. This information is supplied by the network's routers. Exactly how the routers learn this information will be covered in the next section. When a node initializes, it broadcasts a request for the network range to the routers on its subnet. A router will respond with that subnet's network range. The node will pick a network number within the range supplied, then negotiate with other nodes on that subnet for an unused node ID. This means addressing happens dynamically, so manual configuration of node ID is not required.

Routers

An AppleTalk router must know the network range or the subnet it is serving. Depending on the router configuration, this information is supplied by the administrator or learned from other routers. There are three ways an AppleTalk router can be configured: seed, non-seed, and soft-seed. Windows 2000 supports seed and non-seed AppleTalk routers.

You must configure at least one router on each subnet to be a seed router. The seed router contains network range information that has been manually entered by the administrator. When a seed router initializes, it broadcasts "seed ranges" to each subnet it connects. A router that is connected to multiple subnets can seed any or all of those subnets. To provide a measure of fault tolerance, you can also configure more than one seed router on the same subnet, as long as they both provide the same network range information. Assigning two different ranges to the same subnet and assigning overlapping ranges to two subnets are common configuration errors. Another problem is simply entering wrong data into the router. Seed routers provide whatever routing information you enter in the routing table even if it's incorrect, so always double-check your entries. Spelling counts!

Non-seed routers also provide routing information, but this information is not manually entered into the router. Instead, routing table information is collected from other routers in broadcasts sent to every router on the subnet every 10 seconds.

Routing Table Maintenance Protocol (RTMP) is part of the AppleTalk protocol stack. RTMP enables AppleTalk routers to propagate network information to all other routers on a network. RTMP packets are broadcast by every router on a network segment every 10 seconds. Through this process, AppleTalk routers are able to discover locally attached networks, other routers, and remote destinations, and dynamically adapt to changes in connectivity. If a link fails, an alternate network route will automatically be adopted.

Zones

Seed routers are also responsible for the creation and management of groups of nodes called zones. Zones are logical groupings of computers used to organize a network. A single zone can contain multiple networks, and a single network can contain multiple zones. A zone is similar to both a workgroup and a Windows NT or Windows 2000 domain. Like a workgroup, zone membership is voluntary; a user can configure a node to leave one zone and join another at any time. Like a domain, a computer can belong to only one zone at a time.

Demand-Dial Routing

Demand-dial routing allows you to use non-permanent, dial-up WAN lines to transmit data between two separate networks. Perhaps you have a T-1 joining a branch office to your company's headquarters. (See Chapter 10, "Bandwidth and Telecommunications," for a discussion on leased lines, including T-1 lines.) Occasionally, the T-1 becomes saturated with data and you need an alternative route to transmit data between offices. With a demand-dial link, you can use a low-cost alternative at peak times. In this section, we will look at a sample demand-dial network, discuss the connection process and how updates are sent, and wrap up with a look at unnumbered connections.

Demand-dial routing is an uncomplicated concept—you simply activate a link when you need to use it. When the connection is unused for a specific amount of time, the connection will be dropped. However, configuration and the connection process of the demand-dial router are more complex. This is because demand-dial routing makes the following requirements:

- Each end of the connection must be identified by a phone number.
- Each call received by a router must be authenticated. If the caller's account name matches a Windows 2000 account with appropriate dial-up permissions, the router assumes that connection is coming from a remote access client. If the account name matches the name of the demand-dial interface, the incoming call is assumed to be from a router.

- Both ends of the demand-dial connection have to be configured, even if only one end of the connection will ever actually dial the other. This is because communication over the link is bi-directional. If both sides are not configured, proper communication cannot take place.

- Dynamic routes are not recommended over demand-dial links. Instead, you should configure static routes at each end of the connection, or you can use auto-static updates. More on that later in this chapter.

Sample Demand-Dial Network

For this example, we will take a peek at the network of the imaginary law firm of LeBlanc, Prudhomme, and Breaux. The firm's headquarters are in New Orleans and there is a satellite office in Houston. A dial-up link was installed between the offices. The New Orleans office has a Windows 2000 server configured as both a remote access server and demand-dial router. This router (we will call it NewOrleans) has a modem on COM1 and the phone number 504-555-1111. The internal network ID in New Orleans is 192.220.20.0, subnet mask 255.255.255.0. The Houston office also has a Windows 2000 server acting as a remote access server and demand-dial router. The Houston router (we will call it Houston) has a modem on COM2 and the phone 713-555-2222. The internal network ID in Houston is 192.220.30.0, subnet mask 255.255.255.0.

Alice is the New Orleans administrator. Although she could have configured the router manually, she opted to use the wizard Microsoft has provided to help swiftly configure a demand-dial router. The Demand-Dial Wizard will configure everything for you except a static route. With the wizard's assistance, she first created a demand-dial interface named call_Houston. She supplied the equipment information (modem on COM1), phone number (the phone number of the other router, 713-555-2222), protocol(s) used (TCP/IP), and authentication credentials (the name of the other router, call_Houston, and a password). Next, she created a user account that matches the name of the interface on the other router (account name call_NewOrleans, and a password), then she cleared the "User must change password at next logon" check box and checked the "Password never expires" check box. And last but not least, Alice manually configured a static route with the interface (call_Houston), destination (192.220.30.0), subnet mask (255.255.255.0), and metric (1). Because this is a point-to-point link, a gateway is not configured.

David, the administrator in Houston, performs the same steps, substituting the information specific to the Houston site. Figure 4.20 shows the total configuration.

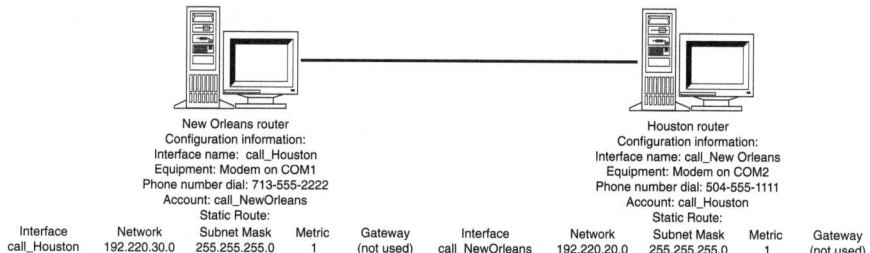

| Interface
call_Houston | Network
192.220.30.0 | Subnet Mask
255.255.255.0 | Metric
1 | Gateway
(not used) | Interface
call_NewOrleans | Network
192.220.20.0 | Subnet Mask
255.255.255.0 | Metric
1 | Gateway
(not used) |

Figure 4.20 Sample demand-dial network.

Connection Process

PPP (Point-to-Point Protocol) is used at the time a demand-dial connection is established. Mike in New Orleans has an IP address of 192.220.20.5, and needs to retrieve a file from Nicholas in Houston. Nicholas's IP address is 192.220.30.8. When Mike tries to connect to Nicholas, the following events happen:

1. Packets from 192.220.20.5 destined for 192.220.30.8 are forwarded to NewOrleans.

2. NewOrleans receives the packet and checks for a route. It finds a route to 92.220.30.8 over the call_Houston interface.

3. NewOrleans checks the call_Houston interface and discovers it is disconnected, so it brings up the configuration of the interface. NewOrleans then dials 713-555-2222 with the modem on COM1.

4. Houston answers the incoming call and requests username and password from the incoming caller.

5. NewOrleans sends the username call_NewOrleans and its password.

6. Houston checks the username and password it receives against Windows 2000 security to be sure that NewOrleans has dial-in permission assigned in the properties of the call_NewOrleans user account and the configured remote access policies. Houston now has to decide if the incoming caller is a remote access client or another router that wants to establish a demand-dial connection.

7. Houston runs through the list of its demand-dial interfaces to see if one matches the username sent by NewOrleans. Houston sees that the demand-dial interface call_NewOrleans matches the username. Houston now changes the call_NewOrleans demand-dial interface to a connected state.

8. NewOrleans forwards the packet from Mike at IP address 192.220.20.5 across the demand-dial connection to Houston. Houston receives the packet and forwards it to Nicholas at IP address 192.220.30.8.

9. The response packet is sent from 192.220.30.8 back to Houston to be forwarded to 192.220.20.5. Houston receives the packet and checks its routing table for a route to 192.220.20.5. The route using the call_NewOrleans interface is selected.

10. Houston checks the call_NewOrleans interface and finds it is in a connected state, so it forwards the packet to NewOrleans.

11. NewOrleans forwards the packet to Mike at IP address 192.220.20.5.

When the connection is made, the static routes on the user account of the calling router are added to the routing table of the answering router. If routing protocols are used to propagate the new static route, there is a delay between the time the connection is made and the time when all the routers on the intranet of the answering router are aware of the new route. Therefore, hosts on the intranet of the calling router might experience a delay between the time the connection is made and the time they begin to receive traffic back from hosts on the intranet of the answering router.

Always Use the Right Name!

Routing problems can result if the username doesn't match the name of the demand-dial interface. The caller could be identified as a remote access client rather than a demand-dial outer. If NewOrleans uses call_Houston as its username credential, NewOrleans will be categorized as a remote access client by Houston, not as a router. Of course, the username has to be associated with a valid account with appropriate dial-in permissions. Packets sent from Mike to Nicholas will be routed just as they were in the example above. However, response packets from Nicholas's computer may not make it back to Mike's computer. This is because the outbound router connection is different than the inbound router connection. The packets are sent to Houston, which looks at its routing table. Houston decides that the appropriate route to Mike's computer is through the call_NewOrleans interface. call_NewOrleans is disconnected, however. Houston calls up the configuration for call_NewOrleans and sees that COM2 is to be used to create the connection. Unfortunately, COM2 is being used at that time for a remote access client called call_Houston. Houston doesn't know that this is a connection to the same place that data needs to go, so it tries to find an unused modem. If Houston finds one, it will dial NewOrleans and forward the packet. If Houston can't find another modem, the response packets from Nicholas to Mike are dropped. The moral of the story: Make sure you configure the user account on your demand-dial router to use the right name!

Updates

It is not a good idea to run routing protocols across dial-up links. Most routing proto-cols rely on periodic announcements to pass along routing information. These adver-tisements force one demand-dial router to call another router every time there is an announcement—every 30 seconds by default for RIP. If your demand-dial link makes a long distance call every 30 seconds, you may get a surprise at the end of the month: a big phone bill that isn't much less than the cost of a dedicated link. How do you get around this? Use static routes instead. These routes identify the network IDs that are reachable over the demand-dial interface. Static routes can be entered manually or automatically with Windows 2000. Automatic entry of static routes is called auto-static updating, and can be used with RIP for IP and IPX, and SAP for IPX. Sorry, but you can't use auto-static updates with OSPF.

An auto-static update is a one-way transfer of routing information that is initiated upon a command issued by an administrator, rather than as a periodic announcement. A demand-dial interface configured for auto-static updates will, upon request, ask for the routes of another demand-dial router across a connection. The requested routes are sent to the soliciting router where they are automatically entered in the routing table as static routes. Auto-static updates behave just like static routes. Even if the link referred to in an entry becomes unavailable or the router is restarted, these entries will remain in the routing table.

It is possible to schedule an auto-static update with the Routemon utility, ensuring that an update will occur at a specified interval. (The use of the Routemon utility is discussed in Chapter 6, "Routing Tools.") Keep in mind, though, that the first thing that happens when you (or your scheduled update task) request an auto-static update is that all current auto-static routes are deleted. After the routes are flushed from the routing table, a request is sent to other routers for updates. If a link is temporarily out of service, the request goes unanswered and the router can be left with an empty rout-ing table (if only auto-static entries were in the table). It can't automatically replace the routes it has deleted. And because auto-static updates are only made upon request, there could potentially be a loss of connectivity to remote networks until the next time the administrator requests an update or a scheduled update task is performed.

Demand-Dial Router Connections

A numbered connection is a demand-dial connection in which the routers at each end of the link have assigned each other an IP address. You use the Routing and Remote Access Service to configure both routers to use the method of IP address assignment appropriate for that network. The default method for IP address assignment is DHCP.

A common pitfall of demand-dial configuration is to forget to set IP address assignment to the appropriate method. If there is not a DHCP server on the network and the RRAS properties are left at the default, no IP address will be given to the other router. This is called an unnumbered connection. If you are using Windows NT 4.0 RRAS, this is a real issue because all demand-dial connections must have a numbered connection. If one router doesn't assign an IP address to the other, the connection will fail. Windows 2000 fixes this problem by adding support for Automatic Private IP Addressing (APIPA) and unnumbered connections.

APIPA allows a router to assign an address to a calling router from a pool of addresses (169.254.0.1 to 169.254.255.254). If you accidentally leave the default of DHCP address assignment, or if your DHCP server goes down unexpectedly, your Windows 2000 router will not be prevented from establishing a numbered connection.

Alternatively, you don't have to use numbered connections at all. With an unnumbered connection, demand-dial routers will still request an IP address from each other while establishing a connection. However, if one of the routers fails to assign an IP address, the connection will still be established. (By the way, you have to use static routes with unnumbered connections because the routing protocols supplied with Windows 2000 don't allow unnumbered connections.) To check whether you are using an unnumbered connection or not, look at the system event log on both servers running a demand-router. If an unnumbered connection was established, you will see a warning stating that one side requested, but did not receive, an IP address.

Unnumbered connections have another use besides acting as a fail-safe mechanism for a missing DHCP server. Your demand-dial router can connect to other routers that just don't assign an IP address upon establishing a connection. Your ISP or ASP (Application Service Provider) may not assign IP addresses to incoming calls because they have more customers than IP addresses.

Summary

As you saw in this chapter, Windows 2000 Routing and Remote Access Service has a plethora of features, making it suitable for use in networks of all sizes. Because it is integrated in the operating system, the Windows 2000 router is a cost-effective routing platform. Beyond the connectivity media required to join the computer running Windows 2000 Server to the network, no additional hardware or software needs to be purchased. Additionally, the Windows 2000 router is RFC-compliant, which enables it to be used in networks where other routing products are also in use. This section will present a brief review of what was covered in this chapter.

A full complement of IP unicast routing services are included with the Routing and Remote Access Service. Static routing, a distance vector protocol (RIP for IP v1 and v2), and a link-state protocols (OSPF) are supported. These provide routing options for the smallest to the largest networks. The DHCP Relay Agent enables administrators to use a single DHCP server on non-contiguous networks. Because

DHCP traffic is not normally routed between networks, the relay agent is used to forward traffic between DHCP clients and DHCP servers in different networks. Windows 2000 includes multicast routing support too. All Windows 2000 computers will listen for and forward IP Multicast traffic by default.

Routing in other network types is easy with the Windows 2000 router. RIP for IPX allows the passing of network route information between routers in an IPX network. Although it is fairly common to see IPX implemented in a Microsoft-networking environment, IPX is the primary LAN protocol in networks with Novell NetWare servers. This allows for easy integration of Microsoft products in an existing Novell environment. To this further the ease of integration, the Windows 2000 router also supports SAP for IPX, which permits advertising of service names and addresses announced by hosts offering services such as file and print sharing. AppleTalk routing is also supported, adding yet another feature to the complement of Macintosh services provided by Windows 2000.

Demand-dial routing is another exciting feature of the Windows 2000 router covered in this chapter. It combines the best of the routing and remote access components to allow for routing on-demand. This allows for two networks to be joined over dial-up lines. Network Address Translation was also discussed as a means to use a private IP addresses in a network that is connected to the Internet. The translation component proxies the data traveling between internal network and the Internet. It does this by translating the private IP addresses into public IP addresses and vice versa. The Windows 2000 router is easily configurable, as the next chapter, Chapter 5, "Configuring the Windows 2000 Router," will demonstrate.

References

The following sources provide additional information on the topics covered in this chapter:

- RFC 1058: Routing Information Protocol
- RFC 1583: Open Shortest Path Version 2
- RFC 1723: RIP Version 2
- RFC 1631: Network Address Translation

These RFCs can be found many places on the Internet, including at: `http://www.cis.ohio-state.edu/hypertext/information/rfc.html` and `ftp://ftp.internic.net/rfc/rfc1700.txt`

- Microsoft TechNet: Technical Information CD. *Windows 2000 Server Internetworking Guide*: Unicast Routing Overview.
- Microsoft TechNet: Technical Information CD. *Windows 2000 Server Internetworking Guide*: Unicast IP Routing.

- Microsoft TechNet: Technical Information CD. *Windows 2000 Server Internetworking Guide*: IPX Routing.

- Microsoft TechNet: Microsoft Knowledge Base CD. Q140859: TCP/IP Routing Basics for Windows NT.

5

Configuring the
Windows 2000 Router

IN THE LAST CHAPTER, WE TALKED ABOUT ROUTING protocols and how they work. In this chapter, installing and configuring the routing protocols that ship with Windows 2000 will be discussed, with one exception: Network Address Translation (NAT), which will be covered in Chapter 11, "Shared Internet Connectivity." In this chapter, you will learn to configure IP, IPX, and AppleTalk routing.

Because different networks have different requirements, this chapter explains the configuration options available for the Windows 2000 router by mentioning when and how a specific option would be configured. The why of network requirements—specific design and architecture issues for different-sized networks—will be covered in Chapter 12, "Network Design."

Configuration Basics

Before you begin installing the Windows 2000 router, all routing hardware needs to be installed and functioning properly. Verify that the hardware is on the Hardware Compatibility List (HCL) before you start the installation process. For the most complete and up-to-date list of devices on the HCL, check Microsoft's Web site (http://www.microsoft.com). After you have installed the network cards, modems, or LAN or WAN adapters on your Windows 2000 server, you need to configure them with the appropriate network protocols for your network. (See Chapter 2, "Remote Access Server," for more information on installing and configuring network devices.)

Install the Windows 2000 Router

The Routing and Remote Access Service is installed when you install Windows 2000 Server, but it is left in a disabled state after installation is completed. You must enable RRAS to configure and use the Windows 2000 router:

1. Open the Routing and Remote Access console.

2. The local server is listed as a server by default, but if you want to add another server, right-click Server Status, then click Add Server. The Add Server dialog box will appear. Click the appropriate option, then click OK.

3. Select the server you want to enable from the list of servers in the console tree. Right-click the server, then click Configure and Enable Routing and Remote Access.

4. The Routing and Remote Access Wizard will appear. You will supply the following information:

   - Specify if you want to do LAN or LAN/WAN routing. (If you opt to enable remote access service at this time, you will be asked questions regarding that as well.)

   - Specify the devices over which you want to enable routing.

5. When prompted, start the Routing and Remote Access Service.

Routing Components

A Windows 2000 router uses interfaces, devices, and ports to create connections, and protocols are used to forward data across those connections.

Interfaces

An interface is a logical or physical connection of a network to a router. In other words, it represents the networks that can be reached over your LAN or WAN adapters. The Windows 2000 router receives data packets from one network and routes or forwards the data to the destination network over the interface. A Windows 2000 server with three NICs installed and configured to forward data between each of the attached networks would be said to have three interfaces. Each installed and configured interface can be accessed through the Routing and Remote Access console. There are three types of interfaces:

- LAN
- Demand-dial
- IP-in-IP tunnel interfaces

The LAN interface is usually indicated by a network card, although a WAN adapter can also be an interface. The LAN interface is always active and does not generally require any type of authentication before it can be used. A demand-dial interface is a point-to-point connection that requires authentication to complete the connection process. A router-to-router VPN and a phone line connected by modems are two examples of demand-dial interfaces. Demand-dial connections can remain continuously connected (also known as a persistent connection), or they can be activated only when needed (on-demand connections). The IP-in-IP tunnel interface is a logical point-to-point connection. It is used for things like forwarding IP traffic (such as IP multicasting) from one area of a network to another area across a network segment that doesn't support that traffic type. LAN, demand-dial, and IP-in-IP tunneling will be covered in this chapter.

The basic process for routing configuration in Windows 2000 is this: Add the protocol, add the interface to the protocol, configure the global protocol options, then configure the interface protocol settings. IP routing is the most complex protocol to configure. By comparison, IPX and AppleTalk routing are much less complicated. Interface management is easily accomplished through the Routing and Remote Access console. Normally, installed and configured network cards will automatically appear in Routing Interfaces. If you need to add another interface, or an interface that is installed does not appear in the list, perform the following steps:

1. Double-click the appropriate server.

2. Select IP or IPX Routing.

3. Right-click General, then click New Interface. The Interfaces dialog box will appear. Select the interface you want to add, then click OK.

4. For IPX routing, the interface is automatically added to all available IPX routing protocols. For IP routing, however, you must add the interface to each IP routing protocol manually. To do so, right-click the desired protocol and select New Interface, then select the interface to be added.

5. If prompted, supply any requested information.

Deleting an Interface

You can delete an interface from a protocol by selecting the interface and pressing the Delete key. You will notice that there is an "Internal" interface in the Routing and Remote Access Console. This is a console object that represents all Routing and Remote Access Devices. It doesn't need to be configured, and it shouldn't be deleted.

Devices and Ports

A Windows 2000 router shows networking hardware as devices and ports. A *device* is a physical card or other piece of equipment that is installed in a computer to connect it to a LAN or WAN. Devices can also be logical, such as a VPN protocol. The device contains one or more ports that create point-to-point connections. Each port allows a single point-to-point connection to be made from a device.

To configure a port or device for routing or remote access, right-click Ports in the RRAS console, then select Properties. Select the appropriate port from the list that appears, then click the Configure button. Supply all requested information, including:

- Whether the device will accept remote access and/or demand-dial routing connections

- The phone number for the device

- The maximum port limit for a device (refer to the manufacturer's documentation for specific details)

Protocols

IP routing protocols are added by right-clicking General under IP Routing. Choose the new routing protocol, then select the desired protocol from the list that appears. IPX routing automatically installs all related protocols. Specific configuration of protocols will be discussed later in this chapter. Each protocol will have a section dedicated to it, titled with the name of the protocol it covers.

Adding a Protocol or Interface

If you add a protocol or an interface and it doesn't show up in the Routing and Remote Access console, exit the console and then launch it again. Your newly added item should appear.

IP Routing

Windows 2000 IP routing offers a full suite of routing protocols. There are seven configurable options found under IP Routing for any given server listed in the Routing and Remote Access console: General, Static Routes, Network Address Translation, IGMP, OSPF, RIP, and DHCP Relay Agent. In this section, the configuration of each of these items will be described.

General

Global IP routing settings are covered in this section of the RRAS console. To begin, let's start with the properties sheet. Right-click General and then click Properties. The General Properties sheet will appear, as shown in Figure 5.1.

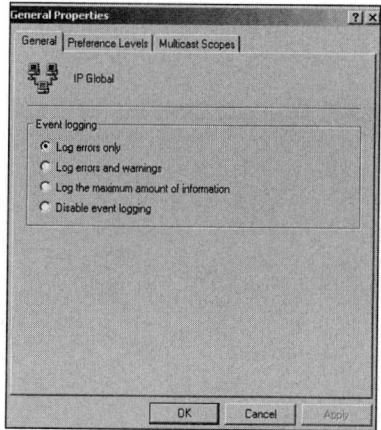

Figure 5.1   IP routing General Properties sheet.

This sheet has three tabs:

- **General.** You'll set Event Viewer logging preferences here. There are four levels of logging to choose from, from no logging to maximum information recorded in Event Viewer.

- **Preference Levels.** You will rank routes according to source on this tab. Routes can be learned in different ways—statically, through routing protocols, and so on. If two routes for the same destination exist, Windows 2000 will select the one with lowest ranking to be placed in the routing table, regardless of hop count. Network conditions in your intranet might dictate that certain routing sources are more reliable than others. For example, you might prefer to use routes learned by OSPF over routes learned auto-statically. You can sort routes according to preference for use by selecting a source and clicking Move Up or Move Down.

- **Multicast Scopes.** If you are using Windows 2000 Server's IGMP Multicasting feature, set the scope for your range of addresses here. Click the Add button, then provide a name for your multicast scope, as well as the IP address and subnet mask for the scope. More details on IGMP will be covered in the section "IGMP" later in this chapter.

You probably noticed that quite a few menu options popped up when you right-clicked General. If you want to add a new interface or a new IP routing protocol, you will do that here (see previous sections on protocols and devices and ports). Additionally, if you want to display various IP routing statistics, or just check that you actually configured what you thought you configured, select the appropriate table from the list.

For further routing and TCP/IP statistics, you can right-click each interface displayed in the right pane of the RRAS console. You can also modify certain aspects of these interfaces by right-clicking the desired interface and then selecting Properties. The properties sheet will appear, as shown in Figure 5.2.

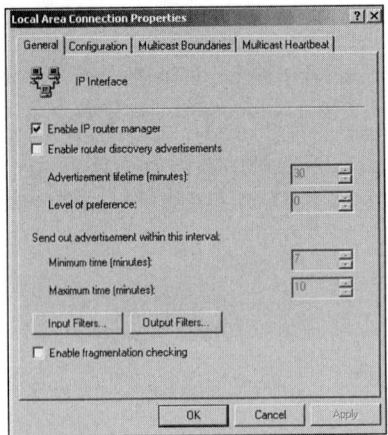

Figure 5.2 IP routing interface properties sheet.

General Tab

The first configuration option is Enable IP router manager. This option is selected by default, and allows you to run IP routing over this interface and view information, such as router discovery options and routing protocols on the specified interface. If you disable this selection, you are disabling IP routing on this interface—if you notice that routing over an interface is failing, make sure the check box for IP router manager is still selected.

Next on this tab are ICMP router discovery options. RFC 1256 provides a standard method for advertising and discovering routers, and the Windows 2000 router conforms to this RFC. Routers advertise their presence on the network, and IP hosts that support Internet Router Discovery Protocol (IRDP) can send router solicitations to aid the detection of an alternate gateway in the event that the client's normal gateway is "dead." Windows 2000 and Windows 98 clients natively support IRDP. Windows NT 4.0 and Windows 95 clients require the following changes: Windows NT 4.0 requires Service Pack 5, and Windows 95 requires Windows Socket update 2. Router solicitations are sent to the IP multicast address 224.0.0.2, and routers that support RFC 1256 reply with an advertisement. The client picks the router with the highest preference level as its default gateway. The higher the number you set here, the more likely this router will be selected. Don't confuse this preference with the preference levels set on the IP Routing General properties sheet. That preference level refers to the route sources a router will prefer, and uses the lowest number to choose between sources.

Router advertisement messages are sent out at a configurable interval. By default this is a random interval between seven and ten minutes. The advertisement includes a lifetime setting that indicates how long a router advertisement will be considered valid. The default is 30 minutes. What this means is that a router advertisement will be considered "good" for a maximum of 30 minutes if no other router advertisement is received. After 30 minutes the router advertised will be regarded as unreachable. This setting can be increased or decreased according to your needs. The preference level can be set in reference to other routers' preference levels. The highest preference level route will be chosen by the client.

Filters are set on the General tab. The last option on this tab, "Enable fragmentation checking," also deals with filtering. This enables the Windows 2000 router to filter incoming fragmented IP packets. Fragmentation filtering will help secure your router against the denial of service attack called the Ping of Death. In attacks of this type, the router is flooded with fragmented packets destined for a host on the other side of the router. The router devotes so much of its resources to dealing with these fragmented packets that it cannot handle any other requests, valid or otherwise.

Configuration

Microsoft has added a feature that is very convenient for administrators: On the Configuration tab, you can change the IP address of an interface without having to go to the Network and Dial-up Connections control panel. You can choose a static or DHCP-assigned address. By clicking the Advanced button you can assign multiple addresses (if using static addressing) and/or gateways (for both static and DHCP addressing) on a single interface.

Multicast Boundaries and Heartbeat

These two tabs will be covered in detail in the section "IGMP." This is where you will set multicast scopes and configure the multicast heartbeat.

Static Routing

You might find it necessary to configure a static route on your Windows 2000 router. To do so, right-click Static Routes, then click Add static route. Provide the following information: Interface, Destination, Network Mask, Gateway, and Metric. If this is an demand-dial static route, you will not need to configure a gateway, but be sure to click the check box at the bottom of the dialog box.

Persistent static routes added through the route command are stored in a separate area of the registry from static routes entered in the Routing and Remote Access console. Routes entered through the console don't appear in the route table until the Routing and Remote Access Service is started.

DHCP Relay Agent

The DHCP relay agent intercepts and forwards DHCP traffic between DHCP clients and servers on separate subnets. DHCP is an offshoot of bootp (bootstrap protocol), which was originally designed to configure diskless workstations with TCP/IP information. Bootp is described in RFC 951 and RFC 1542. Keep in mind that if you run the DHCP relay agent on a Windows 2000 server, that server can't act as a DHCP server or run Network Address Translation (NAT) with automatic addressing enabled.

To configure the DHCP relay agent, follow these steps:

1. Add the protocol (see the "Protocols" section earlier in this chapter).

2. Configure the global agent settings by right-clicking DHCP Relay Agent, then click Properties. Add the IP address(es) of the DHCP servers this agent will service.

3. Add the appropriate interface to the protocol by right-clicking DHCP Relay Agent and selecting New Interface from the context menu. Select the appropriate interface from the list.

4. Configure the interface properties with the following information:

   - If you want to relay DHCP messages over this interface.
   - The maximum number of consecutive DHCP relay agents that will handle DHCP traffic, also called hop-count threshold. The max is 16, default is 4. Using this setting can prevent DHCP messages from getting stuck in a loop while in transit to the DHCP server or client.

- The boot threshold count, which is the number of seconds the DHCP relay agent will wait before forwarding messages. If you have an DHCP server on this network segment, setting it higher will give the DHCP client an opportunity to wait for the server to respond to its request for an IP address.

RIP

To configure a RIP router, first add the protocol as per the instructions in the "Protocol" section earlier in this chapter. Right-click RIP and select Properties from the list. On the resulting properties sheet, you will set global RIP settings that impact all interfaces that are configured for RIP. On the General tab, you will set the following options:

- **Maximum Delay.** This entry indicates the number of seconds a router will wait before it sends a triggered update. The default is 5 seconds. (See Chapter 4, "Routing Protocols," for a discussion of triggered updates in the section "RIP.")

- **Event logging.** You can select what level of logging you would like Windows 2000 to perform, from none to complete logging. All events are stored in the Event Viewer. This is a helpful tool for troubleshooting, but if this is a very busy server, you might want to log only the errors. Logging extra details can over-burden your server—run a performance test if you are unsure of the impact it will have.

On the Security tab, you can instruct that all routers accept or reject specific announcements. You can specify this information at the interface level, but there might be routers in your network that you want all RIP interfaces to ignore.

After you have installed and configured the protocol, add the desired interface(s) to RIP (see the instructions earlier in this chapter in the section "Protocols"). Right-click the interface you want to configure, then click Properties. The interface's properties sheet will appear. You will make configuration changes on each of the tabs as described in the following sections.

General

Under Operation mode, select periodic update or auto-static update. Unless this is a demand-dial connection, you should choose periodic update.

Under Outgoing packet protocol, make your choice based on these qualifications:

- **RIP version 1 broadcast.** Select this option if you only have RIP v1 routers.

- **RIP version 2 broadcast.** Select this option if your network has both RIP v1 and v2 routers.

- **RIP version 2 multicast.** If all neighboring routers support and run RIP v2, select this option.

- **Silent RIP.** If you want your router to listen for RIP announcements from other routers but prevent it from broadcasting its own routes, select this option.

Under Incoming packet protocol, make your choice based on these qualifications:

- **Ignore incoming packets.** Choose this option if you want this router to only announce routes and ignore the routes announced by other routers.
- **RIP version 1 and 2.** Select this option if your network has both RIP v1 and v2 routers and you want this router to accept both types of announcements.
- **RIP version 1 only.** Choose this option if your network has only RIP v1 routers or you only want this router to accept routes from RIP v1 routers. If the only routers in your network use earlier versions of Windows NT, select this option.
- **RIP version 2 only.** Choose this option if your network has only RIP v2 routers or you only want this router to accept routes from RIP v2 routers.

Enter the value for Added cost for routes. This value is added to the hop count for routes over this interface to indicate any additional cost. For instance, a route through this interface might have a "true" hop count of 3, but this interface has an added cost of 3. This brings the total cost of the route to 7. If another route to the same destination exists and it has a lower hop count, it will be chosen over the higher hop count route. This is a good way to detour traffic around high-traffic segments (see Chapter 4 for more information on RIP and hop counts). Remember, the maximum hop count for any route is 15—anything beyond that is considered unreachable.

Tag for announced routes allows you to include a number that identifies routes advertised on this interface. This feature is only supported by RIP v2 routers.

The final option on the General tab allows you to Activate authentication. If you select this, you must include the password you enter in all incoming and outgoing packets (RIP v2 only). All routers connected to this interface will need to use the same password. Keep in mind that the password is transmitted in clear text, so this isn't a security feature, just an identification feature.

Security

On this tab you will set route filters. You can specify which routes your router will accept or reject for both incoming and outgoing packets. Doing so can prevent users from reaching areas of the network where they do not need to be. The default setting is Accept all routes. To configure routes to be accepted or ignored, select the appropriate option, then add the IP address of the routers to be included in the list.

Neighbors

RIP can send announcements to its neighbors three ways:

- Broadcast
- Multicast
- Unicast

The method you use depends on your network and what routing infrastructure you already have in place. Broadcasting or multicasting will reach any routers listening for those types of messages, but if your network does not pass broadcast traffic, you will need to specify the neighbors to which RIP messages must be sent. Otherwise, RIP routes will not be propagated through your network.

Advanced

Advanced is where you set advanced announcement and update information. In Chapter 4, we looked at different ways of ensuring that routing information received was not only up to date, but that does not cause the count-to-infinity problem caused by repeating bad routes to routers where that route was learned. There are quite a few configuration options on this tab, as shown in Figure 5.3.

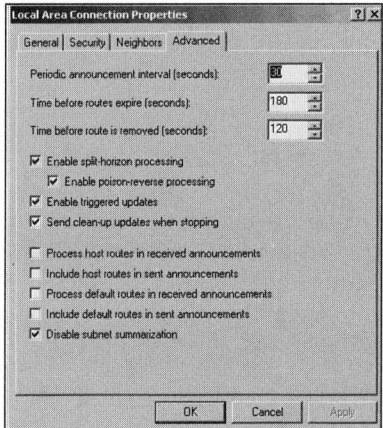

Figure 5.3   RIP Advanced properties.

I will run through the list and tell you what the most commonly used options are, and when or why they should be selected.

- **Periodic announcement interval.** If this router runs in periodic update mode (on the General tab), you can set the number of seconds between updates. The default is 30 seconds, the minimum is 15 seconds, and the maximum is 24 hours (86,400 seconds). If you do not want the added overhead of frequent updates, set this number higher; if your network infrastructure is unstable, or routes frequently change, set this interval lower.

- **Time before routes expire.** This setting sets the duration that a route will be kept in the routing table. The default is 180 seconds, but you can set it as low as 15 seconds and as high as 259,200 (72 hours). If the route is not updated in this time, it expires and is no longer considered a valid route. It will eventually time out of the routing table (see next option). A suggested interval is three times the announcement interval. (This option is only valid for routers running in periodic update mode.)

- **Time before route is removed.** This interval sets how long an expired route stays in a routing table before it is removed. It has the same interval ranges as the expiration interval. You might want to set this at two times the periodic announcement interval, but there are no hard and fast rules governing this setting.

- **Enable split-horizon processing.** Enabled by default, this prevents routers from propagating routes back to the networks on which they are learned.

- **Enable poison-reverse processing.** If split-horizon has been enabled, opt for poison-reverse. This is enabled by default and causes the router to announce that routes learned from a particular network are announced back to that network with an unreachable hop count. This prevents the propagation of bad routes back to the network where they were originally learned.(See Chapter 4 for a review of split horizon and poison-reverse in the section "RIP.")

- **Enable triggered updates.** If you would like this router to send immediate updates of changes received, without waiting for the next periodic update, click this box.

- **Send clean-up updates when stopping.** By default, when a RIP router is stopped, it sends an update stating that any routes reached through it are unreachable. It does this by sending the routes with a metric of 15. The receiving router will up the hop count by 1, which makes that route unreachable. The benefit of this is that other routers do not have to wait for routes to time out before they mark the route through this router as unreachable.

The last five options on this tab are self-explanatory, and all are disabled by default. (For a refresher on host and default routes, check out Chapter 4. The section on RIP covers this in detail.) Unless your network infrastructure requires otherwise, leaving these at the default setting is recommended.

OSPF

To configure an OSPF router, first add the protocol as per the instructions at the beginning of this chapter in the section "Protocols." Right-click OSPF and select Properties from the list. On the properties sheet that appears, you will set global OSPF settings that affect all interfaces configured for OSPF. In this section, the pertinent configuration details on each tab of the OSPF Properties sheet will be covered. For specific information regarding the function and architecture of OSPF routers, see Chapter 4.

General

On the General tab, you will set the following options:

- **Router identification.** Recall from Chapter 4 that OSPF routers are identified by a unique 32-bit number. This number is generally the highest IP address assigned to an interface on the router, although you can choose any unique 32-bit number you want.

- **Enable autonomous system boundary router.** If thisrouter exchanges information with routers in another autonomous system, you can specify that this router acts as an ASBR by clicking this box.

- **Event logging.** Set the level of logging you prefer by clicking the appropriate radio button.

Areas

On this tab, you will define the OSPF areas in your network. To set the areas on a router, click Add and provide the following information on the General tab of the OSPF Area Configuration dialog box:

- **Area ID.** This is a unique 32-bit number, but it does not have to be a specific IP address. It is simply an identifier for the area you are configuring. The only constraint is that it must not be 0.0.0.0, unless you are configuring a backbone area. 0.0.0.0 number is reserved for backbone areas; each backbone can support a maximum of 16 areas.

- **Enable plaintext password.** This is an identification option rather than a security option, as passwords are transmitted in clear text. This is a global area setting—if you decide to use a password in an area, all interfaces on that area must use a password (interfaces on the same network must use the same password, but every network in an area can use a different password). This feature is enabled by default.

- **Stub area.** This option configures an area as a stub area. Backbone areas cannot be configured as stub areas, and virtual links can't be configured through stub areas.

- **Stub metric.** If you configured this area as a stub area, you can assign a cost to routes using this area.
- **Import summary advertisements.** By checking this option, you request the import inter-area summary routes into a stub area. Without this option, all traffic destined outside this area is based on a default route.

The Ranges tab on the OSPF Area Configuration dialog box is the place to specify the destination IP addresses that belong to an area. To add a destination, simply enter the IP address and subnet mask, then click Add. Repeat until all appropriate network destinations are included. When you have finished configuring an area, click OK and you will be returned to the OSPF Properties sheet.

Virtual Interfaces

Virtual interfaces join two routers in a logical link across a common non-backbone area, called the *transit area*. You can use a virtual link in an area without a physical backbone connection to logically join the backbone across an intermediary area (the transit area). The area that is used as a transit area is one of the non-stub, non-backbone areas you have previously configured, and to which the router is physically connected. To create a virtual interface, all you need to do is specify the area the route will cross, then specify the router that is the virtual neighbor of the originating router. Certain other configuration information must match on both ends of the connection, which will be described in the procedures below:

1. Click Add on the Virtual Interfaces tab.
2. Select a Transit area ID from the list of area IDs configured on the router.
3. Enter the Virtual neighbor router ID of the router that is the end point of this virtual link.
4. The next five settings *must match* on the routers at each end of the virtual link or an adjacency will not be formed. The configuration options are as follows:

    - **Transit delay.** This is the number of seconds (estimated) that it takes for a link state update packet to traverse over the network designated as the transit area.
    - **Retransmit interval.** How long a router will wait before retransmitting link updates. This number should be at least double the transit delay number, but it is a good idea to set it even higher than that. The reason is that it is difficult to estimate how long it will take a packet to transit a network—there might be delays due to high traffic volume or other infrastructure problems.
    - **Hello interval.** How long a router will wait between sending Hello packets.

- **Dead interval.** How long an adjacent router will wait after hearing a Hello packet before considering a router to be down. The RFC recommended value is four times the Hello interval.

- **Plaintext password.** The password that will identify each router at the two ends of a virtual connection.

After configuring the adjacency settings for a virtual link, click OK. You will be returned to the OSPF Properties sheet. Repeat this step for each end of any additional virtual links you want to create.

External Routing

If you enabled this router as an ASBR (by clicking the box on the General tab), you can set external route filters based on route source (Auto-static, Local, Static) or protocol (SNMP, RIP v2), or on the source network (click the Route Filters button and provide IP address and subnet mask). As with all RRAS filters, you can choose to exclude or include all but the selected route sources.

After you have configured the global router properties, it is time to move on to the interface properties.

Interface Properties

The interface properties sheet has three tabs: General, NBMA Neighbors, and Advanced, as shown in Figure 5.4. If an interface has multiple IP addresses, you must configure each IP address independently for each of the settings described below.

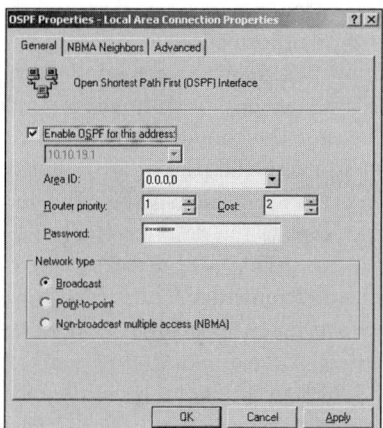

Figure 5.4   An OSPF interface properties sheet.

General

On this tab, you will enable OSPF for this address and assign the interface an Area ID. Remember, an interface can belong to only one area. Next, you will assign router priority, which is used in the election of the designated router (DR). The higher the number, the greater the chance of that interface becoming the DR. You can also assign a cost for traffic passing over this interface. The password is used as a clear text identifier, not for security, and must be the same for all interfaces on the same network if they are in the same area. Interfaces on different networks in the same area can have different passwords.

Network type is used to designate the type of underlying network connectivity. If your network is ethernet, token ring, or FDDI, choose Broadcast. If this is a dial-up link or a high-speed leased line such as a T-1 or T-3, select Point-to-point. The final option, Non-broadcast multiple access (NBMA) is for networks that use ATM, X.25, or frame relay. If you choose this option, you must configure your neighboring routers on the NBMA Neighbors tab.

NBMA Neighbors

On this tab, you will configure NBMA neighbors according to the IP address assigned to the interface. Enter the IP address of the neighboring router and its priority, then click Add. Repeat this step for each neighboring router in the NBMA network.

Advanced

Here you will configure the Transit delay, Retransmit interval, Hello interval, and Dead interval for each IP address assigned to the interface. These settings must match those on the neighboring routers or an adjacency will not be formed (see the section "OSPF" in Chapter 4 for more information).

The Poll interval is set for NBMA interfaces, which is the time that a router will still send Hello packets to a dead neighbor. Although a neighboring router is considered dead, this might be because the connection between the two routers has been severed. By sending an occasional Hello packet, the router can determine if the connection between the routers has been re-established. It is recommended that you set a poll interval at least twice as long as the dead interval.

Maximum transmission unit (MTU) size dictates the maximum size of a datagram that can be sent without being fragmented. This setting is based on the network type; the default setting assumes a 10BaseT or 100BaseT network.

That is all there is to configuring an OSPF router—if you want to view statistics or routing tables, right-click OSPF in the Routing and Remote console and select the desired option from the context menu.

IGMP

Windows 2000 supports Internet Group Management Protocol version 2 (IGMP v2), which allows hosts to join IP multicast groups and receive IP multicast data. IP multicasting allows bandwidth-efficient distribution of media-streaming applications, such as Microsoft NetShow. Multicast clients announce themselves to an IGMP router. The IGMP router listens for these IGMP Membership Report packets and tracks group membership.

Configuring Windows 2000 for IGMP support is very similar to configuring other routing protocols: add the protocol, add the interface, configure global settings, and configure the interface. Use the instructions near the beginning of this chapter in the section "Protocols" to install the protocol and the interface. Then right-click IGMP in the Routing and Remote Access console. The IGMP Properties sheet will appear. Here you will set Event Viewer logging options for IGMP routing, from no logging to logging complete information.

To configure the interface, right-click the desired interface. The properties sheet will appear. On the General tab, you will Enable IGMP on this interface. Next, you will determine if the interface will run in IGMP router or IGMP proxy mode. Remember to enable the IGMP router on all router interfaces where multicast hosts are listening for multicast traffic. If this isn't done, only those networks where the IGMP router was enabled will receive multicast traffic. The IGMP proxy acts as a proxy multicast host. It receives IGMP Membership Report packets on all configured interfaces, and forwards this information over one interface to the upstream router. You must also select the IGMP protocol version you want to run. Select the version that is compatible with the other IGMP routers in your network.

As a reminder, the Windows 2000 IGMP proxy is designed for use only in a single router network or a single network intranet connected to the MBONE.

Multicast Boundaries and Heartbeat

Windows 2000 supports multicast boundaries and multicast heartbeat. This section will demonstrate the configuration of both of these features.

Multicast boundaries prevent the forwarding of IP multicast traffic to scopes based on a range of IP addresses or by the Time to Live (TTL) value. Scope-based boundaries are more effective than TTL boundaries and use less bandwidth. To configure a multicast boundary:

1. Right-click the desired interface, then click Properties.

2. Click the Multicast Boundaries tab.

3. If you want to enable multicast scope boundaries, select a configured Scope from the drop-down list, then click Add (see "General" in the "IP Routing" section earlier in this chapter for instructions on creating a scope).

4. To enable TTL scoping, click the "Activate TTL boundary" check box. Set the TTL value. Packets with a TTL less than the value you set will not be forwarded. If you want to configure a maximum packet forwarding rate to keep from flooding the interface with forwarded traffic, type the desired value in Rate limit (Kbps).

A Windows 2000 router can also be configured to listen for regular multicast notifications to ensure that IP multicast connectivity is present. This is called a *heartbeat*. If the heartbeat is not received within a certain amount of time, an SNMP trap is sent by the router. To configure a multicast heartbeat:

1. In the Routing and Remote Access console, select the desired server. Click IP Routing, then click General.

2. Right-click the appropriate interface, then click Properties.

3. On the Multicast Heartbeat tab, select the "Enable multicast heartbeat detection" check box.

4. Add the IP address of a multicast group you want to use as a Multicast heartbeat group.

5. Configure a "Quiet time before alerting (minutes)." This is the time this interface will wait before issuing an SNMP trap. Configure this variable based on the reliability and traffic levels in your network.

IP-in-IP Tunnel

An *IP-in-IP tunnel* is a logical interface that sends IP packets in tunnel mode. IP packets that don't usually travel over an intranet or the Internet are encapsulated with an additional IP header. The encapsulated IP packets are then sent over the intranet or the Internet. An encapsulated packet is simply a packet with a different header than the payload packet carries. An IP-in-IP tunnel offers no encryption services. After you have created an IP-in-IP interface, you configure it like any other IP interface.

To configure an IP-in-IP tunnel, follow these instructions:

1. In the Routing and Remote Access console, right-click Routing Interfaces and select New IP Tunnel.

2. Provide an Interface name for the tunnel, then click OK.

3. In the console tree, select IP Routing. Right-click General, then select New Interface from the context menu that appears.

4. From the Interfaces list, select the IP-in-IP tunnel you created, then click OK.

5. You will be prompted to provide the Local address (the IP address of this router) and the Remote address (the IP address of the tunnel endpoint). When you are finished providing this information, click OK.

IPX Routing

By now you are completely familiar with the drill of installing a protocol and an interface. With IPX routing, you will get a break from the same old routine. When you enable RRAS, it automatically detects and installs the routing component for any routable LAN protocols running on the host Windows 2000 server. The IPX router will install all IPX components on all interfaces, so you don't have to. All you have to do is configure the global protocol settings, the interface settings, and specific protocol-related settings. Those options are covered in this section.

General Properties

The only global IPX setting is for logging. As I mentioned before, logging the maximum amount of information will cause a slight decline in performance on your server. It is advisable to run a performance test if your Windows 2000 router is already bogged down with performance-draining processes before choosing to log the maximum amount of information. To configure logging, right-click General under IPX Routing, and select Properties from the context menu. The General properties sheet will appear, and you can select the desired level of logging.

There are also several routing and statistics tables that can be viewed from the General context menu. These tables can help you double-check that you have configured your router properly, or ensure that other routers are functioning properly by reading the details included in each table. Right-click General and select the desired table.

NetBIOS Broadcasts

An interface can accept and deliver NetBIOS over IPX broadcasts. These options are configured separately. If you want to accept NetBIOS broadcasts on an interface, select NetBIOS Broadcasts, then right-click the desired interface. The check box to enable broadcast acceptance is found on the interface properties sheet. The default for LAN interfaces is enabled, and the default for demand-dial links is disabled. The delivery options are also found on this properties sheet. There are four choices for delivery of NetBIOS over IPX broadcasts:

- **Always.** This is the default for non-demand-dial interfaces. If this option is selected, this interface will pass broadcasts to all other interfaces except the one from which the broadcast was received, or if the broadcast has already been on the network to which the interface is attached.

- **Never.** This is the default for demand-dial interfaces. When this is selected, the interface will discard all NetBIOS over IPX broadcasts it receives.

- **Only for statically seeded names.** This configuration will pass broadcasts only to names you have statically configured through Static NetBIOS Names (which will be covered later in this section).

- **Only when interface is up.** This specifies that broadcasts will only be delivered when this interface is connected to the network to which it interfaces. It is used with demand-dial connections, to prevent the unnecessary transmittal of broadcast traffic over a potentially expensive link.

Static Routes

To configure a static route, right-click Static Routes and select New Route from the context menu. The Static Route dialog box will appear. You must provide the following information:

- **Network number.** The number assigned to the next hop router.
- **Next hop MAC address.** MAC address of the interface in the next hop router.
- **Tick count.** How long it takes a packet to reach the destination network; one tick equals 1/8 second.
- **Hop count.** How many routers must be crossed to reach the destination network.
- **Interface.** Which interface will be used to forward traffic to the destination network.

Static Services and Static NetBIOS Names

Windows 2000 allows you to enter static services in the SAP table. Static SAP services are usually used to enumerate the services that are available across a dial-up connection without requiring the link to be active for regular SAP advertising. Configuration of these two options is nearly identical in process. When the Only for statically seeded names NetBIOS broadcast delivery option is selected in the NetBIOS Broadcast Configuration dialog box, NetBIOS over IPX broadcasts are only delivered to an administrator-defined set of NetBIOS names. Static NetBIOS names can be used to restrict NetBIOS over IPX broadcast traffic.

To configure a static service entry, right-click Static Services and select New Service. Provide the following information: Service type, Service name, Network address, Node address, Socket address, Hop count, and Interface.

If you want to configure a static NetBIOS name entry, right-click Static NetBIOS Names and select New NetBIOS Name. Provide the following information: Name, Type, and Interface.

RIP for IPX

The only global setting in RIP for IPX is logging. Right-click RIP for IPX under IPX Routing and select Properties. Set the level of logging according to your preference.

To configure interface options, click RIP for IPX, then right-click the preferred interface. Select Properties, and the interface properties sheet will appear, as shown in Figure 5.5.

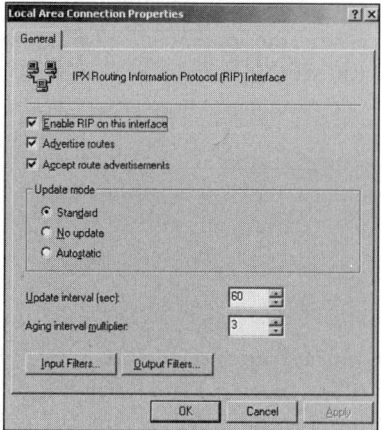

Figure 5.5   RIP for IPX interface properties.

The information to configure on this page is as follows:

- **Enable RIP on this interface.** RIP for IPX is enabled by default. If you want to disable RIP on this interface, remove the check from this box.

- **Advertise routes.** This option dictates if RIP for IPX routes will be advertised on this interface. The default is checked.

- **Accept route advertisements.** RIP for IPX announcements are accepted by default. If you would like this interface to silently discard announcements it receives, remove the check from this box.

- **Update mode.** Depending on the type of link to which this interface is joined, you will select one of the following methods for this interface to advertise its routes: Standard uses the update interval (that topic coming up next in this list) for announcement timing, No update never updates routes on this interface, and Autostatic uses auto-static updates for announcements (the default for demand-dial interfaces).

- **Update interval.** How many seconds this interface will wait between making announcements.

- **Aging interval multiplier.** This number indicates how long a learned route will stay in the routing table before it expires. The formula is n ★ update interval, where n is the multiplier. In other words, given an update interval of 60 seconds and an aging interval multiplier of 3, a route learned over this interface will be considered valid for 180 seconds. If another announcement for this route is not received in that time, the route will expire and be removed from the routing table. When you set this number, keep in mind the update intervals of other routers in your network, and the reliability of the links over which the announcements travel.

- **Filters.** Input and output filters will be covered in the section "Filtering" later in this chapter.

SAP for IPX

Configuring SAP for IPX is nearly identical to RIP for IPX configuration. The only global setting for SAP for IPX is logging. Right-click SAP for IPX under IPX Routing and select Properties. Set the level of logging according to your preference.

To configure interface options, click SAP for IPX, then right-click the preferred interface. Select Properties, and the interface properties sheet will appear. The configurable options on this page are:

- **Enable SAP on this interface.** SAP for IPX is enabled by default. To disable SAP on this interface, remove the check from this box.

- **Advertise services.** This option enables SAP services to be advertised on this interface.

- **Accept service advertisements.** SAP service announcements from other routers are accepted by default. If you would like this interface to silently discard announcements it receives, remove the check from this box.

- **Update mode.** Depending on the type of link to which this interface is joined, you will select one of the following methods for this interface to advertise its services: Standard uses the update interval for announcement (this is the default for LAN interfaces) timing, No update never updates services on this interface, and Autostatic only allows auto-static updates for service announcements (the default for demand-dial interfaces).

- **Update interval.** How many seconds this interface will wait between making announcements.

- **Aging interval multiplier.** This number indicates how long a learned service will stay in the service table before it expires. The formula is n ★ update interval = service expiration time, where n is the multiplier. If another announcement for this service is not received in that amount of time, the service will be removed from the service table.

- **Filters.** Input and output filters will be covered in the section "Filtering" later in this chapter.

Demand-Dial Routing

Demand-dial routing allows you to use non-permanent, dial-up WAN lines to transmit data between two separate networks. With a demand-dial link, you can use additional leased lines to add needed bandwidth at peak times. It can be less expensive than a dedicated connection, but if a long-distance call to the other router is involved, it might be more expensive than you had anticipated. Check out the potential costs involved beforehand to avoid unpleasant surprises when the telephone service bill comes.

Demand-dial routing is a simple concept. A link is activated when it is needed, and when the connection is unused for a specific amount of time, the connection will be dropped. (See Chapter 4 for a detailed look at how demand-dial routing works, and Chapter 7, "Virtual Private Networks," to learn how demand-dial routing is used in router-to-router VPNs.)

There are three basic phases in setting up demand-dial routing:

1. Configure Router A to initiate and receive demand-dial connections from Router B.

2. Configure Router B to initiate and receive demand-dial connections from Router A.

3. Initiate the demand-dial connection from Router A or Router B.

In comparison to the three steps above, actually configuring a demand-dial connection is a complicated, lengthy process. Be sure you double-check your work as you go though the steps involved in setting one up. It is easy to skip a step and difficult to troubleshoot if you don't catch your mistake on the front end. These instructions have been broken into three segments that map to each of the steps above, so you can tell at a glance exactly where you are in the process. Carefully following this procedure will enable you to set up a two-way demand-dial connection.

Part One: Configure Router A

For maximum flexibility, configuring a two-way demand-dial router is best. Two-way means that the router on either side of the connection can initiate a call to the other router. It is possible to configure a one-way demand-dial connection, but this is a less flexible option—only one side of the connection will be able to initiate outbound calls, and only one side will be able to accept incoming calls. (An example of a one-way demand-dial routing scenario is found in Chapter 7, in the section "Router to Router VPNs.") Figure 5.6 shows a two-way demand-dial network.

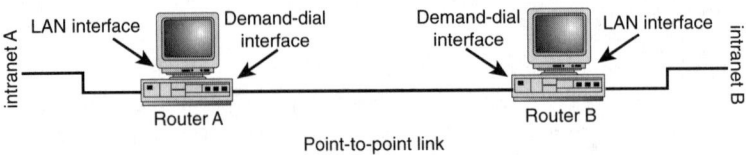

Figure 5.6　A two-way demand-dial network joins two separate intranets over a dial-up link.

Here is a checklist for the first configuration phase. Each of these topics will be covered in detail in this section, but you might find it helpful to check off each of the steps as you complete them.

1.　Configure the connection to the local intranet.

2.　Configure the router for LAN and WAN usage.

3.　Configure ports for demand-dial connections.

4.　Configure the demand-dial interfaces.

5.　Configure static routes.

6.　Configure remote access policies.

Configuring the Connection to the Intranet

The demand-dial router has at least one interface on the internal network. To set this up, install and configure a LAN adapter—Don't forget to check the HCL for compatibility. The adapter must be configured to use the appropriate protocols used on the intranet, including IP address, subnet mask, and name servers.

Router A forwards traffic received from Router B to the local intranet behind Router A, so you must configure static routes or routing protocols to allow accessibility to all intranet resources. Every network in the intranet behind Router A must be reachable from this LAN interface. Use the instructions earlier in this chapter in the section "Interfaces" to configure the appropriate LAN interface with the desired routing protocol (RIP for IP or IPX, OSPF, and so on).

To configure static routes to the resources in the intranet:

1.　In the Routing and Remote Access console, expand IP Routing on the appropriate server.

2.　Right-click Static Routes and select New Static Route.

3.　In the Static Route dialog box, supply the appropriate LAN interface, destination network ID, subnet mask, and metric.

4.　Repeat steps 2 and 3 for each network in the intranet.

Configuring the Router for LAN and WAN Usage

To allow demand-dial connections on Router A, you must configure the certain global settings for the Windows 2000 router. In the Routing and Remote Access console, right-click the appropriate server and select Properties from the context menu. The server's properties sheet will appear. Four tabs on the properties sheet will be accessed. The tabs and options you will select are as follows:

- **General.** Check the Router check box and select LAN and demand-dial routing.

- **Security.** Three options are configured here. First, select the preferred authentication provider, either Windows 2000 or RADIUS. Second, choose the appropriate method of authentication; MS-CHAP or EAP (if you plan to use smart cards or machine certificates) are recommended. Third, if you will be tracking usage of the demand-dial router, select the appropriate accounting provider. Windows 2000 logs activity in files located in the Remote Access Logging folder.

- **IP.** If you are calling a remote router using IP, check "Allow IP-based remote access and demand-dial connections." Select "Use Static Address Pool," then the appropriate IP address range and subnet mask to be assigned to calling demand-dial routers.

- **IPX.** If you are calling a remote router using IPX, check "Allow IPX-based remote access and demand dial connections." Select an IPX network number assignment appropriate for your network.

- **PPP.** If you plan to use multilink capabilities, check Multilink connections. If you also plan to use the bandwidth-on-demand capabilities of BAP or BAPC, check that option. Check the "Link control protocol (LCP) extensions" and "Software compression" check boxes.

Configuring Ports for Demand-Dial Connections

The demand-dial router requires a WAN link. If you do not already have this WAN circuit established, take care of this step first. When you have the infrastructure in place, install and configure the WAN adapter (modem, ISDN adapter, and so on; see Chapter 3, "Dial-Up Networking," for details on hardware installation). After the device is installed and configured, you can begin configuring the ports:

1. In the Routing and Remote Access console, select the appropriate server, then right-click Ports and select Properties from the context menu.

2. In the Ports Properties dialog box, select the desired device and click Configure. The Configure Device dialog box will appear, as shown in Figure 5.7.

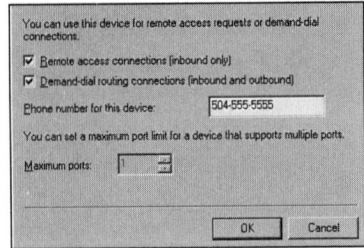

Figure 5.7 The Configure Device dialog box is where you enable demand-dial routing.

3. Put a check in the "Demand-dial routing connections (inbound and out-bound)" check box.

4. If you are using BAP-enabled connections, have configured a Called-Station-ID attribute in the remote access policy, or your phone-line or dial-in hardware/driver doesn't support caller ID, enter the phone number for this device.

5. If your device supports multiple ports, you can configure the number of ports here.

6. Repeat for each demand-dial interface you want to configure.

Configuring Demand-Dial Interfaces

You can create a demand-dial interface by using the Demand-Dial Interface Wizard. Launch the wizard by right-clicking Routing Interfaces for the appropriate server in the Routing and Remote Access console, then select New Demand-dial Interface. The wizard will prompt you for the following information:

- **Interface Name.** Give the interface a name that represents the router that will be calling in, which in this case is Router B. You might want to name the interface RouterB or something similar.

- **Connection Type.** Select "Connect using a modem, ISDN adapter, or other physical interface."

- **Device.** Select the device that will be used to establish the connection.

- **Phone Number.** Enter the phone number (and alternates, if any) of the router this interface will be calling. In this case, you would configure the phone number of Router B. If you are setting up a demand-dial router-to-router VPN, you will supply the address of the remote router here (VPNs are covered in Chapter 7.

- **Protocols and Security.** Choose the appropriate protocols to be routed over this interface, then check the "Add a user account so a remote router can dial in" box.

- **Dial-in Credentials.** Create a user account that will authenticate the calling router (Router B). The name defaults to the name you specified in the first step of the wizard—don't change it or the answering router will assume the connection attempt is from a remote client, not a remote router. If this happens, either the connection attempt will be rejected or demand-dial routing will not work properly. You must also provide and confirm password for this account. Ensure that this password meets any password policies that you have in place for your network (for example, number of characters, mix of upper and lower case letters, and so on). The new account's remote access permission is set to Allow access.

- **Dial-out Credentials.** Provide the user account information used to authenticate this router when it initiates a connection to Router B. (See "Dial-In Credentials" in "Part 2: Configure Router B," later in this chapter for the correct account information.)

Configuring Static Routes

You also need to add static routes so that traffic from the intranet behind Router A is forwarded to the intranet behind Router B using the appropriate demand-dial interface. For each network behind Router B, configure the appropriate demand-dial interface, destination, network mask, and metric.

Why do you have to add static routes instead of using a dynamic routing protocol such as RIP or OSPF? Because RIP and OSPF simply listen for routing updates, and are not designed to initiate a connection when a normal networking path doesn't succeed. You must still have static routes available to force the dialing of a demand-dial connection.

If you would like your demand-dial interfaces to use auto-static updates, configure the demand-dial interfaces to use RIP v2 multicast announcements. (OSPF doesn't support auto-static updates, and Windows 2000 doesn't support the use of OSPF over nonpermanent dial-up links.) Broadcasted RIP announcements are addressed to the subnet broadcast address; each router discards the other router's broadcasted announcement because they are on different subnets. Multicasted RIP announcements are processed regardless of the interface's subnet. (See Chapter 4 for a description of auto-static updates. You can find it in the section "Updates.")

To configure a static route:

1. In the Routing and Remote Access console, expand IP Routing on the appropriate server.

2. Right-click Static Routes and select New Static Route.

3. In the Static Route dialog box, supply the demand-dial interface, destination network ID, subnet mask, and metric.

4. Repeat steps 2 and 3 for each network behind Router B.

To prevent these static routes from causing problems with normal RIP and OSPF operation, give the added static routes higher costs than the regular network connection and adjust the preference levels of routes learned from specific sources (see "Preference Levels" in the "IP Routing" section earlier in this chapter).

Configuring Remote Access Policies

The dial-in properties of user accounts for demand-dial routers are configured to allow remote access by the Demand-dial Wizard. If you want to grant remote access based on group membership, complete the following steps:

1. If this Windows 2000 server is configured as a standalone, set the dial-in properties to Allow access for all users. For a directory services-based Windows 2000 server, set the dial-in properties to Control access through Remote Access Policy for all users.

2. Create a Windows 2000 group containing members that can create demand-dial connections with Router B. Giving this group a meaningful name such as DemandDialRouters can be helpful.

3. Add to this group the user accounts that are used by remote demand-dial routers (RouterB, for example).

4. Delete the default remote access policy Allow access if dial-in permission is enabled.

5. Create a new remote access policy with these properties (see Chapter 2 for complete details on setting up remote access policies):

   - **Policy name.** Assign a meaningful name, such as Allow Demand-dial connection if member of DemandDialRouters, for example.

   - **Conditions to match.** There are two conditions you must select: Windows-Groups (supply the group you created in the previous step—DemandDialRouters, in our example) and NAS-Port-Type (select all types except Virtual).

   - **Encryption.** The default allows IPSec or Microsoft Point-to-Point Encryption (MPPE). If you want to force encryption for demand-dial connections, you'll have to change the encryption configuration on the profile to require encryption. The options are No Authentication, Basic, or Strong.

That ends part one of the demand-dial router setup. Part two is nearly identical, except that the roles are reversed. For the sale of clarity, the entire process will be discussed so that you can easily walk through the configuration of your router.

Part Two: Configure Router B

Here is a checklist for the second configuration phase. Just as before, each of these topics will be covered in detail in this section, but you might find it helpful to check off each of the steps as you complete them.

1. Configure the connection to the local intranet.
2. Configure the router for LAN and WAN usage.
3. Configure ports for demand-dial connections.
4. Configure the demand-dial interfaces.
5. Configure static routes.
6. Configure remote access policies.

Configuring the Connection to the Intranet

The demand-dial router has one or more interfaces on the internal network. Install and configure a LAN adapter. Check the HCL first. Configure the adapter to use the appropriate protocols used on the intranet, including IP address, subnet mask, and name servers.

Router B forwards traffic received from Router A to the local intranet behind Router B, so you must configure static routes or routing protocols to allow accessibility to all intranet resources, as shown in Figure 5.8. Every network in the intranet behind Router B must be reachable from this LAN interface. Use the instructions earlier in this chapter (in the sections "Interfaces" and "Protocols") to configure the appropriate LAN interface with the desired routing protocol (RIP for IP or IPX, OSPF, and so on).

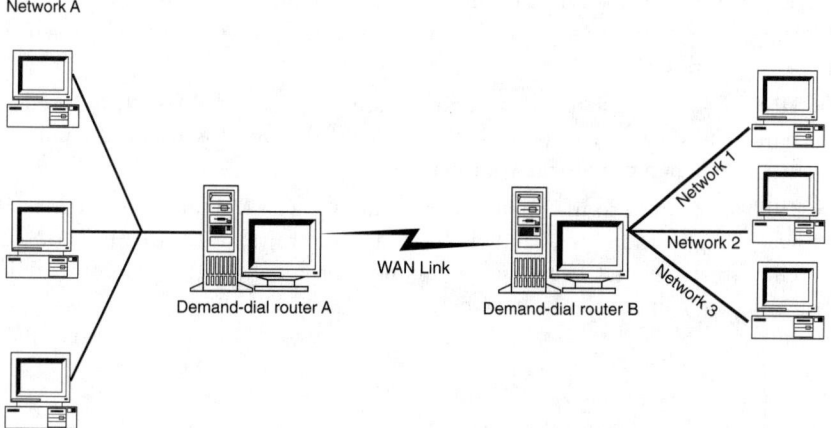

Figure 5.8   Multiple networks behind a demand-dial router.

To configure static routes to the resources in the intranet:

1. In the Routing and Remote Access console, expand IP Routing on the appropriate server.

2. Right-click Static Routes and select New Static Route.

3. In the Static Route dialog box, supply the appropriate LAN interface, destination network ID, subnet mask, and metric.

4. Repeat steps 2 and 3 for each network in the intranet.

Configuring the Router for LAN and WAN Usage

To allow demand-dial connections on Router B, you must configure the certain global settings for the Windows 2000 router. In the Routing and Remote Access console, right-click the appropriate server and select Properties from the context menu. The server's properties sheet will appear. Four tabs on the properties sheet will be accessed. The tabs and options you will select are as follows:

- **General.** Check the Router check box and select LAN and demand-dial routing.

- **Security.** Three options are configured here. First, select the preferred authentication provider, either Windows 2000 or RADIUS. Second, choose the appropriate method of authentication; MS-CHAP or EAP (if you plan to use smart cards or machine certificates) are recommended. Third, if you will be tracking usage of the demand-dial router, select the appropriate accounting provider. Windows 2000 logs activity in files located in the Remote Access Logging folder.

- **IP.** If you are calling a remote router using IP, check Allow IP-based remote access and demand-dial connections. Select Use Static Address Pool, then the appropriate IP address range and subnet mask to be assigned to calling demand-dial routers.

- **IPX.** If you are calling a remote router using IPX, check Allow IPX-based remote access and demand dial connections. Select an IPX network number assignment appropriate for your network.

- **PPP.** If you plan to use multilink capabilities, check Multilink connections. If you also plan to use the bandwidth-on-demand capabilities of BAP or BAPC, check that option. Check the "Link control protocol (LCP) extensions" and "Software compression" check boxes.

Configuring Ports for Demand-Dial Connections

The demand-dial router requires a functioning WAN link. If you don't already have this WAN circuit installed, take care of this step first. When you have the infrastructure in place, install and configure the WAN adapter (modem, ISDN adapter, and so on; see Chapter 3 for details on hardware installation). After the device is installed and configured, you can begin configuring the ports:

1. In the Routing and Remote Access console, select the appropriate server, then right-click Ports and select Properties from the context menu.

2. In the Ports Properties dialog box, select the desired device and click Configure. The Configure Device dialog box will appear.

3. Put a check in the "Demand-dial routing connections (inbound and outbound)" check box.

4. If you are using BAP-enabled connections, have configured a Called-Station-ID attribute in the remote access policy, or your phone-line or dial-in hardware/driver doesn't support caller ID, enter the phone number for this device.

5. If your device supports multiple ports, you can configure the number of ports here.

6. Repeat for each demand-dial interface you want to configure.

Configuring Demand-Dial Interfaces

You create a demand-dial interface with the Demand-Dial Interface Wizard. Launch the wizard by right-clicking Routing Interfaces for the appropriate server in the Routing and Remote Access console, then select New Demand-dial Interface. The wizard will prompt you for the following information:

- **Interface Name.** Give the interface a name that represents the router that will be calling in, which in this case is Router A. You might want to name the interface RouterA or something similar.

- **Connection Type.** Select "Connect using a modem, ISDN adapter, or other physical interface."

- **Device.** Select the device that will be used to establish the connection.

- **Phone Number.** Enter the phone number (and alternates, if any) of the router this interface will be calling. In this case, you would configure the phone number of Router A.

- **Protocols and Security.** Choose the appropriate protocols to be routed over this interface, and then check the "Add a user account so a remote router can dial in" box.

- **Dial-in Credentials.** Create a user account that will authenticate the calling router (Router A). The name defaults to the name you specified in the first step of the wizard—if it is changed, the answering router will think the connection attempt is from a remote client, not a remote router, and the connection attempt will be rejected or will not be connected as a remote router. The new account's remote access permission is set to Allow access.

- **Dial-out Credentials.** Provide the user account information used to authenticate this router when it initiates a connection to Router A. (See "Dial-in Credentials" in the "Part One: Configure Router A" section earlier in this chapter for the correct account information.)

Configuring Static Routes

You also need to add static routes so that traffic from the intranet behind Router B is forwarded to the intranet behind Router A using the appropriate demand-dial interface. For each network behind Router A, configure the appropriate demand-dial interface, destination, network mask, and metric (see "Dial-in Credentials" in the "Part One: Configure Router A" section earlier in this chapter for a discussion on why static routes must be used). To configure a static route:

1. In the Routing and Remote Access console, expand IP Routing on the appropriate server.

2. Right-click Static Routes and select New Static Route.

3. In the Static Route dialog box, supply the demand-dial interface, destination network ID, subnet mask, and metric.

4. Repeat steps 2 and 3 for each network behind Router A.

To prevent these static routes from causing problems with normal RIP and OSPF operation, give the added static routes higher costs than the regular network connection and adjust the preference levels of routes learned from specific sources (see "Preference Levels" in the "IP Routing" section earlier in this chapter).

Configuring Remote Access Policies

The dial-in properties of user accounts for demand-dial routers are configured to allow remote access by the Demand-dial Wizard. If you want to grant remote access based on group membership, complete the following steps:

1. If this Windows 2000 server is configured as a standalone, set the dial-in properties to Allow access for all users. For a directory services-based Windows 2000 server, set the dial-in properties to Control access through Remote Access Policy for all users. This can be found in Active Directory Users and Groups.

2. Create a Windows 2000 group containing members that can create demand-dial connections with Router A. Giving this group a meaningful name like MoreDemandDialRouters can be helpful.

3. Add to this group the user accounts that are used by remote demand-dial routers (RouterA, for example).

4. Delete the default remote access policy Allow access if dial-in permission is enabled.

5. Create a new remote access policy with these properties (see Chapter 2 for complete details on setting up remote access policies):

   - **Policy name.** Assign a meaningful name such as Allow Demand-dial connection if member of MoreDemandDialRouters, for example.

   - **Conditions to match.** There are two conditions you must select: Windows-Groups (supply the group you created in the previous step—MoreDemandDialRouters in our example) and NAS-Port-Type (select all types except Virtual).

   - **Encryption.** The default allows IPSec or Microsoft Point-to-Point Encryption (MPPE). To force encryption for demand-dial connections, change the encryption configuration on the profile to require encryption. The options are No Authentication, Basic, or Strong.

Part Three: Initiate the Demand-Dial Connection

Compared to what came before, this step is a piece of cake. To connect Router A to Router B, or vice versa, right-click the demand-dial interface that connects to the desired remote demand-dial router and then click Connect. If the connection fails, double-check your settings, or refer to Appendix B, "Troubleshooting."

AppleTalk Routing

AppleTalk routing is installed automatically when you configure the AppleTalk protocol on any interface on your server. To enable or disable AppleTalk routing on this router, right-click AppleTalk routing in the Routing and Remote Access console. Select Enable (or Disable) AppleTalk routing from the context menu. To configure AppleTalk seed routing, right-click the proper interface in the right pane of the Routing and Remote Access console. The interface's properties sheet will appear, as shown in Figure 5.9.

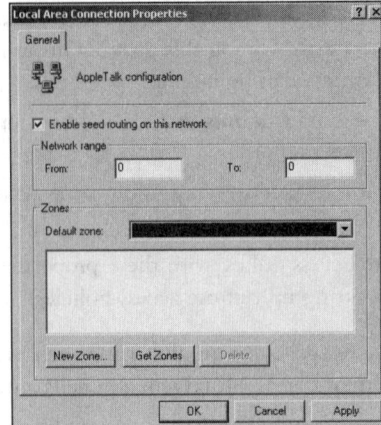

Figure 5.9   AppleTalk seed routing configuration options.

You will need to supply the following information:

- **Enable seed routing on this network.** When this box is checked, this interface is capable of providing AppleTalk network numbers (see Chapter 4 for a discussion of AppleTalk routing). When it is checked, the rest of this properties sheet will become active.

- **Network range.** You can specify the start and end points of a range of network numbers you would like to be distributed by this seed router.

- **Zones.** This area lists the zones included in this network. You can specify a New Zone or Get Zones from other AppleTalk routers present on your network.

Filtering

If you need to prevent your Windows 2000 router from forwarding undesirable traffic into and out of parts of your intranet, you can enable packet filters. One reason you might want to set up a packet filter is if your router has an interface on the Internet. It is possible that any traffic received on the Internet interface could be forwarded into your intranet. To prevent this (and unauthorized network access by unknown users), you must set up filters on the Internet interface of the router. You can also have one particular segment, perhaps the Human Resources department, in your network that must be protected from access by users in other parts of the intranet. You could put those resources on a separate network and set up packet filters. (You could also use IPSec or a VPN to protect these resources. See Chapter 8 or Appendix A, "Technical Overview of RAS Communications," for more information.) You can set both IP and IPX filters with Windows 2000.

Input and output filters are used to regulate traffic coming in and out of a given interface. If the traffic does not meet a particular filter's requirements, it is discarded and not forwarded. To set up packet filters, first determine what types of traffic you would like to limit. Then determine over what interfaces you want these filters to apply. Finally, you will configure the filters according to the instructions below:

1. In the Routing and Remote Access console, click the server name, then click IP Routing or IPX Routing, then click General.

2. Right-click the appropriate interface, then click Properties. The interface properties sheet will appear.

3. On the General tab, click Input Filters. The Input Filters window appears. Click the Add button.

4. For IP filtering: The Add IP Filter dialog box will appear. Select Source network (to filter packets from a particular source) and/or Destination network (to select packets headed for a particular network). In the IP Address field, provide a network or host IP address. In the Subnet mask field, provide the appropriate subnet mask for the IP address you provided above. You can also filter by protocol, with or without specific source or destination information. Provide the desired protocol in the Protocol field. If you selected Other, provide the Protocol number.

5. For IPX filtering: The Add IPX Filter dialog will appear. In the Source (to filter packets from a particular network) and/or Destination network (to select packets headed for a particular network) fields, provide the Network number, Node, Network mask, and Socket. You can also specify the type of packet you want to filter, with or without providing source or destination information.

6. Click OK. You have now added the first input filter, and you will be returned to the Input Filters window.

7. Now you will select the filter action for the input filter you have just created. From the Input Filters window, select Receive or Drop all packets except those that meet the criteria below, then click OK.

8. To configure output filters, you'll perform the same steps, with one exception: in step three, you will select Output Filters.

You have now successfully added filters that will forward only traffic meeting the specific requirements you have set. Be careful what filters you set, however. It is possible to prevent users inside the filtered network from reaching needed resources in other parts of the network.

Conclusion

The Windows 2000 router is easily configured, as shown in this chapter. Rather than wrangling with difficult command line procedures, which must be done with other vendors' routers, Windows 2000 is configured through a series of dialog boxes and wizards. Because of this, it is possible to have a Windows 2000 router up and running in short order. Just as a reminder, be sure you have installed both hardware and WAN links before beginning this process, and collect all pertinent information about other routers in your network. Having this information at your fingertips during the configuration process can make this job even easier.

II

Advanced Administration

6 Routing Tools

7 Virtual Private Networking

8 Windows 2000 Connection Services

9 Internet Authentication Service

6

Routing Tools

THERE ARE SEVERAL TOOLS IN WINDOWS 2000 that you can use to manage and troubleshoot the Routing and Remote Access Service. This chapter will examine Netsh, routemon, mrinfo, pathping, and the Windows 2000 scheduling tools: Scheduled Tasks and the at command.

Netsh

Windows 2000 has a great GUI tool—the RRAS console—for configuring the Routing and Remote Access Service. However, there are times when a command-line utility would be a better tool. NetShell, also known as Netsh, fits that bill very well. You can use it to configure various aspects of Windows 2000 routing, such as interfaces, protocols, filters, routes, and remote access service. Netsh can even be used to script RRAS functions and scheduled to run at a specific time with the Windows Task Scheduler to automate certain routing functions, such as auto-static updates. Another nifty feature of Netsh is that it can save a router's configuration information in a text file for backup purposes or for use when configuring other servers.

Netsh uses a shell interface, similar to what you see when you use FTP at a command line. There are different areas of use for Netsh, and these are broken into service groups called contexts. Contexts provide you with a set of commands for a specific networking component. In this section, we will look at the commands for the ras, routing, and interface contexts. Subcontexts can exist in each context, and they provide specific service-related commands. For instance, in the routing context, there are IP and IPX subcontexts, each of which deals with protocol-specific issues. You can't use Netsh to manage Windows NT 4.0 routers or remote access servers.

Commands

Commands used in Netsh can be used globally or in a context-specific manner. The commands in Table 6.1 can be used at both levels.

Any optional parameters are displayed in brackets ([ ]), while alternative entries are separated by a pipe (|).

Table 6.1 **Global commands**

Command	Function
..	Move up one context level
?	Help
aaaa	Changes to the ras aaaa context. This context handles authentication, authorization, and accounting configuration.
abort	Discard offline mode changes
add	Add configuration entry to table Parameter: [helper]
alias	Add an alias
bye	Exit
commit	Commit offline mode changes
delete	Delete configuration entry from table Parameter: [helper]
Dhcp	Changes to the dhcp context
dump	Dump configuration to screen
exec	Execute script file
exit	Exit
help	Display help
interface	Change to interface context
offline	Set current mode to offline
online	Set current mode to online
popd	Pop context from the stack
pushd	Push current context on stack

Command	Function
quit	Exit
ras	Change to ras context
routing	Change to routing context
set	Set configuration information
	Parameters: [machine] | [mode]
show	Display information
	Parameters: [alias] | [helper] | [mode]
unalias	Delete an alias
Wins	Change to the wins context

Before using Netsh, it is a good idea to create a backup script of your router's configuration. It would be a painful lesson learned to reconfigure it manually if an "accident" happens (and haven't we all been there!).

Use the dump command to output the current configuration to the screen. Simply cut and paste the output into a text file. You can use this script to rebuild a router or to build a new router. By running dump you can also see what the syntax for a complex command should look like, instead of having to fumble and guess your way through various options and command sets.

Netsh has a couple of modes—online and offline—that govern how the commands you issue are treated. When you work in online mode, Netsh commands are executed immediately. When you work in offline mode, commands are queued up and executed as a batch with the commit command. The abort command comes in handy if you have issued a series of commands you no longer want to execute.

Command Line Shortcuts

Instead of having to type a long string of commands, Netsh allows you to shorten the commands to just a few letters. For example, ra aa sh au is the same thing as ras aaaa show authentication.

There is no hard and fast rule about how many characters you must type, as long as there is no confusion about which command you intend to use. For instance, if two commands start with an "s", you need to supply enough characters to differentiate between the two.

Contexts

As mentioned previously, Netsh uses contexts to group related commands together. In this section, you will find tables listing the ras, routing, and interface context and subcontext commands for Netsh. In any context or subcontext, the most useful commands are show, set, add, and delete, with context-specific parameters associated with each command. Additional parameters for each command can be found by typing the command followed by help or ?.

ras Context

The commands listed in Table 6.2 are available for ras.

Table 6.2 **ras commands**

Command	Function
?	Displays help
aaaa	Changes to the ras aaaa context. This context handles authentication, authorization, and accounting configuration.
add	Adds a configuration entry to a table
	Parameters: [authtype] | [link] [multilink] | [registered server]
appletalk	Changes to the ras appletalk context
delete	Deletes a configuration entry from a table
	Parameters: [authtype] | [link] | [multilink] | [registeredserver]
dump	Dumps ras configuration info to the screen
help	Displays help
ip	Changes to the ras ip context
ipx	Changes to the ras ipx context
netbeui	Changes to the ras netbeui context
set	Sets configuration information
	Parameters: [tracing] | [user] | [authmode] |Displays information
show	Displays information
	Parameters: [tracing] | [user] | [authmode] | [authtype] | [link] | [multilink] | [registeredserver] | | [activeservers] | [client] |

In addition to using the global Netsh commands in the ras context, there are also context-specific commands that you can use. These subcontexts are available: ip, ipx, appletalk, and aaaa. After you are in the ras context, type the subcontext to which you would like to enter. In the following table are combinations of commands found in the ras context.

Table 6.3 **ras command combinations**

Command	Explanation
show activeservers	Listens for RAS server advertisements
set/show authmode	Shows the authentication mode
add/delete/show authtype	Displays the authentication types currently enabled
show client	Shows RAS clients connected to this machine
add/ delete/ show link	Shows the link properties PPP will negotiate
add/ show multilink	Shows the multilink types PPP will negotiate
add/ delete/ show	Displays whether a computer registeredserver is registered as a RAS server in the Active Directory of the given domain
set/show tracing	Shows whether extended tracing is enabled for components
set/show user	Displays RAS properties for a user(s)

routing Context

The commands listed in Table 6.4 are available in the routing context.

Table 6.4 **Routing Commands**

Command	Function
dump	Dumps configuration to the screen
help	Displays help
ip	Changes to the routing ip context. The following subcontexts are available: autodhcp, dnsproxy, igmp, nat, ospf, relay, rip, routerdiscovery.
ipx	Changes to the routing ipx context. The following subcontexts are available: rip, sap, netbios.
reset	Resets IP routing to a clean state
show	Displays information
	Parameters: [helper] | [alias] | [mode]
unalias	Deletes an alias

The routing context has ip and ipx subcontexts. For more help on a specific command, type the command followed by help or ?.

Table 6.5 lists command combinations for the IP subcontext.

Table 6.5   **IP Command Combinations**

Command	Explanation
add/ delete/ show boundary	Adds/ deletes/ shows a multicast scope boundary on an interface
add/ delete/ set / show filter	Adds/ deletes/ sets/ shows a packet filter to a specified interface
add/ delete/ set/ show interface	Adds/ deletes/ sets/ shows IP forwarding on an interface
add/ set ipiptunnel	Adds/ sets an IP-in-IP tunnel to the router
add/ delete/ set/ show	Adds/ deletes/ sets/ shows a persistentroute persistent static route
add/ delete/ set/ show preferenceforprotocol	Adds/ deletes/ sets/ shows a preference level for a routing protocol
add/ delete/ set/ show rtmroute	Adds/ deletes/ sets/ shows a non-persistent (NetMgmt) route
add/ delete/ set/ show scope	Adds/ deletes/ sets/ shows a multicast scope
autodhcp	Changes to the routing ip autodhcp context
Dnsproxy	Changes to the routing ip dnsproxy context
Igmp	Changes to the routing ip igmp context
Nat	Changes to the routing ip nat context
Ospf	Changes to the routing ip ospf context
Relay	Changes to the routing ip relay context
Reset	Resets IP routing to a clean state
Rip	Changes to the routing ip rip context
routerdiscovery	Changes to the routing ip routerdiscovery context
set/ show loglevel	Sets/ shows the global logging level
show boundarystats	Shows IP multicast boundaries
show helper	Shows all the helpers below IP
show mfe	Shows multicast forwarding entries
show mfestats	Shows multicast forwarding entry statistics
show protocol	Shows all configured IP protocols
show rtmdestinations	Shows destinations in the routing table
update	Updates auto-static routes on an interface

Table 6.6 lists command combinations for the IPX subcontext.

Table 6.6 **IPX Command Combinations**

Command	Explanation
add/delete/set/show filter	Adds/deletes/sets/shows a packet filter to the list of filters
add/delete/set/show interface	Adds/deletes/sets/shows IPX routing on a demand dial interface
add/delete/set/show staticroute	Adds/deletes/sets/show a static route to the route table
add/delete/set/show staticservice	Adds/deletes/sets/shows a static service to the static service table
Dump	Dumps IPX configuration to a text file
Netbios	Changes to the routing ipx netbios context
Rip	Changes to the routing ipx rip context
Sap	Changes to the routing ipx sap context
set/show global	Sets/shows IPX global configuration
show route	Shows IPX routing table
show service	Shows IPX service table
Update	Updates autostatic routes on an interface

interface Context

The commands listed in Table 6.7 are available in the interface context.

Table 6.7 **Interface Commands**

Command	Function
?	Displays help
add	Adds a configuration entry to a table
	Parameters: [interface]
delete	Deletes a configuration entry from a table
	Parameters: [interface]
dump	Dumps a configuration script
help	Displays help
ip	Changes to the interface ip context
reset	Resets information
set	Sets configuration information
	Parameters: [interface]	[credentials]
show	Displays information
	Parameters: [interface]	[credentials]

There are no subcontexts for the interface context. For more help on a specific command, type the command followed by "help" or "?."

Netsh and Auto-static Updates

Use this code as a starting point for your own script to automate auto-static updates (see Chapter 4, "Routing Protocols," for a discussion of auto-static updates, in the "Demand Dial Routing" section):

```
netsh interface set interface name=DemandDialInterfaceName connect=CONNECTED
netsh routing ip rip update DemandDialInterfaceName
netsh interface set interface name=DemandDialInterfaceName connect=DISCONNECTED
```

The previous script first connects the demand dial interface to its configured telephone number. Then, it updates its RIP routing tables over the connection. Finally, it disconnects the demand dial link.

You can run this as a batch file or a Netsh script file. After the batch or script file is created, schedule it for use with the Windows 2000 Task Scheduler. A batch file is a text file with the .bat extension, while a netsh script file is saved with a .scp extension. To run a set of commands at the netsh command, use the script file with the exec command. To schedule a set of commands to run with the at command or Scheduled Tasks, you can use either the .bat or scp file.

mrinfo

If you use multicast routing, the mrinfo command is a useful command-line tool. It displays the configuration of a Windows 2000 multicast router. The syntax is:

```
mrinfo [-n][-?] [-i address] [-t secs] [-r retries] destination
```

The options are as follows:

- **-n.** Displays IP addresses in numeric format.
- **-?.** Print usage
- **-I.** Specifies the IP address of local interface from which the query is sent.
- **-r.** Specifies how many times an SNMP query will be resent. The default value is 0.
- **-t.** Specifies how long to wait for an IGMP neighbor query reply. The default value is 3 seconds.

mrinfo displays the interfaces on a multicast router and the neighbors on each interface as well as the neighbor's domain name, multicast routing metric, and TTL.

pathping

pathping combines components of ping and tracert and partners it with some additional features to provide you with a handy tool to troubleshoot routing problems. It works by sending packets to each router between the source computer and a final destination over a period of time. It then displays the level of packet loss at each router. You can use this information to figure out where your network reliability problems may be coming from. The syntax is:

```
pathping [-n] [-h maximum_hops value] [-g host-list] [-p value] [-q value] [-w
➥value] final_destination
```

The following switches can be used with pathping:

- **-n.** Do not resolve addresses to hostnames.

- **-h maximum_hops.** Maximum number of hops to search for target (the default is 30 hops).

- **-g host-list.** Loose source route along host-list.

- **-p *period*.** Wait *period* milliseconds between pings (the default is 250 milliseconds).

- **-q num_queries.** Number of queries per hop (the default is 100 queries).

- **-w *timeout*.** Wait *timeout* milliseconds for each reply (the default is 3000 milliseconds).

- **-T.** Test connectivity to each hop with Layer-2 priority tags.

- **-R.** Test if each hop is RSVP aware.

Here are the results of a pathping to yahoo.com:

```
C:\>pathping yahoo.com
Tracing route to yahoo.com [204.71.200.243]
over a maximum of 30 hops:
  0  KCSE-JVNPT5EH5H [154.205.123.146]
  1  bacchus.carrollton.nola.com [154.205.122.2]
  2  endymion.carrollton.nola.com [154.205.94.7]
  3  154.239.29.1
  4  proxy01.iberville.nola.com [154.239.244.7]
  5  206.41.40.5
  6  12.126.29.125
  7  gbr2-a31s7.attga.ip.att.net [12.127.2.170]
  8  gbr2-p40.wswdc.ip.att.net [12.122.3.238]
  9  ar2-a300s3.wswdc.ip.att.net [12.127.1.13]
 10  s1-1-0.br1.iad.globalcenter.net [12.127.45.130]
 11  .pos3-0-155M.cr1.IAD3.gblx.net [206.132.253.17]
 12  pos7-0-622M.cr2.SNV.gblx.net [206.132.151.22]
 13  pos1-0-2488M.hr8.SNV.gblx.net [206.132.254.41]
 14  bas2r-ge2-0-hr8.snv.yahoo.com [208.178.103.58]
 15  img3.yahoo.com [204.71.200.243]
```

```
Computing statistics for 375 seconds...
            Source to Here   This Node/Link
Hop  RTT    Lost/Sent = Pct  Lost/Sent = Pct  Address
 0                                             KCSE-JVNPT5EH5H [154.205.123.146]

                                0/ 100 =  0%   |
 1    0ms    0/ 100 =  0%       0/ 100 =  0%   bacchus.carrollton.nola.com [154.2
➡05.122.2]
                                0/ 100 =  0%   |
 2    0ms    0/ 100 =  0%       0/ 100 =  0%   endymion.carrollton.nola.com [154.20
➡5.94.7]
                                0/ 100 =  0%   |
 3    0ms    0/ 100 =  0%       0/ 100 =  0%   154.239.29.1
                                0/ 100 =  0%   |
 4    0ms    0/ 100 =  0%       0/ 100 =  0%   proxy01.iberville.nola.com
➡[154.239.244.7]
                                0/ 100 =  0%   |
 5    9ms    0/ 100 =  0%       0/ 100 =  0%   206.41.40.5
                                0/ 100 =  0%   |
 6   37ms    0/ 100 =  0%       0/ 100 =  0%   12.126.29.125
                                0/ 100 =  0%   |
 7   32ms    0/ 100 =  0%       0/ 100 =  0%   gbr2-a31s7.attga.ip.att.net [12.12
➡7.2.170]
                                0/ 100 =  0%   |
 8   42ms    0/ 100 =  0%       0/ 100 =  0%   gbr2-p40.wswdc.ip.att.net [12.122.
➡3.238]
                                0/ 100 =  0%   |
 9   47ms    0/ 100 =  0%       0/ 100 =  0%   ar2-a300s3.wswdc.ip.att.net [12.12
➡7.1.13]
                                3/ 100 =  3%   |
10  128ms    6/ 100 =  6%       3/ 100 =  3%   s1-1-0.br1.iad.globalcenter.net [1
➡2.127.45.130]
                                0/ 100 =  0%   |
11  113ms    8/ 100 =  8%       5/ 100 =  5%   pos3-0-155M.cr1.IAD3.gblx.net [206
➡.132.253.17]
                                0/ 100 =  0%   |
12  163ms    7/ 100 =  7%       4/ 100 =  4%   pos7-0-622M.cr2.SNV.gblx.net [206
➡.132.151.22]
                                0/ 100 =  0%   |
13  165ms    3/ 100 =  3%       0/ 100 =  0%   pos1-0-2488M.hr8.SNV.gblx.net [206
➡.132.254.41]
                                2/ 100 =  2%   |
14  158ms    5/ 100 =  5%       0/ 100 =  0%   bas2r-ge2-0-hr8.snv.yahoo.com [208
➡.178.103.58]
                                7/ 100 =  7%   |
15  153ms   12/ 100 = 12%       0/ 100 =  0%   img3.yahoo.com [204.71.200.243]

Trace complete.
```

As you can see from the output, pathping first traces the route to the target destination, then analyzes the traffic running through each hop. If you notice that a particular hop has a significantly larger percentage of lost packets than other hops, you can start troubleshooting that link. There is no magic number for acceptable loss of packets, but double-digit numbers should be a clue that something is going on with a router. Also, keep in mind that testing a particular router for performance should be conducted over time. Testing only during peak or off-peak periods will yield misleading results.

Scheduling Tools

Windows 2000 has two tools you can use to schedule tasks to be automatically executed at a later time and/or date. One is a GUI tool—Scheduled Tasks—and the other is a command-line tool—the at command. This section will cover the use of both tools.

Scheduled Tasks

Scheduled Tasks allows you to easily set up a time and date for a task to run automatically, as illustrated in Figure 6.1 below.

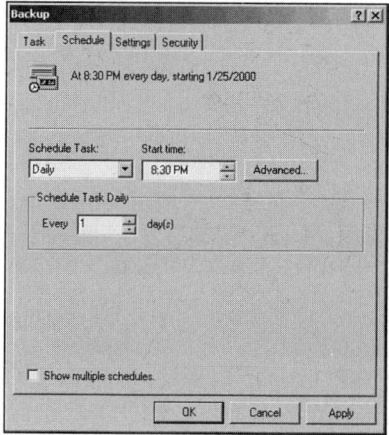

Figure 6.1   Backup scheduled to run every day in Scheduled Tasks.

Scheduled tasks can include auto-statically updating demand-dial routers, automating a backup procedure, or even automatically faxing weekly sales figures to all branch offices every Saturday at midnight.

Scheduled Tasks is found in the Control Panel. To schedule new tasks, simply launch the Scheduled Tasks applet and double-click Add Scheduled Task. The Scheduled Task Wizard will appear. Just follow the instructions on the screen to create a new task. Task Scheduler also enables you to change, delete, disable, or stop tasks.

When you schedule a task, a username and the password of that account must be supplied. This allows multiple users of a computer to have their own scheduled tasks. The task is run under the context of the associated user account, and only users with the proper permission may run, stop, or edit scheduled tasks. The associated user account can be changed at any time by right-clicking the scheduled task and selecting Properties from the context menu. A record of past scheduled activity is stored in %systemroot%\ schedlgu.txt.

at Command

The at command is a holdover from previous versions of Windows NT. The at command doesn't have many of the features of the Scheduled Tasks, but the functionality is essentially the same: scheduling a task to run at a specific time. at command jobs will show up in the Scheduled Tasks window, and you can edit at tasks with Scheduled Tasks. However, if you do this, you won't be able to edit the task with the at command again.

The at syntax is:

```
at [\\computername] [id] [/parameter 1] [/parameter 2] [/parameter 3]…
```

Copying Tasks Between Computers

Tasks are stored as *.job files. You can copy, email, or move these task files between computers to make scheduling tasks even easier.

Starting the Schedule Service

The Schedule service must be running before you can use at. You can start the service from a command prompt by typing

net start "task scheduler"

To view a list of all scheduled at tasks, when the command prompt appears, type at. at parameters are illustrated in Table 6.8.

Table 6.8 **at Parameters**

Command	Function
id	The identification number of a scheduled command.
delete	Cancels a scheduled command. Use with id to indicate a specific command. Otherwise, all scheduled commands are deleted.
yes	When deleting a task, an affirmation of intent is requested. This is used when deleting multiple commands so you don't have to say yes for every command you want to delete.
time	Specifies when the command is to run. Use hours:minutes in 24-hour format, where 00:00 is midnight and 11:59 p.m. is 23:59.
interactive	Enables the job to interact with the desktop of the user who is logged on at the time the job runs.
every:date[,...]	Allows you to schedule a recurring task. Use days of the week (M, T, W, Th ,F , S, Su) or days of the month (numbers 1 through 31). You can use multiple days of the week or month, but be sure to separate multiple date entries with commas.
next:date[,...]	Runs the command on the next occurrence of the day. Use days of the week (M, T, W, Th, F, S, Su) or days of the month (numbers 1 through 31). You can use multiple days of the week or month, but be sure to separate multiple date entries with commas.
command	Specifies which command, program, or batch program is to be run. On local computers, use the entire path, including the drive letter. On a remote computer, use UNC names instead of network drive letters.

The following string demonstrates how to schedule backup to run every day at 8:30 p.m.

```
at \\server1  20:30 /interactive /every:s,m,t,w,t,f,s
➥C:\WINNT1\system32\ntbackup.exe
```

7

Virtual Private Networks

ACCESS TO THE INTERNET IS UBIQUITOUS; ANY PERSON or business with access to a phone line can reach the rest of the world. The Internet provides a cost-effective method to transport data between users or locations. Sometimes this data is very sensitive in nature. It might not be acceptable for that information to be transmitted in plain text across the Internet. If the data is to be moved securely, each endpoint of the transaction must answer these questions:

- How do you keep information private? In other words, how do you prevent others from eavesdropping?
- How do you know that the data sent is the data received? In other words, how do you prevent data modification in transit?
- How do you authenticate the source of the data? How do you know the person or computer sending the data is really who you think he/she is?

Securing sensitive information as it passes through the corporate network is important. That security becomes even more important when you are using the Internet as your pipeline to the corporate network. More and more companies are using the Internet to connect remote users, offices, and even customers and partners. By steering clear of dedicated lines and banks of modems with expensive toll-free access for your remote users, it is possible to reduce your overall connectivity cost.

When the choice is made to connect a network to the Internet, it goes without saying that the perimeters of your network must be defended from attack. Important data transmitted between sites over the Internet is just as vulnerable to attack. Virtual private networks (VPNs) secure communications between two computers by tunneling encrypted information in a virtual point-to-point connection.

Windows 2000 has taken the VPN to a new level of integration with the operating system. Instead of using a separate, third-party VPN solution, Windows 2000 offers an easily configured and even easier to use VPN tool. This chapter will explain how VPNs work and how to set up Windows 2000 to act as a VPN client and server. Specific topics of discussion include Point-to-Point Tunneling Protocol (PPTP), Layer Two Tunneling Protocol (L2TP), VPN routing, VPNs and firewalls, and VPN configuration.

VPN Defined

A private network is run over private LAN and WAN links. It joins users and geographically separate offices, allowing users to access network resources. A VPN also joins users and offices, but it connects them over a public network. Simply connecting to a corporate network over the Internet does not constitute a VPN. A VPN emulates a point-to-point connection by encapsulating encrypted data, then sending that data through the public network. The encrypted data is useless to anyone who does not have the appropriate encryption keys.

A VPN allows your users to connect to the corporate intranet by dialing up the point-of-presence (POP) of any ISP. No special VPN software has to be run on the ISP's equipment or on the intermediary routers a VPN data packet might cross. VPN software is only required on the client and the VPN server that are responsible for authenticating VPN clients. Figure 7.1 illustrates a possible VPN scenario.

The VPN connection is transparent to the user, as is the route through the Internet. The two computers at each end of a VPN connection act as if the connection was a physical point-to-point connection. VPNs can be used to join a remote user with a network, or they can be used to join separate networks with each other. In the latter case, the VPN connection occurs between routers.

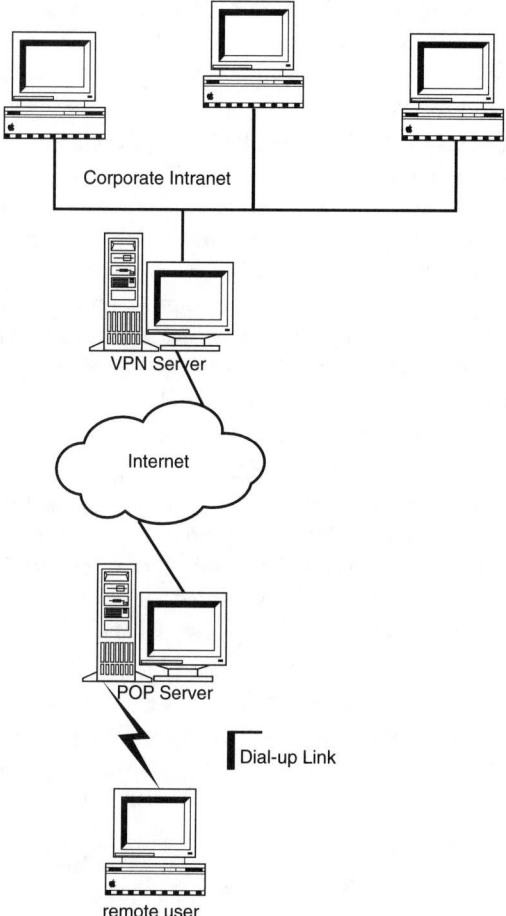

Figure 7.1   Diagram of a VPN.

New Features of Windows 2000 VPNs

VPN support is not new to the Windows family. Previous versions of the Routing and Remote Access Service offer a VPN solution. Microsoft has added several new features to the VPN tools provided with Windows 2000, including:

- **L2TP.**   A second tunneling protocol has been added to offer more choices to administrators. PPTP was previously available, but L2TP can be used with Internet Protocol Security (IPSec) to secure VPN connections. L2TP and PPTP will be described in greater detail in this chapter.

- **Remote access policies.** Support for remote access policies allow the administrator to set and enforce stronger security policies. The policies govern such things as authentication methods and encryption. (For more information on remote access policies, see Chapter 2, "Remote Access Server.")

- **MS-CHAP version 2.** MS-CHAP v2 is the strongest of the Challenge-Handshake Authentication Protocol (CHAP) methods supported by Windows 2000, but it is less secure than Extensible Authentication Protocol (EAP). It allows mutual authentication of clients and servers. The cryptographic key used for challenge response is based on the user's password *and* a random challenge string generated for each connection attempt. In other words, each time a connection is attempted with the same password, a different cryptographic key is used. Different cryptographic keys are created for transmitted and received data, and stronger initial data encryption keys are generated as well.

- **EAP.** EAP is a PPP authentication protocol. It is a flexible protocol that allows the specific authentication mechanism to be swapped in and out to provide a custom authentication solution for any given implementation. EAP authentication mechanisms include MD5-CHAP, smart cards, and token cards. EAP has another added plus: Because the EAP architecture supports plug-in modules, new authentication methods can be created for future security needs. For more information on authentication methods, see Chapter 2.

- **Account lockout.** This security feature prevents users from accessing network resources after a preconfigured number of attempts to input user credentials. Account lockout is most helpful in preventing dictionary attacks, whereby an attacker tries to guess a user's password. (It is always a good idea to set a strong password policy in addition to any other security mechanisms you put in place).

Anatomy of a VPN Connection

A VPN connection is made up of a few basic parts, as depicted in Figure 7.2. Each component serves a specific purpose. The VPN client initiates a VPN connection to a VPN server (the VPN server is also known as a gateway). The VPN client could be a computer running Windows 2000, Windows NT 4, or Windows 9x. The client also could be any third-party PPTP or L2TP/IPSec product making a connection to a Windows 2000 server or Windows NT server 4.0 running Routing and Remote Access Service. The connection also could be made between two routers joining two networks. The server authenticates the client, and depending on the authentication protocol used, the client can authenticate the server as well. This is called mutual authentication.

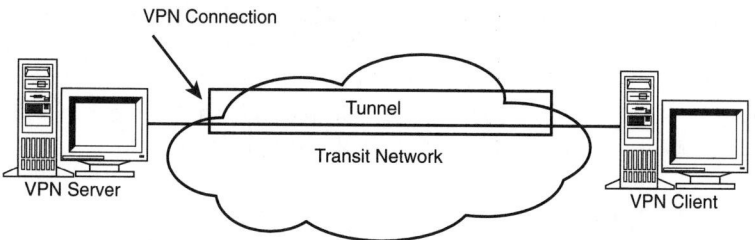

Figure 7.2   Components involved in a VPN connection.

Beyond these components, there are four requirements a connection must meet to be a VPN: encapsulation, authentication, data encryption, and address and name server allocation. If all four of these requirements are not met, the connection is not considered a VPN connection. The following list further explains these requirements:

- **Encapsulation.**   Data that travels over the transit network must be encapsulated with a VPN header.

- **Authentication.**   A VPN authenticates not only the identity of the client (and server if mutual authentication is used), but it also authenticates the data that was sent. Data authentication is important to ensure that the data received originated from the opposite end of the connection and was not intercepted or modified in transit. This protects against spoofing, man-in-the-middle, and replay attacks. It is possible to use user- or machine-based authentication.

- **Data encryption.**   Because data sent over a VPN is actually sent over a public network, it is absolutely imperative that strong encryption be used. No network is guaranteed to be impervious to attack. When you are sending your confidential data over cables and routers that are not controlled by you, you must take extra measures to protect sensitive data.

- **Address and name server allocation.**   The VPN client and server create virtual interfaces over which VPN connections are made. The virtual interfaces are assigned IP addresses, just like a physical interface on a computer. The allocation of these resources happens during VPN connection establishment. The VPN server is responsible for assigning IP addresses and does so by DHCP (the default) or by selecting from a static pool of IP addresses. In addition to assignment of IP addresses, the VPN server also allocates DNS and WINS server addresses to clients. The name servers allocated are the name servers that service the intranet on which the VPN server interfaces.

If DHCP is used to assign IP addresses for VPN clients, the VPN server's virtual interface is assigned the first IP address obtained when requesting DHCP addresses. If a static IP address pool is used, the VPN server's virtual interface uses the first IP address in the static pool. (See the section "TCP/IP" in Chapter 2 for more information on how the Windows 2000 remote access server performs IP address allocations.)

Types of VPNs

VPNs can be used wherever a secure connection is needed between two points, such as accessing personnel records across a private network or across the Internet. There are three types of VPNs: Internet-based, intranet-based, and VPNs that use both Internet and intranet connectivity. This section examines the basics of each type.

Internet–Based VPN Connections

Internet-based VPNs enable companies to leverage the power, availability, and ease of connectivity of the Internet to connect geographically isolated segments. Using local access numbers for ISPs in the area where a VPN connection is initiated can free a company from the expense and administrative burden of maintaining modems for remote access to the corporate network. The initiator of the connection uses the IP connection to the Internet to connect to a VPN server and establish a secure path into a remote network.

VPN connections over the Internet can join individual users to a remote network, or two networks can be joined with a VPN connection. A user simply uses an ISP to make this connection. Networks that want to join together can link with dedicated or dial-up WAN links to a local ISP. In this case, a router from one network forwards packets to another router across a VPN connection. The routers forward data originating from the users of one network to the users of the other network over the VPN connection.

Demand–Dial VPN

A router using a dial-up link to an ISP must connect to a router that has a dedicated link to an ISP, unless the ISP on the receiving side of the connection supports demand-dialing.

Intranet–Based VPN Connections

An intranet-based VPN can protect access to sensitive data in a corporate network. Some data might be so important that it is stored on computers that are isolated from the rest of the network. In this case, the VPN protects the separate segment. The following is an example of such a scenario.

A fictional company called Payroll Systems provides outsourced payroll services to small businesses. Employee information for clients of Payroll Systems is stored on servers on a network physically separate from the rest of the main network. Not all employees who must access this data are located on this separate network, so an intranet-based VPN is set up to provide secured access to resources on that segment. Users on the main network who have the appropriate permissions can establish a remote access VPN connection with the VPN server and access the resources of the protected network. All communication across the VPN connection is encrypted to ensure confidentiality. This type of VPN functions just like an Internet–based VPN.

An administrator can join two different networks in a single intranet over a VPN connection. Two routers are used to forward VPN data between the networks. This is useful when two departments that handle sensitive information exchange data, such as a hospital sending a patient's test information from a lab in the radiology department to the billing department. The lab and the billing department are joined over the hospital intranet by VPN servers that forward protected data between the two networks. When the VPN connection is established, users on computers on either network can exchange sensitive data across the corporate intranet securely.

Internet–Intranet VPN Connections

It is possible to have a hybrid VPN that utilizes both Internet and intranet connections. This is also called a pass-through VPN. Two companies that have formed a strategic alliance might want to have access to selected resources on each other's intranets, as shown in Figure 7.3. VPN connections from one intranet are passed through to the second intranet.

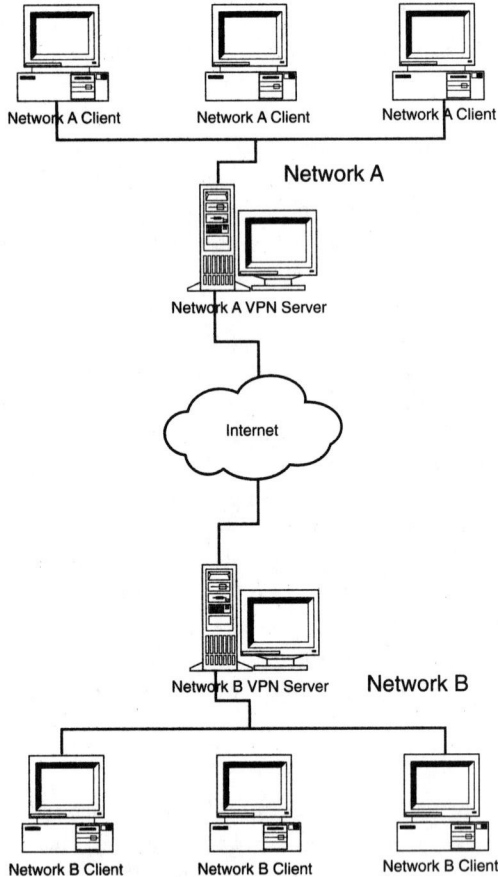

Figure 7.3 A pass-through VPN.

VPN Tunneling Protocols

There are tunnel protocols supplied with Windows 2000: IPSec, PPTP, and L2TP. Only the latter two protocols, however, are true VPN tunneling protocols. This section discusses these protocols.

IPSec

IPSec protocol specifications provide for two types of IPSec packets: Encapsulating Security Payload (ESP) and Authentication Header (AH). ESP provides data encryption, authentication, and integrity. AH provides only data authentication and integrity.

Recall that user authentication is a requirement of a VPN connection. Because of this, IPSec alone is not a true VPN protocol. It can, however, be used in conjunction with L2TP to provide all required properties of a VPN connection. (For more information on IPSec, see Appendix A, "Technical Overview of RAS Communications.")

PPTP

PPTP is an extension of the Point-to-Point Protocol (PPP). PPTP was developed by Microsoft and released in 1996. It supports both client/server and server/server architectures. PPTP provides authenticated and encrypted communications based on username and password. It encapsulates PPP frames in IP datagrams for delivery over an IP network.

Features

PPTP supports several authentication methods. Password Authentication Protocol (PAP), Shiva Password Authentication Protocol (SPAP), CHAP, and MS-CHAP v1 and v2 are supported for Windows 9x and Windows NT 4 remote access clients. Windows 2000 clients can use EAP in addition to these authentication protocols. (See Chapter 2 for more information on authentication protocols.)

The recommended protocols for PPTP authentication are MS-CHAP v2 and Extensible Authentication Protocol- Transport Layer Security (EAP-TLS), both of which offer several benefits to VPN users:

- **Mutual authentication.** Both the VPN client and VPN server are authenticated, preventing an attacker from masquerading as a VPN server. Other forms of authentication only verify the identity of the client.

- **Stronger initial encryption keys.** MS-CHAP v2 uses a unique session identifier *and* user credentials to generate encryption keys. EAP-TLS uses certificates to verify user identity (EAP-TLS can be used with machine-based certificates, but Microsoft recommends that you use EAP-TLS only with smart cards). Older encryption methods use only the username and password to create these keys, making it easier for attackers to determine the keys in use.

- **Separate keys for sending and receiving data.** Each computer uses a different key to encrypt and send data, making it more difficult for attackers to determine which key is used for encryption.

- **Microsoft Point-to-Point Encryption (MPPE).** MPPE uses RSA RC4 stream ciphering and offers 40-bit and 128-bit encryption keys. This gives you the flexibility to use MPPE encryption with both international and domestic (North American) clients. Like authentication method, the encryption key strength also is negotiated during connection establishment. The client and server negotiate with each other for the strongest mutually allowable key. If the server requires a stronger key than that supported on the client, the VPN connection is rejected (MPPE only offers link encryption, however, so if you require end-to-end encryption, use IPSec instead).

Because IP datagrams might not arrive in the same order in which they were sent, the receiving computer must be able to decrypt the packet without regard to the previous packet. Sequencing information is carried in the MPPE header of each packet. If the receiving computer detects that packets have been lost or are received out of order, the encryption keys used to decrypt that packet are shifted to reflect the order and sequence of packets received.

Because it does not require a public key infrastructure, PPTP is easy to set up and administer. PPP is also a good solution for small offices/home offices (SOHOs) that use Network Address Translation (NAT) with a private network IP address scheme. L2TP and IPSec require each end of a VPN connection to use a valid IP address when connecting over the Internet and, as such, are incompatible with NAT. Microsoft plans to continue support and development of PPTP as a VPN protocol for users who do not need more sophisticated VPN solutions, as well as users who must use a NAT-compatible VPN protocol.

Special Requirements

PPTP uses Generic Routing Encapsulation (GRE) to encapsulate PPP frames in IP datagrams for delivery over an IP network. Your ISP might use GRE to forward routing information within its network. If this is the case, the ISP will filter outbound traffic for GRE to prevent private network routing information from being forwarded to Internet routers. This means that PPTP tunnels can be created, but tunneled data will not be forwarded out of the ISP's network. If you discover that data is not traveling from one end to the other of your VPN, contact your ISP to determine whether they filter GRE. If they do, you will not be able to use PPTP with that ISP.

L2TP

L2TP is a best-of-breed PPP tunneling protocol. It combines PPTP with Cisco's Layer 2 Forwarding. The combination came about at the request of the IETF. They were concerned about the possible confusion resulting from two incompatible and competing protocols being available to the public. Although only L2TP over IP is defined as a standard, L2TP can encapsulate PPP frames over X.25, frame relay, and ATM as well. L2TP frames are encapsulated as User Datagram Protocol (UDP) messages. L2TP is used in conjunction with IPSec to encrypt data.

Smart Cards and Domains

If you plan to use EAP-TLS for remote access authentication, your remote access server must be a member of a Windows 2000 mixed-mode or native-mode domain. Windows 2000 remote access servers configured as standalone servers do not support EAP-TLS. This means you will not be able to use smart-card authentication if your remote access server is configured as a standalone.

Authentication

L2TP authentication of a VPN client is a two-phase process. First the computer is authenticated, and then the user is authenticated. The process of establishing an L2TP/IPSec VPN connection is as follows:

1. Both VPN client and server establish an IPSec security association (SA). This SA uses IPSec ESP to agree on encryption algorithm, hash algorithm, and encryption keys. (IPSec ESP provides data encryption where IPSec AH does not.)

2. The VPN client and server perform machine authentication. A computer certificate provides machine authentication and must be installed on both client and server. Computer certificates can be obtained automatically (through Windows 2000 Group Policy) or manually (through a certificate authority).

3. The VPN server verifies the identity of the client user—and vice versa if mutual user-level authentication is used. The user authentication uses standard PPP-based user authentication protocols: PAP, SPAP, CHAP, MS-CHAP, and EAP. IPSec encrypts the entire connection establishment process, so you can use any PPP authentication method with confidence in the security of the connection. Remember, if you want clients and servers to mutually authenticate, use MS-CHAP v2 or EAP-TLS.

Because it is possible for data in transit to be intercepted by an attacker, data sent over a VPN connection also is authenticated. An attacker that intercepts data could modify it and then retransmit it in a man-in-the-middle or replay attack. To ensure that the data a computer receives is exactly the same as the data sent, hash message authentication codes (HMAC) are used to verify the integrity of packets. HMACs combine a hashing algorithm with a previously configured shared secret key to provide a cryptographic checksum that, when properly computed by the recipient, show that the packet is unchanged. A shared secret is known by the parties at each end of a connection. The way it works is as follows: The sender uses a hash function and a shared key to compute and include a checksum with data to be transmitted. The receiving computer performs a hash function on the data received and compares it to the original checksum that came with the data. If it matches, the packet is accepted. If the checksum is different, the recipient rejects the packet. (For more information, see Appendix A.)

Windows 2000 provides two methods of data authentication and integrity. When you set security policies for your VPN, you can choose between two hash functions:

- **HMAC-MD5.** This function uses an algorithm that yields a 128-bit hash. It is stronger, but slower than MD4.

- **HMAC-SHA.** This function uses a longer key—160-bits—and is considered the stronger of these two hash functions.

Encryption

The specific IPSec encryption type to be used by a VPN client and server is agreed upon by the client and server when the security association is formed. Windows 2000 uses Data Encryption Standard (DES) to protect the confidentiality of data passed over an L2TP/IPSec VPN connection. DES uses a 56-bit encryption key. Windows 2000 IPSec provides three DES options for confidentiality. They are listed here, from weakest to strongest encryption:

- **40-bit DES.** This variation only uses 40-bit keys and as such is the least secure method of DES encryption. It is provided for use outside of North America, to meet limits placed on the export of encryption tools.

- **DES.** Straight DES is the "base model" of DES encryption. It uses a 56-bit encryption key. DES is ideal for use in North America in situations where the data transmitted does not need the higher security (and slower performance) of triple DES.

- **Triple DES.** Also called 3DES, it is the strongest of the three DES variations offered in Windows 2000. There is a speed penalty for this extra security, however. Triple DES makes three passes over each data block, slowing performance. Triple DES uses two 56-bit keys and is intended for North American use where a high security encryption method is required.

Two types of encryption are offered by Windows 2000 VPNs: link encryption and end-to-end encryption. Link encryption encrypts the data only from the VPN client to the VPN server. End-to-end encryption encrypts the data from the source host all the way to its final destination, not just to the VPN server.

L2TP Without IPSec

Although it is possible to create and use an L2TP tunnel without encrypting it, it is not a true VPN. Recall that a VPN connection must provide authentication of user and data, IP address and name server allocation, encapsulation, *and* encryption. An L2TP connection without IPSec leaves out the very important element of encryption. You might find it useful, however, to use L2TP without IPSec to troubleshoot the connection process. Elimination of the IPSec authentication and negotiation process can assist in determining where a VPN connection is failing. If a remote user attempting to connect to a VPN server is repeatedly rejected, for example, try to connect using only L2TP. If the connection succeeds, an IPSec problem (such as a configuration mismatch between client and server) is most likely causing the difficulty.

VPN Routing

When a VPN connection is made from a client to a server or from a router to a router, a virtual interface is created on the client. This virtual interface is used to connect to the virtual interface on the VPN server. The virtual interface can also be thought of as a virtual network adapter. The client's virtual interface is assigned an IP address by the VPN server during the connection process and can be a private IP address or a registered IP address.

If a private IP address is used by a VPN client and server, how does data from the VPN client find the VPN server over the Internet? A VPN client and server also have an Internet IP address and a VPN IP address. Data traveling through from a VPN client to a VPN server has an IP header that includes the private network source and destination addresses of the VPN hosts. These data packets have an outer IP header that has the Internet source and destination IP addresses of the client and server. This outer packet is used for routing over the Internet. The entire process is called encapsulation, and is illustrated in Figure 7.4 below.

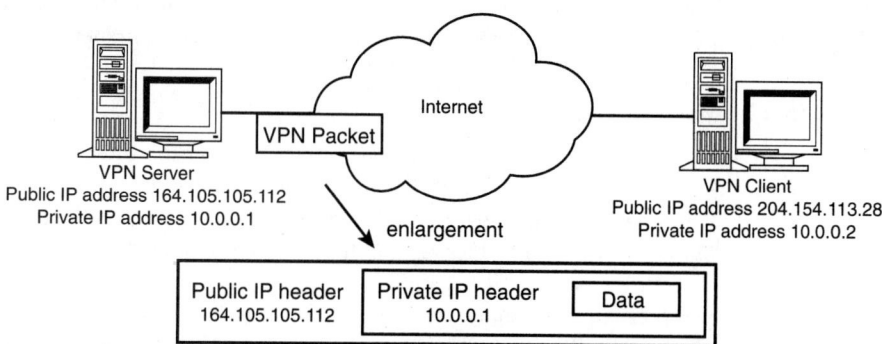

Figure 7.4 VPN packet headers.

Another important configuration change is made on the client during the VPN connection process. The VPN client changes the default route over which traffic is sent through the virtual interface. The default route also can be called the remote gateway. It is the address of the interface over which traffic destined for a host with no known route is sent.

The rest of this chapter will refer to a network protected by a VPN as a red LAN and a network that is not protected by a VPN as a black LAN. These are commonly used and accepted terms to describe the above network types.

A client might need to access resources on red and black LANs simultaneously. Data destined for the VPN-protected network must be sent over the virtual interface. Data destined for unsecured networks must be sent over the appropriate physical interface—which could be a modem or a NIC—for that network. Depending on the configuration of the client, it might be necessary to do a little extra work in order for access to both LANs to be possible. The routes to the black LAN or red LAN must be made known to the client. This is a very important issue to consider for two reasons. First, no administrator wants to discover (or have someone else discover!) that sensitive data has been sent unprotected over the Internet because of a misconfigured route. Second, the connectivity issues that might result from misconfigured routes can cause clients with an established VPN connection to be temporarily unable to access resources previously available when no VPN connection was set up.

This section examines how VPN clients obtain IP addresses and default gateway information when creating connections with PPP servers and VPN servers. It also covers the details of how and when to make routing table changes on VPN clients. Administrators also might find this information helpful when troubleshooting connectivity issues with clients that are attempting to simultaneously access non-VPN Internet and intranet resources through dial-up to an ISP and a NIC in the local intranet.

Dial-Up Clients

Some remote access clients make a remote resource connection over the Internet. Before the connection can be established, a PPP connection must be established with an ISP. In this situation, the client negotiates for and receives an IP address and default gateway information from the ISP. The process is as follows: The remote client attempts to establish a PPP session with the ISP's POP server, during which the client negotiates with the server for an IP address. The ISP then assigns a public IP address to the dial-up client. The public IP address is a registered IP address that is unique on the Internet. The default gateway is not included in this address assignment.

Recall from Chapter 2 that a server that acts as a PPP server is configured only to provide an IP address and subnet mask to dial-up clients. Without a default gateway, the client is unable to reach any resources off its subnet. Because the whole point of dialing up an ISP is to gain access to the Internet in general, this is a problem. To address this, the dial-up client adds a default route to its local routing table. The route uses the interface connected to the ISP. With the default route in place, the client forwards all traffic bound for remote network destinations to the ISP's router, which in turn forwards the traffic to the next appropriate router. (For more information on routing, see Chapter 4, "Routing Protocols.") The default route is created by default in Windows 2000. The route is enabled and disabled through "Use default gateway on remote network" in the TCP/IP advanced settings dialog box of the dial-up networking properties sheet.

If the client only uses a dial-up Internet connection to access remote resources, this is the end of the routing story. If the client also uses a LAN or VPN connection to access resources, however, the story continues and the plot thickens.

Dial-Up Clients on a LAN

Let's consider the case of Ed, a real estate agent at a company called Building Block Realty. Building Block Realty has a LAN with two subnets to connect its employees, but the LAN isn't connected to the Internet. The majority of the resources Ed uses are located on the LAN. The default route for his computer points to a router on the LAN. Occasionally he needs to access the Internet through a dial-up account to an ISP. When the connection is made to the ISP, a new default route is added to the routing table of Ed's computer. The previous default route stays in the table, but the route metric is increased, giving it a higher cost than the route of the ISP. Because the client takes the least-cost route, the ISP's route will always be used for any traffic destined for a network off the local subnet that does not have a static route. This means that, while Ed is dialed into his ISP, he will be able to access all resources on his local subnet and the Internet, but he will not be able to access any resources on the other subnet at Building Block Realty. When Ed ends his dial-up connection, the previous default route is restored, and he is once again able to access the resources on the second LAN.

Simply disabling the creation of the default route does not fix the temporary lack of access to the second subnet at Building Block Realty. If the dial-up default route is not created when Ed dials up the ISP, he will be able to access all resources on the Building Block network, but unable to access the Internet. To overcome this, leave the default route creation setting at its default setting (the option should be selected), and add static persistent routes to resources on the LAN to the routing table of the dial-up/LAN client.

You can use the route add command to add the route, and tack on the –p switch to make the route persistent. The syntax for the command is as follows:

```
ROUTE ADD ]Network ID] MASK [netmask] [IP address of gateway interface} -p
```

The gateway address you use is the address of the interface over which traffic should be sent to reach the destination network specified in the network ID parameter.

You can use the route print command to view static routes. You might not be able to see all the static routes you have configured. If the IP address of the gateway is unreachable, the persistent route is not added or displayed in the routing table until the gateway is accessible. For instance, if a static route points to a red LAN resource, it will not be visible until the VPN connection is established. This characteristic is only true of computers running Windows 2000 and Windows NT 4 Service Pack 3 or later.

Dial-Up VPN Clients

Now that you are familiar with the process of creating a default route for a client with an existing default route, we will explore the implications of the default route for VPN clients.

Dial-up VPN clients are those that connect to the Internet through a dial-up connection before they establish a security association with a VPN server. This is a very common method of establishing a VPN connection. Connection establishment with the ISP and then with the VPN server involves the following addressing and routing processes:

1. The client dials up the ISP. The client obtains an IP address.

2. The dial-up client's default route is changed to reflect the route through the ISP.

3. The client then makes a connection with the VPN server. The VPN server assigns an IP address to the virtual interface of the VPN client. This IP address can be a public or private address.

4. The default route for the client is again changed to reflect the new route though the VPN.

The same situation exists here as in the above example with Ed. When the VPN default route is added, the ISP's default route gets a new, higher metric, and all traffic destined for remote networks passes through the VPN route. This eliminates Internet connectivity during the time a VPN connection is in place, unless you configure static routes on the client.

It is possible that you might have a dial-up VPN client that is connected to a LAN. As each new default route is added, the previously available networks cease to be available, as shown below:

1. A LAN client has an IP address and a default route that enable it to access LAN resources.

2. The LAN client connects to an ISP and gets a new IP address and default route. The client can now access Internet resources, but cannot access resources on remote LAN segments while the Internet connection is up.

3. When the client makes a VPN connection, it gets a new IP address and default gateway. At this point, the client is now only able to access resources on the VPN network. Internet resources are unavailable while the VPN connection is in place. Further, the LAN resources that were made unavailable during the ISP connection are still unavailable.

In order for black LAN (off-VPN) resources to be reachable, you must make several configuration changes. First, you must prevent only the VPN connection from creating the default route. On the TCP/IP Advanced Settings dialog box, reached through the properties sheet of the VPN connection, configure the connection to *not* use the remote gateway, by removing the check mark from the check box. The dial-up connection used to access the ISP will still use the remote gateway. Second, you must create static routes to resources on the client to reach resources on the VPN and the

LAN. To configure static routes to access networks on the LAN, use the IP address of the gateway on the LAN as the gateway. To access the VPN, the `route add` command uses the IP address of the virtual interface of the VPN server as the gateway.

VPNs and Firewalls

VPNs and firewalls can be used in conjunction with each other. There are two basic configurations for a VPN installed with a firewall: The VPN server sits in front of the firewall, and the VPN server sits behind the firewall. (Other configuration options beyond these two scenarios are possible.) This chapter will briefly examine the differences between the two basic options and the packet filters that must be put in place to allow VPN traffic into and out of the intranet secured by the firewall and VPN.

VPN Server in Front of the Firewall

The first configuration we will examine is the VPN in front of the firewall, shown in Figure 7.5.

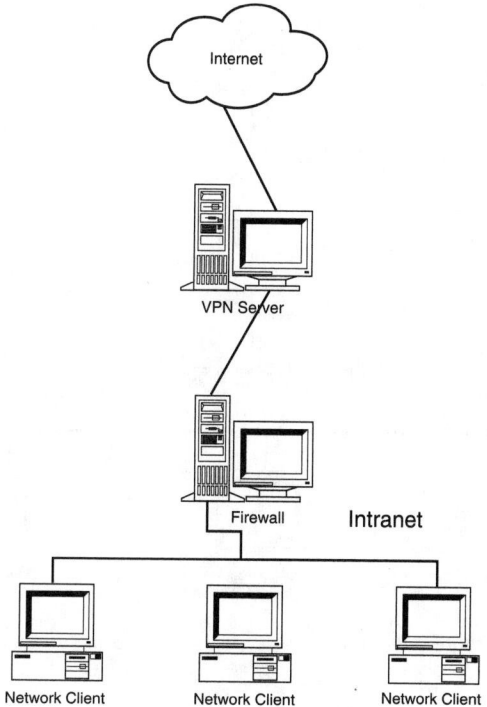

Figure 7.5 The VPN server sitting outside the firewall.

In this architecture, the VPN interfaces with the Internet and the firewall, and the firewall interfaces with the VPN and the intranet. The only Internet traffic allowed into the private intranet is funneled first through the VPN, where it is authenticated or rejected. The authenticated traffic is then forwarded on through the firewall. Packet filters must be configured on the firewall to permit traffic only from the VPN server to enter the intranet. For L2TP VPNs, filter UDP ports 1701 and 500. For PPTP VPNs, filter TCP port 1723.

VPN Server Behind the Firewall

This architecture reverses the above schema. The VPN server interfaces with the intranet and the firewall, and the firewall interfaces with the VPN and the Internet, as depicted in Figure 7.6.

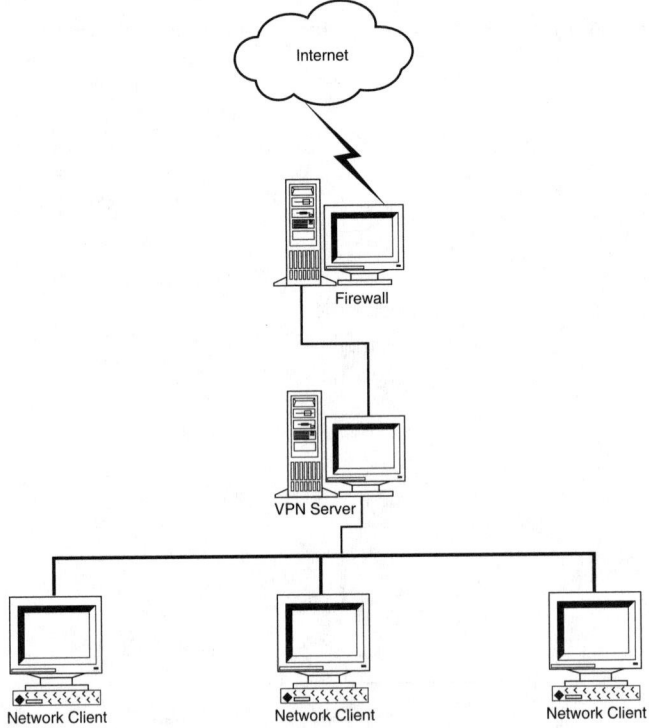

Figure 7.6 The VPN server sits behind the firewall.

Firewall Filters

The firewall only filters VPN traffic based on the header data. The firewall does not have the encryption keys needed to decrypt and filter the passing traffic. As a result, all tunneled data passes through the firewall. This is not as much of a security problem as it seems, however, because the inbound traffic is destined for a VPN server, where it must be authenticated before it is forwarded.

Internet traffic that enters through the firewall must be filtered to permit both the tunnel maintenance and tunnel data traffic to reach the VPN server. Ensure that filters allow traffic passing through the firewall to reach only the resources you intend. For L2TP VPNs, filter UDP ports 1701 and 500. For PPTP VPNs, filter TCP port 1723.

VPN Configuration

This section covers how to set up both L2TP and PPTP VPN servers, for both remote access VPNs and router-to-router VPNs. It also runs through the procedure for setting up the VPN client.

Design Considerations and Recommendations

Before you begin setting up your Windows 2000 VPN server, you need to sit down and think about what you want to do with your VPN. You should consider the needs of the remote users, the level of security you want to enforce, and administrative requirements. The last thing you want to do is set up a high-maintenance VPN that requires several hours of administration each day.

Some issues to carefully plan are:

- **Location of user accounts.** In the interest of ease of management and centralized administration, it is recommended that you store all VPN user accounts on a domain controller or a RADIUS server.

- **User access.** You can control user access to the VPN individually or by remote access policy. Depending on the number of users you are supporting, you might prefer to administer them individually or as a group.

- **Authentication.** VPN users can be authenticated by Windows 2000 authentication methods or by a RADIUS server. If you want to use L2TP over IPSec, you have to set up machine certificates on the clients and servers that will be making VPN connections. EAP or MS-CHAP v2 authentication is recommended.

- **Logging connections.** You might want to set up an accounting system to determine which departments are utilizing the VPN. It is not uncommon for IS departments to "bill" other departments for their use of the network infrastructure, so that departments using more bandwidth, disk space, or administrative time are carrying the cost of their heavier use. Windows 2000 or a RADIUS server can act as a VPN accounting provider.

- **Number of ports.** How many users will be connecting at any given moment? By default, Windows 2000 VPN servers install five PPTP and L2TP ports. If more than five users will be connecting simultaneously, and your hardware supports it, you can add additional ports. If you don't have enough ports, remote users attempting to connect will be denied access until a free port is available.

- **Client connection configuration.** Ten to fifteen remote users can most likely be managed manually. Anything larger than that might require something a little more elegant and hands-off in terms of administration. You might want to consider using Connection Manager and the Connection Manager Administration Kit to provide preconfigured VPN connection dialers to your users.

- **Encryption.** Should every connection to the intranet be encrypted, and if so, how strong should your encryption policy be? If you are in North America, you can use strong encryption. If you have international clients connecting to your VPN server, you will want to use export-friendly encryption.

- **Filtering.** Be sure you have configured appropriate filters to ensure that the data entering or exiting your intranet is secure. A VPN server acts as a router, which can send all kinds of unwanted/unsecured Internet traffic into your intranet. If the purpose of the VPN is to keep unidentified users out of your network, failing to filter traffic has rendered your VPN useless in terms of secure access to your intranet. Filtering is done on an exceptions basis—all packets are allowed except for type x, or only packets of type x are allowed.

- **IP addressing.** You can use DHCP or a static pool of addresses for a VPN server to assign to clients. If you have a DHCP server configured on your network, you can go ahead and use it for VPN client IP address assignment. DHCP is certainly the easiest method of addressing.

Remote Access VPNs

Now let's get down to the business of actually setting up and configuring the VPN server. This section will show you how to set up both an L2TP and a PPTP VPN server to be used by remote users. Router-to-router VPNs will be covered in the section "Router-to-Router VPNs" later in this chapter.

L2TP Server

If your security policy requires your remote users to connect to the corporate intranet with IPSec, you need to configure your Windows 2000 VPN server to use L2TP. This involves configuring both internal and external interfaces, enabling routing and L2TP ports and access, and setting filters and policies. For this and similar processes, the rest of this chapter will walk you through configuring a VPN server from start to finish.

Configure the Internet Interface

First things first: If you haven't yet gotten a WAN connection to the Internet installed, give your access provider a call. Next, install and configure the WAN adapter according to the manufacturer's instructions. (Hint: Don't forget to make sure it is on the HCL!) Then configure the adapter with the IP address, subnet mask, and default gateway provided to you by the ISP. This is the black LAN side of the VPN and will be the interface used as an entrance point for VPN traffic. All data that moves beyond this point must be secured.

Configure the Intranet Interface

You also must install and configure a LAN adapter to interface with the intranet. This is the red LAN or secure side of the server. You need to install and configure a network card with IP address, subnet mask, and name servers (DNS and/or WINS) for the network to which it is attached.

Configure the Remote Access Server to Act as a Router

VPN traffic from the Internet must be forwarded to the intranet and vice versa. To make this happen, the remote access server must be configured as a router, with the appropriate protocols and static routes for destination hosts on either side of the router.

You also need to configure multicast routing. To do so, add Internet Group Management Protocol (IGMP) version 2,. Configure the interface for IGMP router mode. (Note: In this step, Internal interface does *not* refer to the intranet LAN. Instead, it refers to the interface selected when you add IGMP to your IP routing protocols.) Next, you must add an IGMP interface that represents the intranet LAN adapter and configure it in IGMP proxy mode. (For more information on routing, see Chapter 4 and Chapter 5, "Configuring the Windows 2000 Router.")

Allow L2TP Clients

The VPN server must be configured to allow L2TP clients to access it. In the Routing and Remote Access console, right-click the server you want to enable as an L2TP server. Now click Properties. The properties sheet for the server appears, as shown in Figure 7.7.

IP Address Identification

If you ever need to know what IP addresses are assigned to the red LAN and black LAN interfaces, and you don't know this information right off the top of your head, the following procedure can be used to find the information you need. In the Routing and Remote Access console, click the server name, then click IP Routing, then click General. In the right pane, scroll over to the IP Address column, and write down the IP address assigned to the appropriate interfaces.

IGMP Proxy Mode

A Windows 2000 router will support IGMP proxy mode on only a single interface.

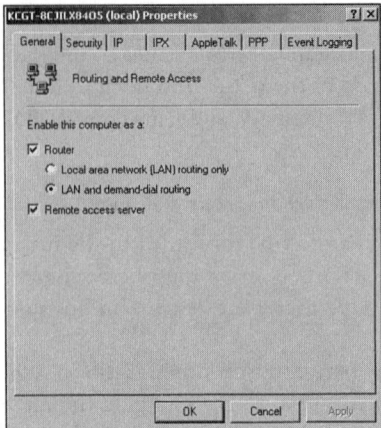

Figure 7.7   The remote access server properties sheet.

You make configuration choices on several of the tabs on the properties sheet:

- **General.**   Make sure there is a check in the "Remote access server" check box.

- **Security.**   There are three choices to be made here: authentication method, authentication provider, and accounting provider. First, select Windows 2000 or RADIUS for your authentication provider. If you want to use a RADIUS server to provide authentication, but you have not set up your RADIUS server, this would be a good time to do that. (See Chapter 9, "Internet Authentication Service," for more information.) Next, select the appropriate authentication methods. Make sure you choose methods that will be supported by your clients or that provide the level of authentication you require. MS-CHAP v2 and EAP are recommended (EAP is required for smart card authentication). Finally, if you are planning to track client usage for billing or activity analysis purposes, select your accounting provider here too.

- **IP.**   Check the "Enable IP Routing" check box and select "Allow IP-based remote access and demand-dial connections." You also must specify the preferred method of IP address and name server assignment. If you have a DHCP server setup on your intranet and want to use it, select Dynamic Host Allocation Protocol (DHCP). If not, or you want to use a range of static addresses instead, click Static address pool and include the range of IP addresses and the subnet if necessary (be sure that the IP addresses are not already in use on your network). If you are using a separate subnet, make sure the intranet's routers have a static route configured to this range of addresses. If you don't add this route, VPN clients won't receive traffic from hosts on the intranet.

Configure L2TP Ports

Configure as many L2TP ports as needed. By default, only five ports are enabled, so consider the number of remote clients you will be supporting at a time. If your hardware supports it, you can increase the number of ports. You should configure all the L2TP ports for remote access. To perform this task:

1. In the Routing and Remote Access console, click the name of the VPN server. Next, right-click Ports, then click Properties. The Ports Properties dialog box appears.

2. Select the appropriate device, then click Configure. The Configure Device dialog box appears.

3. To enable remote access, put a check mark in the "Remote access connections (inbound only)" check box.

Configure L2TP over IPSec Filters

You should prevent your VPN server from forwarding undesirable traffic into and out of the intranet you are trying to protect. Because the VPN server has been configured as a router, it is possible that any traffic received on the Internet interface would be forwarded into your private network. To prevent this, you must set up L2TP over IPSec filters on the Internet interface of the VPN server.

To properly secure your VPN server, you must set input and output filters. Four L2TP over IPSec filters combine to execute L2TP over IPSec filtering. These filters are:

- UDP Port 500, Input- used for IKE (Internet Key Exchange)
- UDP Port 1701, Input- used for L2TP connections
- UDP Port 500, Output
- UDP Port 1701, Output

If all four filters are set up, L2TP over IPSec input and output filtering is secure. Further, if no other filters are set, the only traffic permitted in and out of the configured interface is L2TP over IPSec traffic between VPN server and client. To set up the filters, follow this procedure:

1. In the Routing and Remote Access console, click the server name, then click IP Routing, then click General.

2. Right-click the Internet interface, then click Properties. The interface properties sheet appears.

3. On the General tab, click Input Filters. The Input Filters window appears. Click the Add button.

4. The Add IP Filter dialog box appears. Select the "Destination network" check box.

5. In the IP Address field, type the IP address of the Internet interface.

6. In the Subnet mask field, type `255.255.255.255`.

7. In the Protocol field, select UDP.

8. In the Source port field, type `500`.

9. In the Destination port field, type `500`.

10. Click OK. You have now added the first input filter, and you will be returned to the Input Filters window.

11. To add the second input filter, click the Add button.

12. In the Add IP Filter dialog box, select the Destination network check box.

13. In the IP Address field, type the IP address of the Internet interface.

14. In the Subnet mask field, type `255.255.255.255`.

15. In the Protocol field, select UDP.

16. In the Source port field, type `1701`.

17. In the Destination port field, type `1701`, then click OK. You have now added the second input filter, and you will be returned to the Input Filters window.

18. Now you will select the filter action for the input filter you have just created. From the Input Filters window, select "Drop all packets except those that meet the criteria below," then click OK.

You have now successfully added two input filters that will forward only traffic meeting the specific requirements you have set. You must now configure the output filters that will prevent any L2TP over IPSec traffic from exiting the intranet through this interface.

1. In the Routing and Remote Access console, click the server name, then click IP Routing, then click General.

2. Right-click the Internet interface, then click Properties. The interface properties sheet appears.

3. On the General tab, click Output Filters. The Input Filters window appears. Click the Add button.

4. The Add IP Filter dialog box appears. Select the "Source network" check box.

5. In the IP Address field, type the IP address of the Internet interface.

6. In the Subnet mask field, type `255.255.255.255`. This will block connection attempts to subnets behind the interface unless specified in the static routes of the computer attempting to connect.

7. In the Protocol field, select UDP.

8. In the Source port field, type `500`.

9. In the Destination port field, type `500`.

10. Click OK. You have now added the first output filter, and you will be returned to the Output Filters window.

11. To add the second Output filter, click the Add button.

12. In the Add IP Filter dialog box, select the "Source network" check box.

13. In the IP Address field, type the IP address of the Internet interface.

14. In the Subnet mask field, type `255.255.255.255`.

15. In the Protocol field, select UDP.

16. In the Source port field, type `1701`.

17. In the Destination port field, type `1701`, then click OK. You have now added the second output filter, and you will be returned to the Output Filters window.

18. Now you will select the filter action for the output filter you have just created. From the Output Filters window, select "Drop all packets except those that meet the criteria," then click OK.

It is important to double-check your work when configuring filters. If all four filters are not set up properly, VPN traffic will not be secured.

Install Machine Certificates

L2TP over IPSec VPNs require a machine certificate on both the VPN client and server. You have to have a certificate authority (CA) to issue these certificates. When you have a CA up and running, you can either automatically allocate computer certificates to computers in a Windows 2000 domain or you can use Certificate Manager to collect a computer certificate. (See Chapter 2 for details on how to perform this step.)

Configure Remote Access Policies

Now you need to set appropriate user access permissions or remote access policies, depending on the user administration model you prefer.

If you are controlling access by user, set the remote access permission to Allow access on for the users who will need VPN access to the intranet. If you want to administer user access based on remote access policies, you will need to modify existing (or create new) policies. The policies must include these settings:

- **NAS-Port-Type.** Set to Virtual.

- **Grant remote access permission.** Selected.

- **Default remote access policy** (called **A**llow access if dial-in permission is enabled). Must be deleted or moved after the new policy.

- **Encryption.** Must be set to No Encryption, Basic (56-bit DES IPSec or 40-bit MPPE), or Strong (56-bit DES IPSec or 56-bit MPPE), depending on your security requirements.

For more information on setting remote access policies, see Chapter 2.

PPTP Server

If you opt to use your Windows 2000 VPN server to provide PPTP access for remote clients, you will configure the server in much the same way as an L2TP server. To assist you with the configuration task, step-by-step instruction in included in this section as well.

Configure the Internet Interface

Assuming that you already have a functioning WAN connection to the Internet, you will install and configure the WAN adapter according to the manufacturer's instructions. Check the HCL before you buy—You can save yourself a lot of headaches. Then configure the adapter with the ISP's IP address, subnet mask, and default gateway. Just as a reminder, this is the black LAN side of the VPN, the interface remote clients will use to enter the red LAN/intranet. All data that moves beyond this point must be secured.

Configure the Intranet Interface

You also must set up a LAN adapter on the VPN server that will interface with the intranet. Install your NIC and configure it with an IP address, subnet mask, and DNS and/or WINS for the network to which it is attached.

Configure the Remote Access Server to Act as a Router

VPN traffic from the Internet has to be routed to the intranet and vice versa. The remote access server has to be configured as a router to make this happen. The appropriate protocols and static routes for destination hosts on each side of the router must be configured as well.

You also will need to configure multicast routing. To do so, add IGMP version 2, on the Internal interface. Configure IGMP on the Internal interface for IGMP router mode. Next, you must add an IGMP interface for the intranet LAN adapter and configure it for IGMP proxy mode. (For more information on routing, see Chapters 4 and 5.)

Allow PPTP Clients

The VPN server must allow PPTP clients to access it. In the Routing and Remote Access console, right-click the server you want to use as a PPTP server, then click Properties.

You need to make configuration choices on several of the tabs on the properties sheet:

- **General.** Make sure there is a check in the "Remote access server" check box.
- **Security.** You make three choices here: authentication method, authentication provider, and accounting provider. First, select Windows 2000 or RADIUS for your authentication provider. Next, select the appropriate authentication methods. MS-CHAP v2 and EAP are recommended. Finally, if you will be tracking VPN client usage, select your accounting provider.

- **IP.** Check the "Allow remote systems running" IP check box and select "Access entire network." You also must pick the preferred method of IP address and name server assignment. If you have a DHCP server, select "Dynamic Host Configuration Protocol (DHCP)." If you want to use a range of static addresses instead, click Static address pool and include the range of IP addresses and subnet if necessary.

Configure PPTP Ports

Configure as many PPTP ports as needed. By default, only five ports are enabled, so consider the number of remote clients you will be supporting at a time. If your hardware supports it, you can increase the number of ports. It is recommended that you configure all PPTP ports for remote access. To perform this task:

1. In the Routing and Remote Access console, click the name of the VPN server. Right-click Ports, then click Properties. The Ports Properties dialog box appears.

2. Select the appropriate device, then click Configure. The Configure Device dialog box appears.

3. To enable remote access, put a check mark in the "Remote access connections (inbound only)" check box.

Configure PPTP Filters

You need to prevent your VPN server from forwarding undesirable traffic into and out of the intranet you are trying to protect. Because your VPN server also acts as a router, it is possible that any traffic received on the Internet interface could be forwarded into your intranet. To prevent this, you must set up PPTP filters on the Internet interface of the VPN server. To properly secure your VPN server, you must set input and output filters based on well known port numbers and protocols. Six PPTP filters are used to properly secure your intranet. If all six filters are set up, PPTP input and output filtering is secure. Further, if no other filters are set, the only traffic permitted in and out of the configured interface is PPTP traffic between VPN server and client.

1. In the Routing and Remote Access console, click the server name, then click IP Routing, then click General.

2. Right-click the Internet interface, then click Properties. The interface properties sheet appears.

3. On the General tab, click Input Filters. The Input Filters window appears. Click the Add button.

4. The Add IP Filter dialog box appears. Select the "Destination network" check box.

5. In the IP Address field, type the IP address of the Internet interface.

6. In the Subnet mask field, type 255.255.255.255.

7. In the Protocol field, select Other.

8. In the Protocol name field, type 47.

9. Click OK. You have now added the first input filter, and you will be returned to the Input Filters window.

10. To add the second input filter, click the Add button.

11. In the Add IP Filter dialog box, select the "Destination network" check box.

12. In the IP Address field, type the IP address of the Internet interface.

13. In the Subnet mask field, type 255.255.255.255.

14. In the Protocol field, select TCP.

15. In the Source port field, type 0.

16. In the Destination port field, type 1723, then click OK. You have now added the second input filter, and you will be returned to the Input Filters window.

17. To add the third input filter, click the Add button.

18. In the Add IP Filter dialog box, select the "Destination network" check box.

19. In the IP Address field, type the IP address of the Internet interface.

20. In the Subnet mask field, type 255.255.255.255.

21. In the Protocol field, select TCP (established).

22. In the Source port field, type 1723.

23. In the Destination port field, type 0, then click OK. You have now added the third input filter, and you will be returned to the Input Filters window.

24. Now you will select the filter action for the input filter you have just created. From the Input Filters window, select "Drop all packets except those that meet the criteria below," then click OK.

You have now successfully added three input filters that will forward only traffic meeting the specific requirements you have set. You must now configure the output filters that will allow only PPTP traffic to exit the intranet over this interface.

1. In the Routing and Remote Access console, click the server name, then click IP Routing, then click General.

2. Right-click the Internet interface, then click Properties. The interface properties sheet appears.

3. On the General tab, click Output Filters. The Output Filters window appears. Click the Add button.

4. The Add IP Filter dialog box appears. Select the "Source network" check box.

5. In the IP Address field, type the IP address of the Internet interface.

6. In the Subnet mask field, type 255.255.255.255.

7. In the Protocol field, select Other.

8. In the Protocol name field, type 47.

9. Click OK. You have now added the first output filter, and you will be returned to the Output Filters window.

10. To add the second output filter, click the Add button.

11. In the Add IP Filter dialog box, select the "Source network" check box.

12. In the IP Address field, type the IP address of the Internet interface.

13. In the Subnet mask field, type 255.255.255.255.

14. In the Protocol field, select TCP.

15. In the Source port field, type 1723.

16. In the Destination port field, type 0, then click OK. You have now added the second output filter, and you will be returned to the Output Filters window.

17. To add the third output filter, click the Add button.

18. In the Add IP Filter dialog box, select the "Source network" check box.

19. In the IP Address field, type the IP address of the Internet interface.

20. In the Subnet mask field, type 255.255.255.255.

21. In the Protocol field, select "TCP (established)."

22. In the Source port field, type 0.

23. In the Destination port field, type 1723, then click OK. You have now added the third output filter, and you will be returned to the Output Filters window.

24. Now you will select the filter action for the output filter you have just created. From the Output Filters window, select "Drop all packets except those that meet the criteria below," then click OK.

It's wise to double-check your work when you have finished configuring the filters. If all six filters are not set up properly, VPN traffic will not be secured.

Configure Remote Access Policies

Now you need to set appropriate user access permissions or remote access policies, depending on the user administration model you prefer.

If you are controlling access by user, set the remote access permission to Allow access on for the users who will need VPN access to the intranet. If you want to administer user access based on remote access policies, you will need to modify existing (or create new) policies. The policies must include these settings:

- **NAS-Port-Type.** Set to Virtual.
- **Grant remote access permission.** Selected.
- **Default remote access policy (called Allow access if dial-in permission is enabled).** Must be deleted or moved after the new policy.
- **Encryption.** Here you will select 40-bit, 56-bit, or 128-bit encryption, depending on your needs and your geographic location.

For more information on setting remote access policies, see Chapter 2.

Client Setup

Configuring a remote access VPN client is a snap with the Network Connection Wizard. Click Start, then Settings, and then Network and Dial-up Connections, then Make New Connection. The Network Connection Wizard appears. Run through the wizard's prompts and supply the following information or select the following options:

1. Select "Connect to a private network through the Internet."

2. Specify if you want to automatically dial the Internet connection and which dial-up connection to use (if any).

3. Supply the FQDN or IP address of the VPN server to which you want to connect.

4. Specify whether the connection is to be available for all users or only the user under whose profile the connection was configured.

5. Specify whether you want to use Internet Connection Sharing (optional).

6. Name the VPN connection you have just created and add a shortcut to it on your desktop (optional).

After the connection is created, you can go back and modify the connection options if necessary. In Network and Dial-up Connections, right-click the connection icon and select Properties from the context menu. The properties dialog box is where you can modify the settings you chose during connection creation. You can also add or change network and tunneling protocols to be used, authentication, and encryption, and specify whether a dial-up connection to the Internet should be initiated before a VPN connection is attempted.

Router-to-Router VPNs

Two separate networks can be joined over a VPN connection. These types of VPNs are called router-to-router VPNs because they are established between two routers. Typically, traffic going though this type of VPN does not originate at the client-side router. Instead, traffic originates from nodes on the network behind the initiating router destined for nodes behind the end-point router. These types of VPNs are not difficult to set up, but—just like remote access VPNs—they require proper advance planning. Considerations, such as security policies, maintenance, and the needs of the users at each end of the VPN connection, are just a few of the things to think about. The list that follows starts the ball rolling by identifying the major points you need to know before you start configuring your VPN:

- **Connection type.** This issue deals with the type of Internet connectivity each site has. There are two types of router-to-router VPNs: on-demand and persistent. Each type has infrastructure-based requirements. On-demand connections enable the initiating router to use either a permanent or a dial-up connection to the Internet, but the answering router is required to have a dedicated Internet connection. If you opt to use an on-demand connection, you might want to limit when or how a connection is made. You can set the dial-out hours when a router may or may not make a connection, or you can set filters that permit only certain types of traffic to initiate a router connection. Persistent connections are used when both VPN routers are connected to the Internet with permanent WAN links.

- **Connection initiation.** One or both routers can initiate a VPN connection. You might want only one network to be able to establish a VPN, or you might want both sides to be able to establish a connection. A connection that is initiated from only one side (one-way initiated connection) enables the calling router to use a dial-up Internet connection. The answering router must use a permanent Internet connection. If you want to enable either side of the connection to initiate the VPN, both sides must use a permanent Internet connection.

- **Number of required ports.** The default number of L2TP or PPTP ports added is five. You might need more ports than this if you are supporting a large number of remote sites. Check the manufacturer's documentation to determine the number of ports your hardware allows.

- **Routing information.** Both routers must be configured with static or dynamic routes to enable traffic to be forwarded from one side of the VPN connection to the other. Routes can be added manually, by auto-static updates, or by dynamic update (recommended only if the demand-dial interface is permanently connected to the Internet). Keep in mind that you can't use the default route for the VPN's demand-dial interface to summarize routes on the intranet. The default route for this interface has to summarize Internet routes. (See Chapter 4 for more information on default routes.) As a convenience, however, the connection across the Internet can be virtualized as a single hop, no matter how many Internet routers are actually used.

- **Remote access policies.** Policies enable you to require specific encryption strength and/or authentication type, and manage VPN routers as a group, instead of individually. If you connect several sites with identical security requirements, you might find it easier to deal with groups rather than individual sites.

The remainder of this section will detail the processes involved in configuring L2TP and PPTP router-to-router VPNs.

L2TP Router-to-Router VPN

There are three basic steps to set up an L2TP router-to-router VPN: configuring the answering router (which acts as the VPN server), configuring the calling router (which acts as the VPN client), and establishing a connection between routers. We will start with the answering router.

Configuring the Answering Router

A simple example of an answering router is found in the following scenario. A company with multiple locations allows employees at these locations to access the corporate intranet through a router-to-router VPN. The answering router fields the incoming VPN connections initiated by the calling routers at the company's remote locations. Configuring the answering router is a rather intensive process. If you use the following configuration instructions, however, it shouldn't be too painful.

Configure the Internet Connection

The answering router requires a dedicated WAN link to the Internet. If you do not already have this WAN circuit to an ISP established, take care of this step first. If you have ever worked with a local telephone company and an ISP to install a dedicated line, you know that it is never too early to start this process. When you have the infra-structure in place, install and configure the WAN adapter in the VPN server with the ISP's IP information: IP address, subnet mask, and so on.

Configure the Intranet Connection

The answering server also must interface with the internal network. Install and config-ure a LAN adapter; don't forget to check the HCL for compatibility. The adapter must be configured to use the appropriate protocols used on the intranet, including IP address, subnet mask, default gateway, and name servers.

Install Machine Certificates

L2TP over IPSec VPNs require a machine certificate on both the VPN client and server. You have to have a certificate authority (CA) to issue these certificates. When you have a CA up and running, you can automatically allocate computer certificates to computers in a Windows 2000 domain, or you can use Certificate Manager to collect a computer certificate. (See Chapter 2 for details on how to perform this step.)

Configuring the Routing and Remote Access Service

The Routing and Remote Access Service on the answering VPN router must be configured with the following options. To set this information, right-click the server name in the Routing and Remote Access console and select Properties. The tabs that appear are governed by the protocols installed on the server. In this case we will use these tabs:

- **General.** Check the Router check box and select LAN and demand-dial routing.

- **Security.** There are three options to configure here. First, choose the appropriate method of authentication, either Windows 2000 or RADIUS. Second, select the authentication method of preference. MS-CHAP v2 or EAP-TLS is recommended. Third, if you will be tracking usage of the VPN server, select the appropriate accounting provider.

- **IP.** Check "Allow remote access clients to use" and select Entire network. Select DHCP or Use Static Address Pool, then enter the appropriate IP address range and subnet mask to be assigned to VPN clients. Only use IP addresses that are not already in use on your network.

- **PPP.** Check "Link control protocol (LCP) extensions" and Software ompression check boxes.

Configuring Ports

Five L2TP ports are configured by default. If you need more, and your hardware supports it, you can configure additional ports. In the Routing and Remote Access console, right-click Ports, then select Properties. Click the L2TP device, then click the Configure button to set the desired number of ports.

Configuring Demand-Dial Interfaces

Now it is time to set up a demand-dial interface. You will set up one interface for each remote router that will be making a connection to the answering router. First, launch the Demand-Dial Interface Wizard from the Routing and Remote Access console by right-clicking Routing Interfaces, then selecting New Demand-Dial Interface. The wizard prompts you for the following information:

- **Interface Name.** Assign a name to the interface that will answer the call from the calling router. You might find it helpful to give the interface a meaningful name. For instance, the interface might answer calls from your mid-city office. In this case, you might name the interface MidCity or something similar.

- **Connection Type.** Select Connect using virtual private networking (VPN).

- **VPN Type.** Select Layer 2 Tunneling Protocol (L2TP).

Tip

Demand-dial connections can be on-demand or persistent. Persistent demand-dial connections use a dial-up link but are left in a connected state at all times. Persistent demand-dial connections can include local calls that use analog phone lines and flat-rate ISDN.

- **Destination Address.** This is not required, because the answering interface will be receiving, not initiating connections. If you were configuring a two-way demand-dial connection, you would provide this information. Entering it as an IP address can help identify the connection later.

- **Protocols and Security.** Select the appropriate protocols to be routed over this interface, then check the "Add a user account so a remote router can dial in" box.

- **Dial-in Credentials.** Now you add the user account for the remote router. Provide the password for the account that will authenticate the calling router. (The name defaults to the name you specified in the first step of the wizard—don't change it or the answering router will consider the connection attempt to be from a remote client.) The account is created at this point. The new account's remote access permission is set to Allow access.

- **Dial-out Credentials.** Set credentials that match those on the remote router.

Configuring Static Routes

The server also acts as a router between the VPN and the internal network, so you must configure static routes or routing protocols to allow accessibility to all intranet resources. Each network in the intranet that has resources required by remote users must have a static route configured on the demand-dial interface.

1. In the Routing and Remote Access console, expand IP Routing on the appropriate server.

2. Right-click Static Routes and select New Static Route.

3. In the Static Route dialog box, supply the demand-dial interface, destination network ID, subnet mask, and metric.

Configuring L2TP over IPSec Filters

You must configure input and output filters on the Internet interface to allow only L2TP over IPSec traffic to be forwarded into the intranet. Use the instructions in the previous section on L2TP remote access VPNs.

Configuring Remote Access Policies

Finally, you set the remote access policies that control access by remote routers attempting to make a connection. Follow these guidelines for setting up the remote access policy:

1. Configure user accounts on the router for remote access. On a standalone, set all users' dial-in properties to Allow access. On a router that uses the Active Directory, set users' dial-in properties to Control access through Remote Access Policy.

2. Create a group made up of user accounts that represent the calling router(s). The accounts in this group are the accounts that will be used by the initiating routers.

3. Build a remote access policy that allows access by the group you created in the last step. It must contain the following properties:

   NAS-Port-Type.   Set to Virtual.

   Grant remote access permission.   Selected.

   Default remote access policy (called Allow access if dial-in permission is enabled).   Must be deleted or moved after the new policy.

   Encryption.   Require IPSec encryption by clearing the check from No Encryption. The other encryption options are Basic (56-bit DES IPSec or 40-bit MPPE) and Strong Encryption (56-bit DES IPSec or 56-bit MPPE). This setting must match on both ends of the connection.

For more information on setting remote access policies, see Chapter 2.

Configure the Calling Router

Now that you have the answering router configured, you can move on to the calling router. The steps to configure the calling router are similar to the steps involved with the answering router. In an attempt to not be redundant, this section will use general descriptions for steps that were detailed in the answering router section.

- **Configure the Internet connection.**   Assuming that your WAN link to he Internet has been installed, you will first install and configure the device that will interface with the Internet. Include the IP information provided by your ISP.

- **Configure the intranet connection.**   Install and configure a LAN adapter. Include the appropriate IP information: address, subnet mask, name servers, and so on. You also need to configure routing with static routes or a routing protocol, such as RIP or OSPF, as appropriate for the intranet. This ensures that all networks in the intranet are accessible from the router.

- **Install a computer certificate.**   L2TP over IPSec VPNs require machine certificates on both the client and the server.

- **Configure a demand-dial interface.**   Use the Demand-Dial Wizard to configure the following information:

   Interface Name.   The name you would like to assign to the connection.

   Connection Type.   Select "Connect using virtual private networking (VPN)."

   VPN Type.   Select "Layer 2 Tunneling Protocol (L2TP)."

   Destination Address.   The name or IP address of the answering router.

   Protocols and Security.   Select the desired protocols.

   Dial-out Credentials.   Use the credentials you provided for dial-in credentials on the answering router.

- **Configure static routes.** Add static routes to the demand-dial interface so that all networks on the intranet are reachable.
- **Configure L2TP over IPSec filters.** Add the appropriate input and output filters to the Internet interface so that undesirable traffic is not forwarded into your network.

That's it for configuring the calling router. The final step in creating a router-to-router VPN is next.

Initiate the VPN Connection

Compared to what came before, this step is a breeze. You direct the calling router to connect to the answering router through the Routing and Remote Access console. Right-click the appropriate demand-dial interface and select Connect. If both the client and the server have been configured properly, the VPN tunnel will be established and L2TP over IPSec data will pass securely between both networks over the Internet. If you experience difficulties establishing the connection, double-check the configuration of the calling and answering routers. You also can refer to Appendix B, "Troubleshooting," for more information.

PPTP Router-to-Router VPN

The process for setting up a PPTP server is nearly identical to setting up an L2TP server. Because different networks have different needs, you might choose to use a PPTP VPN. The three parts of setting up a PPTP router-to-router VPN are the same: configuring the answering router, configuring the calling router, and establishing a connection between routers. Because this is intended as an aid for installation and configuration, it will seem redundant if you just read the section on L2TP VPNs. Even if you don't use this VPN type, this is a good reinforcement of the process you learned in the last section.

Configuring the Answering Router

The answering router acts as the VPN server and handles the incoming VPN connections initiated by the calling routers. The process to set it up is lengthy but not too difficult.

Configure the Internet Connection

The answering router requires a dedicated WAN link to the Internet. When you have the infrastructure in place, install and configure the WAN adapter (don't forget to check the HCL for compatibility) in the VPN server with the IP information provided by the ISP.

Configure the Intranet Connection

Install and configure a LAN adapter to interface with the intranet. The adapter must be configured to use the appropriate protocols used on the intranet, including IP address, subnet mask, default gateway, and name servers.

Configuring the Routing and Remote Access Service

The Routing and Remote Access Service on the answering VPN router must be configured with the following options. To set this information, right-click the server name in the Routing and Remote Access console and select Properties. Four tabs on the properties sheet are accessed. The tabs and their options are as follows:

- **General.** Check the Router check box and select LAN and demand-dial routing.

- **Security.** Select the authentication method of preference. MS-CHAP v2 or EAP-TLS are recommended. Next, select the appropriate authentication method, either Windows 2000 or RADIUS. Finally, select the appropriate accounting provider if you will be tracking client usage.

- **IP.** Check "Allow remote access clients to use" and select Entire network. Select DHCP or Use Static Address Pool, then enter the appropriate IP address range and subnet mask to be assigned to VPN clients.

- **PPP.** Check "Link control protocol (LCP) extensions" and "Software compression" check boxes.

Configuring Ports

Five PPTP ports are configured by default. If you need more, and your hardware supports it, you can configure additional ports. In the Routing and Remote Access console, right-click Ports, then select Properties. Click the PPTP device, then click the Configure button to set the desired number of ports.

Configuring Demand-Dial Interfaces

Set up one demand-dial interface for each remote router that will be making a connection to the answering router. Launch the Demand-Dial Interface Wizard from the Routing and Remote Access console by right-clicking Routing Interfaces, then selecting New Demand-Dial Interface. The wizard prompts you for the following information:

- **Interface Name.** Assign a name to the interface that will answer the call from the calling router.

- Connection Type. Select "Connect using virtual private networking (VPN)."

- **VPN Type.** Select "Point to Point Tunneling Protocol (PPTP)."

- **Destination Address.** This isn't required, because the answering interface will be receiving, not initiating connections. (If you were configuring a two-way demand-dial connection, you would provide this information.)

- **Protocols and Security.** Select the appropriate protocols to be routed over this interface, then check the "Add a user account so a remote router can dial in" box.

- **Dial-in Credentials.** Now you will add the user account for the remote router. Provide the password for the account that will authenticate the calling router. (The name defaults to the name you specified in the first step of the wizard—Don't change this or the answering router will treat the calling router as a remote access client.) The account is created at this point. The new account's remote access permission is set to Allow access.

- **Dial-out Credentials.** The answering router will not initiate connection, so you can enter any user account information here. (If you are configuring a two-way demand-dial connection, provide this information.)

Configuring Static Routes

Because this server also acts as a router between the VPN and the internal network, you must configure static routes or routing protocols to allow access to all intranet resources. Each network in the intranet that has resources required by remote users must have a static route configured on the demand-dial interface.

1. In the Routing and Remote Access console, expand IP Routing on the appropriate server.

2. Right-click Static Routes and select New Static Route.

3. In the Static Route dialog box, supply the demand-dial interface, destination network ID, subnet mask, and metric.

Configuring PPTP Filters

You must configure input and output filters on the Internet interface to allow only PPTP traffic to be forwarded into the intranet. Use the instructions in the previous section on PPTP remote access VPNs.

Configuring Remote Access Policies

Finally, you will set the remote access policies that will control access by remote routers attempting to make a connection. Follow these guidelines for setting up the remote access policy:

1. Configure user accounts on the router for remote access. On a standalone, set all users' dial-in properties to Allow access. On a router that uses the Active Directory, set users' dial-in properties to Control access through Remote Access Policy.

2. Create a group made up of user accounts that represent the calling router(s). The accounts in this group are the accounts that will be used by the initiating routers.

3. Build a remote access policy that allows access by the group you created in the last step. It must contain the following properties:

    NAS-Port-Type—Set to Virtual.

    Grant remote access permission—Selected.

    Default remote access policy (called Allow access if dial-in permission is enabled)—Must be deleted or moved after the new policy.

    Encryption—Select the preferred method of encryption.

For more information on setting remote access policies, see Chapter 2.

Configure the Calling Router

The steps to configuring the calling router are nearly identical to the steps involved with the answering router. This section will use general descriptions for steps that were detailed in the answering router section.

- **Configure the Internet connection.** Install and configure the device that will interface with the Internet. Include the IP information provided by your ISP.

- **Configure the intranet connection.** Install and configure a LAN adapter. Include the appropriate IP information: address, subnet mask, name servers, and so on. Also, configure routing with static routes or a routing protocol, such as RIP or OSPF, as appropriate for the intranet. This will ensure that all networks in the intranet are accessible from the router.

- **Configure a demand-dial interface.** Use the Demand-Dial Wizard to configure the following information:

    Interface Name—The name you would like to assign to the connection.

    Connection Type—Select "Connect using virtual private networking (VPN)."

    VPN Type—Select "Point to Point Tunneling Protocol (PPTP)."

    Destination Address—The name or IP address of the answering router.

    Protocols and Security—Select the desired protocols.

    Dial-out Credentials—Use the credentials you provided for dial-in credentials on the answering router.

- **Configure static routes.** Add static routes to the demand-dial interface so that all networks on the intranet are reachable.

- **Configure PPTP filters.** Add the appropriate input and output filters to the Internet interface so that unwanted traffic is not forwarded into your network.

Initiate the VPN Connection

To connect the calling router to the answering router, launch the Routing and Remote Access console. Right-click the appropriate demand-dial interface and select Connect. If you experience difficulties establishing the connection, double-check the configuration of the calling and answering routers. You also can refer to Appendix B for more information.

References

Here are some helpful sources on topics covered in this chapter:

Administering Certificate Services. Microsoft TechNet.

Internet Protocol Security, Windows 2000 Server Resource Kit. Microsoft Press.

IP Security for MS Windows 2000 Server. Microsoft TechNet.

MS Privacy Protected Network Access: Virtual Private Networking and Intranet Security. Microsoft TechNet.

MS Windows 2000 TCP/IP Implementation Details. Microsoft TechNet.

Remote Access Server, Windows 2000 Server Resource Kit. Microsoft Press.

The Security Support Provider Interface. Microsoft TechNet.

Setting Up Certification Authority Trust for a Domain. Microsoft TechNet.

Smart Card Certificate Enrollment. Microsoft TechNet.

Smart Card Logon. Microsoft TechNet.

Smart Card Reader Installation. Microsoft TechNet.

Virtual Private Networking, Windows 2000 Server Resource Kit. Microsoft Press.

Windows 2000 Security—Default Access Control Settings. Microsoft TechNet.

8

Windows 2000 Connection Services

WINDOWS 2000 SUPPLIES TWO TOOLS TO EASE THE ADMINISTRATIVE burden of supporting many users with dial-up and VPN connection requirements. The first tool is Connection Manager version 1.2 and its Administration Kit. The second tool is Connection Point Services. These two tools could probably fill an entire book by themselves, but this chapter will give you just the basics of each. I will cover the function of each and how they work together, and then explain how to set up these services from start to finish.

Connection Manager is a preconfigured dialing tool for remote users. It contains all the settings and options required to connect a computer to a particular service. This service could be a private remote access server, a commercial ISP, or a VPN connection. The Microsoft Network uses Connection Manager to distribute its connection information to its subscribers, and you can do the same thing with your network services, whether they are ISP, RAS server, or VPN based.

The Connection Manager is configured with the Connection Manager Administration Kit (CMAK). The CMAK contains a wizard to assist you in compiling all the pertinent information needed to put together a fully functional Connection Manager profile for your users. After a Connection Manager profile has been customized to suit your service's requirements, it can be distributed as a self-contained installation package. Another ease-of-use feature is the level of integration with Internet Explorer 5.0. You can use Internet Explorer Administration Kit 5 (IEAK 5) to distribute your Connection Manager profile at the same time you are distributing Internet Explorer 5. In fact, you can use IEAK 5 to handle most of the configuration of Connection Manager and Internet Explorer 5. This chapter, however, will only explore Connection Manager version 1.2 from the CMAK point of view. Systems requirements and configuration instructions for Configuration Manager and the CMAK will be covered later in this chapter, in the section called "Connection Manager Configuration."

Connection Point Services (CPS) allow you to automatically update client or customer phone book files. Phone book files contain information on access numbers for POPs or RAS servers for your users. This means that when you add or remove access numbers, users can automatically download these updated files. CPS has two parts: Phone Book Service (PBS) and Phone Book Administrator (PBA). PBS is an IIS extension and requires Internet Information Services 5.0. It is used to provide phone book files to your users. PBA can be used on a server or a workstation, and it is used to create and maintain phone book files. A phone book is a collection of point-of-presence servers and the access number for each. PBA uses the FTP service to publish these files to the PBS.

When a user's Connection Manager profile has been configured to permit automatic downloading of files, every time he or she dials in using that profile, Connection Manager will check for the presence of a new phone book file on the server running PBS. If one is found, it is downloaded to the client computer, without requiring user interaction. The WWW service handles the connection by Connection Manager clients. By providing this service, you can free your helpdesk or administrative staff from answering customer questions about current local access numbers.

In the overview of this chapter, I covered Connection Manager first and Connection Point services second. Now, I am going to reverse positions and cover CPS configuration first. Connection Point Services and Connection Manager have a sort of "which came first, the chicken or the egg?" air about them. It is difficult to talk about CPS without first discussing Connection Manager, but it is difficult (though not impossible) to use the phone book function of Connection Manager without first setting up CPS. The goal of this chapter is for you to end up with a fully functional set of connection services. To that end, I will cover these topics in the order in which they should be configured.

Connection Point Services

Connection Point Services can be a big help for you and your users if your network adds or changes access numbers on a regular basis. Many ISPs, ASPs, and VPN vendors regularly provide monthly or quarterly phone book updates. In the past it was difficult to distribute this information among all the users needing it. Through Connection Manager, users can automatically download new phone books containing the updated information. This section will cover the configuration and administrative tasks of Connection Point Services—creating and maintaining phone books.

Install and Configure Connection Point Services

This section will cover the basics of setting up CPS, including some recommended practices and security precautions you should take.

System Requirements

CPS requires IIS 5.0 to be installed on the CPS server. Further, both the WWW and FTP services must be present. If, for security reasons, you prefer to not have the FTP service running, you can stop the FTP service through the Internet Service Manager. To publish new phone books, FTP must be running. You can start and stop this service as needed to make phone book updates. (Alternatively, you could add and remove the Write permission from the FTP directory. Instructions for this are in the upcoming "Configuration" section.) Uninstalling FTP will uninstall CPS. You should install and configure Internet Information Services before proceeding to the next section, "Installation." For more information on IIS 5.0, refer to Windows 2000 Help.

Installation

Installation Connection Point Services is a snap. It is installed through the Windows Components Wizard, using the following procedure:

1. Click Start, Settings, Control Panel. The Control Panel appears.
2. Double-click the Add/Remove Programs applet, then click Add/Remove Windows Components. The Windows Component window appears.
3. Select Management and Monitoring Tools, then click the Details button. The Subcomponents dialog box appears
4. Put a check in the Connection Manager Components check box. Click Next.
5. Click Finish the complete the wizard.

Next, you will install the Phone Book Administrator.

1. On the Windows 2000 Server CD, navigate to the \VALUEADD\MSFT\MGMT\PBA directory and double click PBAINST.exe. This will launch the Phone Book Administrator Installer.
2. Click Yes when prompted to verify that you wish to install Phone Book Administrator.
3. Click OK when the installation is completed.

Configuration

When CPS is installed, you will need to secure your server. This section will cover setting permissions on CPS folders and creating FTP accounts for the users who need to be able to create and upload phone books.

1. The first thing to do is grant administrator-only access for these folders:

   ```
   C:\Program Files\Phone Book Service
   ```

   ```
   C:\Program Files\PBA
   ```

2. Right-click the folder, then Properties, then click the Security tab. Add the appropriate users or groups and remove the check mark for "Allow inheritable permissions from parent to propagate to this object." Repeat this process for both folders.

3. Next, you will enable write access to the FTP virtual directory used for Phone Book Services. Note that for security purposes you might want to perform this step just before you post a phone book, and then remove the permission as soon as you are through posting. This step is accomplished through the Internet Services Manager. Click Start, Programs, Administrative Tools, Internet Services Manager. The Internet Services Manager console will appear.

4. In the left pane, double-click Internet Information Services, then double-click the appropriate server name.

5. Double-click Default FTP Site, then right-click PBSData. Select Properties from the context menu.

6. Click the Virtual Directory tab and place a check mark in the Write check box, as shown in Figure 8.1.

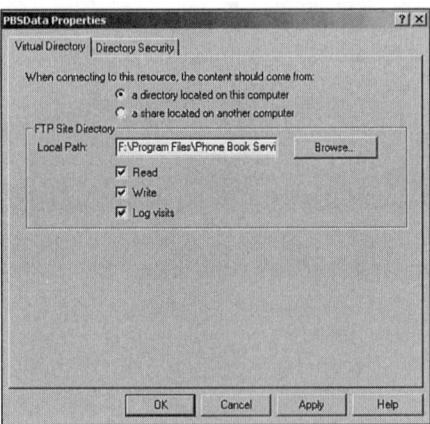

Figure 8.1   Setting write access on the FTP virtual directory for the Phone Book Service.

7. Click OK. Leave the Internet Service Manager console open for the next step.

8. The last part of the Connection Point Services configuration process is to configure the FTP service to allow access based on Windows 2000 user credentials for those users who will need to publish phone books to the CPS server. Right-click Default FTP Site and select Properties from the context menu.

9. Select the Security Accounts tab, as shown in Figure 8.2. Remove the check mark in the Allow Anonymous Connections check box. When prompted to verify this action, click Yes.

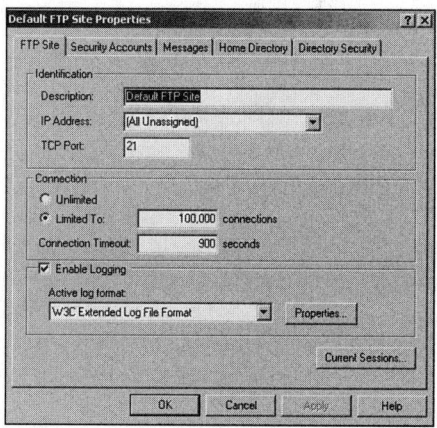

Figure 8.2 Preventing anonymous FTP connections.

10. Click the Add button. Add the appropriate names of those users who will be publishing phone books. Click OK when done.

At this point you should have successfully configured Connection Point Services on your server. From here, we will move into the administrative tasks.

Administering Connection Point Services

Administering Connection Point Services has two basic parts: first creating and then publishing a phone book. This section will give you the instructions to perform both of these tasks.

Create a Phone Book

To create a new phone book containing the access numbers of your service:

1. Launch Phone Book Administrator by clicking Start, Programs, Administrative Tools, Phone Book Administrator.

2. Select the File menu, then click New Phone Book. The Add New Phone Book dialog box appears, as shown in Figure 8.3.

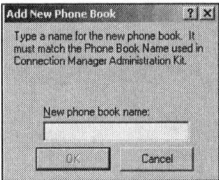

Figure 8.3 Adding a new phone book.

3. In the New phone book name field, give the phone book a name. The phone book name can't be longer than eight characters, and can't include the following characters: ★ = \ / : ? ' " < > |. Click OK. Note: This is the name that is referenced in the Connection Manager when configuring phone book support (see the upcoming "Connection Manager" section for more information).

4. In Phone books, select the new phone book. Select the Tools menu, then click Options. The Options dialog box will appear. Fill in the CPS server address and the username and password of the account to be used to FTP phone books to the server specified.

5. Next, you will add a point-of-presence (POP) server to the phone book you just created. Select the new phone book in the Phone books list.

6. Select the Edit menu, then select Add POP.

7. On the Access Information tab, include the following information:

   - **POP name.** Identifies the point-of-presence server
   - **Country/ Dependency.** The country where the POP server is located
   - **Region.** Optional identifier you can use if your service is geographically divided
   - **Area code.** Area code of the POP server
   - **Access number.** Phone number of the POP server
   - **Status.** Allows you to specify if a POP server is In Service or Not In Service

8. Repeat for each POP in your network. Click OK when finished.

Publish a Phone Book

When your phone book is complete, you must upload it to the serve by publishing it. If you have not set write access for the PBSData FTP virtual directory for an extra measure of security, you must set it before you can proceed with these steps. To publish your phone book:

1. Open Phone Book Administrator.
2. In Phone books, click the appropriate phone book.
3. Select the Tools menu, then click Publish Phone Book. The Publish Phone Book dialog box will appear, as shown in Figure 8.4.

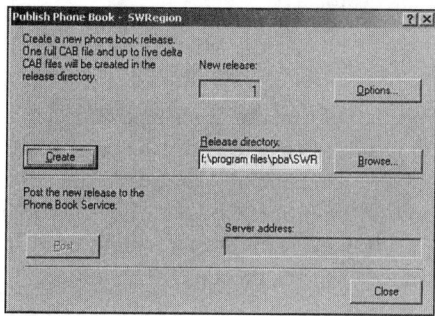

Figure 8.4 Publishing a new phone book.

4. Specify or browse to the Release directory. This is the directory where phone book files will be stored.
5. Click Create, then click Post.

Now that you have gone through the process of installing and configuring Connection Point Services and creating and publishing phone books, you are ready to do the same for your own service. The next section will cover Connection Manager, which is used in conjunction with CPS. Connection Manager can, among many other things, automatically download phone books to a client computer.

Connection Manager

In this section, you will learn the requirements for installing and running Connection Manager. Then you will actually walk through the step-by-step configuration of a Connection Manager profile.

Requirements

Connection Manager is supported on Windows 2000, Windows NT 4.0, Windows 98, and Windows 95. In addition to the required operating system, a client must have a minimum of 1MB free disk space, a service profile, and the Connection Manager software. The service profile is built with the Connection Manager Administration Kit. The profile and Connection Manager software can be distributed together in a self-contained installation package.

If you plan to use Phone Book Service (PBS) to update client phone books, those should be ready to be included in the service profile. If they are not, the service profile can be edited at a later date to include support for PBS. The service profile can then be redistributed to your clients for use.

Service Profiles

Service profiles contain all the information a client will need to connect to your service. You can also use the service profile to automate tasks a user would typically do manually both before and after connecting, or to distribute custom Help files. The wizard will configure most of the profile for you, based on the information you provide, but there are certain advanced features that require manual configuration of the file (a later section, "Advanced Service Profile Configuration," will cover this topic).

Connection Manager Configuration

In this section, we will cover the process of creating a profile with the CMAK Wizard and the available configuration options. When configuring service profiles in a production environment, you might find it helpful to compile all the information requested by the wizard ahead of time.

1. To begin, you will install the Connection Manager Administration Kit. Open Control Panel and launch the Add/Remove Programs applet.

2. Select Add/Remove Windows Components and follow the onscreen directions. Select Management and Monitoring Tools, then click the Details button. Put a check mark in the Connection Manager Components check box. Click OK, then click Next. Finish the wizard by following the onscreen instructions.

Profile File Size

The amount of required disk space varies with the size of the service profile and any other files included with the profile, such as pre- and post-connections action files.

3. To start the CMAK Wizard, click Start, Programs, Administrative Tools, Connection Manager Administration Kit. The Connection Manager Wizard will start. Be prepared—this is a rather lengthy wizard. You will need to supply information in the corresponding panel for each of the options below.

- **Service Profile Source.** You must choose whether to create a new profile or edit an existing profile. You can create as many profiles as needed to support your clients. For instance, you may want to provide different support files for different operating systems, or some clients might use VPN connections and others might not. You can also edit existing profiles to reflect recent changes to your service.

- **Service and File Names.** The wizard asks you for a service name and a file name. The service name can be about 40 characters, depending on capitalization, punctuation, spacing, and the specific characters used. It identifies your service to clients—you can use your company name or organization name as a service name. The service name is displayed prominently in several areas, including the Connection Manager title bar, dialog boxes, and taskbar when the program is running. The file name identifies the files created by the wizard, and can be a maximum of 8 characters (these files are described at the end of this section). When specifying this name, use the standard rules for "8.3" file names: don't use spaces or special characters such as ! , ; ★ = / \ : ? ' " < > or extended character sets. Both service and file names must be unique among other service and file names on the same computer. You can use the same name for both service name and file name as long as the naming parameters for each are followed.

- **Merged Service Profiles.** The CMAK allows you to combine existing service profiles to create a new profile in a process called merging. Merging profiles allows you to consolidate profile information to make your service appear to be one single service, rather than several separate services. Let's say your company maintains an RAS server for users in the local area, but outsource dial-up access for users in remote areas to an ISP. If you merge the service profiles for local and remote users, you can combine the access numbers for those users. The resulting profile makes your service seem as if it offers all access numbers, even those that belong to the ISP. This allows a single profile to support a wide array of users. (Note that this example assumes that the ISP is also maintaining a service profile and shares it with your company.) Merging profiles can also support multiple realm names in the event that your service spans multiple networks or ISPs.

- The profile that includes information from other profiles is the referencing profile, and the profile that has its information merged into another service profile is called a merged profile. The following properties of a service profile are taken from the merged profile: file name, merged profiles, realm name, Network and Dial-up Connections entries, phone books, download phone book, and URL for downloads. All other properties must be specified within the referencing profile.

- **Support Information.** On this panel, you can enter a line of information to be displayed in the logon dialog box. It can be about 50 characters (once again, depending on the characters used, capitalization, spaces, and so on). An example of such an entry is "For customer support, call 1-800-555-1234."

- **Realm Name.** This name provides the necessary information to route user authentication requests to the appropriate authenticating server, such as an IAS or RADIUS server. (See Chapter 9, "Internet Authentication Service," for more information on realm names and RADIUS.)

- **Dial-Up Networking Entries.** In this panel of the wizard, you will customize the Network and Dial-up Connections in the phone book you would like to use. These entries correspond to the Network and Dial-up Connections you have previously specified in the Phone Book Administrator of Connection Point Services (the name of the entry must match exactly—spelling counts!). You can further customize the way these entries are treated by Connection Manager by providing a particular set of DNS and/or WINS servers to be used, and indicating if a particular script should be run if this connection is used. This is shown in Figure 8.5.

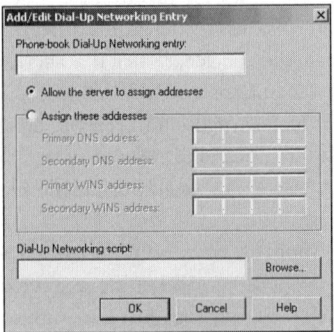

Figure 8.5   Dial-Up Networking Entry configuration.

- **VPN Support.** If you want to specify support for VPN connections, the CMAK Wizard can help you with that. Select whether you want to add VPN support for this service profile or, if this is a merged profile, select for merged service profiles. If you do not want to include support for VPN connections, you should skip the next item in this list and move on to the Connect Actions item.

- **VPN Connection.** On this panel, you tell the wizard the address of the VPN server (either IP address or Fully Qualified Domain Name (FQDN)). The wizard supports VPN connections using PPTP (the default) and L2TP (Windows 2000 clients only). If you want to use L2TP as the tunneling protocol, you'll have to configure this through advanced service profile configuration (see the "Advanced Service Profile Configuration" section later in this chapter). You may also opt to allow the VPN server to assign name servers or indicate specific DNS or WINS servers for the client to use. The final option on this panel is whether or not clients use the same username and password for a VPN connection as for a dial-up connection; otherwise they will be prompted for both sets of credentials.

- **Connect Actions.** The CMAK Wizard can integrate specific actions to be taken at various points in the connection process, including pre-connection, pre-tunnel (if you are using a VPN connection), post-connect, and disconnect actions. For instance, you may select as a post-connect action for your users to automatically download new phone book entries from a phone book server. You can choose any combination of these that fits your needs. You are then prompted to supply the following information for each action you have selected: a description of the program to run, the path to the program itself, and any parameters required for program execution, as shown in Figure 8.6.

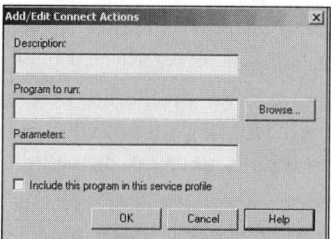

Figure 8.6   Configuring connect actions.

As another convenience, you can distribute the program to be run with this profile by selecting the Include this program this in service profile option at the bottom of the dialog box. Other connect actions are available by editing the profile directly (see "Advanced Service Profile Configuration"), including pre-dial, on-cancel, and on-error.

- **Auto-applications.** Auto-applications are similar to post-connect actions, except they are run after the dial-up or VPN tunnel has been established. Auto-applications are run every time a user connects to your service. When the auto-application is closed, Connection Manager will automatically start to disconnect the user from the service. Perhaps your company has a proprietary database front-end that connects to a back-end over an RAS dial-up link. Let's also say that you don't have enough modems to support the simultaneous connection of all remote users to the network, but statistically speaking, there should be enough so that a user is able to get a connection most of the time. You can use the auto-disconnect feature to free up unused connections by disconnecting those users who are no longer using the database, but who have not closed their dial-up connection to the RAS server.

- **Custom Graphics.** You can use the provided bitmap graphics in the Logon and Phone Book dialog boxes or you can replace them with your own graphic, such as a corporate logo or other bitmap. This feature offers the most tangible customization of your service, at least as far as the user is concerned. The first thing they see when the connection manager launches is the logo you have provided. The recommended logon bitmap size is 330×141 pixels, while the phone book bitmap is 114×304 pixels. Your graphics do not have to be these exact sizes, but they will display at this size. To prevent distortion, match the dimensional proportions of your replacement graphics to the display sizes above. Bitmaps must use a 256-color (halftone) palette.

- **Phone Book.** There are three options for providing a phone book for your users with the CMAK Wizard:
  - Include a phone book in the profile, with support for automatic upgrades. To do this, select "Automatically download phone-book updates" in the Post-Connect Actions dialog box. In the Phone Book dialog box, provide the path to and name of the phone book file you want to use. In the Phone Book Updates dialog box, supply the IP address or FQDN of the Connection Point Services server where upgrades can be found.

  - Include a phone book in the profile, but don't support automatic upgrades. Simply provide the path to and name of the phone book file you want to use in the Phone Book dialog box.

  - Don't include a phone book in the profile, but support users downloading the phone book and upgrades at a later time. This is helpful if you haven't finished compiling all the access numbers at the time you need to deploy Connection Manager to your users. To do this, select "Automatically download phone-book updates" in the Post-Connect Actions dialog box. Then, in the Phone Book Updates dialog box, supply the IP address or FQDN of the Connection Point Services server where upgrades can be found.

- **Icons.** Three icons are used in conjunction with Connection Manager: the program icon, the title bar icon, and the status area icon. You can specify your own graphic for one, two, or all three of these icons. The program icon is 32×32 pixels, and the title bar and status area icons are 16×16 pixels. All are limited to 16 colors, and should remain proportionally similar to the display sizes listed above.

- **Status-Area-Icon Menu.** When a user right-clicks the status-area icon, a pop-up menu appears. You can customize this menu to provide your users with shortcuts to tasks or programs frequently used in association with this connection, such as email or browser applications. Provide the name of the command as you want it to appear in the context menu, the full path to the program to be run, any necessary parameters, and whether to include the program in the profile.

- **Help Files.** As an alternative to the built-in Connection Manager Help files, you can create custom Help files to provide your users with solutions to typical problems. Building custom Help files is beyond the scope of this chapter, but you may find it helpful to know this feature is available. If your helpdesk or administrative staff has created a knowledge base of users' problems and their solutions, you could integrate this into the Connection Manager profile you are distributing.

- **Connection Manager Software.** If the users to whom you are distributing this service profile are not currently using Connection Manager version 1.2, you can include it in this profile.

- **License Agreement.** If you are using CMAK to create profiles for a commercial service—that is, you are an ISP using CMAK to distribute connection information and software to your customers—you can include a license agreement with the profile. This license agreement requires that a user agree to the terms of your service before the profile will be installed.

- **Additional Files.** If you want to include any other software or documentation in this profile that has not been included elsewhere, you can do so here. For instance, you may want to include "bonus software" for signing up with your service, or a new screen saver featuring your company's logo.

Creating Keyboard Shortcuts

By preceding a letter in the display entry on the menu with an &, you can create a keyboard shortcut. For example: &Outlook would display as <u>O</u>utlook. Outlook can then be launched by pressing O. To use an "&" in a menu item, use "&&".

When you have entered all the requisite information, the wizard will compile the data and build a profile. Each service profile is made up of multiple files, stored in the `\Program Files\CMAK\Profiles\`*`ServiceProfileFileName`* folder. The CMAK Wizard creates the following files for each profile:

- The folder containing the files required to install Connection Manager and the associated service profile
- A .cms file, containing the administrator-specified configuration data for Connection Manager
- A .cmp file, which stores client-specified information
- An .exe file, which is the self-extracting executable for distribution
- An .inf file, used to set up and install Connection Manager on the client computer
- An .sed file, which specifies how to compress the service profile files when the profile is created

The only file required for distribution to your clients is the .exe file. This can be distributed any way you want: burned on a CD, copied to a floppy, emailed, downloaded from a Web site, and so on. Just keep in mind the size of the executable when determining the manner of distribution. The more files you included in the service profile, the larger the distribution file will be.

Advanced Service Profile Configuration

You can edit the service profile files directly to include additional service features that are not supported through the wizard, such as L2TP VPN tunneling. To do this, first run the wizard and provide the requested information, then edit the files that were created by the CMAK Wizard. This will only affect the service profile you are editing. Alternatively, you could edit the template files that are used by the CMAK Wizard to build the service files. This method will affect all future profiles created with those template files. After editing a service-profile file, you must run the CMAK wizard again to rebuild the service profile with your customized settings.

There are many changes that can be made to these files; for a complete list of them, see "Customizing Additional Features" in the Connection Manager Administration Kit Guide. Here is one change you may find useful. It allows you to modify the VPN protocols required in a profile.

Always Work With a Safety Net!

Always make backup copies of a file before editing it directly!

Set VPNStrategy= to one of the following:

0 = Automatically select the primary protocol (default)

1 = Use Point-to-Point Tunneling Protocol (PPTP) only

2 = Try PPTP first

3 = Use L2TP only

4 = Try L2TP first

Built Files

To edit built service profile files, navigate to the `\Program Files\CMAK\Profiles\` *ProfileFileName* folder. All profile files have the name *ProfileFileName*, which you specified in the CMAK Wizard. The files you edit and their functions are as follows:

- **.cms files.** These files contain most of the configuration information for a profile. This is where you will do the majority of editing.

- **.cmp files.** These contain user-supplied information, which means that any changes you make here can be overwritten by users once the profile is installed. Don't spend the time to change this file.

- **.inf and .sed files.** .inf files contain the installation information for the profile. .sed files contain the information required to build an .exe. It is possible to edit both of these files, but Microsoft cautions against it, due to the difficulty of troubleshooting any resulting problems.

After you edit the files, you must rerun the wizard so that the changes are incorporated (or built) into the profile.

Template Files

The Connection Manager Administration Kit uses a template version of each of the preceding file types. These templates contain the default options for the CMAK Wizard. The files are located in the `\Program Files\CMAK\Support` folder, and are called `Template.cms (or .cmp, .inf, .sed)`. Changes made to any of these files (following the recommendations in the Built Files section) affect any future profiles built with the wizard.

References

For more information on Connection Manager and Connection Point Services, check out these sources:

Microsoft TechNet: Client Utilities CD. Internet Explorer 5.0 Administration Kit Guide.

Microsoft TechNet: Technical Information CD. Administration Guide—Connecting Point Services

Microsoft TechNet: Technical Information CD. Administration Reference—Connecting Point Services

Microsoft TechNet: Technical Information CD. Connection Manager Administration Kit Guide.

9

Internet Authentication Service

INTERNET AUTHENTICATION SERVICE (IAS) IS A WINDOWS 2000 add-on component that provides authentication, authorization, and accounting services to remote access dial-in and VPN clients. IAS uses the IETF standard RADIUS protocol (Remote Authentication Dial-In User Service, RFCs 2138 and 2139) to forward authentication requests from a network access point, such as a remote access server, to a RADIUS server. The IAS server then compares the user's credentials to a client database to verify identity. IAS supports standard PPP authentication protocols, offering a flexible remote access solution for both heterogeneous and homogeneous networks of any size, from standalone servers to large corporate intranets.

In this chapter, we will cover the basics of IAS, including how it works, its features, things to consider when planning your IAS implementation, and suggested best practices. We'll wind things up with step-by-step instructions for configuring IAS for dial-up and VPN access.

Overview of IAS

As previously stated, RADIUS is a standard protocol for authentication, authorization, and accounting services in a dial-up or VPN network. RADIUS uses a client/server configuration. The RADIUS client is not the actual user requesting access, however. Instead, the RADIUS client is the Windows 2000 remote access server, another dial-up server, such as that used by an Internet service provider (ISP), or even another

RADIUS server forwarding requests to an IAS server. This server is called the Network Access Server (NAS). The NAS sends the user's credentials to the RADIUS server, which performs the tasks of authentication, authorization, and accounting. Windows 2000 includes both the client (a component of RRAS) and server (IAS) components.

The Windows 2000 Routing and Remote Access Service allows you to separately configure accounting and authentication providers (see Chapter 2, "Remote Access Server"). You can enable a RADIUS server to handle both tasks. Alternatively, you can use the Windows 2000 or Windows NT 4.0 domain user accounts database to authenticate users, and use RADIUS only for accounting. By using RADIUS for both tasks, you can use an IAS server to integrate authentication, authorization, accounting, and remote access policies management into a single administrative tool. Keep in mind that the Windows 2000 IAS server does not have the ability to create its own database of user accounts and passwords, like the IAS server found in the Internet Connection Services for Microsoft RAS, Commercial Edition.

To answer the question at the top of everyone's list of concerns, yes, RADIUS is fault tolerant. You can set up backup RADIUS servers that are automatically used in the event that the primary RADIUS becomes unavailable.

Functionality

Let's take a detailed look under the hood at how IAS works. IAS acts as a clearinghouse of sorts for authentication and/or accounting services for remote access servers. Because IAS is an RFC-compliant RADIUS server, it can accept such requests from many types of network access servers, not just Windows 2000 remote access servers. In the network illustrated in Figure 9.1, you see two network access servers, one a Windows 2000 remote access server and one that belongs to an ISP. The RADIUS client requests from both dial-up servers are treated identically by the IAS server.

VPN and IAS

The Windows 2000 remote access server can also be the endpoint of a VPN tunnel, accepting requests for authentication from VPN clients over the Internet.

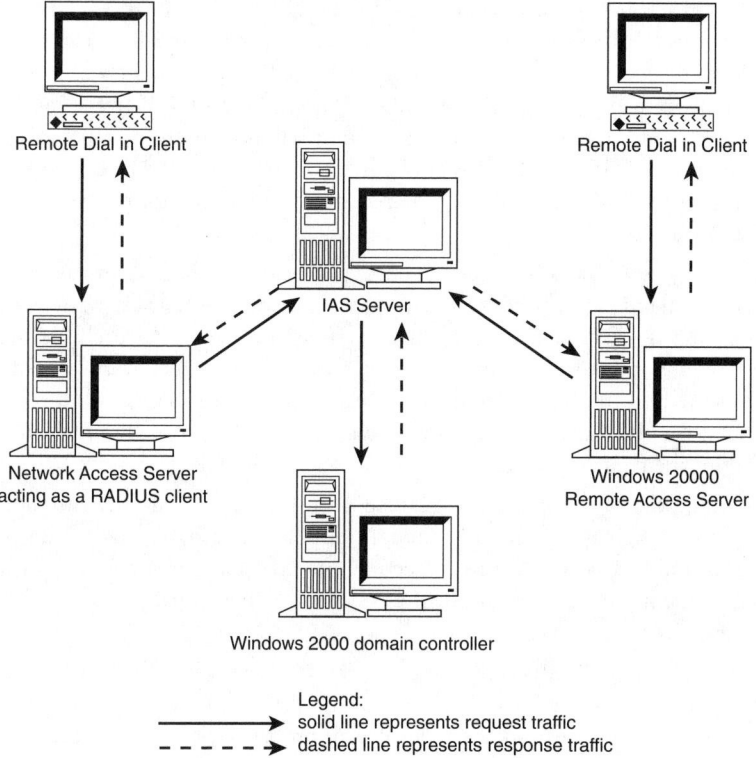

Remote Dial in Client

Remote Dial in Client

IAS Server

Network Access Server
acting as a RADIUS client

Windows 20000
Remote Access Server

Windows 2000 domain controller

Legend:
solid line represents request traffic
dashed line represents response traffic

Figure 9.1 A remote access network using IAS for authentication in a Windows 2000 domain.

Upon initialization, a network access server sends the IAS server an accounting-start packet. This lets the IAS server know that a particular RADIUS client is open for business. While the network access server is running, all requests, responses, and interim messages are logged on the IAS server. When the NAS is stopped, an accounting-stop packet is sent to the RADIUS server.

The connection and authentication process is as follows:

1. A remote user accesses the NAS, by dialing in to it or by connecting to it over the Internet (in the case of a VPN client).

2. The NAS negotiates with the client for a mutually acceptable authentication protocol. The NAS works from the list of authentication protocols it has been configured to accept, from strongest to weakest. If no mutually acceptable protocol is found (if, for example, the server will only accept EAP, and the remote client has only been configured with MS-CHAP), the connection attempt is refused. If an authentication protocol is successfully negotiated, the NAS moves to the next step.

3. An access–request packet is generated by the NAS. This packet contains the user's name and password. The packet is sent to the first IAS server in the list of RADIUS servers configured on the NAS. The RADIUS client will attempt to send the message for a specific amount of time (the default is five seconds). If the IAS server does not respond, the request will be retried. If subsequent attempts also fail, the request will be directed to the next RADIUS server configured on the NAS. If the NAS receives no response from any server, it will disconnect the remote user.

4. The IAS that receives the access–request packet first authenticates the sending NAS. Authentication is in the form of a shared secret—basically, a password. The NAS is configured with the appropriate shared secret for each IAS server with which it needs to connect. This shared secret must match the shared secret configured on the IAS server, or the IAS server will silently discard the access–request packet. If this happens, the sending NAS will eventually time out and attempt the next RADIUS server in its list, if applicable.

5. Assuming that the shared secret matched, the IAS server will then attempt to connect to the appropriate domain controller to be authenticated against the user accounts database. If the connection attempts fails, the access–request packet will be silently discarded. The RADIUS client will eventually time out and try another RADIUS server.

6. If the user credentials are authenticated, the IAS server will determine whether the user is authorized for remote access. The decision is based on both the remote access policies and the user's dial-in properties. The conditions of at least one policy that grants access to the user must be met (for more information, see the section "Remote Access Policies" in Chapter 2). If access is granted, the IAS sends an access-accept packet. An access-accept packet not only informs the NAS that the remote user is permitted to connect to the network, it also announces what the user is authorized to do, according to the user's profile and remote access policies. If the remote user does not match conditions in at least one access-granting policy, or if the user matches conditions in a policy that denies access, an access-reject packet is sent to the NAS. The NAS will then disconnect the remote user.

Why Use IAS?

IAS offers administrators several features and benefits, including:

- **Authentication.** IAS uses the PPP authentication protocols supported by Windows 2000 (see Chapter 2 for a complete list and explanation of the Windows 2000 PPP authentication protocols). From clear text passwords to smart-card authentication, IAS has an authentication protocol for nearly every situation and every network. AppleTalk Remote Access Protocol (ARAP) authentication is also included to support remote Apple Macintosh clients. IAS can authenticate users in Windows NT 4.0 and Windows 2000 domains as well as Windows 2000 local accounts databases.

- **Authorization.** By using remote access policies, IAS can streamline the job of administering remote access permissions for users. Policies enable you to control access based on many different variables, such as group membership, time of day, or connection type.

- **Accounting.** The RADIUS protocol provides for the logging of communication between all network access servers and the IAS server. This information can be imported into a database and examined for such things as authentication success, rejection statistics, and account lockout statistics to track attempted fraudulent access. This information can be used for budgeting or billing purposes as well.

- **Remote access services from commercial ISPs.** Instead of setting up and maintaining banks of modems to enable remote users to access the corporate network, you can leverage the nearly universal availability of the Internet to provide network access through an ISP. IAS can still be utilized even if you do not provide the network access. It is possible to contract with an ISP to have the authentication and accounting requests from your users connecting to its NAS forwarded to your IAS server.

Planning Your IAS Deployment

Planning is an important part of any deployment. Performance and security should definitely be considered when you are setting up IAS for your network. Logging is another important consideration—after all, it provides a terrific source of data that can be used for planning upgrades or modification of network services. This section will look at each of these issues and provide some suggested best practices, before moving on to the actual configuration of IAS.

Performance

Network and server performance are issues in any environment. Because authentication and accounting traffic are passed from RADIUS client and RADIUS server, the obvious network bottlenecks must be considered. Certain segments might become saturated with a high volume of IAS traffic. Upgrading the network infrastructure to support the level of data transmission is a key factor in supporting remote user requests in a timely fashion. Server performance is also an important factor. A slow IAS server or domain controller can slow down remote user authentication just as much as a busy network. Here are some tips for minimizing network latency and improving throughput/performance of IAS in your enterprise:

- When IAS authenticates users against a native mode Windows 2000–based domain controller, authentication speed will be improved if the domain controller contains the Global Catalog. For even better performance, run your IAS server on a domain controller with a Global Catalog.

- The number of user authentications per second achieved are dependent on the sizing of the hardware used for the domain controller. Generally speaking, a faster domain controller should yield a better throughput. More memory, a faster processor, and minimal network bottlenecks will contribute positively to the improvement of IAS performance.

- If possible, use separate IAS servers for authentication and accounting. This eases load on the server performing each of these tasks.

Security

As with any other computer in your network that is potentially open to attack, you should take care to protect your IAS server. Certain configuration options, firewalls, passwords that are difficult to guess, and physical security are all possible parts of a good security plan. Here are some practical suggestions for your IAS server.

Use long, difficult to crack phrases for the shared secret used between a NAS and IAS. Use a combination of up to 255 upper- and lowercase letters, numbers, and special characters. A phrase like "ThEH0use1s0nf1Re!" is an ideal shared secret. It uses random uppercase letters, substitutes zeros for the letter "o" and ones for the letter "i," and includes a special character (the exclamation point).

Use the most secure authentication protocol possible. Using EAP or MS-CHAP is much more secure than other protocols that send passwords in clear text, or in a form that is easily unencrypted or does not require a password, such as PAP, SPAP, or ANI/CL1. Disable all protocols you do not plan to use—If authentication protocols are negotiated in order of strength, a rogue RADIUS client could slip in with a less secure protocol than you had intended for use in your network, or passwords could be passed in the clear text format for eavesdroppers to pick up.

Use the account lockout feature to limit the number of attempts a remote user can make at authentication. If the remote user fails to authenticate in the set number of attempts, the account will be denied access. This can help prevent dictionary attacks. To enable account lockout, you must decide how many attempts are allowed before lockout, and how long the user must wait before the counter is reset (the default is 48 hours). Balance the need for security with the administrative overhead you might incur when valid users are locked out inadvertently by typing mistakes or forgetting a password. To enable account lockout, edit the registry on the Windows 2000 computer that provides remote access user authentication. This will be either the RAS or IAS server, depending on the RAS configuration you have selected. Make the following changes:

1. Set the value of HKEY_LOCAL_MACHINE\SYSTEM\CurrentControlSet\ Services\RemoteAccess\Parameters\AccountLockout\MaxDenials to the number of attempts you will allow. The default is zero, indicating that account lockout is disabled.

2. Set the value of HKEY_LOCAL_MACHINE\SYSTEM\CurrentControlSet\ Services\RemoteAccess\Parameters\AccountLockout\ResetTime (mins) to the number of minutes you wish the account to be locked out before it is automatically reset.

It's a good idea to set up a dedicated IAS server that has no other important data on it. This reduces the risk of exposure if the system is successfully hacked. Also, it's always a good idea to physically secure any server. Putting your servers in a locked room or other inaccessible place and/or running in headless mode (no mouse, monitor, or keyboard) can prevent unauthorized access and modification.

An IAS server can be used with a firewall. This is especially important when you are using an IAS server to authenticate Internet-based remote user requests for VPN connections. Be sure that your firewall allows UDP packets coming from or going to the IAS server. The default ports are 1812 and 1645 for authentication and 1813 and 1646 for accounting.

Logging

Coming up with a good logging strategy is important. You need to decide which RADIUS requests are pertinent to your needs and how often to start a new log. Requests should be logged in an easily analyzed format, so you will also need to determine which format is the best for you. Log files are stored by default in the %systemroot%\system32\LogFiles folder, however, you can certainly choose to store then in a different location. Don't forget to periodically back up these files.

What to Log

Excessive logging can cause a decline in performance of your server, so only log those options you really need. When you don't need a particular type of log data any longer, stop recording it. For security monitoring, you can get by with just authentication logging. You might want to add accounting data to this for a clearer picture of resource usage. It is recommended that you do not log anything until you know that your IAS server and all network access servers are functioning as intended. When you log authentication and accounting traffic, the following information is recorded to form a solid basis for auditing IAS usage:

- **Accounting-on requests.** Announcement that a NAS is online and available to service incoming connection attempts.

- **Accounting-off requests.** Announcement that a NAS is stopping and will not be available to service incoming connection attempts.

Account Lockout

The remote access account lockout feature is unrelated to the account lockout property of a user account. If you need to manually reset a locked remote access user account, delete the subkey that corresponds to the user's account name: HKEY_LOCAL_MACHINE\SYSTEM\CurrentControlSet\Services\ RemoteAccess\Parameters\AccountLockout*domain name:user name*

- **Accounting-start requests.** Packet from a NAS to announce the start of an authenticated user session.

- **Accounting-stop requests.** Packet from a NAS to announce the end of an authenticated user session.

- **Authentication requests.** Remote user authentication requests forwarded by the NAS.

- **Authentication accepts and rejects.** Packet from IAS to inform a NAS that a remote user connection attempt should be accepted or rejected.

When to Start New Logs

You can start new logs on a daily, weekly, or monthly basis. You can also start a new log when the log file becomes a certain size. You can change the logging option at any time, but because of the way log files are named, it is possible you could overwrite an existing log file by doing so. Back up existing logs files before changing the logging start options.

File Format

You can log IAS data in ODBC-compatible format or IAS format. The data saved in the ODBC-compatible format can be imported into an ODBC database (such as Microsoft SQL Server) and analyzed, and the results can then be output in user-friendly format such as a report, chart, or graph. IAS logs are less easily analyzed, because that format makes no attempt to ensure that the data collected displays consistent or uniform characteristics.

Installation and Configuration

Now we'll get down to the business of configuring an IAS server and RADIUS clients. You can use the steps in this section as a checklist for completing the setup of your own IAS server.

1. Install IAS by going to Start, Settings, Control Panel.

2. In Control Panel, click Add/Remove Programs. The Add/Remove Programs applet will start.

3. Click Add/Remove Windows Components. The Windows Components Wizard will start, as shown in Figure 9.2.

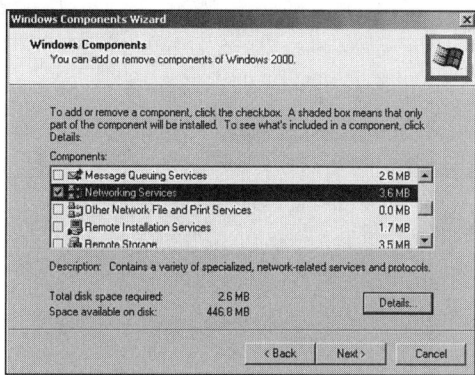

Figure 9.2   The Windows Components Wizard.

4. Click Networking Services, then click the Details button. The Networking Services dialog box will appear.

5. Put a check in the box next to Internet Authentication Service, then click OK. The Windows Component Wizard reappears.

6. Click Next. The Windows Component Wizard will begin to install IAS. Insert the Windows 2000 Server CD-ROM if prompted to do so. When the configuration process is finished, click Close. You are now ready to begin configuring IAS.

7. Launch the IAS console by clicking Start, Programs, Administrative Tools, Internet Authentication Service.

8. To configure the IAS server, right-click Internet Authentication Service in the left pane of the IAS console. Select Properties from the context menu. The Internet Authentication Service properties sheet will appear, as shown in Figure 9.3.

Starting and Stopping IAS

Although the default on installation is for the Internet Authentication Service to be started, it might be necessary at some point to start and/or stop the service. To do so, click the Action menu in the IAS console, then select Start Service or Stop Service, as appropriate for the situation.

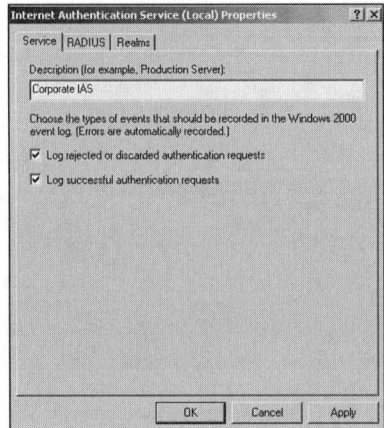

Figure 9.3   The IAS properties sheet.

9. There are three tabs on the Internet Authentication Service properties sheet.
    Each one has the following configurable options:

    - **Service tab.** On this tab you can input a description, a title to describe
      this IAS server. You also can choose to log rejected or discarded authenti-
      cation requests and/or log successful authentication requests.

    - **RADIUS tab.** Here you can provide a specific UDP port to use for
      accounting and authentication. Different NAS vendors might use different
      ports, so be sure you input all appropriate ports for all network access
      servers in your network. The defaults are ports 1812 and 1645 for authen-
      tication, and ports 1813 and 1646 for accounting.

    - **Realms.** A realm identifies the network to which the object bearing a
      realm name belongs—for instance, `user@supernet.com`, where
      `supernet.com` is the realm. Earlier in this chapter we took an example of
      using an ISP to provide Internet access for your users, and having the ISP's
      NAS hand off the requests from your users to your network. The realm
      name is used in conjunction with the user credentials, so the NAS knows
      which traffic goes where. Realm names, if used, must be removed from the
      user's credentials before IAS sends them on to a domain controller for
      authentication. If they are not removed, domain authentication will fail
      because the username and password do not match that stored on the
      domain controller. On the Realms tab, shown in Figure 9.4, you can cre-
      ate the rules that will be used to process usernames for accounting and
      authentication requests. This process is called realm replacement.

To configure a realm replacement rule, click Add and supply the realm name to be replaced and what it is to be replaced with. The Find string cannot be blank, but the Replace string can be blank.

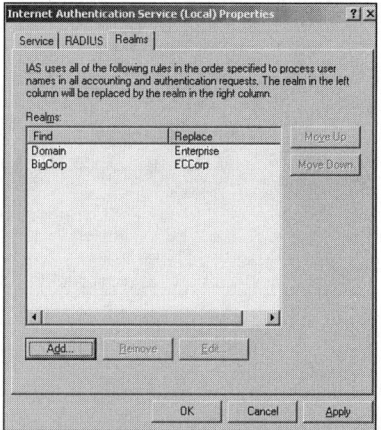

Figure 9.4   Realm replacement in IAS.

10. The next step is to add RADIUS clients to the IAS server. Right-click Clients in the left pane of the IAS console. Click Add in the context menu. The Add Client Wizard will appear.

11. Provide a friendly name for the client, and select the appropriate protocol for that client. The default is RADIUS. Click Next.

12. On this panel, you will provide the address (IP or DNS) and the vendor of the client NAS. The default is RADIUS Standard. Put a check in the box for "Client must always send the signature attribute in the request to use EAP authentication." Finally, put in your shared secret and click Finish.

13. To configure logging, click Remote access logging in the left pane of the IAS console. In the right pane, right-click Local File, then select Properties from the context menu. On the Settings tab, select the desired logging options, as shown in Figure 9.5.

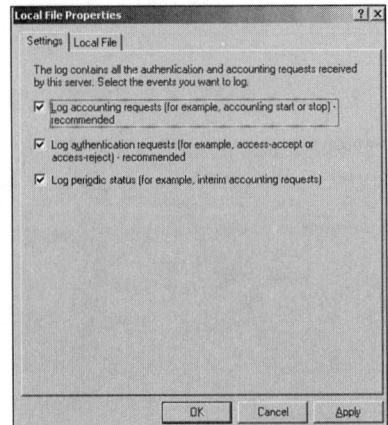

Figure 9.5 Options for logging specific IAS traffic.

14. On the Local File tab, you can configure additional specific logging preferences regarding the frequency of log file creation, file type, and file location, as shown in Figure 9.6.

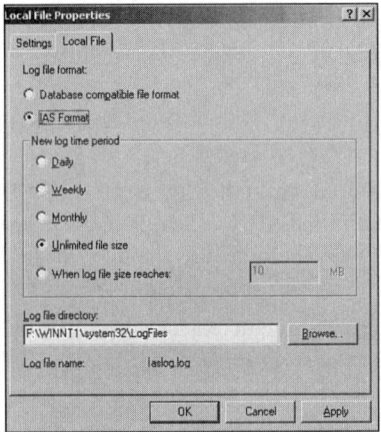

Figure 9.6 IAS log file options.

15. Now you are ready to configure remote access policies. Right-click Remote Access Policies in the left pane of the IAS console. From the context menu, select New, Remote Access Policy. You will then specify the policy name, the policy conditions, whether permission is granted or denied based on this policy, and the specific user profiles that must be matched to complete the connection. See Chapter 2 for full details on configuring remote access policies.

That is just about it for a quick and easy IAS configuration. If you will be installing a backup IAS server, wait until you have completely configured the primary server. That way you can export a copy of the complete server setup—configuration, remote access policies, logging, and all—to the server (or servers) you have designated as backup. To do this:

1. Copy %SystemRoot%\system32\ias\ias.mdb from the primary IAS to the same location on the backup IAS.

2. On the backup server, make a small change to remote access policy and/or logging settings to force the server to read from the new configuration file configuration. It doesn't matter what you do—remove or add an option to a policy and/or logging (do both if you are using both), apply the change, then undo the change. Alternatively, you can restart your server, but if the server is in use at the time, that might not be a practical option.

Testing IAS

It is a good idea to test that your IAS server is working properly before you implement remote access policies on it. That way you can be sure it is the policy that is causing the problem rather than IAS.

IAS Scenarios

There is a wide variety of configuration options for IAS, for every size and type of network. This section will briefly describe two IAS architectures: one small and the other larger and more complex.

Small IAS deployment

ABC Computer Consulting has decided to implement IAS. The company has 30 consultants, all of whom spend 50% of their time on the road. They have used a very simple, straight-forward approach to IAS. Because ABC is a small company with relatively few users, they have decided to piggy-back IAS on the existing server that also acts as the only Windows 2000 domain controller. Remote users dial in to the ABC Windows 2000 remote access server, which has been configured to use RADIUS as its authentication and accounting provider, as illustrated in Figure 9.7.

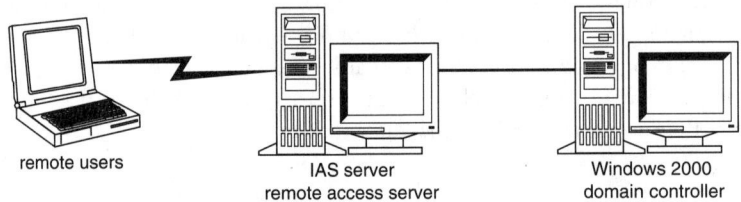

remote users   IAS server   Windows 2000
remote access server   domain controller

Figure 9.7   ABC Computer Consulting IAS implementation.

Large IAS deployment

Farm and Home Insurance has over 300 field agents that travel around the country handling claims resulting from natural disasters. The company also has 1000 users in its corporate headquarters. Farm and Home has partnered with a national ISP to allow the remote users to use local POPs for access to the corporate intranet. The ISP has configured its RADIUS servers to forward Farm and Home authentication requests to the Farm and Home IAS server. The realm name is used to differentiate Farm and home traffic from the traffic of other customers of the ISP. The Farm and Home IAS server also runs on a Windows 2000 domain controller, one of three in the Farm and Home intranet. The accounting processes are offloaded onto another server in the network to improve user authentication throughput. Figure 9.8 illustrates this architecture.

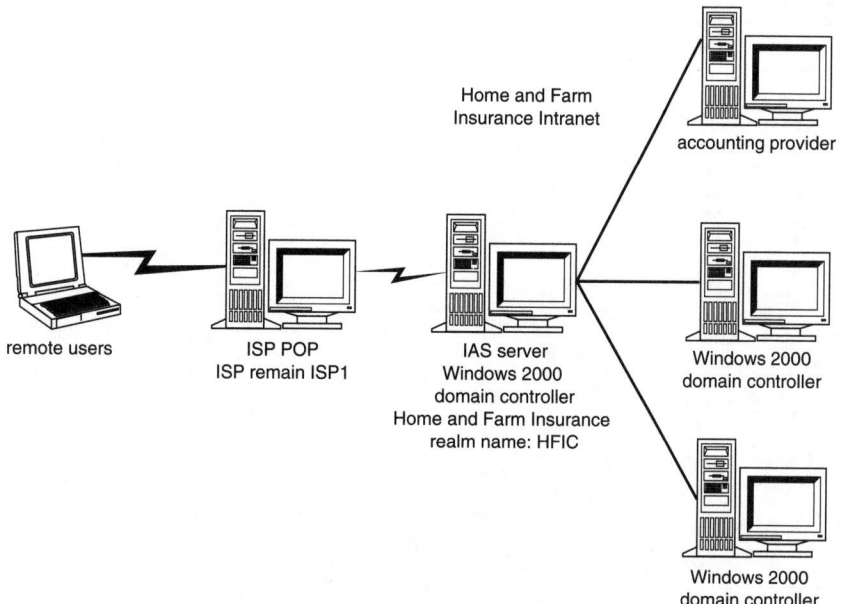

Figure 9.8   Farm and Home Insurance IAS implementation.

For more information regarding large-scale implementations of IAS, consult the Microsoft Commercial Internet System documentation and resource kit. Both can be found on the Microsoft TechNet Technical Information CD.

References

Here are some great sources for more information about RADIUS and Internet authentication services:

- Internet Engineering Task Force, RFC 2138, "Remote Authentication Dial-In User Service (RADIUS)"
- Internet Engineering Task Force, RFC 2139, "Radius Accounting"
- Internet Engineering Task Force, RFC 2548, "Microsoft Vendor-specific RADIUS Attributes"
- Microsoft KnowledgeBase Article Q168667, "RADIUS: Remote Authentication Dial-In User Service"

III

RRAS Planning

10 Bandwidth and Telecommunications

11 Shared Internet Connectivity

12 Network Design

Bandwidth and Telecommunications

THIS CHAPTER IS INTENDED AS A GUIDE FOR NETWORK administrators, to be used when considering making changes or upgrades to the WAN links in your network. The first part of this chapter has two sections. The first section deals with features built into Windows 2000 that can help you use existing bandwidth more efficiently. The second presents basic concepts of performance and utilization monitoring. Network Monitor and the Performance console are introduced in this section. These two tools help you gather the statistics needed to make decisions about how and when to upgrade your WAN links.

The second part of this chapter concerns WAN technologies. The basics of these telecommunication services are presented so you can begin to make an informed decision about upgrading the infrastructure of your network. The basics of Plain Old Telephone Service (POTS), ISDN, T-carrier, ATM, and frame relay are covered in this section. At the end of this chapter, you will find a list of helpful sources on these and other telecommunication services.

Bandwidth and Usage Statistics

In this section, we will explore the features Microsoft has built into Windows 2000 for efficient bandwidth usage, including Multilink, Bandwidth Allocation Protocol (BAP), Bandwidth Allocation Control Protocol (BACP), and RAS Idle Disconnect. Tools and suggestions for gathering and analyzing traffic data for your network will also be covered. Use the data you collect to create a usage baseline and continue monitoring over time. Doing so will enable you to project future usage and budget for additional bandwidth. Another benefit is that you will be able to troubleshoot network problems more easily if you have an idea of what is typical network activity and what is not. We will begin with bandwidth features and move on to network analysis.

Windows 2000 Bandwidth Control Features

Windows 2000 supports several features to enable you to efficiently manage the bandwidth available to remote clients. The first feature we will examine is Multilink.

Multilink

Multilink protocol is defined in RFC 1990. It is used to bundle multiple physical links (PPP links) into one logical link. You might already be familiar with a common multilink connection: ISDN BRI, which uses Multilink to join two separate channels into a single logical channel (an explanation of BRI is found later in this chapter in the "ISDN" section). Windows 2000 remote access clients and remote access servers support Multilink, giving you the capability to use two or more lines as if they were a single line.

There are a couple of caveats to Multilink. The first is that it must be supported on both ends of the connection. The second has to do with Multilink used in conjunction with callback. Because only one number can be stored in a user account, Multilink functionality can be lost under most circumstances. If a remote client uses Multilink to dial a server that is configured to call that user back, only one phone number will be called back. Unless you are using dual-channel ISDN with the same phone number for both channels, Multilink can't be used successfully with callback. In this case, you will have to evaluate your security requirements and balance them with the need for additional bandwidth. If you are using remote access policies, Multilink usage must be enabled in the policy profile, as well.

Multilink is configured on a per server basis. To enable or disable Multilink:

1. In the Routing and Remote Access console, right-click the desired server, then click Properties.

2. Click the PPP tab, then put a check mark in the Multilink check box.

Bandwidth Allocation

BAP and BACP are used in conjunction with Multilink connections to dynamically add or drop links as needed. Both protocols are PPP Link Control Protocols (LCP). BAP monitors link usage to determine when to add or drop links. BACP handles peer priority determination in the event that multiple BAP requests are made simultaneously.

A BAP-enabled Windows 2000 RAS server can provide dial-up clients with additional remote access phone numbers when additional bandwidth is needed. When a dial-up client that has been configured to use BAP requests another connection, the RAS responds with a message containing the phone number of another modem. The benefit of using server-provided phone numbers is that dial-up clients only need to know one access number. If you add additional access numbers, you will not be required to reconfigure all the existing clients to take advantage of the new numbers.

BAP and BACP are configured on a per server basis. To enable or disable BAP/BAPC:

1. In the Routing and Remote Access console, right-click the desired server, then click Properties.

2. Click the PPP tab, then put a check mark in "Dynamic bandwidth control" using the BAP or BACP check box.

If you want to configure the remote access server to provide BAP-enabled clients with additional access numbers:

1. In the Routing and Remote Access console, right-click Ports for the desired server, then click Properties.

2. Select the appropriate remote access port and click Configure.

3. Input the phone number of the modem connected to this port in the "Phone number for this device" field.

4. Repeat this procedure for additional modem ports.

BAP client usage requirements are enforced using remote access policies. Through these policies you can set the maximum number of ports a user can dial, limit Multilink connections to BAP-enabled clients only, and set the point at which additional lines should be dropped (based on usage and the duration of connection). Complete details for configuring these policies are found in Chapter 2, "Remote Access Server."

RAS Idle Disconnect

This is another option that is dictated and enforced under a remote access policy. If you choose to do so, you can opt to have an unused RAS connection disconnected from your RAS server after a specified number of minutes have passed. This can free up connections for other users, as well as be part of your security program. If a user leaves his computer unattended while it is dialed in to your network, anyone who uses that computer has that user's access to the network. If you force a disconnect after 5–10 minutes of idle time, you narrow the window of opportunity for a would-be attacker. However, you should weigh the need for security against the needs of your users. It is inconvenient for remote users to be repeatedly disconnected. A window of 30 to 45 minutes of idle time should be adequate for most users.

WAN Analysis

Monitoring and analyzing your WAN traffic on a regular basis offers you the opportunity to manage your network proactively rather than reactively. If you are able to anticipate and plan for bandwidth needs in advance, you will maintain or increase user productivity. Further, by collecting and analyzing this information over time, you will be able to spot problem areas before they become bottlenecks. Finally, you can use this data to determine whether the network security you have in place is working. Tracking normal usage patterns can help determine if a particular increase in activity is a potential attack.

Windows 2000 Server provides two tools to assist you in collecting network usage statistics: Network Monitor and Performance Monitor. An overview of these tools is provided in this section. Before you can begin to collect data, you have to determine what you are looking for. We will begin with how, when, and where to monitor network performance and usage.

Best Practices

The best way to start any project is by gathering the requirements. To perform a valid analysis of the network, you need to determine what services, protocols, and communications methods (WAN, LAN, or dial-up) are in use on your network. Here are a few items that are commonly run over WAN links:

- **Services.**   File and printer sharing, faxing, HTTP and FTP hosting
- **Applications.**   Web browsing, email, database access, proprietary applications
- **Protocols.**   TCP/IP, IPX/SPX, SNA
- **Basic service traffic.**   User login, password changes, DHCP, WINS, replication
- **Management traffic.**   Remote administration, SNMP tools and messages

You also need to know when this traffic is expected to travel over the WAN link. Many of these services, such as Web and email hosting, require full-time connectivity. Other services add additional load only at certain times of the day, such as user logins between 8:00 and 9:00 a.m., or only once a week, such as weekly sales report updates.

To get a complete picture of usage, you will need to find out the answers to these questions:

- What is the total bandwidth?
- What are peak usage times?
- How much bandwidth is used during these peak times?
- What services are in use during these peak times?
- How many users/computers does this link support?
- How many users/computers can be supported before expansion is required?
- Do all services require constant connectivity?
- Could some services be relegated to dial-up service?
- Are there enough inbound lines to service remote access users?
- Do any applications require encryption? The additional overhead this imposes should be considered.

You might find that to balance costs with usage requirements you need to change the way some services use the WAN link. You might also find out that the WAN link you have in place is capable of handling the needs of users, provided you shuffle the times that non-essential services use the WAN link. Scheduling some services, such as WINS replication for off-peak times, or modifying the way you handle SNMP or remote administration can make a difference in the amount of bandwidth required at peak times. Installing a proxy server can also cut down on the total amount of bandwidth required for Web browsing.

As mentioned earlier in this section, data analysis should be an ongoing project, not just a one-time activity. Set up a regular schedule—perhaps every 30 to 60 days—to monitor the complete network. Collect data at various times of day. It is important to track the range of usage with varying loads and components in use. Compare the collected data to previous records to determine if any trends are beginning to manifest. Always take new usage surveys when new components, applications, or major configuration changes have taken place.

Plan Ahead

If you are planning a major rollout of software in the next year, don't forget to consider the requirements of the new software when the rollout is complete, as well as the bandwidth required to support any rollout tasks over WAN links. Any plans and changes you make should support the needs of users for a minimum of 18 months.

Network Monitor

Network Monitor is a packet-sniffing tool that can be used to capture packets directly from the network media. When captured, Network Monitor can filter, display, and save the captured frames. The version of Network Monitor that comes with Windows 2000 is very basic. It only monitors traffic to and from the local computer on which it is running. The version of Network Monitor that comes with Systems Management Server (SMS) is a fully functional packet analyzer. The SMS version requires that the network cards in the computer on which it is running can be placed in promiscuous mode (check with your manufacturer to determine whether yours can).

Even though Windows 2000 Network Monitor is a simple tool, you can still use it to trace data as it flows in and out of your network over a Windows 2000 router. Figure 10.1 shows the results of a packet capture.

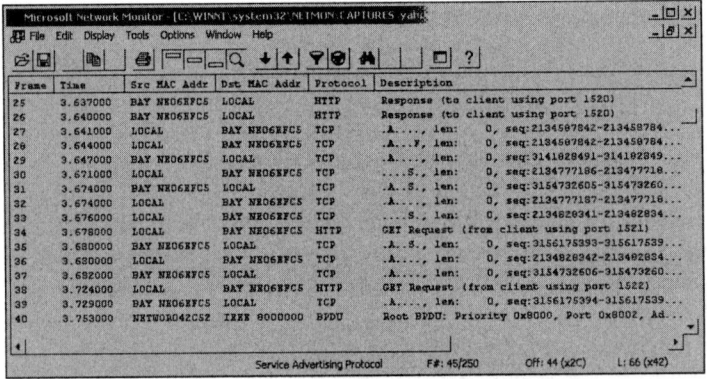

Figure 10.1   Results of a packet capture.

To run a capture on your Windows 2000 server:

1. Launch Network Monitor by clicking Start, Programs, Administrative Tools, Network Monitor. On a multihomed computer, you will be prompted to select which network you would like to monitor (simultaneous monitoring of multiple networks is not supported).

2. On the Capture menu, click Start. Captured frames will begin to appear in the Capture window.

3. To temporarily halt the data capture, select the Capture menu, then click Pause.

4. To stop the data capture, select the Capture menu, then click Stop.

5. To display the captured frames, select the Capture menu, then click Display Captured Data. The Frame Viewer window will appear.

Using the traffic statistics you collect with Network Monitor, you can determine the type, time, and amount of traffic passing through your router. You can save the capture files from monitoring sessions by going to the File menu, then selecting Save. Provide the name and storage location for the file. For more information about Network Monitor, refer to the online Help. (Running packet sniffers can have certain security implications. See Appendix A, "Technical Overview of RAS Communications," for more information.)

Performance Console

The Performance console can be used to gather specific performance and usage statistics from your Windows 2000 router and remote access server. The data you gather can be formatted as a report, log, or graph, or it can trigger an alert. Counters are used to specify what types of data will be captured. The counters that will be of most interest to you when checking WAN utilization are Network Segment and Network Interface. Run these counters under different loads and at different times of day to get a clear picture of the load on your Windows 2000 router or remote access server. After you have collected data, you can export it to a database for further analysis. Figure 10.2 shows a chart created in the Performance console.

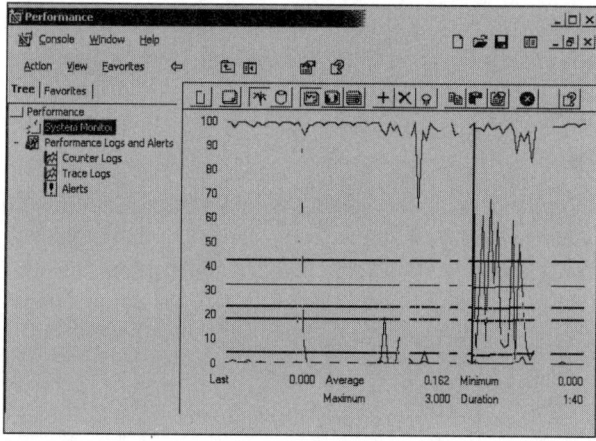

Figure 10.2 A Windows 2000 performance chart.

To run the Performance console:

1. Launch the console by clicking Start, Programs, Administrative Tools, Performance.

2. Double-click System Monitor in the left pane. The System Monitor window will appear in the right pane.

3. Click the + symbol in the toolbar of the System Monitor window. Select the counters you would like to add, then click Close. Statistics will immediately begin to display.

For more information about running the Performance console and the specific performance counters available, refer to the online Help.

Telecommunication Services

Being familiar with the technologies available will help you decide on the appropriate solution when it comes time to upgrade the WAN links in your network. Armed with the data you collect using the suggestions in the last few sections, you will be able to narrow down the list of possible WAN connectivity candidates to one or two choices that fit in your budget. However, different services are available in different areas, even when offered by the same provider, and available features can vary widely. That means selecting a telecommunication link isn't necessarily as easy as selecting a long distance provider. Knowing your requirements and sharing them with your provider can make the task a little easier.

In this section, we will cover five common WAN technologies:

- Plain Old Telephone Service (POTS)
- ISDN
- T-carrier
- ATM
- Frame relay

This chapter is not meant to be the definitive source for information on the listed technologies—whole books could be written on each of these topics! Rather, it offers an overview of each service and sources for more information on each technology. We will start with the most common service type: POTS, also known as analog dial-up.

POTS

Plain Old Telephone Service is the analog dial-up service used for basic voice and data service. It is also known as Public Switches Telephone Network (PSTN). This type of service is widely used for dial-up remote access or access to an ISP. POTS can transmit data between 52 and 56Kbps on two-wire analog copper cable, with send and receive functions sharing the same pair of wires. One or more PSTN lines can provide the right amount of bandwidth for smaller networks.

You might find that aggregating multiple dial-up lines with Multilink (see the "Multilink" section earlier in this chapter for more information) can provide a cost-effective alternative to leased high-speed lines. You might also discover that certain network services can be offloaded to dial-up lines to alleviate periodic congestion on high-capacity circuits. For example, the production department at your company might send status reports twice daily to a remote location. The time these reports are sent coincides with shift changes when several hundred users are logging on to the network over WAN links. Due to company business process policies, it is not possible to change the timing of the shift changes or the status report update. After examining the WAN traffic, you might determine that the best possible alternative is to use a dial-up line to transmit the status reports, freeing up bandwidth for users logging on to the network. For more information on POTS, consult `http://www.webopedia.com`.

ISDN

Integrated Services Digital Network (ISDN) is a high-speed, digital dial-up alternative to analog telephone service. The majority of the telephone networks in existence today are entirely digital except for what is called the "last mile." The last mile refers to the span of telephone cable that joins your home or office to the telephone company's central office or local exchange.

During the 1960s, telephone companies began to replace their analog equipment with digital equipment, but bringing digital service to the customer site was prohibitively expensive. ISDN was introduced in 1972 as a cost-effective solution for digitizing that last segment. ISDN offers speeds up to 128Kbps and can send voice, video, and data over existing copper telephone wiring.

ISDN uses logical groups of channels to transmit data from end to end in a circuit. There are two types of channels:

- **B-channel.**   This channel is used for sending a voice, video, or data payload. Also known as the bearer-channel, a single B-channel typically offers throughput of 64Kbps, but it is not uncommon to find telephone companies that offer 56Kbps or 65Kbps B-channel service.

- **D-channel.**   This channel is used for call setup and tear-down and other maintenance functions. By segregating this function to the D-channel, the B-channel bandwidth can be used exclusively for data transmission. The size of a D-channel is dependent on the number of B-channels it is supporting.

Grouping B-channels into specific configurations enables phone companies to offer standardized ISDN service. These groupings are called access interfaces. There are two main access interfaces: Basic Rate Interface (BRI) and Primary Rate Interface (PRI). BRI is best suited for use by small offices and home offices (SOHO), and PRI is suited for businesses that have higher bandwidth needs due to application or data requirements, such as the need to send large graphics files or real-time video over WAN links.

BRI uses two B-channels with a 16Kbps D-channel, and for this reason this access interface is often referred to as 2B+D. Assuming that 64Kbps B-channels are used, BRI offers a total of 144Kbps throughput. Keep in mind, however, that only 128Kbps is available for actual data transmission, as the D-channel is used for call maintenance. Some telephone companies only offer one B-channel as basic BRI service.

PRI uses 23 B-channels and one 64Kbps D-channel. This offers a total bandwidth of 1.536Mbps, of which 1.472Mbps is available for data transmission. This is very nearly equal to the 1.544Mbps throughput offered by T-1 service (T-carrier service is covered in the next section).

If you would like to learn more about ISDN, visit `http://www.iti.ch`. This is the Web site of the International Telecommunications Union, where you will be able to find the standards governing ISDN. For information about installing ISDN adapters in a computer running Windows 2000, see Chapter 3, "Dial-Up Networking."

T-Carriers

The term "T-carrier" refers to the category of high-speed digital telecommunication services that includes T-1, T-3, and Fractional T-1. All these point-to-point services rely on one or more 64Kbps channels to transmit voice, video, and data. These leased line services can deliver the following speeds:

- **Fractional T-1.**   Also known as DS-0, this service enables the customer to order the number of 64Kbps channels needed to fulfill bandwidth requirements.

- **T-1.**   Also known as DS-1, this service offers 1.544Mbps bandwidth.

- **T-3.**   This service offers huge amounts of bandwidth: 44.736Mbps! T-3 service is also called DS-3.

T-carrier services are sometimes referred to as private network services because leased line services are used to join two sites. The customer provides the equipment to forward traffic to the site at other end of the leased line. All this bandwidth is not cheap—If you find that your network traffic needs are more "bursty" (meaning that they do not occur at a steady rate), you might be paying for dedicated bandwidth you don't need. Fractional T-carrier provides a more budget-conscious choice for companies that need more bandwidth than dial-up service provides, but less than a full T-1 line. Fractional T-carrier service provides a portion of the bandwidth of a T-carrier line at a portion of the price. The next section covers packet-switched services, which might also be better for you and your budget. For more information on T-carrier services, see `http://www.t1.org`.

Packet-Switched Services

From here, we will move into the realm of packet-switched services and talk about ATM and frame relay. These services provide permanent (also known as "nailed-up") connections that are comparable to ISDN or T-carrier services. However, instead of point-to-point connections, virtual circuits are used. Multiple customers share the backbone area, which is also known as a cloud. Because of this shared service, the costs of packet-switched services are quite competitive with T-carrier-class circuits.

ATM

ATM is a high-speed network data transfer technology capable of transmitting data and real-time voice and video through both public and private networks. That means ATM is an attractive alternative for Windows 2000 LANs and WANs with high-bandwidth requirements. Windows 2000 supports the use of ATM adapters, bringing ATM right to the desktop. This section will highlight ATM's features, how it works, and its drawbacks. If you would like to learn more about ATM, go to `http://www.trillium.com` and `http://www.3com.com`. Both sites have several detailed whitepapers about the subject. If you would like more information on configuring Windows 2000 for ATM use, refer to the list of suggested reading at the end of this chapter.

ATM Features

ATM is a flexible, scalable, and reliable networking technology that can provide large amounts of bandwidth for your users. It can travel a kilometer without a problem, making it suitable for long runs between buildings in a campus area network or a metropolitan area network. ATM is also flexible in terms of what type of media it will travel over. It runs over single or multimode fiber cable or unshielded twisted pair (UTP) copper cable at the following speeds:

- 1.544Mbps to 25Mbps
- 155Mbps, also called OC3
- 622Mbps, also called OC12
- 2.488Gbps, also called OC48

Another ATM feature is quality of service (QOS). QOS enables you to fine-tune network response for applications, such as real-time video, that do not tolerate delays in transmission well. You can also set up switched virtual circuits (SVCs) or permanent virtual circuits (PVCs) with fixed endpoints. ATM works in ethernet and token ring networks as well, which is made possible by LAN emulation (LANE).

How ATM Works

ATM uses fixed-length cells to transmit data over one or more full-duplex (bidirectional) connections. Each cell contains a 48-byte data payload and a 5-byte header. An ATM connection is called a virtual channel. This channel (or path) from source to destination is determined before the packet is sent. Routing information for the path, called the Virtual Path Identifier/Virtual Channel Identifier (VPI/VCI), is included in the header of each ATM cell. Each header also contains congestion and error checking information. Cells transmitted on the same virtual channel are sent in sequence and should arrive that way, too. This provides a level of error correction by ensuring that all packets are received. If packet number two is received before packet number one, it is assumed packet one is lost.

ATM cells are forwarded by switches. The switch's equivalent of an interface is called a port. When an ATM switch receives a cell, it reads the header and determines the port over which it should be sent. Latency at junctures between networks due to routing table analysis is therefore, eliminated.

ATM provides several service choices, including:

- **Constant Bit Rate (CBR).**   Guarantees a fixed bit rate; data is sent in a steady stream.

- **Variable Bit Rate (VBR).**   Guarantees a specific throughput over time; data is not guaranteed to be sent at an even speed.

- **Unspecified Bit Rate (UBR).**   Throughput is not guaranteed.

- **Available Bit Rate (ABR).**   Guarantees minimum throughput, but data is sent at higher capacities when bandwidth is available (also known as bursting).

ATM Drawbacks

ATM is not available in all areas, and it can be quite expensive where it is available. Although ATM is governed by industry standards, several standards exist. Hardware vendors might support different versions of LANE—one might support only LANE v1, another might support only LANE v2, and another might support both. Service providers might offer features that are not supported by your ATM-based LAN, and your LAN might offer features that are not supported by your WAN ATM provider. This can make it difficult to integrate your network seamlessly into the network of your provider. Consult the manufacturer for complete information about your hardware when attempting to integrate your LAN with a WAN. Make sure your service provider is familiar with your equipment and needs, and can provide acceptable levels of support and service based on your requirements.

Frame Relay

Frame relay service gives you speeds of 56Kbps, 1.544Mbps, and 45Mbps without the cost associated with leasing a dedicated high-speed line, such as a T-1 or T-3. Frame relay uses virtual circuits through the cloud of existing T-1 and T-3 lines owned by the telephone service provider. Virtual circuits to an endpoint do not take a dedicated route, but instead are routed through the cloud over available links. Many users can send data over logical point-to-point circuits and share the cost of the cloud area. The way frame relay allocates bandwidth enables this.

Frame relay leverages the bursty nature of data transmissions to offer bandwidth on demand. Data is transmitted in spurts, which means there are silences between transmissions. These silences occur between packets when the interface is waiting for an opportunity to put data on the cable. Bandwidth in a dedicated link—such as a T-1—is allocated for the duration of the connection whether data is being sent or not, and goes unused during these silences. Frame relay uses logical circuits rather than physical circuits, and is able to dynamically allocate bandwidth from unused circuits as needed, on a packet-by-packet basis, rather than when the connection is established. In other words, bandwidth is not allocated until data is actually sent, preventing the allocation of bandwidth to silence. This is known as statistical multiplexing.

Occasionally, bandwidth demand can exceed the amount of available bandwidth. Switches along the path to the destination can store the data to be transmitted when the bandwidth becomes available. Additionally, frame relay has no error-recovery functions, reducing latency caused by checking for errors in transit. The source and destination devices are responsible for ensuring that data is received error-free.

For more information about frame relay, including industry standards, refer to `http://www.motorola.com/networking/frame-relay/`. You will find numerous whitepapers and technical analyses of the technology at this site.

References

Many telephone companies also provide data about their services on their Web sites. Check out your local telephone company's Web site for details about the services they offer in your area.

Another useful site is the MIT Internet & Telecoms Convergence Consortium (ITC). It is made up of corporations and academics working together to research issues related to the Internet and telecommunication. You will find numerous whitepapers on various aspects of the two subject areas covered by the group at `http://itel.mit.edu`.

In addition to the Web sites mentioned previously, the following two resources offer useful information:

Lewis, Chris. *Wide Area Systems & Services: What's Cooking With T1 Bandwidth?* Manhasset, New York: CMP Media Inc., 1997.

Weeks, Andy. *Network Infrastructure: Moving to Gigabit Ethernet and ATM.* First published in TechRepublic's Windows NT Enterprise Strategies, and now found on the Microsoft TechNet Technical Information CD.

11

Shared Internet Connectivity

Providing access to the Internet is an important function of most networks. Up to now, this book has examined dial-up and routed network connectivity options. This chapter focuses on connecting your network to the Internet using Windows 2000. The chapter presents two options for multiple users sharing a single connection point to the Internet: Network Address Translation (NAT) and Internet Connection Sharing (ICS). Both connectivity methods work by allowing multiple users on a private network to reach the Internet through a single access point with a single public IP address (although it is possible to use multiple public addresses), as shown in Figure 11.1.

These two methods differ in the amount of flexibility of configuration. Their workings, differences, and configurations are discussed in the following sections.

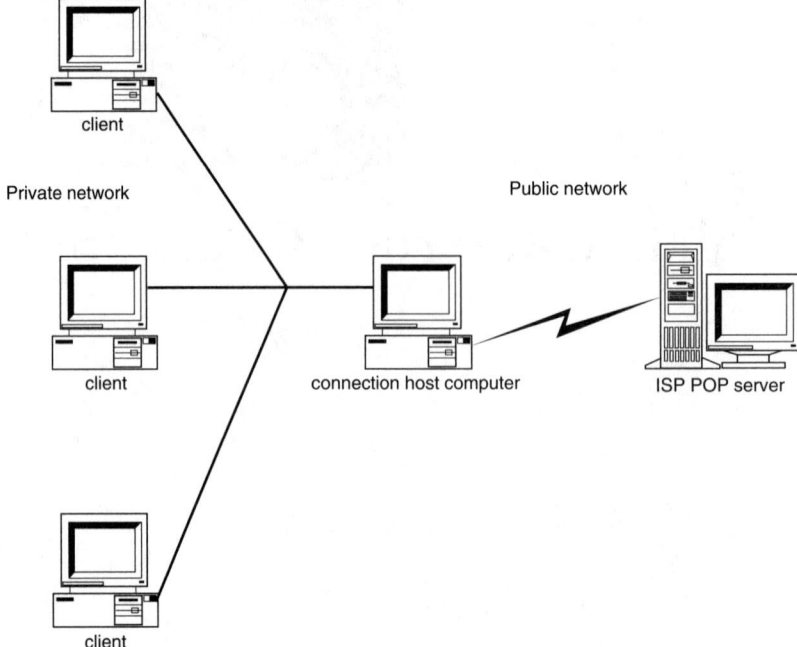

Figure 11.1   A shared Internet connection.

Network Address Translation Protocol

If you have a small home or office network (also called a SOHO network) that you would like to connect to the Internet, the Network Address Translation protocol (NAT) might be an option for you. NAT enables you to use a private IP address scheme for your internal network and a public IP address scheme for the interface that connects to the Internet. As you might recall from Chapter 4, "Routing Protocols," NAT essentially proxies connection requests between internal and external networks by translating private IP addresses to public IP addresses and vice versa. It tracks source and destination IP addresses by mapping these addresses to TCP/UDP port numbers. Because of the way NAT performs IP address assignment, it also eases the administrative tasks of client TCP/IP configuration.

NAT can be divided into three independently configurable functions that are essential for address translation to happen properly:

- Translation
- Addressing
- Name resolution

This section covers these functions, as well as instructions for configuring NAT on the client and server, with special emphasis placed on the addressing component.

Translation Component

The function of the translation component is mapping private internal addresses to public external addresses. It converts an IP address to a valid address appropriate for the internal or external network and edits the IP header information to reflect this. As mentioned earlier, Chapter 4 contains information on translation in a section called "Network Address Translation (NAT)." For more information on the translation component, refer to that chapter. A computer running NAT has an interface on the internal network and an interface on the Internet.

Addressing Component

NAT can act as a basic DHCP server for the other computers on its internal network interface. The same TCP/IP configuration information supplied by a standard DHCP server is also provided by NAT. Specifically, this includes:

- **An IP address.** A private address in the 192.168.0.0 range (the default)
- **A subnet mask.** 255.255.255.0 (the default)
- **A default gateway.** The IP address of the internal network interface on the NAT computer
- **WINS and/or DNS servers.** The IP address of the internal network interface on the NAT computer (the next section covers the way name resolution works with NAT)

Private Addresses

One of the benefits of NAT is that it helps alleviate the dearth of IP addresses. IP addresses come in two types: public and private. Public addresses are unique IP addresses that can be used on the Internet. Private addresses are ranges of IP addresses reserved by InterNIC for use on networks that are not connected to the Internet (see Chapter 4 for a list of private address ranges). The NAT computer assigns private addresses to the clients on the internal network. Because these addresses cannot be used on or receive traffic from the Internet, the NAT translation component must convert private and public addresses.

NAT can be configured to dynamically assign the following private networks:

- **Class A.** 10.0.0.0 with a subnet mask of 255.0.0.0.
- **Class B.** You have two choices for a private class B address. The first is the Microsoft-reserved private network ID of 169.254.0.0 with a subnet mask of 255.255.0.0 The second choice is 172.16.0.0 with a subnet mask of 255.240.0.0.
- **Class C.** 192.168.0.0 with a subnet mask of 255.255.255.0.

You also can specify exclusions for private network addresses that are already in use on your network.

Public Addresses

Your ISP must assign the NAT computer's Internet interface one or more public IP addresses. A single public address is the default for Windows 2000 NAT, but you can configure additional addresses as needed. If the range of addresses can be used with a single subnet mask, you can express this range as a single IP address (the starting address) and the appropriate subnet mask for the range. Otherwise, you can express the range or ranges by the starting and stopping addresses for each range.

Name Resolution Component

The NAT computer also can be configured to provide name resolution services for the internal network clients. It does this by assigning the IP address of the internal NAT interface to clients as the WINS and/or DNS server for that network. The NAT computer is not actually configured as a WINS or DNS server for the internal network. Instead, it forwards the name resolution request to the WINS and DNS servers the NAT computer is configured to use for its own name resolution needs. The name server to which NAT forwards name resolution requests must be on the Internet interface network. In addition to providing name server IP addresses, NAT assigns the M-node NetBIOS type to its clients. This means clients use the following services in the order listed to resolve names:

1. Local cache
2. Broadcast
3. WINS
4. LMHOSTS
5. HOSTS
6. DNS

Issues and Considerations

NAT is not intended as a general replacement for a routed connection to the Internet. Instead, it is provided as a tool that can be used by SOHO administrators to connect their networks to the Internet without requiring extensive knowledge of routing or IP addressing schemes. When deciding to implement NAT, however, there are still a few things to keep in mind:

- **DHCP.**   Because NAT provides addressing components, you cannot use NAT on a private network where DHCP is already in use. There is no way for DHCP clients to differentiate between NAT and a standard DHCP server. The same goes for the DHCP relay agent. It can't be used on the private network where NAT is assigning addresses because it is possible it will forward DHCP traffic to a DHCP server on another network.

- **WINS and DNS.** If you enable name resolution services for NAT, you cannot run a WINS or DNS server on the same private network as NAT.

- **Inbound connections.** Connections initiated from within the private network are automatically able to receive traffic from the Internet host they have contacted. If Internet users must be able to access resources within the private network, however, you must configure NAT with a static mapping that permits this (specific how to lists are covered in the upcoming "Configuring NAT" section).

- **Application configuration.** If you want to run applications over the Internet, you must configure NAT to use these applications. Be aware that not all applications function properly when run with NAT.

- **NAT editors.** Not all protocol packets will be translated properly by NAT. Specifically, any packet that contains source or destination address data in the data payload or that does not use a TCP or UDP header will require extra assistance to be properly translated. This assistance comes in the form of NAT editors, which can scour the entire packet for information required for successful translation and delivery. Windows 2000 includes NAT editors for FTP, ICMP, and PPTP, but you might need editors for other services, such as SNMP or LDAP. Keep in mind, too, that not every protocol is translatable. IPSec is one such protocol. H.323 is another, which means you can't use NetMeeting over a translated connection.

- **VPN connections.** PPTP VPN connections can be used with NAT, but as stated previously, IPSec does not work with NAT. Clients behind a NAT, therefore, will not be able to use L2TP over IPSec VPNs.

Configuring NAT

To set up NAT in your network, you must set up both client computers and the Windows 2000 router acting as a NAT. The instructions in this section walk you through the whole process. Let's start with the server.

Following these instructions will help you successfully set up the computer that provides network address translation services for your network.

1. Install and configure the network card that interfaces with the internal network. This card needs to be configured for TCP/IP as follows:

    IP address—This must match the range of private IP addresses you plan to use in your network. Assuming that you plan to use the default NAT address scheme, you would select an address from the 192.168.0.0 range. Using the first address of a range of addresses for the NAT computer is common practice. For instance, if you use the default range of addresses, you would use 192.168.0.1 for the NAT computer.

Subnet mask—This must be appropriate for the network address range you have selected for your internal network. If you plan to use the default range, this would be 255.255.255.0.

Default gateway—Leave this blank.

2. Enable the Routing and Remote Access Service. Click Start, then Programs, then Administrative Tools. Right-click the appropriate server, then click Configure and Enable Routing and Remote Access. Complete the Routing and Remote Access Wizard. Start the service when prompted to do so.

3. If you are not using a dial-up connection to the Internet, skip to step 4. If you are using a dial-up connection, follow these instructions:

   Install and configure your modem. (See Chapter 3, "Dial-Up Networking," if you need assistance with this step.)

   After the modem is configured, enable routing over the port(s) in that device. In the Routing and Remote Access console, select the appropriate server, then right-click Ports. Select Properties from the context menu that appears. The Ports Properties sheet appears, as shown in Figure 11.2.

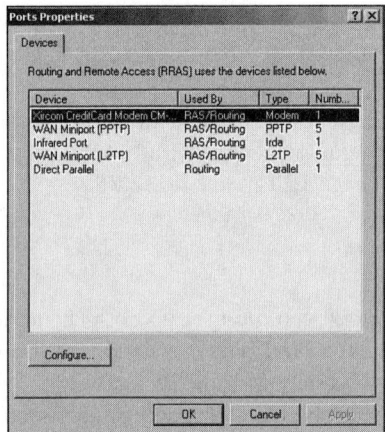

Figure 11.2 The Ports Properties sheet displays the devices available to the Routing and Remote Access Service.

Select the appropriate device, then click the Configure button. The Configure Device dialog box appears.

Put a check in the "Demand-dial routing connections (inbound and out-bound)" check box. Click OK to close this dialog box, then click OK to close the Ports Properties sheet dialog box.

Create a demand-dial interface that connects the NAT computer to your Internet service provider. In the Routing and Remote Access console, click the appropriate server. Right-click Routing Interfaces and select New Demand-dial Interface from the context menu that appears.

The Demand Dial Wizard starts. Provide the information that is requested in the Wizard. (You can find more information on demand-dial routing in Chapter 4 and in Chapter 5, "Configuring the Windows 2000 Router." Each chapter has a section devoted to that topic.)

4. If you are using a permanent connection to the Internet, you must install and configure the interface that attaches the NAT computer to the Internet. (If you use a dial-up connection, you can skip this and proceed to step 5, configuring a default static route.) This interface could be an ISDN adapter, a network card, or other device. It must be configured with the appropriate TCP/IP information for the network to which it is joined. Your ISP will supply this data.

5. Regardless of what type of connection you have to the Internet—demand-dial or permanent—you must configure a default static route that uses the Internet interface. To do this:

    In the Routing and Remote Access console, select the appropriate server, then double-click IP Routing. Right-click Static Routes and select New Static route from the context menu. The Static Route dialog box appears, as shown in Figure 11.3.

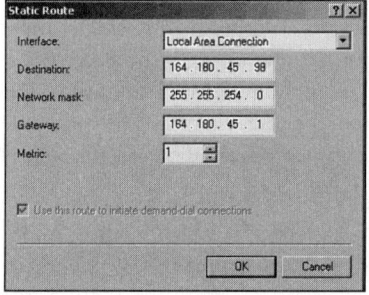

Figure 11.3 The Static Route dialog box.

Select the appropriate interface from the Interface list box.

Enter `0.0.0.0` in the Destination field.

Enter `0.0.0.0` in the Network mask field.

The type of interface determines what you enter for Gateway. If the interface is a permanent connection, enter the IP address of the Internet interface for the device selected. If you are using a demand-dial interface, however, do not enter a gateway address. Instead, put a check in the "Use this route to initiate demand-dial connections" check box. This option is only available if you have selected a demand-dial interface in the Interface list box.

Enter 1 as the Metric for this route.

6. You have now completed the "prep work" involved in configuring network address translation. At this point you actually start working with NAT-specific configuration issues. The first thing to do is add network address translation to the Routing and Remote Access Service. To do so, double-click the appropriate server in the Routing and Remote Access console, then double-click IP Routing. Right-click General and select New Routing Protocol from the context menu. The New Routing Protocol dialog box appears. Select Connection Sharing (NAT) and click OK.

7. Add and configure the Internet interface:

   Right-click Network Address Translation (under IP Routing in the RRAS console) and select New Interface. Select the appropriate Internet interface from the list presented. The interface properties sheet appears.

   Put a check in the "Public interface connected to the Internet" check box. If you are using only one public IP address on this interface, put a check in the "Translate TCP/UDP headers" check box.

   Click the Address Pool tab and click the Add button to add the range of IP addresses and the associated subnet mask your ISP has assigned you. If you are using a single address, enter it as both the Start and End address. If you specified an entire range of IP addresses, but one or more of those addresses are already in use by other devices, click the Reservations button. Enter the public IP address and the private network address of the device that is assigned this reserved address. If the device must be reachable from the Internet, place a check in the "Allow incoming sessions to this address" check box.

   Click the Special Ports tab. If you have any special mappings for specific port traffic received by your interface or for a specific IP address, enter that information here.

8. Now you add the internal interface. (Note: The order in which the interfaces are added does not matter—just be sure you add both!) Right-click Network Address Translation (under IP Routing in the RRAS console) and select New Interface. Select the appropriate internal interface from the list presented. The interface properties sheet appears. Specify that this is a "Private interface on a private network" by checking the appropriate box.

9. To configure NAT, right-click Network Address Translation and select Properties. The NAT Properties sheet appears. This sheet contains four tabs:

   General—Various levels of logging are available. Logging can assist with troubleshooting NAT problems, but logging too much information can cause a decrease in performance on your NAT computer. It is recommended you log the maximum amount of information until you have NAT running properly, and then switch to Log errors only.

Translation—On this tab, you can vary the timeout for TCP and UDP mappings. The default time a TCP mapping remains in the translation table is 24 hours, although the default UDP timeout is 1 minute. You also set parameters for applications that must be run over the Internet. To do so, click the Applications button. Provide the following information requested in the shared access application dialog box, shown in Figure 11.4:

Name of application—Enter the name of the application. This can be a friendly name.

Remote server port number—Enter the port number of the computer on which the application resides. Also specify whether the port is TCP or UDP.

Incoming response ports—Enter the TCP or UDP ports on your internal network to which the remote application must connect.

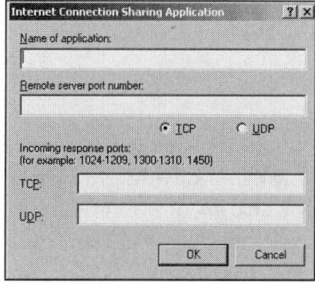

Figure 11.4   Configuring remote application access.

Address assignment—Check the "Automatically assign addresses by using DHCP" check box. If you want to use a different network address, specify that in the IP address and Mask fields. You also can specify any exclusions for addresses that have been assigned to devices already on the network (such as those assigned to database servers).

Name resolution—To enable name resolution using WINS and DNS, put a check in the appropriate box on this tab. If you are using a demand-dial interface, you can specify that a client request for DNS name resolution will begin the demand-dial process.

Name Resolution and Applications

Not all applications run successfully over a demand-dial interface.

With a demand-dial interface, there can be a lengthy delay between the time a name resolution request is issued by a client and the time the name is resolved. It is possible that applications initiating a request for name resolution independently of the operating system can time out while waiting for the connection to be dialed. This can result in the application returning a "remote host not found" type of message or simply failing to run as designed.

Configuring the client end of NAT is a breeze: All you have to do is configure your Windows 2000, Windows NT, Windows 98, and Windows 95 computers as DHCP clients. Because DHCP is the default for these operating systems, you might not even have to do that!

Internet Connection Sharing

Internet Connection Sharing (ICS) is the second network address translation service offered with Windows 2000 and Windows 98. In fact, it is a simplified version of NAT—it works the same way, but it does not allow any configuration changes as NAT does. ICS is a feature of dial-up networking and is ideal for use in very simple small office or home office networks. It is a quick and easy way to set up a small TCP/IP network with dynamically allocated IP addresses and name resolution services. ICS also enables you to create a single Internet gateway through the Windows 2000 computer running the connection-sharing service.

ICS Configuration

ICS can be configured on a network, dial-up, or VPN connection at the time the connection is created or after the fact by modifying the connection's properties.

To enable Internet connection sharing at the time the connection is created, click Start, then Settings, then Network and Dial-up Connections, then Make New Connection. The Network Connection Wizard appears. You are prompted to specify whether you want to share this connection. Simply click the box to indicate that you want to do so. If you want this connection to be dialed on demand, click that box too, as shown in Figure 11.5.

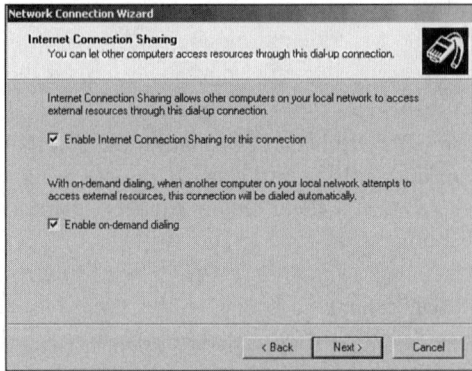

Figure 11.5   Enabling connection sharing and demand
dialing through the Network Connection Wizard.

To enable connection sharing on an existing connection, open the Network and Dial-up Connections folder. Right-click the desired connection and select Properties. Click the Internet Connection Sharing tab and check the box to "Enable Internet Connection Sharing for this connection," as shown in Figure 11.6. Enable on-demand dialing as well, if desired.

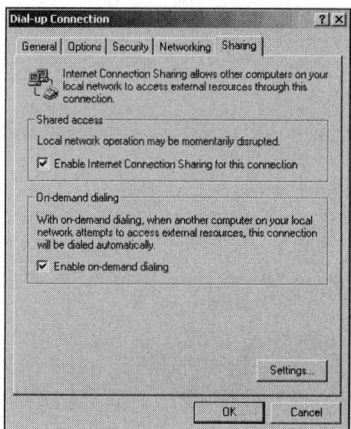

Figure 11.6   Enabling connection sharing and demand dialing through the connections properties sheet.

Applications and services that run over a shared connection might need to be tweaked for use over ICS. To do so, click the Settings button on the Internet Connection Sharing tab of the connection properties sheet (shown in Figure 11.6). The Internet Connection Sharing Settings dialog box appears. Click the Applications tab, then click the Add button. Provide the following information for each application you want to configure to run over ICS:

- **Name of application.**   Enter the name of the application. This can be a friendly name.

- **Remote server port number.**   Enter the port number of the computer on which the application resides. Also specify whether the port is TCP or UDP.

- **Incoming response ports.**   Enter the TCP or UDP ports on your internal network to which the remote application must connect.

To provide a specific user service that will run over this connection, click the Services tab. Provide the following information for each service you want to configure to run over ICS:

- **Name of service.**   Enter the name of the service. This can be a friendly name.

- **Service port number.**   Enter the port number of the computer on which the service resides. Also specify whether the port is TCP or UDP.

- **Name or address of server computer on private network.**   Enter the name or TCP/IP address of the computer on your internal network where the service resides.

ICS Considerations

Internet Connection Sharing is not configurable beyond simply enabling or disabling its use and setting up applications and services to run over the connection. Although this makes for an easy job for the administrator, it might make ICS unusable in your network. It is important to be aware of how it assigns addressing and performs name resolution functions, as well as its potential impact on the current networking services on your network. Keep the following things in mind when you are considering using ICS in your network:

- The range of IP addresses assigned to the internal network cannot be changed. It always uses the 192.168.0.0 network and a subnet mask of 255.255.255.0.

- If any devices on the network require a static IP address, you should use NAT instead, which enables you to reserve specific private IP addresses.

- The internal interface of the computer configured for ICS is automatically set to 192.168.0.1. This setting overwrites whatever static IP address had been assigned to this device previously. This means that any TCP/IP connections between this computer and any other device on the internal network will be broken when you enable ICS and must be subsequently re-established.

- You can't specify more than one public IP address for use on the Internet interface. If you want to use multiple public IP addresses, you should use NAT instead.

- The ICS computer intercepts all requests for name resolution and forwards them to a DNS server on the Internet. You cannot disable this feature.

Basically, you can sum up the preceding caveats with a simple rule of thumb: If all you need to do is give Internet access to three or four computers in a very simple SOHO network over a single gateway, you can use ICS. ICS is still bound by the same restrictions as NAT, however. Not all applications or protocols can be translated, including IPSec and H.323 (that is, you can't use L2TP over IPSec VPNs or NetMeeting with ICS).

References

For more information about private IP addressing, see RFC 1597, "Address Allocation for Private Internets."

For more information about the Network Address Translation protocol, see RFC 1631, "The IP Network Address Translator."

For more information about the Dynamic Host Configuration protocol, see RFC 2131, "Dynamic Host Configuration Protocol."

12

Network Design

THERE ARE MANY WAYS TO CONNECT PRIVATE networks to each other and to the Internet. When implementing Routing and Remote Access Service in your network architecture, you'll need to take into consideration what type of connectivity you will have, the network infrastructure in place and what you might be adding, and what intranet and Internet resources must be available to your users. This chapter will build on the information that has been presented thus far on the routing, remote access, and dial-up networking components of Windows 2000. Note that this chapter focuses on the implementation of the Routing and Remote Access Service, not on the how and why of name resolution or the Active Directory, both of which can impact the final architecture selection. For the purposes of this discussion, the placement and configuration of those services has already been determined.

You will find several example networks in this chapter. Each scenario describes the Routing and Remote Access Service framework for a variety of network sizes and configurations. Table 12.1 displays a rule-of-thumb sizing guide for networks.

Table 12.1   **Sizing Guide for Networks**

SOHO Network	Medium-sized Network	Large Network
2 to 15 workstations	16 to 100 workstations	More than 100 workstations
1 server	2 servers	3 or more servers
1 site	2 sites	3 or more sites
1 network segment	2 network segments	3 or more network segments

Generally, a network is considered a particular size if it meets at least two of the qualifications for that size.

From the information in this chapter, you should be able to create a custom solution to meet your connectivity requirements. The chapter is structured based on sizing, as shown in the preceding table. We'll start with the Small Office/Home Office (SOHO) network, then work our way up through medium-sized and large networks.

Small Office/Home Office Networks

Smaller networks are generally uncomplicated by nature and are probably the easiest to design and configure. When planning a small network, however, you always want to take into consideration possible future growth and be sure that the plans you make do not preclude such growth. The following example shows the current configuration of a very small network and presents options for its upgrade and growth to a slightly larger, slightly more complex network.

Current Configuration

The fictional Shady Grove Animal Clinic is a small veterinary office that has not changed much about its computers or network since they were installed. The network is very simple: There are five workstations running Windows 95 and one server running Windows NT 4. NetBEUI is the LAN protocol for this 10BaseT LAN. Internet access is available only on the workstation in the office manager's office, through a dial-up account to a national ISP. The clinic uses Noah's Ark, a software package for veterinary offices that provides electronic storage of patient medical information, accounting and billing, and inventory of supplies and equipment. The owner, Dr. Smith, has decided it's time to upgrade the infrastructure and has made up the following wish list:

- **Three additional workstations.**   Dr. Smith has expanded the staff at the clinic and needs the additional workstations.
- **Internet access from every computer.**   There are quite a few reasons why everyone at the clinic needs to have Internet access. However, a dial-up account for everyone in the office is not practical. A faster connection, such as ISDN (integrated services digital network), is desired.

- **Faster network speeds.** The 10BaseT network has served well, but adding additional computers and Internet access from every desktop will make the additional bandwidth a welcome addition. Because category 5 unshielded twisted pair cable was originally planted in the office, this upgrade will only require new network interface cards (NICs) in the workstations, plus a server and a new hub/switch.

- **Easy to configure and maintain.** Because the staff at the clinic will be responsible for maintaining the new network after it is in place, it should be as easy to support as possible.

Because this is an opportune time to do so, Dr. Smith has also decided that the server must be upgraded from Windows NT 4 to Windows 2000 Server. With Windows 2000 Server, there are two options that can meet the requirements Dr. Smith has set forth in his wish list. One involves a translated connection to the Internet, and the other involves a routed connection to the Internet. Both options, however, will require that new 100Mbps or 10/100Mbps cards are installed in all computers, all cabling is in place, and the high-speed link to the Internet has been installed.

Option One: Translated Connection

A translated connection will provide two important services for the users at the clinic. In addition to providing the users with access to the Internet, it will also handle client IP addressing by giving each client a private IP address, a subnet mask, and a default gateway. The default private network address range is 192.168.0.0, with a subnet mask of 255.255.255.0. The internal network interface of the Network Address Translation (NAT) server is assigned the private IP address of 192.168.0.1, with no default gateway. (A static default route over the Internet interface is used instead.) The NAT server is also configured to provide name resolution services. Figure 12.1 shows the network as it would be deployed using NAT.

It is also possible to use Internet Connection Sharing (ICS) successfully in this scenario. (For specific information on the configuration of NAT or ICS, see Chapter 11, "Shared Internet Connectivity.") The drawback to using a translated connection is that not all types of application traffic will pass through the NAT computer successfully. The elimination of the need to configure public IP addresses, however, can outweigh the need for guaranteed passage for all application types into and out of the network.

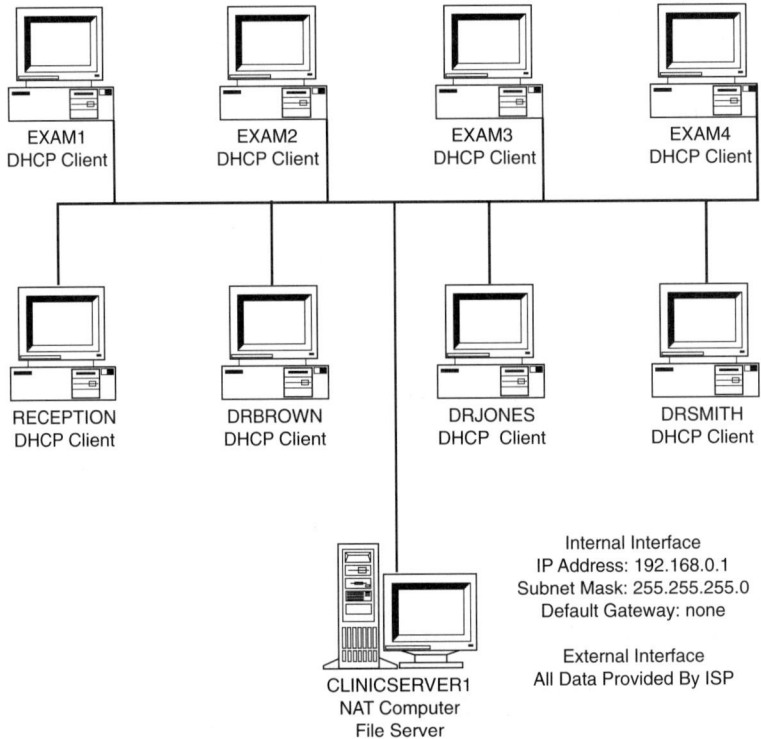

Figure 12.1 A small network using NAT.

Option Two: Routed Connection

A routed Internet connection offers the users at the clinic the capability to use all types of applications over the Internet connection, including NetMeeting. However, it requires the use of public IP addresses on all computers in the network. Toward this end, a DHCP server can be set up, or static IP addresses can be assigned manually. Because the network is small—only nine computers—and has trained administrator onsite, a DHCP server might prove easier than manually assigning static IP addresses in the long run.

For this example, we will assume that the server has been configured with the Routing and Remote Access Service, and all computers have been assigned public IP addresses from the x.x.x.x range, as shown in Figure 12.2. The workstations use the IP address of the server, which acts as a router. The server itself is not configured with a default gateway, but with a default static route over the Internet interface instead, just as with the translated connection.

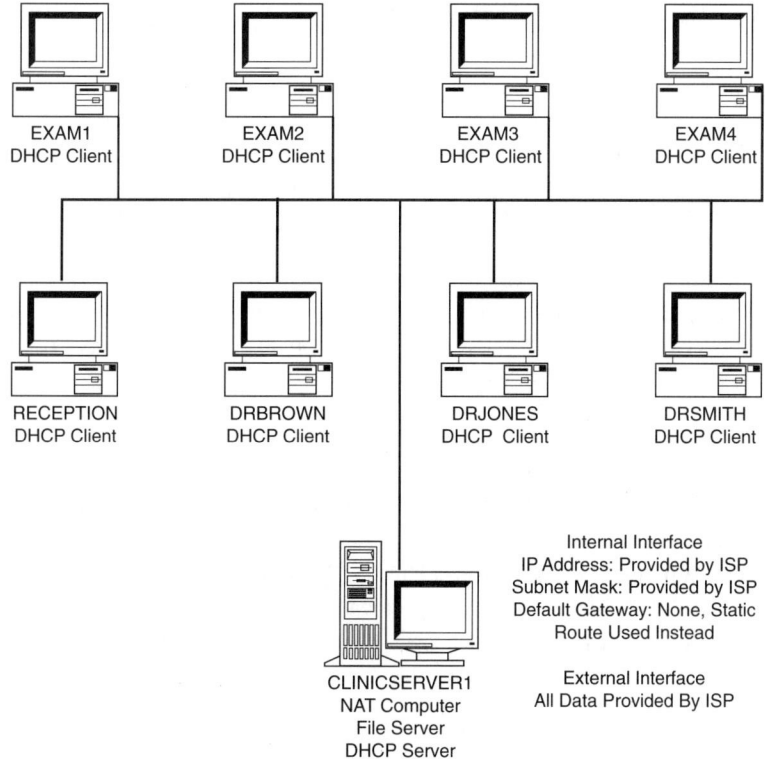

Figure 12.2 A small network using a routed Internet connection.

Both the translated connection option and the routed connection will allow for continued growth and expansion of the network. If the routed connection is used and the network grows beyond the number of IP addresses that it has been assigned by the ISP, a possible solution is to expand by adding a second subnet and a router between the two networks.

Medium-sized Networks

The medium-sized network requires more thought and planning than the SOHO network. The medium-sized network typically joins two network segments that might be located in two different locations. The two networks might be joined over a single backbone or, in the case of two separate locations, over leased lines. The leased lines can be dedicated routed connections, demand-dial connections, or VPN-based connections. The medium-sized network can also require remote access for mobile users through dial-up or VPN connections. This section will look at one possible option for using Routing and Remote Access Service in a medium-sized network.

Overview of Current Infrastructure

The Alexandrian Imports Company specializes in importing antiques from around the world. The corporate offices and showroom are located downtown, and the company's warehouse is located across town. Currently, the company has a single network at each location with no connectivity between the sites. Alexandrian Imports also employs eight agents who travel to various locations to examine and purchase antiques from estate sales and private antique collections. Several users at the warehouse and the corporate offices have dial-up Internet access, as do the traveling agents. These users communicate and send files to each other by email.

The board of directors has decided to upgrade the infrastructure to provide connectivity between sites. This will facilitate the use of an application that tracks the inventory, shipping, buying, and selling of the company's merchandise. This application will also allow the remote users to access inventory information and make purchasing decisions based on the current inventory levels of products.

The two administrators employed by Alexandrian Imports surveyed each site. Their observation revealed the following information about the warehouse network:

- **Type and number of hosts.**   Two servers providing file and print services running Windows NT 4 Server and 15 client workstations running a mix of Windows NT 4 Workstation and Windows 98.

- **LAN protocols in use.**   Internetwork Packet Exchange (IPX)/Sequenced Packet Exchange (SPX) is used on this network.

- **Internet access.**   Two users have dial-up Internet access.

A survey of the corporate network uncovered the following information:

- **Type and number of hosts.**   One server running Windows NT 4 Server and 11 client workstations running a mix of Windows NT 4 Workstation and Windows 98.

- **LAN protocols in use.**   Internetwork Packet Exchange (IPX)/Sequenced Packet Exchange (SPX).

- **Internet access.**   Two users have dial-up Internet access.

The remote users are currently using laptops running Windows 98. The users access the Internet through a national ISP with local numbers in most areas. If an agent needs access in an area that has no local number, the ISP provides an 800-number for an additional per minute charge.

RRAS Deployment Options

The board of directors has decided they would like to link both sites over a cost-effective high-speed link, while providing secure remote access for the agents in the field. They also want to provide Internet access for all employees. The company's administrators came up with the following plan to fulfill the requirements set forth by the board of directors.

The administrators decided to implement a demand-dial link to route traffic between sites and a dedicated link to the Internet from each site. The administrators decided to use a faster link for the ISP connection and a less expensive digital line between sites. Because keeping costs down was a priority for this implementation, and because the ISP provides numerous local access numbers, the administrators decided against maintaining a bank of modems for remote access by the field agents. The cost of the long distance calls to the RAS server would be greater than the cost of an occasional 800-number call to the ISP. As a result, the remote users will be given VPN access (using PPTP) to the network over the existing ISP. Connection Manager Administration Kit was used to create the dial-up networking service profiles used by the remote users.

Before the telecommunications infrastructure was put in place, the administrators upgraded the servers at each site to Windows 2000 Server and implemented TCP/IP as the primary LAN protocol. IPX/SPX was originally implemented because of its ease of configuration and because previous upgrade plans had included a Novell server. The Novell server was never implemented, so it was decided to scrap IPX/SPX in favor of TCP/IP. All servers and clients were configured with IP addresses provided by the ISP. A DHCP server was set up at one site and a DHCP relay agent was set up at the other site. This configuration was fully tested (and previously existing mapped drives were remapped). The ISP's domain name system (DNS) server provides name resolution for both sites. Figure 12.3 shows the architecture of this network after the plan has been implemented.

For specific details on implementing demand-dial routing, see Chapter 4, "Routing Protocols," and Chapter 5, "Configuring the Windows 2000 Router." There is a demand-dial section in each of those chapters. For more information on VPNs, see Chapter 7, "Virtual Private Networking." Finally, see Chapter 8, "Windows 2000 Connection Services," for more information about using the Connection Manager Administration Kit.

In the real world, the option selected by the board and the administrators would depend on several variables, such as the actual cost of the communications circuit, likelihood for growth over the next 18 months, and the cost of administrative support of the new infrastructure. This scenario might not be appropriate for use in your network, due to the variance of the actual cost of deployment from location to location.

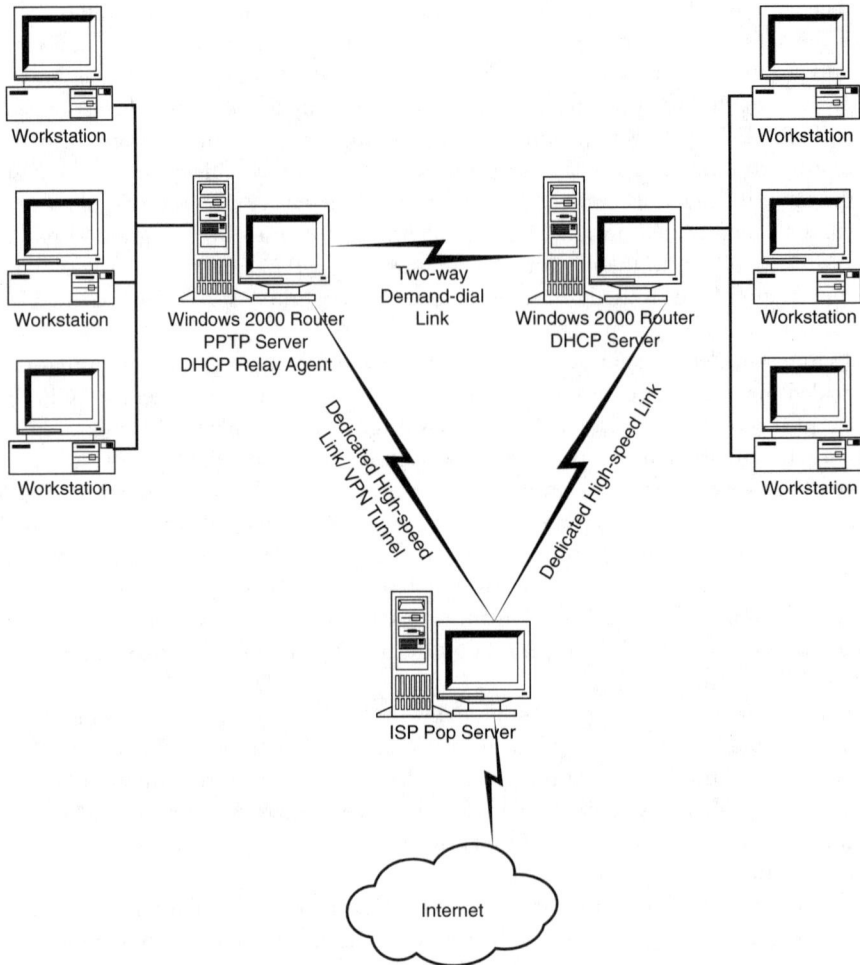

Figure 12.3 The Alexandrian Imports RRAS implementation.

Large Networks

The large network requires the most planning of all network types. Large networks typically link multiple network segments in multiple locations and are complex in nature. The network example in this section joins several sites over dedicated links using Open Shortest Path First (OSPF), and links remote users through dial-up networking connections to a Windows 2000 remote access server.

The Shangri-La Nursery Company specializes in tropical plants, which they sell over the Internet to wholesale customers and through their own stores. The company is headquartered on a 100-acre working plantation. On the plantation, there are four buildings, each of which has a single network. The buildings are linked by a fiber backbone configured as a mesh network, to provide a measure of fault tolerance. A DHCP server is used to provide IP addressing information to the 200-plus workstations. There are a total of 13 company-owned stores which reach the company intranet over dial-up links. There are also a number of employees and wholesale customers who access the Shangri-La intranet by dialing into a bank of modems.

Windows 2000 routers are placed in each building to provide several services in the Shangri-La intranet, as illustrated in Figure 12.4.

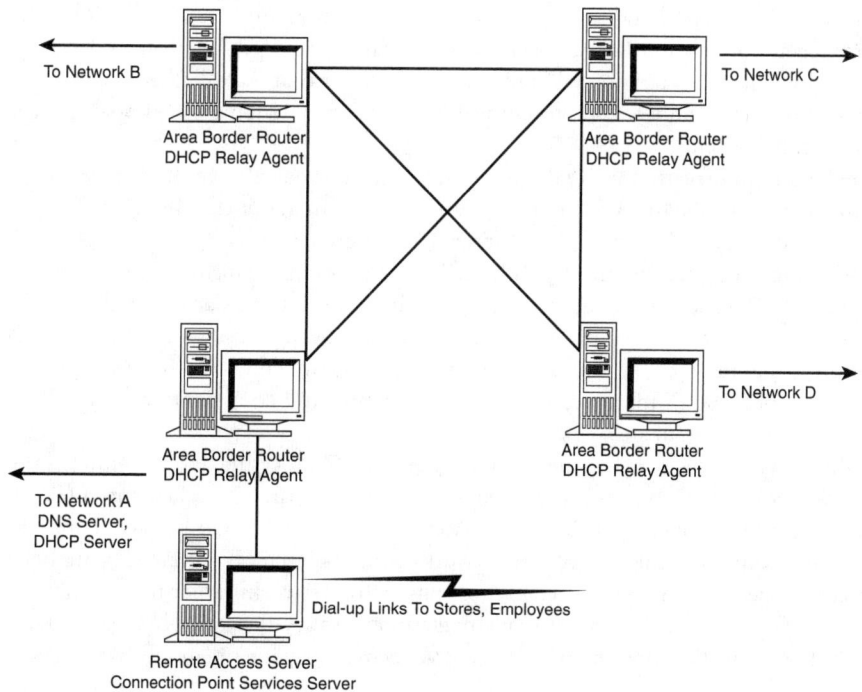

Figure 12.4 The Shangri-La corporate intranet.

Each of the four networks is joined by a Windows 2000 router that is configured as an area border router. On one of the networks, a DHCP server has been set up. Each intervening router between DHCP clients and a DHCP server must be configured with the relay agent, because DHCP traffic is not ordinarily broadcast between networks. As a result, each Windows 2000 router on each of the networks has been configured to act as a DHCP relay agent to facilitate the dynamic IP addressing of the clients located in each building.

A separate Windows 2000 router in Building A has been configured as a remote access server to provide dial-up access to the mobile users, wholesale customers, and company-owned stores that require access to the Shangri-La intranet. Future plans for expansion include allowing dial-up users to access the network through local points of presence (POPs) owned by ISPs, and using Internet Authentication Service (IAS) to provide authentication and accounting services. For this reason, the Connection Manager Administration Kit has been used to create service profiles that can be easily updated when this expansion takes place. Connection Point Services have been installed on the Windows 2000 router in Network A to provide phone book updates to the remote clients.

For more information on OSPF and the DHCP relay agent, see their respective sections in Chapters 4 and 5. Configuration information about the Windows 2000 remote access server is covered in Chapter 2, "Remote Access Server," and dial-up networking is covered in Chapter 3, "Dial-Up Networking." Finally, IAS is covered in Chapter 9, "Internet Authentication Service," and Connection Manager and Connection Point Services are covered in Chapter 8. Security is an important consideration in any network, so you might wish to refer to Appendix A, "Technical Overview of RAS Communications," for information and configuration instructions to further protect your network.

Variations on this scenario are practically infinite. Connecting additional networks with Windows 2000 routers can create even larger networks, also called enterprises. In place of private connections between networks, the Internet could be used as a backbone, and communications between networks could be secured within VPN tunnels. Enterprise networks are often managed as clusters of networks rather than a single large network. The actual cost of implementation can vary from area to area, so you might find that other options are more cost-effective for your organization.

References

For more information on designing the network infrastructure of your company, refer to the following sources:

Managing Infrastructure Deployment Projects. Microsoft TechNet, Technical Information CD, 1999.

Network Services Architecture Strategic Plan for XYZ Communications. Microsoft TechNet, Technical Information CD, 1999.

Planning for Windows 2000 in the Enterprise. Microsoft TechNet, Technical Information CD, 1999.

WAN Design at Shinozaki Automotive Corp. Microsoft TechNet, Technical Information CD, 1999.

IV

Appendixes

A   Technical Overview of RAS Communications

B   Troubleshooting

C   Glossary

Technical Overview of RAS Communications

After you have set up Routing and Remote Access Service on your network, you need to take a step back and evaluate how RRAS has enabled users to access resources that might have been previously inaccessible. Securing network resources involves more than just setting up user accounts and putting a firewall between your network and the Internet. There are all kinds of ways an attack on your network can be launched.

This appendix will take a look at Windows 2000's built-in security features, why you need them, and how to implement them. We also will spend some time examining Internet Protocol Security (IPSec).

Detailed information on hacks and attacks—and how to detect and avoid them—is beyond the scope of this book. You will come away from this chapter with a solid foundation of knowledge of Windows 2000 security and how it can make your job as administrator easier.

Windows 2000 Security

Windows 2000 security features are numerous, and all are designed for ease of use for both the administrator and the user. Some even offer savings in the form of cost-avoidance, because additional applications or user training are not needed to implement these security features. Additionally, Windows 2000 security offers the flexibility needed to connect your company's intranet to the Internet or to the intranet of partner companies while still maintaining a secure network environment.

The following list is a brief introduction to Windows 2000 Distributed Security features. We will cover them in more detail later in the appendix.

- **Integration of domain security and account information.**   The Active Directory acts as a storage depot for all domain security policy and account information. It can be remotely managed, and because it can be replicated to other domain controllers, the Active Directory makes security policies available domain-wide. The multiple master model that Active Directory replication uses enables you to make account changes and updates to the directory on any domain controller, not just the primary domain controller (PDC).

- **Hierarchical name space.**   The Active Directory allows hierarchical name-space for user, group, and computer account information. Accounts can be grouped according to your company's logical or physical organization, instead of just by a group that implies some function within the organization. Windows NT 4 (and earlier) allows only flat domain account namespace. Microsoft recommends creating a structure that effectively supports the corporate organization, rather than creating one that exactly duplicates the corporation's structure. The latter option can become an administrative burden to maintain if there is a high level of turnover in a company.

- **Delegation of administration.**   You can delegate administrative rights to manage accounts to other users and groups within the enterprise. Granular security can grant certain individuals or groups the right to reset passwords, but not to modify other account information. Other users or groups can have full account modification access rights.

- **Domain hierarchy and transitive trusts.**   The Active Directory supports a multilevel hierarchy tree of domains, much like DNS domain namespace organization. Trust management between domains is facilitated by a tree-wide transitive trust.

- **Encryption.**   Operating-system-level support of encryption permits use of digital signatures to authenticate data streams. Application Programming Interfaces (APIs) allow developers to develop other digitally signed applications.

- **Authentication protocols.**   Windows 2000 authentication includes support for Kerberos Version 5 and Transport Layer Security (TLS). It also supports Windows NT LAN Manager authentication protocols for backward compatibility with non-Windows 2000 computers or trusted domain members. Additionally, Windows 2000 supports smart cards for user logons, allowing strong domain authentication.

- **Public key infrastructure.**   Microsoft Certificate Server enables companies to issue public-key certificates to their users, whether they are employees or business partners. Windows 2000 can use standard format certificates issued by either the Microsoft Certificate Server or a commercial Certificate Authority (CA). The benefit is that users who don't have a Windows 2000 account can use trusted public-key certificates for authentication. Secure channel security protocols, such as Secure Sockets Layer (SSL) 3.0/Transport Layer Security (TLS), enable strong client authentication by mapping user credentials (public-key certificates) to existing Windows NT accounts. The certificate is mapped to a Windows account that specifies what resources are accessible.

Active Directory

With Windows 2000, user, group, and computer account information is stored in the Active Directory. This is an improvement over the Windows NT directory services implementation for many reasons, which will be covered in this section. Active Directory offers a hierarchical namespace and enhanced performance and scalability. It also combines security management with account management, and eases the administrator's job with GUI tools to perform these tasks. Batch scripts also can be used to automate accounts administration.

User, group, and machine accounts are organized into containers called organizational units (OUs). There is no limit on the number of OUs in a single domain. You can use your company's organization chart to organize the account namespace to accurately reflect departmental and employee hierarchy. You can name and rename OUs and accounts as your company grows and changes. Another improvement over the Windows NT directory services model is the number of objects that can be supported in the user directory. The Windows NT directory services database is stored in the registry, limiting the number of user, group, and computer accounts in the security accounts manager (SAM) database. The maximum size of the SAM is 40MB, or 40,000 user accounts. Compare that to the Active Directory, which can hold more than one million objects! And here is another plus: Not storing the Active Directory in the registry leads to better performance.

Because the Active Directory can support one-million-plus objects, your Windows 2000 domain architecture is not tied to a specific number of accounts. You can create and join domains in a very complex organizational structure to better serve today's distributed networks. The Active Directory can include a single domain or multiple domains. The Active Directory also supports multiple copies of account information, which means you can make changes on any domain controller, not just the PDC. Remote locations are now able to participate in the enterprise domain structure and handle their own account administration tasks more easily. The administrator at a remote facility doesn't have to be sure the PDC is available over a WAN link to make a change in a user account. Replication of accounts information still takes place, but it uses a different mechanism to propagate this information through the enterprise. Check out http://www.microsoft.com for more information on accounts synchronization.

Users and groups are treated as objects in the Active Directory. Granularity of control is maintained for read and write access to objects in the directory. Access can be granted to the entire object or to specific individual properties of the object. A human resources staff group, for example, can be granted write access to user account properties related to contact information without assigning full Account Operator or Administrator privileges. Group management is simplified by combining local and global groups into a single group object, which can be used for domain-wide or local resource access purposes. Windows 2000 provides API support for global and local groups to ensure backward compatibility.

In addition to account-related information, domain security policy information is stored in the Active Directory. This information includes properties that enable users to have direct use of the system—passwords are an example of the type of security information stored here. Care must be taken that these security objects are protected from unauthorized access. To this end, security and directory services are tightly tied to each other. The Active Directory is protected by Windows 2000 object-based security and access control. A unique security descriptor is assigned to each object in the directory. The descriptor defines what permissions are needed to read or update directory object properties. If permissions are configured for the object, its security descriptor contains a discretionary access control list (DACL) with SIDs for the users and groups who are allowed or denied access. If auditing is configured for the object, its security descriptor also contains a system access control list (SACL) that controls how the security subsystem audits attempts to access the object. As mentioned previously, this security can be defined granularly, so that a user who has permission to change one object property might not have permission to change other object properties. The operating system enforces access control, rather than the directory itself. In order for Windows 2000 to enforce access control, it has to assume that the access information in the directory can be trusted. Accordingly, security-related object properties are stored in a secure area of the directory, which requires a certain level of permission to access.

Domain Trust Relationships

You can organize Windows 2000 domains hierarchically. The resulting domain tree resembles a DNS domain structure. As you know from Windows 4.0 and earlier, trust relationships between domains allow users with accounts defined in one domain to be authenticated in another domain. In Windows NT, these trust relationships are established by creating one-way trusts between domains. Maintaining trust relationships between account domains and resource domains on a large distributed network can be an arduous task. This is especially true if there are multiple trusts, multiple locations, multiple administrators, and not a lot of communication between people or computers.

Windows 2000 Active Directory creates transitive trusts between domains. This simplifies the administration of interdomain trust accounts. All domains in a tree establish a two-way trust relationship with their parent domain in the tree, and every domain trusts every other domain in the tree. Windows 2000 also supports Windows NT 4 one-way trusts to ensure backward compatibility.

Delegating Administrative Duties

To facilitate the administration of very large enterprises, it is possible to allow certain users to perform specific Active Directory updates and changes. Delegation of administration makes it possible for companies to restrict administration to defined portions of the entire domain. The Directory Service Administration console is used to view and modify delegation information. Adding new delegation of permissions is done simply by selecting the users you want to delegate permission to, and then selecting which permissions they are to be given. A Delegation of Control Wizard makes this task even easier. Permissions are delegated at three levels:

- To change properties on a particular container
- To create and delete child objects below the OU level (such as users or groups)
- To update specific properties on child objects below the OU level (such as updating a user's telephone number or changing a password)

After you have delegated responsibility to specific administrators, you must then grant access rights for specific operations, such as updating contact information. The granularity of Windows 2000 security enables you to assign just the permissions you want, such as changing a password, without granting permission to do other things you don't want, such as creating new accounts.

Previously, we looked at Windows 2000 security descriptors. These are used to control object access. Each object in the Active Directory has a unique security descriptor that contains a list of entries granting or denying specific access rights. This is called an Access Control List (ACL). Access rights can be defined for the entire object, a subset of properties within an object, or only to a specific property of an object. The creator of an object is granted read/write access to all properties by default.

Administrators for one OU aren't necessarily able to administer another OU within a domain. Domain-wide access rights can be effective everywhere in the tree, however, depending on access rights inheritance. Be sure that you have granted subadministrators rights to manage users or groups that are appropriate for their area of responsibility. It is possible to accidentally delegate responsibility for users and groups that are outside the scope of a subadministrators' responsibility. The accounting department managers group, for example, needs to be able to change passwords for the accounting department employees. The human resources department and the accounting department have been placed in a common group because they are located in the same building. The administrator delegating authority needs to be sure that the group that contains both accounting and human resources is *not* included in the groups the accounting department managers are able to manage. If this were the case, they would then have the authority to change the human resources department's passwords as well.

Support for Many Security Protocols

Windows 2000 supports several security protocols. There are many advantages of doing this:

- Interoperability and compatibility with existing applications
- Stronger security
- Forward compatibility with new standards-based security mechanisms

In short, it offers you, the administrator, the flexibility to choose a security scheme that meets the needs of your company and the company's business partners while supporting the infrastructure and software you have already deployed.

Windows 2000 supports the following security protocols:

- **Windows NT LAN Manager (NTLM) authentication protocol.** NTLM is used by Windows NT version 4.0 and earlier for user and computer authentication and authorization. By supporting NTLM, Windows 2000 allows your existing Windows NT computers to stay in place until you decide to upgrade.

- **Kerberos Version 5 authentication protocol.** Kerberos replaces NTLM for client authentication and authorization for access to resources located in Windows 2000 domains. The next section will discuss Kerberos in detail.

- **Distributed Password Authentication (DPA).** DPA is a shared secret authentication protocol. A shared secret is a previously configured password that is known to the parties at each end of a connection. It is included in Microsoft Commercial Internet System (MCIS) services. It allows access to membership-based Internet services such as the Microsoft Network (MSN) without users having to reenter username and password every time they access a different resource through the service.

- **Public-key protocols.**   Public-key protocols enable private Internet communication. Secure Socket Layer (SSL) is one common public-key protocol. It is the industry standard security method used to secure transactions between browsers and Web site servers. Public-key certificates are issued by a trusted CA. The certificate is considered proof of identity, eliminating the requirement for a server to perform user authentication. These certificates can be mapped to user accounts to allow external users access to a network's resources. Later in this appendix, we will examine public keys more closely.

Kerberos and Authentication

Authentication means proving that an object is genuinely what it purports to be. When you authenticate something, such as a piece of art or a person, you go through a process to verify the identity of that object. When an art dealer authenticates a work of art, he or she verifies that the object in question was indeed executed by the artist. When you write a check at the grocery store and the cashier asks to see your driver's license, he or she is verifying that you are who you say you are. Users who log on to a Windows 2000 domain must be authenticated before they can access any domain resources. Kerberos authentication protocol is the default authentication protocol for Windows 2000 clients (Windows NT 4.0 and Windows 9x still use NTLM). The Windows 2000 Kerberos implementation is based on the Internet RFC 1510 definition of the Kerberos protocol. A list of RFCs can be found at `www.cis.` `ohio-state.edu/hypertext/information/rfc.html`.

Kerberos gets its name from a three-headed dog that guarded the gates of the underworld in Greek mythology. It provides a means for authentication between a client and a server before a network connection is opened between them. Kerberos works under the presumption that communication between clients and servers, at least initially, is not secured, and that any unsecured information on the network can be monitored by others. This information can be used by an attacker to masquerade as a client or a server. Parties wanting to communicate share secret authentication information (such as a password) with each other, but they do not share this information with anyone else. Both parties use this information to verify the other's identity.

There is a catch with using the password. Let's say Melissa and Max want to email each other. If the network is presumed to be unsecured, the secret password can't be transmitted in any manner that could be detected by an attacker. How do they prove they are who they say they are without divulging their secret password over the network? By using an encrypted key called an authenticator. The authenticator must be different each time authentication takes place. If it is not, the authenticator could be used by anyone eavesdropping on the communication. When Melissa receives an authenticator from Max, she decrypts it to discover the secret password. If the authenticator is decrypted successfully, Melissa knows that Max is the person who sent it. If the authenticator does not decrypt successfully, the communication is not from Max and can be rejected.

There are other problems with this method, however. How do Melissa and Max get a secret key? If they communicate with other computers, they need a secret key for each one that requires secure communications. Where these keys are granted, stored, and managed is a logistical issued solved by Kerberos. Kerberos protocol uses a trusted third party to negotiate between the two parties who want to communicate. The trusted intermediary is known as the Key Distribution Center (KDC). The KDC runs as a service on a secure server and holds a database of account information and cryptographic keys for the security principals in its realm. (A Kerberos realm is an organizational unit comparable to a Windows 2000 domain.) Because the user and the KDC both know the secret password, it is called a shared-secret protocol. Kerberos defines the way clients, the KDC, and servers get and use these keys, also known as tickets. For more information on Kerberos, refer to "Windows 2000 Kerberos Authentication" which can be found on Microsoft TechNet.

Windows 2000 Public-key Infrastructure

Public Key Infrastructure (PKI) is a system that uses digital certificates, Certificate Authorities, and other registration authorities to authenticate users who want to use secure communication. No single standard PKI is used by everyone in the world, but there are industry standards for individual components of public-key security. Microsoft has designed a PKI that integrates public-key security with the security offered by Windows 2000, including a Certificate Server, a secure channel security provider that implements SSL/TLS protocols, the Secure Electronic Transaction (SET) secure payment protocol for credit card transactions, and CryptoAPI components for certificate management and administration. These features are based on RSA, X.509, and Public Key Cryptography Standards (PKCS), all of which are industry standards for public-key security. A good source for more information on these security standards is www.securityfocus.com. You can also read more about PKI in the book *Understanding Public Key Infrastructure* by Carlisle Adams and Steve Lloyd, published by MTP (1-57870-166-x).

Windows 2000 includes the following public-key features:

- **CryptoAPI.**   A set of application programming interfaces that provide support for developers designing solutions for key generation and exchange, digital signatures, and data encryption.

- **X.509 certificates and PKCS.**   These standards have been supported since Windows NT 4.0 SP3. X.509 and PKCS also are supported by Internet Explorer 4.0 and later.

- **Authenticode.**   Authenticode announces to users the identity of publishers of Internet content and assures that the software in question has not been altered or damaged.

- **Client Authentication with SSL 3.0.**   SSL 3.0 based on public-key certificates obtained from a Microsoft Certificate Server or other supported CA.

- **Certificate Server.**   This Microsoft CA issues certificates to Windows 2000 domain accounts.

Internet Protocol Security

In addition to the other new security features included in Windows 2000, support for Internet Protocol Security (IPSec) has been added as well. IPSec is an open cryptographic standard for privatizing and securing IP communications over public and private networks. Windows 2000 implementation of IPSec was jointly developed by Microsoft and Cisco Systems and is based on Internet Engineering Task Force (IETF) IPSec RFCs (A list of RFCs can be found at www.cis.ohio-state.edu/hypertext/information/rfc.html). IPSec offers internal and external security for data traveling over an IP network, but its primary benefit is protection against internal attacks. Simply using access to resources based on passwords doesn't protect data traveling across a network, as demonstrated in the previous example of the salesman.

Data on both the Internet and private networks is vulnerable to attack by unauthorized users. A hacker breaking into a corporate Web site and plastering it with graffiti is the stereotypical network intrusion scenario. You are just as vulnerable, if not more so, to attack from inside the network. What about that salesman who plugs his laptop into a customer's network and grabs an IP address from DHCP? He's not a threat—all he can do is surf the Web site, because he doesn't have a user account in the domain, right? Well, how do you know he's not running a sniffer on his laptop? Although you think he is just checking his Internet email account, he is actually reading your company's employees' email as it passes through the network. And here is another shocker: you have repeated the phrase "Don't put your password where others can see it" about 600 times, but some of your users have shared their password in emails, which the sneaky salesman has read. Now he has access to other sensitive data on your network. Scary to think about, isn't it?

Hacks and Attacks

There are many different ways your network and data can come under attack. Active attacks are launched for the purpose of damaging or destroying data and networks. Passive attacks, on the other hand, don't do physical damage. Instead, these are more of a "fishing trip"—The attacker is just snooping around to see what he or she can see. The sneaky salesman sniffing the network is an example of a passive attack. It is imperative that you plan and implement a security system for your network to avoid both kinds of attacks. IPSec is a mainstream solution for securing data. Not only does it provide internal and external protection, but it is also easy to use.

IPSec uses cryptography-based services, security protocols, and dynamic key management to protect IP packets and networks. IPSec can protect computers in various environments and organizational configurations: entire private networks, domains, workgroups, remote sites, dial-up clients, and individual computers can be configured to use IPSec. It also can filter specific incoming or outgoing traffic.

IPSec provides end-to-end transaction security. The source and destination computers manage their own security and assume that the network they are communicating over is not secure. They are the only computers involved in the transaction. In fact, other computers or routers that forward data from source to destination don't even have to support IPSec. That means IPSec can be successfully deployed in existing networks using your existing hardware. How's that for a cost savings? Further, IPSec supports LAN, WAN, and RAS connections, in any configuration: client/server, client/client, or network/network (router/router).

Defending Your Network

IPSec by itself—or any other single means of security, for that matter—is not a complete security solution. Instead, IPSec is a fine addition to an extensive, well-thought-out network security plan, including access control and perimeter security methods. Typical security schemes emphasize blocking external attacks with firewalls and/or routers. Perimeter security keeps the bad guys from coming into your network, but it doesn't do anything about the bad guys within. Even access control-based security measures, such as smart cards, are not enough protection from a majority of network-level attacks. Why? Because usernames and passwords used with these systems can be shared, stolen, cracked by brute force, or hijacked. (Another convenient means of access to network resources is any computer left logged on and unattended.) Network resources can't know that a password is being used fraudulently, so the resources accessible with those credentials are there for the taking by the attacker. There are physical-level protection strategies that can protect network cabling from unauthorized access. Unless the entire data path is protected from source to destination, however, this is not a complete solution either.

The following sections provide an overview of typical hacks and network attacks and how IPSec can thwart them.

Eavesdropping and Data Modification

When you listen in on someone else's private conversation, you are eavesdropping. Eavesdropping can happen in a network too—remember the sneaky salesman? Because most network communications are transmitted in clear text, any person who has gained access to the network can listen for and read network traffic. Eavesdropping also is called sniffing or snooping because a sniffer is used to capture and read data packets or to monitor data exchanges. Without encryption, the contents of these packets are literally as easy to read as the daily paper. Even encapsulated packets can be broken open and read.

Let's say an attacker has sniffed some data off the network. Now, the intruder can tamper with it, and the sender and receiver will never know. Matters of confidentiality aside, if you are sending data in clear text format on the network, modification of data can cause many problems. If the previously mentioned salesman intercepts an order for items he is selling your company, it is possible for him to modify the quantity or price of a product. To prevent tampering, IPSec uses a checksum for each IP packet. A checksum is a calculated value used to test data for changes that occurred when data was transmitted. An invalid checksum indicates to the receiving computer that the packet was modified in transit. The keys used by the source and destination computers are the only keys that can decrypt the checksum, making it impossible for an intruder to modify the checksum.

IPSec doesn't keep the bad guys from sniffing a network. That is accomplished by establishing physical-layer security, but it is an expensive and uncommonly used security practice. IPSec Encapsulating Security Payload (ESP) protocol encrypts data to make it extremely difficult or impossible for an intruder to interpret. DES (Data Encryption Standard) or 3DES (Triple DES) can be used to provide multiple levels of encryption from 40- 128-bits.

Identity Attacks

Attacks based on false identities, such as spoofed IP addresses and fraudulently acquired passwords, can be avoided by using an authentication mechanism that does not reveal the identity of the users over the network. Man-in-the-middle attacks are another form of identity attack. In this scenario, an attacker between the valid sender and receiver intercepts and reroutes data to another destination by pretending to be the true receiver. IPSec enables secure authentication between parties using public-key certificates, thus preventing intruders from impersonating valid users on the network.

Application-layer and Denial-of-Service Attacks

An application-layer attack exploits a fault in an operating system or application. This results in the attacker gaining the capability to bypass normal access controls. The attacker can then take control of the application, system, or network, and can make whatever changes or modifications he or she wants, including destroying data and making security changes that allow other attackers into the system.

A denial-of-service attack is one that attempts to prevent authenticated users from using the network or a specific computer.

IPSec public-key certificate-based authentication and packet filtering can eliminate these attacks by allowing only specific users, IP addresses, protocols, or ports to access resources on your network.

Security Association

A security association (SA) must be established between two computers before a secured data exchange can take place. An SA is an agreement between two computers that covers how they will exchange and protect information. The SA identifies the security services, mechanisms, and keys that will be used to protect the transmission of data. Each computer can have several associations simultaneously with one or more remote computers. To differentiate between these SAs, a unique number is used to identify each association. This is called the security parameters index (SPI). The receiving computer uses the SPI to determine which SA is to be used for data that comes from a specific source.

A standard way to establish SAs and manage key exchange has been defined by the IETF. It is called Internet Key Exchange (IKE), and it combines the Internet Security Association and Key Management Protocol (ISAKMP) and the Oakley key generation protocol. ISAKMP is used for security association management, and Oakley is used to generate and manage the keys used to secure the information. (IKE was formerly known as ISAKMP/Oakley.)

Implementing IPSec

There are three stages in an IPSec implementation:

1. Define a security policy.

2. Assign the security policies to the resources you have selected.

3. Manage those policies over time to ensure that they are still effectively protecting your network.

Before you can begin setting up IPSec in your Windows 2000 network, however, you have to determine what you want to secure and what level of strength you want applied to those resources. You'll need to weigh the requirements for security against the ability of users to access resources easily. You might find that different users and different resources need different levels of security applied to them. Because Windows 2000 IPSec is policy-based, you have the flexibility to apply security however you see fit—In some places you may need a little more security, and in some places you may need a little less security. If you want to allow all users to access the internal corporate Web site, for example, you can specify a minimal security policy. The server that contains personnel records, however, might require a more secure policy that prohibits most users from accessing it. And finally, the server that contains the results of product testing your company has been conducting on The Next Big Thing might require the most security of all.

After you have decided on your security scheme, you then need to define your security policy. By default, IPSec is disabled. The administrator must enable it by defining and assigning security policies. Windows 2000 comes with default security policies that cover most situations. These policies can be modified, but Microsoft recommends that if you make more than the most basic changes you should create a new policy.

The basic structure of a policy is as follows: Policies contain one or more rules, each of which contains filter lists and filter actions. Each filter list is composed of one or more filters. What each component does, as well as how to configure them, will be covered in this chapter.

Predefined IPSec Policies

Windows 2000 ships with a group of predefined IPSec policies. These preset policies are specifically designed for Windows 2000 domain members, but can be modified for use with non-domain members. The default options cover the needs of most low to medium security networks, saving the administrator the time and effort involved in creating custom rules. It is a good idea to test any IPSec policy, however, before it is put into production use. You don't want to find out that your users suddenly can't access resources they regularly use, nor do you want to discover (possibly days later) that assets needing the most security are accessible by just about everybody on the network.

The predefined security policies are described in the following sections.

Client (Respond Only)

This policy is ideal for most computers that don't need to secure communications most of the time. Clients in the marketing department, for example, might not require IPSec unless requested by another computer. The predefined Respond Only policy enables the computer on which it is configured to respond to requests for secured communications. The policy contains a default response rule, which allows the client to negotiate with computers requesting IPSec. The only traffic secured in this policy is the requested protocol and port traffic.

Server (Request Security)

Any computer that needs secure communications most of the time can use this policy. Servers that transmit sensitive data, such as sales or inventory information, could be secured in this way. This policy actually requests security from the initiator of the communication. The server accepts unsecured traffic, but it will always try to secure further communications by requesting security from the original sender. This policy gives you the flexibility to permit an entire communication to be unsecured if the other computer does not use IPSec, but enabling IPSec to be used wherever required.

Secure Server (Require Security)

The Secure Server policy is ideal for those computers that always require secure communications. No unsecured communications take place, which means that non-IPSec computers are not able to access resources on computers protected with this policy. A server that stores human resources or payroll information, for example, should be protected from access by anyone but the employees in that department. This policy rejects any unsecured inbound communications, and outbound traffic is secured.

Predefined Rules

The default response rule also is included as a convenience for administrators. It allows an unsecured computer to respond to another computer's request for secured communications. The default rule is automatically added to each new policy you create, but it isn't activated unless you opt to do so. It can be enabled as-is, or you can modify it to fit your security needs. The default response rule cannot be removed.

Predefined Filter Actions

Two predefined filter actions are provided in a new or pre-existing rule. They can be activated as they are or you can modify them. The rules cover low to high security requirements.

- The Require Security rule is for high security environments or situations. No unsecured communication with this computer is permitted when this rule is activated.

- The Request Security (Optional) rule is for use in cases of low to medium security. When you activate this rule, you are permitting unsecured communication with computers that don't use or support IPSec. It also allows this computer to engage in insecure communications with other computers that do attempt to negotiate IPSec.

IP Security Policy Management Console

Now we will get down to the business of creating and configuring IPSec policies. For all actions that are performed on an IPSec policy, you must be logged on with an account that is a member of the local system Administrators group or that has Group Policy administrator rights. Click Start, then Run, then type MMC, and click OK. In the MMC window, select the Console menu, then select Add/Remove Snap-in. Click the Add button. Select IP Security Policy Management from the list, and click Add. A window appears prompting you to select the computer for which you want to manage IPSec policies. Because IPSec is managed on a computer-by-computer basis, you must pick one of the following options:

- **Local Computer.**   Only manage the computer on which this console is running

- **Manage domain policy for this computer's domain.**   Manage IPSec policies for domain members

- **Manage domain policy for another domain.** Manage IPSec policies for a domain where the computer running this console is not a member

- **Manage a remote computer.** Manage a computer on which this console is *not* running

Click Finish, and you return to the Add Snap-in window. Click Close, then click OK. Repeat this process for each of the options listed above that you would like to include in this console. Save the console (select the Console menu, then select Save). You can even create a new console for each computer, domain, or some combination of computers that represents your organizational structure. If you choose to create multiple consoles, be sure to save each with a console name that is meaningful to you. That will make it easier to find the policy you are looking for later. To open a saved console, double-click the console icon, or you can open the MMC and select Open from the Console menu.

Add or Update Policies

Now, you are ready to create a new policy or edit an existing one. To define a new policy, right-click IP Security Policy on Local Machine, and select Create IP Security Policy from the context menu. A wizard will guide you through the process. You will be asked to provide a name and description for your policy, whether you would like the default response rule to be activated, and to provide an authentication method. The choices for authentication are:

- **Windows 2000 default(Kerberos V5 protocol).** The computer on which you create this rule must be a member of a Windows 2000 domain.

- **Use a certificate from this certificate authority (CA).** You must provide the name of a CA.

- **Use this string to protect the key exchange (preshared key).** This method uses a shared secret for authentication.

The specifics of these options will be covered later in this section. For now, you can select any authentication method. When you are done, the Properties dialog box appears for the policy you just created.

The properties sheet is where you can fine-tune or modify existing IPSec policies. To access the properties sheet later, right-click a policy and then click Properties. You can also double-click the policy to achieve the same result. Figure A.1 illustrates the properties sheet.

Tip

Hint: You can refresh, rename, or delete any policy by right-clicking it and selecting the appropriate option.

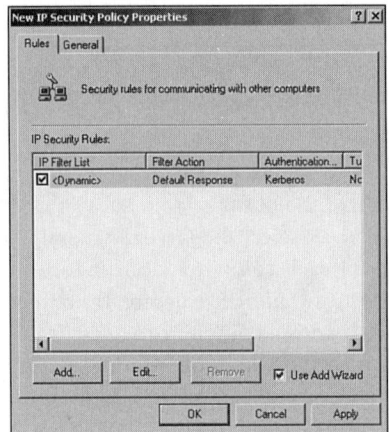

Figure A.1   The policy properties sheet is where you will modify IPSec policies.

If you have several policies, using the Description field on the Rules tab of the properties sheet is a good way to keep track of what policy does what and to which computers it applies. It is also a good idea to describe why it was set up. This can
potentially help resolve possible policy conflicts or serve as an aid to new administrators that join your company in the future. Selecting "Check for policy changes every
X minute(s)" enables you to specify how often this computer checks for Group Policy
updates. This method is only used for computers that are members of a domain. There
is also a Key Exchange button used to set specific options for exchanging keys. This
feature will be discussed in the upcoming section "Key Management."

If you have modified the default policies and would now like to restore the default
settings, select the IP Security Policies folder. Select the Action menu, select All Tasks,
and click Restore Default Policies. When prompted, click Yes. This will discard all
changes you have made to the default policies and can't be undone, so make sure you
mean to do this before you click Yes!

The predefined policy settings are covered at the end of this chapter.

Rules

IPSec rules govern the securing of communication. Each policy can contain one or
more rules. You can activate any or all rules in a policy simultaneously. Doing so permits different security actions to be applied to the same object for different communications types. You might have a single policy for a server that uses different security
actions for communications originating from different computers. A Windows 2000
router, for example, might have a policy containing two rules: one allowing all
communication from a range of addresses assigned to the internal network, and one
rejecting all communication from computers with IP addresses outside that range.

A rule determines how and when security is used, based on source or destination address or traffic types. You can set your own rules, or you can use the default rule automatically included in every new IPSec policy. A rule includes options for filter lists, filter actions, authentication methods, IPSec tunnel settings, and connection types. These specific options are covered later in this section.

To create a rule, you can use the Security Rules Wizard, or you can edit the properties sheet directly. Right-click the policy you want to change and select Properties, then click the Rules tab. To use the Security Rule Wizard, check the Use Add Wizard check box. Click Add and follow the wizard's instructions. To add or edit a rule without the wizard, clear the Use Add Wizard check box. Click Add or Edit and define the appropriate settings for IP Filter List, Filter Action, Connection Type, Authentication Methods, and Tunnel Setting. To deactivate a rule, clear the check box for that rule. Figure A.2 shows an activated rule.

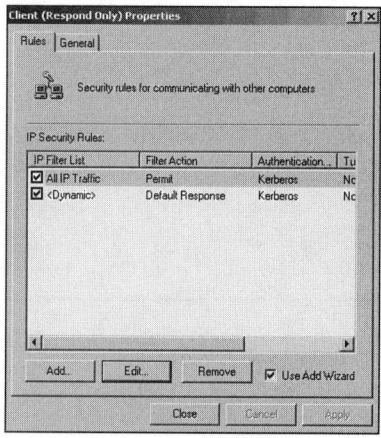

Figure A.2   To activate a rule, place a check mark in the box by the appropriate rule.

After a policy and its rules have been defined, you must enable it before it becomes effective. Policy are enabled when you assign the policy. Right-click the policy you want to activate, and click Assign. If you want to unassign an IPSec policy from a computer, just right-click the policy and click Unassign. To disable IP security, you can disable the IPSec Policy Agent Service on that computer. To do so, click Start, then Programs, then Administrative Tools, then Service. In the Services console, locate IPSec Policy Agent Service. Double-click this service and click the stop on the properties sheet that appears. If you need to, you can also configure this service to be manually started, instead of automatically started. This is done in the Startup type field on the service properties sheet.

Rules versus Policies

Don't confuse rules with policies. Rules are contained within policies and can be individually activated or deactivated. The status of rules has no effect on the active or inactive status of the policy as a whole. In other words, deactivating a rule does not disable a policy and vice versa.

To assign IPSec policy to a Group Policy object, open your Group Policy management console. If the Group Policy snap-in has not been added to your MMC console, on the MMC console's menu bar, click Console, and then click Add/Remove Snap-in. On the Standalone tab, click Add. In the Add Standalone Snap-in dialog box, click Group Policy, and then click Add. In the Select Group Policy object dialog box, click Local Computer to edit the local Group Policy object, or browse to find the Group Policy object you want. Click Finish, and then click OK. In the MMC console select the Group Policy object to which you want to assign an IPSec policy. Select Computer Configuration, then Windows Settings, then Security Settings. Then click the IP Security Policies folder. Right-click the policy you want to assign, and click Assign. This is shown in Figure A.3.

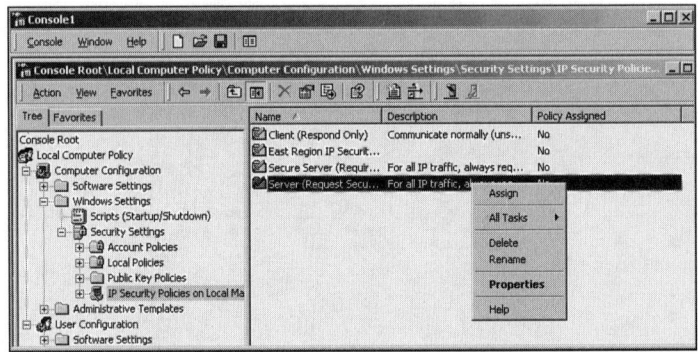

Figure A.3 Assigning IPSec policy through the Group Policy console.

An IPSec policy will stay active even after you delete the Group Policy object to which it is assigned, so be sure you unassign the IPSec policy before you delete the object. If you don't, the IPSec Policy Agent will think it just can't find the policy and will use a cached copy.

Importing and Exporting Policies

Windows 2000 Server allows you to copy policies between computers. This is especially helpful in networks where you have defined complex policies that are to be used on several computers. You can export the policy from one computer and import it into another.

To export an IPSec policy, click the IP Security Policies folder. Click Action, select All Tasks, then click Export policies. Now, specify the name of the file and the location where the exported policy should be saved.

To import an IPSec policy, click Action, select All Tasks, then click Import policies. Supply the path and filename of the policy you are importing. If you want this policy to override all existing security policies, check the "Delete all existing policy information" check box.

If you would like to have a list of the IPSec policies you have created and assigned to various computers, you can export a list of these policies. Remember it is only a text listing of policies, not the actual policies. Right-click the IP Security Policies folder, select Export List, and save the export file.

IPSec Authentication

Each rule specifies acceptable methods for identity verification in communications associated with that rule. You can configure as many authentication methods as you would like on a computer, but only one method will be used between any two computers. This means that any pair of computers using IPSec to communicate must use the same authentication method. By creating multiple authentication methods, however, you raise the chances for a pair of computers to find a common authentication method.

As part of the rule-definition process, you need to specify what type of authentication you would like to use. In IP Security Policy Management, open the properties sheet of the policy you want to change. Select the desired rule and click Edit. Click the Authentication Methods tab and click Add or Edit, depending on whether you want to add a new authentication method or modify an existing authentication method. The configuration dialog box is shown in Figure A.4.

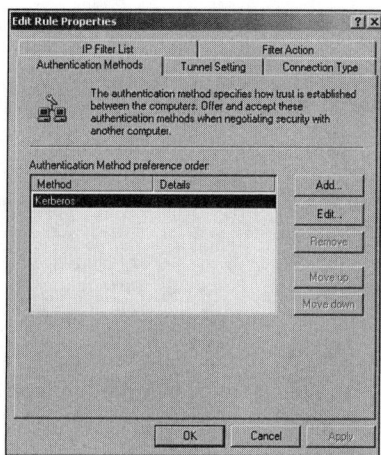

Figure A.4 IPSec authentication methods are a subset of the rules properties sheet.

The available authentication methods:

- **Windows 2000 default.** This method uses the default Kerberos security for authentication. Select this option if this rule will be applied to computers that are members of a trusted domain or that use Kerberos V5.

- **Use a Certificate from this certificate authority (CA).** This method allows you to use a public-key certificate for authentication. If you select this option, you must enter the name of a CA. This is helpful is situations where a computer accessing a resource does not use Kerberos V5. Windows 2000 includes a CA you can use to provide certificates, or you can use one of several commercial certifying authorities.

- **Use this string to protect the key exchange (preshared key).** This method allows you to include a key to be used for authentication. If you choose this option, ensure that both partners in the communication use the same key or authentication will fail. You might want to use this if computers that will access this resource do not use Kerberos and a CA is not available.

IPSec Connection Types

A policy can be applied to specific network connections. Right-click the policy you want to modify, then click Properties. Select the rule you want to change, then click Edit. Click the Connection Type tab and select one of the following options:

- All network connections
- Local area network (LAN)
- Remote access

IP Filtering

An IP filter list triggers security negotiations according to the source, destination, and type of IP traffic. By using an IP filter list, a network administrator can define exactly what IP traffic will be secured, because a single list can contain many different filters. Remember from the "Implementing IPSec" section, each rule has one or more filter lists. Each IP filter list contains one or more filters that define source and destination IP addresses and traffic types to filter. Outbound filters govern outgoing traffic and kick off a security negotiation that takes place before traffic is sent. Inbound filters govern incoming traffic and permit the receiving computer to reply to secure communication requests. An inbound and an outbound filter must be specified on each computer in the filter list.

IP Filter Lists

Open the properties sheet for the policy for which you want to specify a filter. Click the rule to which you want to add the new IP filter list, and click the Edit button. Now click Add or Edit to create a new filter list as shown in Figure A.5.

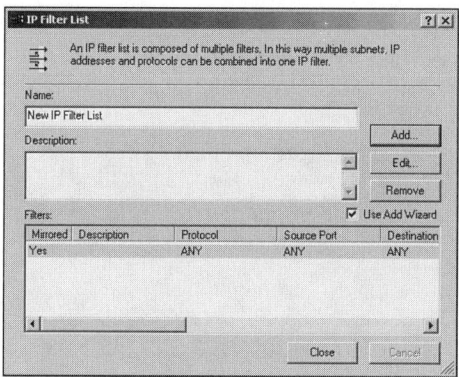

Figure A.5 The IP Filter List dialog box.

IPSec Filters

To create or edit a filter, edit the rule that contains the IP filter list you want to modify. On the IP Filter List tab, click Add or Edit. You can use the IP Filter Wizard to create a filter, or you can configure the filter manually. Specify Source and Destination Address and place a check in the Mirrored check box to automatically create the reverse of the filter you are working with. A mirror is a filter that is created for incoming and outgoing traffic. If you are using IP tunneling you must manually create these reverse filters. Continue filling in the blanks for this filter by supplying a description and any protocols or ports you would like to filter. If you chose to manually configure this filter, use the IP Filter Properties dialog box shown in Figure A.6.

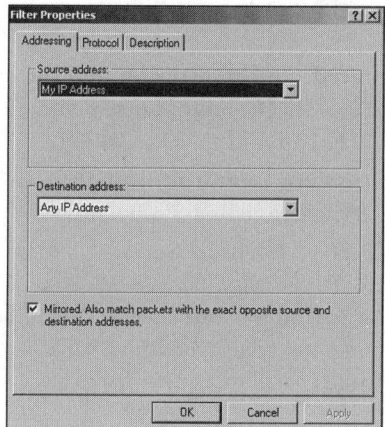

Figure A.6 Configure IPSec filters in the Filter Properties dialog box.

Filter actions define the action to be taken when traffic that matches the parameters in the filter is encountered. They are defined manually or with a wizard. Click the Filter Action tab of the desired rule. The Filter Action dialog box is illustrated in Figure A.7.

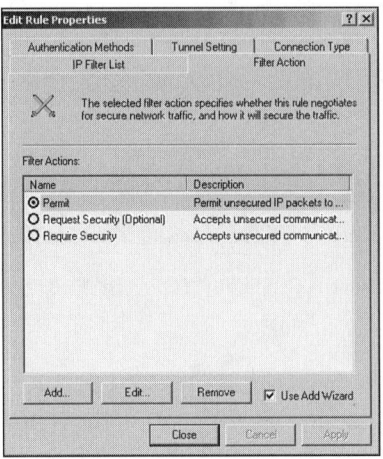

Figure A.7   The Filter Action dialog box is accessed through the Edit Rule Properties sheet.

Whether you use the wizard or manually configure the action, you must choose one of the following negotiation policy methods:

- **Permit.**   Allow *all* incoming communications.
- **Block.**   Prohibit *all* incoming and outgoing communications.
- **Negotiate security.**   Negotiate security according to a custom method or one of the following options:
    - **Accept unsecured communication, but always respond using IPSec.**   Do not block incoming, unsecured traffic, but secure outgoing messages.
    - **Allow unsecured communication with non–IPSec aware computers.**   Allow communication with non-IPSec computers.
    - **Session key Perfect Forward Secrecy.**   Master keys and master keying material will not be reused when generating session keys. This does add additional CPU overhead because periodic reauthentication is required. As a rule, the stronger the security method, particularly with encryption, the bigger the demands made on system resources.

Key Management

To configure key exchange methods, open the properties sheet of the policy you want to modify. Click the General tab, then click the Advanced button. The following options are available:

- **Master key Perfect Forward Secrecy.**   Master keys and master keying material will not be reused.

- **Authenticate and generate a new key after every X (minutes).**   Require reauthentication and generation of a new key at the specified time interval.

- **Authenticate and generate a new key after every X (sessions).**   Sets a limit on how many times a master key or master keying material can be reused to generate session keys. When the limit is reached, reauthentication and new key generation will be forced.

By clicking the Methods button on the Key Exchange Settings dialog box, you can create or edit key exchange security methods. Doing so allows you to specify which security algorithms are used for key exchange. This is demonstrated in Figure A.8. Windows 2000 supplies MD5 (128-bit) and SHA (160-bit) integrity algorithms and DES, 3DES, and 40-bit DES confidentiality algorithms.

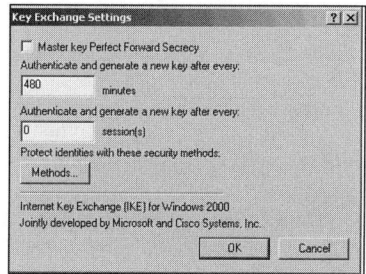

Figure A.8   You can select specific key exchange security algorithms.

Diffie-Hellman groups determine the prime numbers used during key exchange. The stronger the Diffie-Hellman group, the stronger the keying material.

- **Group 1 (low).**   Protects 768 bits of keying material
- **Group 2 (medium).**   Protects 1,024 bits of keying material
- **Export.**   Used when data is exchanged outside the United States

Use caution when specifying groups on different computers. If each computer in attempting to negotiate security uses a different group to generate the keying material, negotiation will fail. The Diffie-Hellman group selected will not dynamically fall back to a matching group during the negotiation process.

References

To find out more about securing your network and related topics, take a look at these sources.

End-to-End Security: An Introduction to Internet Protocol Security (IPSec). Microsoft TechNet, 1999.

IP Security for MS Windows 2000 Server. Microsoft TechNet, 1999.

Microsoft Windows 2000 Server Resource Kit. Microsoft Press, 1999.

MS Privacy Protected Network Access: Virtual Private Networking and Intranet Security. Microsoft TechNet, 1999.

MS Security Configuration Tool Set. Microsoft TechNet, 1999.

MS Windows 2000 Public Key Infrastructure. Microsoft TechNet, 1999.

MS Windows 2000 TCP/IP Implementation Details, Microsoft TechNet, 1999.

Secure Networking Using Windows 2000 Distributed Security Services. Microsoft TechNet, 1999.

The Security Support Provider Interface. Microsoft TechNet, 1999.

Understanding Public Key Infrastructure. MTP, 1999.

Windows 2000 Kerberos Authentication. Microsoft TechNet, 1999.

Windows 2000 Security—Default Access Control Settings. Microsoft TechNet, 1999.

B

Troubleshooting

THIS APPENDIX DIVES INTO THE MOST COMMON PROBLEMS you might have while using Routing and Remote Access Service for Windows 2000. The list in this appendix is in no way a comprehensive list of problems you might encounter with RRAS. However, it is a handy guide for many problems commonly encountered. To use this appendix, find the appropriate section covering the component of RRAS with which you are having a problem. The topics covered in this appendix are:

- Remote Access Server and Dial-Up Networking
- VPN
- Routing Problems, including:
    - RIP for IP
    - OSPF
    - DHCP Relay Agent
    - IP Multicast
    - RIP and SAP for IPX
    - Demand-Dial Routing
    - Network Address Translation

After you have identified the appropriate section of the appendix, then scan the problems listed in each section. Possible causes and solutions will be presented for each problem presented in the appendix. Before trying any of the solutions presented however, always run through a quick check of the basics: power is on, cables connected, and intermediary infrastructure is not causing problems (for example, cables are not damaged or phone service has not been interrupted). Doing so can save a lot of time troubleshooting a faulty network connection.

Remote Access Server and Dial-Up Networking

This section will deal with both the remote access server and dial-up networking components of Windows 2000. The problems identified in this section can be caused by the server or the client. Where it makes sense, the client and server side of a problem will be covered in the same subsection here (see Chapter 2, "Remote Access Server," or Chapter 3, "Dial-Up Networking," for specific configuration instructions or more information).

The Problem: Connections Are Not Established

If you aren't able to establish a connection with a remote access server and you are getting a specific error message, such as "PPP peer not responding," you will have a basis for starting the troubleshooting process. However, if you are *not* getting a specific error message, such as "PPP peer not responding," you have to determine if the problem is at the server or the client. First, we will look at what can happen on the server to prevent a successful remote connection.

Server Side Issues

The following things can cause the server to refuse a connection:

- *The modem might be malfunctioning.* Run through this checklist:

    Is the modem on the Windows 2000 Hardware Compatibility List? This can lead to flaky or intermittent problems. Contact the vendor to determine whether any issues exist with its product on Windows 2000. The manufacturer might have a workaround in place.

    The modem might be installed improperly. Double check that the modem is physically installed correctly and all necessary drivers are installed.

    The modem might be powered off. Your modem might have a power switch to be turned on, or an external power supply that must be connected to both the modem and an electric current.

    The modem might be configured incorrectly. The modem might have been installed on an incorrect port or configured to use incorrect dialing properties. Special modem strings might be required by your ISP or your modem for use. Contact your service provider or your manufacturer to determine whether these strings are required.

- *The phone service between routers might have been disrupted.* Try using a normal phone to call the remote device. If the device does not answer, this eliminates the problem from the originating end.

- *Routing and Remote Access Services might have not been enabled or started.* Enable, configure, and start the service.

- *The appropriate ports might have not been enabled for inbound remote access connections.* Configure the ports for inbound connections.

- *All available inbound remote access ports might already be in use.* Add additional remote devices and configure the ports for inbound connections.

- *The static IP address pool might be too small.* Configure a larger pool of addresses.

- *There might be a configuration mismatch between the remote access clients and the remote access server.* Be sure that the remote clients and the remote access server use at least one common LAN protocol, authentication method, and encryption method.

- *The user account or the remote access policy might not permit a remote access connection.* Run through the following checklist:
  Verify that the remote client been granted remote access permission.

  Ensure that the remote client meets the conditions of the user's property sheet, such as callback options.

  Verify that the remote client meets the conditions of one or more remote access policies, if required.

- The remote access policy might conflict with the remote access server configuration. They must both contain common settings for all separately configurable options such as authentication methods and bandwidth utilization.

- Remote client configuration options conflict with server or policy configuration. Remove any conflicting requirements.

- The authentication provider, either RADIUS or Windows 2000, is offline or configured improperly. Verify that the authentication provider is available and functioning correctly.

Client-Side Issues

If the server appears to be configured properly, perhaps the problem is with the client. Try connecting to the same server with another client computer to see if the same problem happens when a different computer tries to connect. Also, try connecting to other servers with the same client experiencing the problem.

Several things could cause the remote client to fail to connect with the server. The possible culprits include:

- *The remote client might not have a valid user account and/or remote access permission.* Be sure that the client account has not expired and that appropriate dial-in permissions have been granted.

- *The client's credentials might have not been entered properly.* Check that the user is entering the proper username and password. Remember, spelling counts, and passwords are case-sensitive.

- *The dialing properties of the remote client might not have been configured with the correct access number and/or any prefixes required to dial an outside number.* Correct any incorrect entries.

- *The modem might be set at a bps rate that is too high for the server's modem.* Reduce the bps rate on the client.

- *The remote client might not be able to negotiate with the modem on the server.* Older servers might use hardware that cannot negotiate with newer 56K modems. If this is the case, consult the documentation for the client modem to disable certain incompatible features, such as v.90.

- *The client's login settings might not match the server's.* There are still a few companies and government agencies using remote access or POP servers that require a client to log in through a terminal window. Contact your service provider to verify what settings or features should or should not be enabled. Also, some older servers do not run scripts as well as newer servers. If you are running a script on the client, disable the script and attempt to manually login. If the manual login works, check with the provider what script changes need to be made.

The Problem: No Access to Resources on the Remote Network

If a remote client cannot access resources beyond the remote access server, check the following things:

- Incorrect LAN protocols might have been configured on the client. Be sure that network access has been enabled for the appropriate LAN protocol.

- Routes back to the remote client might not have been entered in the routing tables of the routers in the remote network. You can enter this information as a static route or you can enable routing on the remote access server. Make sure that the routing type you enable on the remote access server matches the routing method in use in the remote network.

- Packet-filtering settings in remote access policies might be preventing specific traffic from or to a remote client. Make sure that filters enabled for a policy do not restrict needed traffic types.

The Problem: ISDN Connection Attempts Result in "No Answer"

If an ISDN connection attempt fails because the server did not answer, the following list can help you narrow down the cause of the problem:

- *The remote access server you are attempting to reach might be out of service or experiencing hardware problems.* Check with the administrator of the server to be sure that the server is online and the connection hardware is functioning properly.

- *The ISDN adapter at the client end might not be functioning properly.* Check the physical installation and the configuration of the adapter.

- *The line you are calling might be busy or the condition of the line might be poor.* Try the connection again in a few minutes.

- *The line-type configuration on the adapter might be incorrect.* Check that line-type negotiation is enabled.

- *The SPID or phone number of the ISDN is configured incorrectly.* Contact the telephone company to verify that the SPID you are using is correct.

- *The telephone company ISDN switching facility might be temporarily overloaded.* Wait a few minutes and try again.

Virtual Private Networks (VPNs)

This section addresses problems encountered in both client-to-server and router-to-router VPNs. We will start with the client-to-server, or remote access VPN.

Remote Access VPNs

The remote client attempting to tunnel into a private network might encounter the errors in this section. These errors might require reconfiguration of the client or the server.

The Problem: VPN Connection Attempts Fail

If a remote access client can't get a VPN connection with a VPN server, check the following configuration options that might be causing the problem:

- *The Routing and Remote Access Service might not be started on the server.* Enable this service if it is not running.

- *The PPTP and/or L2TP ports on the server might not be enabled for inbound remote access, or all ports might be currently in use.* Confirm that the ports are configured to enable inbound remote access. Check port usage in the Routing and Remote Access console by selecting the appropriate server, and then clicking Ports. If your hardware supports it, consider adding additional ports.

- *The LAN and tunneling protocols on the client and server might not match.* Be sure that the client and server have at least one LAN and tunneling protocol in common.

- *There might be too few static IP addresses in the static pool on the server.* Increase the number of addresses to accommodate the number of expected users.

- *The remote access policy on the server might require an authentication or encryption method or dial-in permission that the client does not have.* Either change the policy on the server to match the client, or change the client's configuration to match the server.

- *The remote access policy on the server might require an authentication or encryption method or dial-in permission that the server is not configured to use.* Either change the policy or change the server's configuration.

- *The client might be using improper credentials.* Make sure that users are aware of their usernames and passwords.

- *The authentication provider of the server might be set incorrectly.* Verify that the authentication provider matches what is actually present on your network.

The Problem: The VPN Client Doesn't Receive Return Traffic

If a VPN connection is made, but traffic never returns to the client, one of the following things might be the cause of the problem:

- Packet filters might have been set incorrectly. The PPTP and L2TP filters must be set properly, and any other IP filter that is set must also have appropriate input and outputs. Double-check that the filters set do not block the traffic you are trying to receive from the internal network.

- Incorrect or missing routes back to the client. Routes from the VPN intranet interface must be set to allow traffic to reach the rest of the network, and the other routers in the network must be configured with routes to the VPN server, otherwise traffic can't find its way back to the client. Check all routers for appropriate routes within the intranet.

Router-to-router VPNs

If you are unable to make a router-to-router VPN connection, or if traffic does not return to the calling router, verify the configuration on both routers. Router-to-router VPNs are as susceptible to configuration problems as remote access VPNs. Run through the preceding list of possible solutions, as well as examining the following options:

- The wrong demand-dial interface might have been added to the routing protocol. The appropriate demand-dial interface must be added to the protocol you want to route. If you have more than one demand-dial interface, make sure that you added the right interface to the right routing protocol.

- A route to the opposite VPN router might not have created, or might be incorrect. A router-to-router VPN connection does not create a default route, so there aren't routes on each side of the routers that allow bidirectional traffic flow. You must create these routes statically, through regular routing protocol updates, or autostatically.

- The name of the demand-dial interface might not match the user credentials assigned to it. Verify that the name of the demand-dial interface of the answering router is *identical* to the username in the credentials assigned to the calling router. If the interface name and the user account name do not match, the remote access connection will be treated as a remote client rather than a remote router.

You might find the "Demand-dial Routing" section later in this appendix to be helpful, too.

Routing Problems

This section covers general routing problems. If you don't see the problem you are experiencing, check the subsections that follow for the specific routing protocol you are using.

The Problem: Traffic Is Not Routed between Networks

If traffic is not being forwarded between networks, verify the following things are not the cause of this problem:

- The Routing and Remote Access Service might not be started. Check that the Routing and Remote Access Service is started.

- Routing might not be enabled on the correct server. Routing must be enabled on the server's Routing and Remote Access properties sheet.

- Routing for the correct LAN protocol might not be enabled. For example, if you are using IP routing, IP routing must enabled on the IP tab for the server's properties sheet.

- The router might not be receiving routed from other routers. View the routing table to see that the router is receiving routes from other routers. (Right-click Static Routes in the RRAS console for the appropriate server. Select the routing table for the appropriate protocol.) If you see anything other than Local in the Protocol column, the router is receiving routes from routing protocols. If no routes are received, double-check the rest of the settings in this section and then jump to the subsection for the appropriate protocol.

- The wrong routing protocol might have been installed, or the correct routing protocol might have been installed on the incorrect interface. The right routing protocol must be installed on the right interface.

- The TCP/IP configuration for the computer might be incorrect. TCP/IP must be configured properly for this computer, using the right IP address and subnet mask.

- The default route might be incorrect or missing. If you are using default routing, the default route must be learned through routing protocols or statically configured on the router over the correct interface.

RIP for IP

A common problem with RIP for IP is incorrect routing table entries. If wrong or inconsistent routes are found in routing tables or routes are missing, one of the following things might be the culprit:

- An incorrect version of RIP might be in use. If you are running in a mixed RIP v1 and v2 environment, make sure that your RIP v2 routers are configured to broadcast rather than multicasting announcements, and are receiving both RIP v1 and v2 announcements.

- Silent RIP hosts might not be receiving routes. Make sure that the version of RIP that your Silent RIP hosts are using matches the version the RIP routers are using. Also, keep in mind that not all Silent RIP hosts support both RIP v1 and v2.

- The subnetting scheme on your network might be incompatible with your routing infrastructure. Because RIP v1 routers do not interpret the Subnet Mask field in the route, Variable Length Subnet Masking (VLSM), supernetting, and disjointed subnets cannot be used in mixed RIP v1 and V2 environments. Either switch all routers to OSPF or change your subnetting scheme.

- A router might be using an incorrect password. Make sure that all router passwords match.

- Route filters might be too restrictive. If route filtering is used, be careful not to exclude necessary network IDs.

- Packet filters might be too restrictive. If packet filtering is used, make sure that UDP port 520 is not excluded.

- Neighbors (if used) might have been incorrectly configured. Verify that neighbors have been configured with the proper IP addresses.

- Default routes might not be propagated. If you must use default routes, change the settings on the Advanced tab of the properties of a RIP interface to process received default routes. Be sure to configure the interface to include default routes in announcements.

Open Shortest Path First (OSPF)

Not forming adjacencies is the most common problem area with OSPF networks. If adjacencies do not form, routing information will not be properly propagated through the network. These suggestions might help you find the cause of the adjacency problems:

- OSPF might not be enabled on the desired interface. Verify that the correct interface has been configured for OSPF.
- The neighboring router might be unreachable. Use ping to test accessibility.
- All OSPF settings might not match on each of the neighboring routers. Does the OSPF configuration, including authentication and password settings, match on both routers? Logging OSPF errors can help troubleshoot this problem.
- The stub area configuration or area ID on neighboring routers might not match. Verify that the area ID is identical on each router.
- NBMA interfaces might not be configured with OSPF neighbors' IP addresses. Check that the correct IP address for the neighbor is entered.
- There might not be a *designated router* (DR) for the network. At least one router must have a priority of 1 or greater. If all router interfaces are set to a router priority of 0, no router can become the DR for the network.
- Packet filtering might be too restrictive. If packet filtering is used, OSPF traffic (IP protocol number 89) should not be filtered out.

Other potential problems include wrong or missing routes and virtual links that won't form. Here is a list of possible causes:

- Summarized routes might not be configured properly. If you aren't receiving summarized OSPF routes for an area, or if you are getting both summarized and individual routes for an area, check that all the ABRs for the area are configured with the correct ranges of destination network and subnet masks that summarize that area's routes.
- ASBR (autonomous system boundary router) source or route filtering might be too restrictive. If it is , it could actually filter out the routes that should be propagated into your AS. Check to be sure that you haven't excluded addresses that really should be included. Open the OSPF properties sheet, then click the External Routing tab.
- Virtual links might be incorrectly configured. ABRs (area border routers) must be physically or logically connected to the backbone by using a virtual link. For virtual links problems:

    Check that the router ID of a virtual link neighbor is correct.

    Make sure that virtual link neighbors are configured for the same transit area ID.

    Confirm that the transit area ID is correct.

    Check that the retransmit interval is long enough to allow for large, busy networks.

DHCP Relay Agent

If the DHCP relay agent is not passing DHCP traffic between networks, use this list to double-check your settings:

- The DHCP relay agent might not have been enabled on the correct interface or might not have been configured to relay DHCP packets. Check these settings to verify that they are correct.

- The IP address of the DHCP server might have been entered incorrectly. Make sure that the IP addresses of the DHCP servers configured on the DHCP relay agent properties sheet are correct and that all the required DHCP servers are listed.

- Network connectivity issues or an offline DHCP server might be causing the problem. Verify that the DHCP servers in question are online and reachable over the network by pinging the DHCP server in question.

- Packet filters might be too restrictive. If filters have been configured, be sure they do not prevent DHCP traffic (UDP ports 67 and 68) from being forwarded. Check any hardware routing devices for access via these ports, as well.

IP Multicast

If IP multicasting is not functioning as expected and the Windows 2000 router has been configured as an IGMP router, the problem could be your network card. To use the IGMP router component, your network card must support multicast promiscuous mode. When Windows 2000 initializes the IGMP router, it puts the network card into multicast promiscuous mode. If your network card does not support this, IP multicasting will fail. To determine if this is indeed the problem, check the System Event Log in Event Viewer. You will see Event ID: 20127, "The interface [interface name] could not be enabled for multicast. IGMP router will not be activated over this interface." Check with your manufacturer to determine whether your hardware supports this feature. The manufacturer might have an updated Windows 2000 driver that will support this functionality.

RIP and SAP for IPX

Misconfiguration is a common cause of problems for all routing and remote access components and features, and RIP and SAP for IPX are no different in this regard. If you are having trouble, double-check the following possible causes:

- The Routing and Remote Access Service might not be running. Verify that the service is running.

- The correct routing protocol might not be installed on the correct interface. Make sure the correct IPX protocol (RIP for IPX or SAP for IPX) is enabled on the correct interface.

- The interface might not be operational for RRAS. Verify that the interface's Administrative State in the RRAS console is set to Enabled, and that the interface's Operational State (also in the RRAS console) is set to Up. If it is disabled, enable it by right-clicking the interface and then clicking Enable.

- The router's IPX network number might be incorrect. Verify that your router is configured for the correct external network number, frame type, and internal network number. You can use the `ipxroute config` command to display your IPX configuration.

- The update interval might be set at a different interval than the other routers in the network. Check that the update interval matches the rest of the routers on that network. It is recommended that all routers in a network have the same update interval.

- A manual update might not have been performed for the first update. If you are using autostatic updates, be sure to perform a manual update for the first update. If you do not, autostatic updates will fail.

- Packet filters might be too restrictive for the required traffic types. If you set up packet filtering, be sure that the filters you set do not prevent the passing of types of traffic that will be traveling over your network (And while you're checking, it's a good idea to make sure the filters are not too loose either).

Demand-Dial Routing

Demand-dial routing has a lengthy and complex configuration process. As with any other routing configuration, all settings must be correct. Always check your work as you go, because it can be difficult to find an error later on. The two most common demand-dial problems are:

- You are unable to make a demand-dial connection.

- You can make a connection, but you can't reach resources beyond the demand-dial router.

To troubleshoot these problems, start by checking the Unreachability reason in the RRAS console. To do this, double-click the appropriate server, then double-click Routing Interfaces. Right click the interface and select Unreachability reason from the context menu. If that does not provide an adequate solution, run through the following list and check that your routers match the suggested configuration:

- RRAS might not be started. Routing and Remote Access Service must be started on both the calling and answering routers.

- Routing might not be enabled. LAN and demand-dial routing must be enabled on both the calling and answering routers.

- The LAN protocols might not be configured for demand-dial access. Remote users must be permitted to access the demand-dial router and the remote network (if desired) through the proper protocol. Check the IP and IPX tabs on the calling and answering routers' properties sheets in the RRAS console.

- The demand-dial interface might not be enabled. Confirm that the demand-dial interface is enabled on both calling and answering routers.

- Dial-out hours might be set incorrectly. Verify that dial-out hours for the demand-dial interface on the calling router are not preventing the connection attempt.

- Static routes might be incorrect or missing. If you use static routes, verify that the correct static routes are configured.

- Filters might be too restrictive. Make sure that any filters you are using do not filter out demand-dial traffic.

- There might not be enough free ports. Verify that there are enough free ports to make or answer the call. All the ports on the calling or answering router might already be in use by connected remote access clients or other demand-dial routers. For VPN connections—if necessary and if your hardware supports it—increase the number of PPTP or L2TP ports. The default number of PPTP and L2TP ports is 5.

- VPN protocols might be mismatched. Both answering and calling routers must support a common VPN protocol, if you are using VPN connections.

- The demand-dial connection might not match user permissions or policy requirements. The demand-dial connection on the calling and answering routers must have dial-in permissions through the user account properties and remote access policies. In order for the connection to be established, the settings of the connection attempt must match all the conditions of at least one remote access policy that grants access. Remote access policies can be tricky. It is a good idea to make sure the routers will call and answer as intended before you implement a remote access policy.

- The user account associated with the demand-dial interface might be incorrectly configured. The user account on the calling router must match exactly the interface name on the answering router.

- Authentication credentials or provider might be incorrectly configured. Verify that the user account information of the calling router is correct. Test this by logging on to the answering router with those credentials. It is also possible that your authentication provider is configured incorrectly. If you are using IAS or another RADIUS server as an authentication provider, be sure that it is functioning properly.

Tip

Use Event Viewer to help narrow down the reason that a router is not functional. The error messages can help you troubleshoot by providing clues to the nonfunctional component. Increase the error logging level to log the maximum amount of information to gather the most data.

- There might not be enough free IP addresses available. If you use a static pool of IP addresses, make sure that you have enough static addresses in the pool to service the number of simultaneous inbound requests.

Network Address Translation

Misconfiguration of the Routing and Remote Access Service can prevent you from successfully connecting to the Internet or to another LAN using NAT. Verify the following settings if you are having difficulty:

- An interface might not have been installed. Verify that you have added both internal and external interfaces to the Network Address Translation protocol in the Routing and Remote Access console.

- An interface might have been incorrectly configured. Verify that you have configured the internal and external interfaces properly. The internal network interface should be configured as a private interface, and the external interface should be configured as a public interface. Right-click each interface in the RRAS console and select Properties from the context menu. Click the General tab and verify that the appropriate box has been checked for the interface.

- Private address range configuration might be incorrect. Confirm that the range of private addresses and the associated subnet mask is configured correctly.

- Public address range configuration might be incorrect. Make sure that you have configured the range of public addresses properly and reserved any necessary addresses. If you are using more than one public IP address, be sure there is a check in the "Translate TCP/UDP headers (recommended)" check box.

- There might be no method of name resolution configured. Make sure you have provided a method of name resolution. Verify that there is a check mark in the WINS and/or DNS name resolution boxes on the Name Resolution tab of the NAT Properties sheet. If name resolution requests should initiate a demand-dial connection by the NAT computer, verify that the "Connect to the public network when a name needs to be resolved" box is checked, and that the proper demand-dial interface is selected.

- Demand-dial routing, if used, might be configured incorrectly. Double-check that this is not the culprit. Use the preceding "Demand-Dial Routing" section as a guide to demand-dial troubleshooting.

C

Glossary

ABR   See *area border router*.

access control   The prevention of unauthorized users from using resources. This can be accomplished many ways, including through policies, permissions, or packet filtering.

account lockout   The period of time an account will be locked after a user unsuccessfully attempts to supply the correct username and password to log on to a computer or domain.

ACK   See *acknowledgment message*.

acknowledgment message (ACK)
The acknowledgment of receipt of TCP or other protocol data packets. ACKs offer reliability of packet delivery, but at the cost of additional network overhead in the form of extra traffic. To offset the potential doubling of traffic on the wire,

most hosts ACK at predetermined intervals, such as every x packets or every x seconds or milliseconds.

Active Directory   The directory service included with Windows 2000 Server. It is based on X.500 standards and offers a level of administrative granularity not available in Windows-based directory services up to now.

Active Directory Users and Computers   The utility used to manage users and computers on a Windows 2000 computer that runs the Active Directory.

adapter   The logical representation of a network card or other device, such as a (WAN) adapter, that physically links a computer to a network segment.

address classes The Internet Engineering Task Force (IETF) has defined groups of Internet addresses. Each class of address identifies networks of a certain size. The range of network numbers in an IP address is based on the address class. Class A addresses include IP addresses with the first octet in the range of 1-126 and can have more than 16 million hosts per network. Class B addresses are in the range of 128-191, and have a max of 65,534 hosts per network. Class C addresses range from 192-223 and can host up to 254 nodes per network.

address pool The range of IP addresses that have been designated for use by a Dynamic Host Configuration Protocol (DHCP) server or an RRAS server to be assigned to their clients.

Address Resolution Protocol (ARP) The TCP/IP protocol responsible for converting an IP address into a physical address, such as a media access control (MAC) address.

adjacency The relationships between neighboring routers for the purposes of synchronizing the link-state database (LSDB) are called adjacencies. Adjacencies are used to compile entries in the LSDB. Adjacencies are set-up between selected routers to eliminate the network overhead of every router sending its routing information to every other router in an autonomous system. Failure to establish adjacencies results in convergence problems in Open Shortest Path First (OSPF) networks.

APIPA See *Automatic Private IP Addressing*.

AppleTalk The built-in networking protocols and related components in Apple Macintosh computers. AppleTalk also refers to networks running the AppleTalk protocol.

AppleTalk Phase 2 An AppleTalk network architecture that supports multiple zones in a network and extended network addressing capacity.

AppleTalk protocol The network protocol used in AppleTalk networks.

area Administrative groups made up of adjoining networks and their hosts. An autonomous system is made up of one or more areas.

area border router (ABR) A router that interfaces with multiple areas. An area border router holds the topological database for each area to which it is attached.

ARP See *Address Resolution Protocol*.

AS See *autonomous system*.

ASBR See *autonomous system boundary router*.

asymmetric encryption Also known as public-key encryption, asymmetric encryption uses two different keys for each user: one private key known only to the user and one public key, which is known by both users.

asynchronous communication Data bytes sent asynchronously have a start and stop bit. Compare with synchronous communication, which uses timing information instead of start and stop bits.

auditing Logging the activities of users or access on a specific resource.

authentication   Validation of a user's identity, such as when a user logs on to a computer. This can be accomplished many ways, including through a username and password combination, smart cards, or machine certificates. Authentication should not be confused with authorization to access a resource. Authentication only proves the identity of a user.

authorization   Verification of the user's permissions to use the resources he or she is attempting to access. Authentication only verifies the identity of a user; authorization uses the identity of a user to determine if sufficient rights or permissions are in place for the requested activity or resource.

Automatic Private IP Addressing (APIPA)   A Windows 2000 feature in which the Remote Access Server can automatically assign remote clients an IP address from a pool of private, internal IP addresses.

auto-static routes   These types of routes are a hybrid of static and dynamic routes. They are learned from other routers, but remain in the routing table even if the router is rebooted or goes down.

auto-static updates   When a router is configured for auto-static updates, it requests and inherits auto-static routing information from another router. Typically used in demand-dial scenarios.

autonomous system (AS)   A group of areas joined by routers under a single administrative authority that exchange routing information.

autonomous system boundary router (ASBR)   A router that exchanges routing information with routers that belong to other autonomous systems (ASs). The ASBR advertises external routes inside its own AS.

backbone   In an Open Shortest Path First (OSPF) network, the backbone is responsible for spreading routing information between all attached areas. The backbone is a contiguous group composed of area border routers (ABRs) and routers of networks not wholly contained in any area.

backbone router   Any router that is connected to the backbone.

backup domain controller (BDC)   A computer that contains a backup copy of the domain directory database.

bandwidth   The data-transfer capability of a network, usually expressed as a measurement of data over time, such as megabits per second.

Bandwidth Allocation Protocol (BAP)   A Point-to-Point Protocol (PPP) used to dynamically add or remove links in a multilink dial-up connection.

BAP   See *Bandwidth Allocation Protocol.*

BDC   See *backup domain controller.*

BGP   See *Border Gateway Protocol.*

BOOTP   See *bootstrap protocol.*

bootstrap protocol (BOOTP)   A protocol used to assign BOOTP clients an IP address, default gateway, name server address, and other related information.

Border Gateway Protocol (BGP)
A routing protocol used to exchange routing information between autonomous systems.

broadcast Data destined for all hosts on a given network.

CA See *certification authority*.

callback number The number a remote access server will dial to reach a client when a client attempts to establish a dial-up link with that server.

callback security When configuring a remote access connection, a feature that requires a server to disconnect the calling client and call them back at a number preconfigured by the administrator or set by the user.

certificate A digital guarantee of identity.

certification authority (CA) A trusted third-party organization or company that issues certificates. The CA authenticates the identity of the person who is assigned the certificate. X.509 is the most widely used standard for certificates.

Challenge Handshake Authentication Protocol (CHAP)
A challenge response authentication protocol that requires an encrypted response. Windows 2000 supports CHAP and MS-CHAP versions 1 and 2.

CHAP See *Challenge Handshake Authentication Protocol*.

clear-text passwords Passwords transmitted in plain text.

client A remote computer that requests resources from another computer. A user accessing an RAS server over a dial-up line is a client.

connection-oriented Data transmission that occurs over a pre-established connection. The connection is maintained while data is transmitted and is dropped when the data transmission is completed. Connection-oriented communication offers reliable packet delivery. Compare to connectionless communication.

connectionless Data is sent to a host without first establishing a connection. This offers less overhead than connection-oriented delivery, but at the expense of reliable delivery.

container object An object, such as Active Directory Organizational Units (OUs), that can contain other objects, such as contact objects, computer objects, group objects, and many other object types.

convergence The point at which all routers in a network have the correct routing information in their routing tables.

count-to-infinity A loop that happens between routers when a link goes down. Routers on the network advertise bad routes as good routes, and send these updates to the source from which it was originally learned. The routing data is exchanged until the hop count reaches 16 or infinity. Infinity is the point at which a route is considered unreachable.

cryptography The science of data encryption.

default gateway The router that is automatically used by a host to forward packets to other networks.

demand-dial connection   A dial-up network connection that is not activated until it is needed. Demand-dial connections can pass routing information or data.

demand-dial routing   A method by which a router can forward traffic over a wide area network (WAN) link on a dial-as-needed basis.

dial-up networking   The mechanism by which a computer uses a phone line and a modem to connect to a remote computer or network.

DHCP   See *Dynamic Host Configuration Protocol.*

DHCP client   A computer that requests—and is dynamically assigned—IP address, default gateway, and related information from a DHCP server.

DHCP relay agent   Forwards DHCP messages between DHCP clients and DHCP servers on different networks.

DHCP server   A server that provides IP address, default gateway, and related information to clients that request this data.

dial location   The area code and any other location-specific information needed to dial out from a specific place—for example, 9 to reach an outside line or ★70 to disable call waiting.

dial-up connection   A connection to a remote network that is made by a dial-up line and a modem rather than by a network interface card (NIC).

dial-up line   A telephone line that is used to dial a remote network.

direct cable connection   A connection between two computers using null modem cable or another connective device, instead of a standard network or dial-up connection.

DNS   See *domain name system.*

DNS name server   A server that stores a database of host names mapped in a hierarchical manner to the IP addresses of those hosts.

domain   An administrative group of computers running Windows NT or Windows 2000 that uses a single directory services database. Copies of this database are stored on and can be centrally administered from each domain controller instead of a separate database stored and individually administered on each computer in the network.

domain controller   A computer that maintains a copy of the domain directory services database.

domain name system (DNS)   The system that enables users of a TCP/IP network to use friendly names instead of IP addresses to locate other hosts. See *DNS name server.*

Dynamic Host Configuration Protocol (DHCP)   A protocol that runs on a server that dynamically assigns IP address, default gateway, and related information to requesting computers.

dynamic routing   Routing using automatic updates of network topology changes. These changes are learned from other routers rather than from an administrator.

EAP   See *Extensible Authentication Protocol.*

encapsulation   Formatting data in a different manner than usual to enable the data to pass from one network to another. Typically this is because the network the data is being transported over does not support the traffic type transiting the wire. In this case, the data is wrapped in a new header of a different protocol.

encrypted password   A password sent in a scrambled format, making it difficult for eavesdroppers to decrypt and use.

encryption   Scrambling of data before transmission to make it difficult for eavesdroppers to understand the contents of the transmission.

event logging   Tracking and recording specific events in the Event Viewer for analysis or trouble-shooting.

Extensible Authentication Protocol (EAP)   An extension of the Point-to-Point Protocol (PPP) that permits user authentication by means of security devices, such as smart cards or certificates. EAP is a flexible protocol and allows the introduction of new user authentication modules.

filter   A means of monitoring traffic and excluding specific types of traffic from entering or exiting a network. Filters can be set to work on the basis of exclusion or inclusion.

firewall   A security system that prevents unauthorized access into a network. These systems can be hardware- or software-based and function in a manner similar to filters.

fragmentation   Data packets may be broken into pieces smaller than normal. This is called fragmentation. These frag-ments may pass through a filter even if their type has been specifically excluded, unless you opt to filter packet fragments.

gateway   A device that connects two networks together and forwards data between them.

Group Policy   A policy that describes the permitted actions of users on that computer.

Group Policy object   The collection of Group Policies that affect computers and users locally or in a domain.

Hardware Compatibility List (HCL)   A list of hardware that has been tested and approved for use with the Windows family of operating systems.

Hash-based Message Authentication Code (HMAC)   A method of utilizing cryptographic hash functions to authenticate messages.

HCL   See *Hardware Compatibility List.*

heartbeat   A periodic announcement that is sent for the specific purpose of advertising that a device is still in service.

HMAC   See *Hash-based Message Authentication Code.*

host   A computer that provides services or data to other computers.

host ID   The portion of an IP address that identifies the host. The subnet mask is used to separate the network ID from the host ID.

host name   The friendly name of a computer. The friendly name is mapped to an IP address in the HOSTS or LMHOST file, or in a Windows Internet Name Service (WINS) or domain name system (DNS) server.

IANA See *Internet Assigned Numbers Authority.*

IAS See *Internet Authentication Service.*

ICMP See *Internet Control Message Protocol.*

IETF See *Internet Engineering Task Force.*

IGMP *Internet Group Management Protocol.*

interface The logical point of connection between a network and a network adapter card.

internal network number In an Internetwork Packet Exchange (IPX) network, this number identifies a virtual network running inside a computer.

internal router A router that is connected only to networks in a single area.

international prefix The number that must be dialed before dialing an international call. Also called a country code.

Internet The public worldwide TCP/IP network.

Internet address The unique address that identifies hosts on the Internet, or a non-unique address that identifies hosts on a private network.

Internet Assigned Numbers Authority (IANA) The central coordinating agency for the assignment of unique values for Internet protocols.

Internet Authentication Service (IAS) An authentication provider for remote access clients and demand-dial routers.

Internet Control Message Protocol (ICMP) An error-reporting and diagnostic utility used by routers, hosts, or other devices to send updates or error information to other routers, hosts, or devices.

Internet Engineering Task Force (IETF) The organization of engineers, vendors, computer scientists, and other interested parties dedicated to developing architectural and operational standards for the Internet and related technologies.

Internet Group Management Protocol (IGMP) The protocol used by IP multicast hosts to announce their membership in multicast groups to IGMP routers.

Internet Network Information Center (InterNIC) The coordinating agency for DNS registration and IP address acquisition.

Internet Protocol (IP) A TCP/IP protocol that provides connectionless delivery of packets. It offers best effort, not guaranteed packet delivery.

Internet Protocol Security (IPSec) A set of open standards for private and secure communications over IP networks using cryptographic security.

Internet service provider (ISP) A company that provides access to the Internet for a fee.

Internetwork Packet Exchange (IPX) A communications protocol commonly used in Novell and Microsoft networks.

intranet A private TCP/IP network that uses Internet technology.

IP See *Internet Protocol.*

IP address The unique 32-bit binary number used to identify hosts and other devices on a TCP/IP network. It is expressed in dotted decimal form.

IPSec See *Internet Protocol Security*.

IPX See *Internetwork Packet Exchange*.

IPX/SPX Internetwork Packet Exchange/Sequenced Packet Exchange. A suite of protocols used in Novell and Microsoft networks.

ISP See *Internet service provider*.

ISDN interface card Hardware that connects a computers to an Integrated Services Digital Network (ISDN).

Kerberos V5 The default for network authentication on computers with Windows 2000. It replaces the NTLM (NT LanMan) authentication used in Windows NT.

key The portion of a cryptographic algorithm used to generate encrypted data.

L2TP See *Layer 2 Tunneling Protocol*.

LAN See *local area network*.

latency The delay between start and finish of an activity, such as propagating routing tables between routers or sending a data packet across a network.

Layer 2 Tunneling Protocol (L2TP) One of the two virtual private network (VPN) protocols integrated into Windows 2000. L2TP encapsulates data and tunnels it across a network (such as the Internet). This tunnel allows companies to securely send private data across public networks.

lease The duration during which a client's server-assigned IP address is valid.

link state database A database of the topology of an Open Shortest Path First (OSPF) network. It is updated after every change in network topology.

local account A user or computer account residing only on the local computer.

local area network (LAN) A group of computers connected over private network links, usually contained in a single building.

local computer The computer a user is physically interacting with, as opposed to interacting over a network or dial-up connection.

LocalTalk The built-in networking equipment and protocols found in Apple Macintosh computers.

log file A file kept to record events related to specific activities, such as routing logs.

MAC address See *media access control (MAC) address*.

media The wiring used to connect computers on a network and the protocols used to put data on the cable.

media access control (MAC) address The unique physical address assigned to a network card.

member server A server that is a member of a domain, but does not host a copy of the domain directory services database.

Message Digest Four (MD4) A 128-bit hash algorithm developed by RSA Data Security, Inc.

Message Digest Five (MD5) A one-way 128-bit hash algorithm developed by RSA Data Security, Inc.

metric   The number of hops to the destination network. Also called the cost of a route.

Microsoft Management Console (MMC)   The utility used to manage various aspects of Windows 2000.

Microsoft Point-to-Point Compression (MPPC)   A compression protocol used with Microsoft Point-to-Point Encryption (MPPE), Point-to-Point Protocol (PPP), and Point-to-Point Tunneling Protocol (PPTP).

Microsoft Point-to-Point Encryption (MPPE)   Provides data confidentiality between a remote access client and the remote access or tunnel server. It is offered as an alternative to Internet Protocol Security (IPSec).

minimum password length   The fewest characters required in a password. The more characters required, the more secure the password.

modem   The device used to connect a phone line to a computer. Converts digital signals from the computer to analog signals to be sent over the phone line.

MPPC   See *Microsoft Point-to-Point Compression.*

MPPE   See *Microsoft Point-to-Point Encryption.*

MPR   See *multiprotocol routing.*

MS-CHAP   See *Challenge Handshake Authentication Protocol.*

multicast   Data destined for multiple hosts that are members of a multicast group.

multicasting   Transmission of network data to multiple hosts according to group membership rather than only to specific hosts or to every host on the network.

multihomed computer   A computer that is assigned more than one IP address or has more than one network card installed.

multilink dialing   A dial-up connection to a single remote host, created with multiple phone lines and multiple modems.

multiprotocol routing (MPR)   The capability to route multiple protocols.

NAS   See *network access server.*

NetBEUI   See *NetBIOS Enhanced User Interface.*

NetBIOS Enhanced User Interface (NetBEUI)   A broadcast-based nonroutable communications protocol commonly found in small networks.

network access server (NAS)   A server that accepts Point-to-Point Protocol (PPP) connections from remote clients and then acts as a gateway to a network for the remote client.

network adapter card   See *network card.*

network card   The local area network (LAN) or wide area network (WAN) device that physically attaches a computer to a network.

network ID   The portion of an IP address that identifies the network on which a host is located. The subnet mask is used to separate the network ID from the host ID.

Network Interface Card (NIC) See *network card*.

network number The address or range of addresses assigned to an AppleTalk network.

NIC (Network Interface Card) See *network card*.

node A host or other device on a network.

null modem cable A cable used to link two computers in a direct connection, in place of a modem or a network card.

Open Shortest Path First (OSPF) A routing protocol that eliminates some of the problems with propagation of routing information found in the Routing Information Protocol (RIP). It is used in medium to large networks.

OSPF See *Open Shortest Path First*.

packet Data that is sent as a single unit over a network. A packet can also contain protocol information.

packet assembler/disassembler (PAD) A device used to connect a computer to an X.25 network.

packet header The portion of a data packet sent over a network that contains its protocol and addressing information.

packet filtering A method used to prevent certain types of traffic from entering or leaving a network, based on the packet type.

PAD See *packet assembler/disassembler*.

PAP See *Password Authentication Protocol*.

password The phrase used in conjunction with a user ID to log on to a Windows 2000 computer.

Password Authentication Protocol (PAP) An authentication protocol that uses plain text passwords to verify a user's identity.

PDC See *primary domain controller*.

ping A test used to verify that a host is reachable over a TCP/IP network, or to determine that the gateway or other device between the local host and remote host is reachable. ICMP echo request and ICMP echo reply packets are used to determine that the destination address is reachable.

PKI See *public key infrastructure*.

Plain Old Telephone Service (POTS) Refers to the public switched telephone network (PSTN).

point of presence (POP) The access point for a network, such as the Internet.

Point-to-Point Protocol (PPP) A set of protocols used to negotiate and establish point-to-point connections, such as a dial-up connection. It is much more robust and feature-rich than its predecessor, Serial Line Internet Protocol (SLIP).

Point-to-Point Tunneling Protocol (PPTP) One of the two VPN protocols that are integrated into Windows 2000. PPTP encapsulates data and tunnels it across a network (such as the Internet). This tunnel allows companies to securely send private data across public networks.

poisoned reverse A technique used in Routing Information Protocol (RIP) networks in conjunction with split horizon advertising. It allows all networks to be advertised, but networks learned in a specific direction are advertised with a hop count that indicates the network is unavailable. This improves convergence of routing information.

policy A set of conditions, rules, or other parameters that must be met by users or computers to which the policy applies.

POP See *point of presence*.

POTS See *Plain Old Telephone Service*.

PPP See *Point-to-Point Protocol*.

PPTP See *Point-to-Point Tunneling Protocol*.

primary domain controller (PDC) In a Windows 2000 or Windows NT domain, the computer that holds the master copy of the domain directory services database.

private key An encryption key known only by one user, used in conjunction with a public key.

private network A network that utilizes leased lines and local area network (LAN) connections. Access to this network is limited to specific authorized users.

protocol The common communication method between computers.

public key An encryption key that is known by both parties that are communicating with each other. It is used in conjunction with a private key.

public key cryptography Encryption using both public and private keys.

public key infrastructure (PKI) The servers, certificates, and other related items used to authenticate users in a Windows 2000 or other network.

public network A collective network, such as the Internet, where data from multiple entities travels between hosts.

Public Switched Telephone Network(PSTN) Public analog telephone lines.

PSTN See *Public Switched Telephone Network*.

RADIUS See *Remote Authentication Dial-In User Service*.

RADIUS proxy A RADIUS server used to forward authentication to an Internet Authentication Service (IAS) server.

RAS See *remote access server*

realm name The name used to identify and route authentication request traffic from one network to another, such as from an ISP POP to an Internet Authentication Service (IAS) server in a private network.

remote access Network access by a remote client over a dial-up connection to a remote access server.

remote access server A server that accepts dial-up connections from remote clients for the purpose of allowing them to access specific resources or an entire network.

Remote Authentication Dial-In User Service (RADIUS) A standard protocol and provider for remote access and virtual private network (VPN) client authentication.

remote computer   A geographically separate computer that is not connected to a local area network (LAN) until it establishes a Point-to-Point Protocol (PPP) connection to a remote access server.

Request for Comment (RFC)   An official publication of the Internet Engineering Task Force (IETF) that specifies the standards for specific protocols to be used on the Internet.

RFC   See *Request for Comment.*

RIP   See *Routing Information Protocol.*

RIP for IP   A version of the Routing Information Protocol for IP networks.

RIP for IPX (RIPX)   A version of the Routing Information Protocol for IPX networks.

roaming   The capability to use the point-of-presence (POP) servers of other Internet service providers to access the Internet while in a geographic area outside one's own normal location.

router   A computer that forwards data between networks.

routing   The process of forwarding data between networks.

Routing Information Protocol (RIP)   A routing protocol that allows routers to exchange information with each other. It is used in small to medium-sized networks.

routing protocol   A method of learning and propagating network information between routers.

routing table   The table of routes to networks, maintained by routers.

SAP   See *Service Advertising Protocol.*

Secure Hash Algorithm (SHA-1)   A 160-bit hash algorithm.

seed router   The router responsible for defining the network numbers and zones for an AppleTalk network.

Serial Line Internet Protocol (SLIP)   An older remote access protocol. It does not provide a means for compression, error control, or negotiate for IP address assignment. Point-to-Point Protocol (PPP) is its successor.

Service Advertising Protocol (SAP)   A method for servers on an IPX network to advertise services.

set-by-caller callback   The process in which a remote access server is configured to disconnect a remote client attempting to establish a Point-to-Point Protocol (PPP) connection and then call the client back at the number specified by the client.

SHA-1   See *Secure Hash Algorithm.*

shared secret   A secret that is known by both sides of an authentication request. A password is a shared secret.

Simple Network Management Protocol (SNMP)   A protocol used to centrally manage network components and computers. Applications such as Computer Associates' Unicenter and Microsoft's Systems Management Server use SNMP to manage enterprise and network assets remotely.

SLIP   See *Serial Line Internet Protocol.*

smart card   A small certificate storage device used in conjunction with a PIN to authenticate users logging on to a computer.

smart card reader   A device used to read the certificates stored on a smart card.

SNMP   See *Simple Network Management Protocol.*

sniffer   A network device that views and monitors packets sent over a network.

split horizon   A configuration in Routing Information Protocol (RIP) routing used to configure a router to only advertise routes in a single direction, away from the router where the information is learned. This helps prevent loops.

SSL   See *Secure Sockets Layer.*

standalone server   A computer that is not a member of a domain and maintains its own directory services database.

static routes   Routes that are manually entered into a routing table by an administrator.

subnet mask   A 32-bit binary value, expressed in dotted decimal notation, used to distinguish the network ID from the host ID of an IP address.

symmetric encryption   A form of encryption that requires the same secret key to be used for both encryption and decryption. It is also called secret key encryption.

TCP/IP   See *Transmission Control Protocol/Internet Protocol.*

ticket   Data used to verify a user's identity. Kerberos V5 uses tickets to authenticate Windows 2000 users.

time-to-live (TTL)   A value that indicates how long a packet is considered valid. When the TTL is reached, the packet is discarded.

TLS   See *Transport Layer Security.*

topological database   The "map" of the geography of a network that is maintained by routers.

topology   The geographical layout of networks and routers and their location relative to each other.

Transmission Control Protocol/Internet Protocol (TCP/IP)   A suite of protocols used on the Internet.

Transport Layer Security (TLS)   A protocol that provides security and privacy over network connections.

triggered update   Updates of changes in routing information that occur when a routing change is learned.

TTL   See *time-to-live.*

tunnel   A secure communications channel across a public or private network used to secure data transmissions.

unicast   Data destined for a single host.

virtual link   A logical link between two routers that have an interface to a single common non-backbone area.

virtual private network (VPN)   A logical private connection created over a public network to allow the secure transmission of data between two locations. VPNs eliminate or reduce the need for expensive point-to-point links.

VPN   See *virtual private network.*

WAN   See *wide area network.*

wide area network (WAN)   A network that spans geographically separate sites and is joined by leased lines or public networks such as the Internet.

Windows Internet Name Service (WINS)   A name resolution service supported by Microsoft clients. A WINS server maintains a dynamic database mapping IP addresses with NETBios names of nodes in a network.

WINS   See *Windows Internet Name Service.*

X.500   A set of directory services standards incorporated in Windows 2000.

X.509   The most widely used standard for defining digital certificates. Because X.509 has not been officially defined or approved, companies have implemented the standard in different ways.

Zone   A logical group of resources in an AppleTalk network, arranged for easy browsing by users.

Index

Numerics

2B+D, 255
3DES, 184
40-bit DES, 184

Symbols

? Command (Netsh), 160
  interface context, 165
  ras context, 162

A

aaaa command (Netsh), 160–162
abbreviating commands, 161
abort command (Netsh), 160
ABR (available bit rate), 258
ABRs (area border routers), 100–101
accepting external routes, 104
access interfaces, 255
access methods
  analog phone connections, 50
  cable modems, 50
  dial-up networking, troubleshooting, 316
  ISDN, 50
  X.25, 51
accounting, 6, 230–233
accounts
  callback options, 40
  caller ID verification, 40
  configuring, 39
  lockout, 176, 234
  OUs, 291
  remote access permission, 39
  remote access policies, 41
    conditions, 43
    creating, 42
    permissions, 43
    profiles, 44-46
  SAM, 291
  static IP address assignment, 40
  synchronization, 292

ACLs (Access Control Lists), 293
activating rules, 305
active attacks, 297
Active Directory, 291–292
  administrative duties, delegating, 293
  cross-forest authentication, 38
  domains
    security policies, 292
    trust relationships, 293
  objects, granularity, 292
add command (Netsh), 160
  interface context, 165
  ras context, 162
add/delete/set/show filter command (Netsh), routing context, 164
add/delete/set/show interface command (Netsh), routing context, 164
add/delete/set/show preferencefor protocol command (Netsh), routing context, 164
add/delete/set/show persistentroute command (Netsh), 164
add/delete/set/show rtmroute command (Netsh), routing context, 164
add/delete/set/show scope command (Netsh), routing context, 164
add/delete/show authmode command (Netsh), ras context, 163

add/delete/show boundary command
(Netsh), routing context, 164

add/delete/show link command
(Netsh), ras context, 163

add/delete/show registeredserver
command (Netsh), ras context, 163

add/set ipiptunnel command (Netsh),
routing context, 164

add/show multilink command (Netsh),
ras context, 163

adding
    interfaces, 123
    IPSec policies, 303-304
    static routes, 128
        demand-dial routing, 147-148, 152
        persistent static routes, 187

address translation
    ICS, 270
        affect on network services, 272
        configuring, 270-272
    NAT, 262-263
        addressing component, 263
        configuring, 265-270
        name-resolution component, 264
        translation component, 263
        troubleshooting, 325

adjacencies, 94-95
    BDRs (backup designated routers), 99
    forming, 96-98
    point-to-point networks, 97
    uncontrolled, 98

administrative duties (Active
Directory), delegating, 293

administrative router shutdown, 80

advanced configuration,
    service profile, 226
    connections, 62
        operator assisted dialing, 63
        preferences, 63-64
    RIP, 131-132

Advanced Security Settings
dialog box, 61

advertisements, 127
    RIP, 78
        convergence, 81
        for IPX, 110

    silent hosts, 87
    timers, 80
    SAP for IPX, 111

AH (Authentication Header), 180

algorithms
    Dijkstra, 95
    SPF (Shortest Path First), 92

alias command (Netsh), 160

analog phone connections, 50

analyzing WANs
    network requirements, 250-251
    traffic, 250

ANI/CLI (Automatic Number
Identification/Calling Line
Identification), 34-35

announcements, 7
    multicast, RIP v2, 91

APIPA (Automatic Private IP
Addressing), 17, 118

APIs (Application Programming
Interfaces), 67
    TAPI, 13

AppleTalk, 20, 52, 111
    configuring, 153
    network number, 112
    nodes, 112
    ranges, 112
    routers, 8, 112
    RTMP (Routing Table Maintenance
        Protocol), 113
    seed routers, 112
    zones, 113

appletalk command (Netsh), ras
context, 162

Application Programming Interfaces.
See APIs

application-layer attacks, 299

applications
    auto-applications (Connection
        Manager), 224
    configuring over Internet, 265
    Connection Manager, 9
    multicasting, 75
    name resolution, 269
    Network Monitor, 252

architecture, 13
   OSPF, 102

area code rules, 57-58

areas (OSPF)
   configuring, 133-134
   inter-area routing, 100
   partitioning, 100
   topology, 100
   virtual links, 102

AS (autonomous system)
   areas, 100
   external routes, 92
   LSAs, flooding, 94-95
   stub areas, 104

ASBRs (Autonomous System Boundary Routers), 101
   default gateways, 103
   enabling, 133
   external routes, filtering, 104

assigning
   cost to interfaces, 95
   IP addresses, 17
   IPSec policies to Group Policy
      object, 306
   multicast addresses, 76
   policies to Group Policy object, 306
   ranges, 112
   static IP addresses, 18, 40

Asynchronous Trasfer Mode. See ATM

at command, 170

ATM (Asynchronous Transfer Mode)
   cells, 257
   features, 257
   line speeds, 257
   services, 258
   switches, 258
   versions, interoperability, 258
   Web sites, 257

attacks
   application-layer, 299
   denial of service, 299
      Ping of Death, 127
   eavesdropping, 298
   identity attacks, 299
   IPSec, 297-298

auditing IAS usage, 235

authentication, 5–6, 21
   account lockout, 234
   challenge-response protocols
      CHAP, 27-28
      MS-CHAP, 29-30
      MS-CHAP v2, 30-31
      PAP, 32-33
      SPAP, 32
   direct access, 51
   DPA, 294
   EAP, 22
      EAP-MD5, 23
      EAP-TLS, 23-24
      smart cards, 24-26
   IAS, 8, 229-232
   identity attacks, 299
   IPSec, 307-308
   KDC, 296
   Kerberos, 295–296
   key management, 311
   L2TP, 183
   mutual authentication, 176-177, 181
   PPP, 20
   PPTP, 181
   preshared keys, 308
   profiles, 45
   RADIUS, 39
   realm names, 238
   RIP, configuring, 130
   RIP v2, 90-91
   shared secrets, 234
   simple password authentication, 92
   SLIP, 49
   smart-card authentication, standalone
      servers, 182
   VPNs, 177
   Windows 2000, 36
      cross-forest, 38
      member servers, 37
      standalone servers, 37
   Windows NT 4.0
      Service Pack 3, 38
      Service Pack 4, 38
   See also unauthenticated access, 33

Authentication Header (AH), 180

Authenticode, 296

authorization, 6, 21
   direct access, 51
   IAS, 233

remote access policies, 41
  conditions, 43
  creating, 42
  profiles, 44-46
  remote access permission, 43
user accounts
  callback options, 40
  caller ID verification, 40
  configuring, 39
  remote access permission, 39
  static IP address assignment, 40

auto-applications, 224

auto-enrollment (certificates), configuring, 25

auto-static updates, 117
  scripts, 166

autodhcp command (Netsh), routing context, 164

autodial, 61, 64

automatic hangup, 61

Automatic Number Identification/Calling Line Identification. See ANI/CLI

Automatic Private IP addressing. See APIPA

AutoNet addresses, 17

autonomous networks, 78

available bit rate. See ABR

B

B-channels, 255

backbone
  MBONE, 75
  OSPF, 100–101
  transit areas, 102
  tunnels, 75

backup servers (IAS), exporting data to, 241

backward compatibility, RIP v2, 89

BACP (Bandwidth Allocation Control Protocol), 249

bandwidth
  bursty, 256
  consumption, 5
  Frame Relay, 258
  multilink, 50
  POTS, 50
  RIP v1, 87
  WANs, requirements, 250-251

BAP (Bandwidth Allocation Protocol), 5, 50, 249

batch files, auto-static updates, 166

BDRs (backup designated routers), 99

bitmap graphics (Connection Manager), customizing, 224

black LANs, 185
  IP addresses, identifying, 193
  reachability, 188-189

Bluetooth, 51

boot threshold count (DHCP), 129

bootp (bootstrap protocol), 128

boundaries
  autonomous networks, 78
  multicasting, 74

BRI (Basic Rate Interface), 248, 255

broadcast networks, OSPF, 97

broadcasts, 74
  MAC-level, 87
  NetBIOS, IPX configuration, 139-140
  RIP, bandwidth consumption, 87

brute force attacks, 36

building
  Custom Help files, 225
  LSDB (link state database), 94-95
  routing tables, 95

built-in guest account, unauthenticated access, 35-36

bundling links, 248

burstiness, 256

bye command (Netsh), 160

C

CA (certificate authority), 24

cable modems, 50

cables
last mile, 255
Parallel Technologies, 51

calculating maximum adjacencies, 97

callback, 20, 64

Caller ID verification, 40

calling routers (router-to-router VPNs), configuring, 207

capturing
frames, 252
packets, 252

CBR (constant bit rate), 258

cells (ATM), 257

certificates
auto-enrollment, configuring, 25
installing on RAS, 24-25
public-key, 295

challenge-response protocols
CHAP, 27
caveats, 28
implementing, 28
MS-CHAP, 29
implementing, 30
version 2, 30-31
PAP, 32-33
SPAP, 32

channels (ISDN), 255

CHAP (Challenge Handshake Authentication Protocol), 27
caveats, 28
EAP-MD5, 23
implementing, 28

charts, Performance console, 253

checksums, 299

CIDR (Classless Inter-Domain Routing), 87-88

Class D addresses, 76

Classless Inter-domain Routing. See CIDR

clear text, 234

CLI (command-line interface), 68

clients
demand-dial routing, usernames, 116
dial-up, 186
LANs, 187
VPNs, 188
remote access VPNs, setup, 202

cloud, 256

CMAK (Connection Manager Administration Kit), 9, 213
installing, 220
template files, 227
wizard, starting, 221

combining
commands
IP subcontext, 164
IPX subcontext, 165
RIP versions, 91

Command field (RIP v1 messages), 86

command-line utilities
Netsh, 159
global commands, 160-161
optional parameters, 160

commands
abbreviating, 161
at, 170
IP subcontext, combinations, 164
IPX subcontext, combinations, 165
mrinfo, options, 166
Netsh, contexts, 162
route add, 187
route print, 187

commit command (Netsh), 160

comparing
multicast forwarding and multicast routing, 76
RAS and remote control software, 12

compatibility, RIP v1 and RIP v2, 92

compiling LSDB (Link State Database), 94

conditions, remote access policies, 43
profiles, 44-46
remote access permission, 43

Configuration tab (IP routing General Properties sheet), 127

configuring
 account lockout, 234
 advanced connection parameters, 62
  operator assisted dialing, 63
  preferences, 63-64
 AppleTalk, 153
 auto-static updates, 166
 Connection Manager, 220-225
  connect actions, 223
  dial-up networking entries, 222
  profiles, 221
  service name, 221
 CPS, 216
 demand-dial routing, 117
  remote access policies, 148–152
 devices, 124
 dialing rules, 56-58
 dialup connections, X.25, 61
 DNIS, 34
 guest accounts, 35
 IAS server, 237-239
 ICS, 270-272
 IGMP v2, 137
 incoming connections, 64
 IP routing
  DHCP relay agent, 128
  IGMP, 137
  IP Routing General Properties sheet,
   126-128
  OSPF, 133-136
  RIP, 129-132
  static routing, 128
 IP-in-IP tunnels, 138
 IPSec filters, 309-310
 IPX
  NetBIOS broadcasts, 139-140
  RIP for IPX, 140
  SAP for IPX, 142
  static routes, 140
 multicast routing
  boundaries, 137
  heartbeats, 138
 NAT, 265-270
  default static route, 267
  demand-dial interfaces, 266
  dial-up connections, 266
  internal interface, 268
  Internet interface, 268

  name resolution, 269
  network card, 265-266
  permanent connections, 267
  remote application access, 269
 OSPF
  external routing, 135
  interfaces, 135-136
  virtual interfaces, 134-135
 packet filtering, 154-155
 ports, 124
 remote access VPNs
  client setup, 202
  L2TP servers, 192-197
  PPTP servers, 198-201
 RIP, authentication, 130
 router-to-router VPNs, 202-203
  connections, 203
  L2TP, 204-207
  PPTP, 208-211
 RRAS, 15-16
 smart cards, 24-26
 TCP/IP
  assigning IP addresses, 17-18
  name resolution, 18
 user accounts, 39
  callback options, 40
  caller ID verification, 40
  remote access permission, 39
  static IP address assignment, 40
 VPNs, 191
  server behind firewall, 190
  server in front of firewall, 189

Connection Manager, 9, 213
 auto-applications, 224
 bitmap graphics, customizing, 224
 configuring, 220-225
 Help Files, building, 225
 icons, 225
 installing, system requirements, 220
 profiles, 214
  advanced configuration, 226
  editing, 227
  license agreement, 225
  merging, 221

Connection Point Services. See CPS

connection protocols, 49

connections
advanced, configuring, 62-64
ATM, 257
demand-dial, 115-117
configuring, 143-145, 149-151
static routes, 147-148, 152
troubleshooting, 323-324
dial-up networking, troubleshooting, 314-316
establishing, 14
inbound, 265
interfaces, 122
Internet-based VPNs, 178
Internet-Intranet, 179
Intranet-based VPNs, 179
IPSec, 308
ISDN, troubleshooting, 317
large networks, 282–284
medium-sized networks, 279-281
multilink, 248
point-to-LAN remote access connectivity, 11
point-to-point remote access connectivity, 11
PPP, negotiation, 20
remote-access VPNs, troubleshooting, 317-318
router-to-router VPNs, 203, 318-319
sharing, 6, 271
SOHO networks, 276-277, 279
unused, disconnecting, 249
VPNs, 174–176, 265

consoles, IPSec policy management, 302-303

constant bit rate. See CBR

contexts, 160–162

Control Panel, Phone and Modem Options
Dialing Rules tab, 56
modem installation, 53-54

controlling network access, 51

convergence (RIP), 81

converting private addresses to public addresses, 106

copying
dial-up connections, 64
modem properties, 55
task files, 170

cost
RIP, hop count, 79
unitless measurements, 95

count-to-infinity
RIP, 81
split horizon, 84

counters, Performance console, 253

CPS (Connection Point Services), 9, 214
configuring, 216
installing, 215
phone books
creating, 218
publishing, 219
system requirements, 215

creating
filters, 309-310
Help files, 225
IPSec policies, 303-304
keyboard shorcuts, 225
phone books, 218
remote access policies, 42
rules (IPSec), 305
user accounts, 36

cross-forest authentication, 38

CryptoAPI, 296

customizing
Help files, 225
phone books, 224

D

D-channels, 255

DACL (discretionary access control list), 292

data encryption, 5, 177

data modification, security risks, 298

Database Description Packets, 96

Database Exchange Process, 96

databases
  LSDBs, 92
    building, 94-95
    Database Description Packets, 96
    Database Exchange Process, 96
    synchronization, 95
  routing tables, 69
    dynamic routing, 72
    RIP, 79
    RIP for IPX, 110
    RTMP, 113
    static routing, 71

datagrams, MTU, 136

Dead Interval, 96, 135

decryption, hashed passwords, 27

dedicated links (Frame Relay), bandwidth, 258

default gateways, ASBRs, 103

default response rule
  IPSec, 302

default routes, 70, 104

default static route (NAT), configuring, 267

delegating administrative duties, 293

Delegation of Control Wizard (Active Directory), 293

delete command (Netsh), 160
  interface context, 165
  ras context, 162

deleting interfaces, 123

Demand Dial Wizard, 267

demand-dial routing, 4, 143-145, 149-150
  auto-static updating, 117
  example, 114
  interfaces, 123
    configuring, 146, 151
    NAT, 266
  numbered connections, 117
  ports, configuring, 145, 151
  PPP (Point-to-Point Protocol), 115-116
  remote access policies, configuring, 148, 152

  requirements, 113-114
  static routes, 147-148, 152
  troubleshooting, 323-324
  updates, 117
  usernames, 116

denial-of-service attacks, 299
  Ping of Death, 127

deploying IAS
  large-scale, 242-243
  logging, 235-236
  performance issues, 233
  security issues, 234-235
  small-scale, 242

DES (Data Encryption Standard), 184

designated router. See DR

designing
  networks, connectivity
    large-scale, 282–284
    medium-scale, 279-281
    SOHO, 276-279
  VPNs, 191-192

Destination Unreachable messages, 79

Device Manager, 55

devices, 124
  cable modems, 50
  interfaces, 122
  ISDN adapters, installing, 55
  modems
    dialing rules, 56
    installing, 53-54
    selecting, 54
  routers
    AppleTalk, 112
    failover, 80-81
    IGMP, 77
  X.25 cards, installing, 55

DHCP (Dynamic Host Configuration Protocol), 109, 264
  assigning IP addresses, 17
  hop-count threshold, 128
  relay agent, 7
    configuring, 128
    troubleshooting, 322

dhcp command (Netsh), 160

DHCPINFORM messages, 19

Dial-Up Connection Properties sheet
General tab, 59
Networking tab, 62
Options tab, 60-61
Security tab, 61

dial-up networking
access to resources, troubleshooting, 316
clients, 186
LANs, 187
VPNs, 188
connections
autodial, 64
callback, 64
copying, 64
NAT, configuring, 266
operator assisted dialing, 63
preferences, 63-64
properties, 59
troubleshooting, 314-316
X.25, 61

**Dialed Number Identification Service.
See DNIS**

dialing rules, area codes, 56-58

dialog boxes
Advanced Security Settings, 61
Internet Connection Sharing Settings
(ICS), 271
IP Filter List, 308
Modem Configuration, 60
New Static Route, 267
Options, 218
OSPF Area Configuration, 133

dictionary attacks, preventing, 234

Diffie-Hellman groups, 311

Dijkstra algorithm, 95

direct access, 51
security, 51
serial connections, 51
wireless, 51

**directory services (Windows 2000),
Active Directory, 291-293**

DirectParallel driver, 51

disabling
BAP, 249
IPSec Policy Agent Service, 305
Multilink, 248

disconnecting unused connections, 249

discovery, heartbeats, 138

**discretionary access control list
(DACL), 292**

displaying
scheduled tasks, 171
static routes, 187

**Distance Vector Multicast Routing
Protocols. See DVMRP**

**Distributed Password Authentication.
See DPA**

**Distributed Security Features
(Windows 2000), 290-291**
Active Directory, 291-293
Kerberos, 295
multi-protocol support, 295
PKI, 296

**DNIS (Dialed Number Identification
Service), 34**

DNS servers, assigning, 19

**dnsproxy command (Netsh), routing
context, 164**

domain controllers, throughput, 234

domains
logon process, smart cards, 25
OUs, 2915
security, 292
See also AS, 100
trust relationships, 293

downstream routing, 77

**DPA (Distributed Password
Authentication), 294**

DRs (designated routers), 96–97
election, 98
fault tolerance, 99
star configuration, 98
See also BDRs

DS-0. See Fractional T-1

dump command (Netsh), 160–161
interface context, 165
ras context, 162
routing context, 163–165

**DVMRP (Distance Vector Multicast
Routing Protocols), 75**

**Dynamic Host Configuration Protocol.
See DHCP**

dynamic routing, 72

E

EAP (Extensible Application Protocol), 22, 176
EAP-MD5, 23
smart cards
authentication, 182
configuring, 25-26

EAP-TLS (Extensible Authentication Protocol-Transport Layer Security), 23–24, 181

eavesdropping, 298

editing
filters, 309-310
Incoming Connections properties sheet, 65
IPSec policies, 303-304
profiles, 227
Registry, account lockout configuration, 234
RRAS properties, 15-16

editors (NAT), 107

EGRPs (exterior gateway routing protocols), 100

electing DRs (designated routers), 98

enabling
account lockout, 234
ASBR, 133
BAP, 249
EAP on RAS, 26
Multilink, 248
RRAS, 15, 122
rules, 305

encapsulation, 185

encryption, 5
clear text, 234
end-to-end, 184
keys, MS-CHAP v2, 181
L2TP, 184
MPPE, 29, 181
VPNs, 177

end-to-end encryption, 184

enrollment (certificates), configuring, 25

ESP (Encapsulating Security Payload), 180, 299

establishing
adjacencies, 96-97
connections, 14

event logging (OSPF), 133

Event Viewer, logging options, 137

examples, demand-dial routing, 114

exclusion, area code rules, 57

exec command (Netsh), 160

exit command (Netsh), 160

expiration interval (RIP), 132

exporting
data to backup IAS servers, 241
IPSec policies, 306-307

Extensible Application Protocol. See EAP

Extensible Authentication Protocol-Transport Layer Security. See EAP-TLS

external routes, 92, 103
filtering, 104
OSPF, configuring, 135
static routes, 104

extranets, 3

F

failover
links, 80-81
RIP for IPX, 111

Family Identifier field (RIP v1 messages), 86

fault tolerance
AppleTalk routing, 112
DRs, 99
RADIUS, 230

features
ATM, 257
RIP, 85

fields
OSPF packets, 93
RIP v2 messages, 89-90

files
  log files, formats, 236
  tasks, manipulating, 170
filters (traffic), 154–155
  creating, 309-310
  external routes, 104
  firewalls, 190
  fragmented packets, 127
  IP, 308
    IPSec filters, 309-310
    predefined actions, 302
firewalls, VPN configuration
  server behind firewall, 190
  server in front of firewall, 189
flexibility, PPP (Point-to-Point Protocol), 49
flooding LSAs (link-state advertisements), 94–95
forcing disconnections, 249
formats
  RIP v1 messages, 86
  RIP v2 messages, 89
forming adjacencies, 96–98
forwarding. See multicasting
Fractional T-1, 256
fragmentation, packet filtering, 127
Frame Relay, 258
  bandwidth, 258
  line speeds, 258
  logical circuits, 258
  Web site, 259
frames, capturing, 252
functionality, IAS, 230

G

gateways
  address, 71
  NetBIOS, 14
General Properties sheet (IP routing), 125
  Configuration tab, 127
  General tab, 126-127
  Heartbeat tab, 128
  Multicast Boundaries tab, 128

General RIP Requests, 80
General tab
  Dial-Up Connection Properties sheet, 57–59
  IP routing General Properties sheet), 125-127
    Enable IP router manager options, 126
    Fragmentation checking options, 127
    ICMP router discovery options, 127
global addresses, 106
Global Catalog, 233
global commands (Netsh), 160-161
graph theory, 95
GRE (Generic Routing Encapsulation), 182
Group Policies
  assigning, 306
  updates, 304
groups (Diffie-Hellman), 311
guest accounts, unauthenticated access, 35-36
GUIs
  MMC (Microsoft Management Console), 68
  Scheduled Tasks, 169-170

H

hacks, IPSec, 297-298
hardware
  ISDN adapters, installing, 55
  modems
    installing, 53-54
    selecting, 54
  X.25 cards, installing, 55
hashing, 27
HCL (Hardware Compatibility List), 121
headers
  ATM cells, 257
  OSPF, 93
Heartbeat tab (IP routing General Properties sheet), 128

heartbeats, 138

Hello packets, 96, 134

help command (Netsh), 160
   interface context, 165
   ras context, 162
   routing context, 163

Help files, creating, 225

hierarchical structure, OSPF, 100

HMAC-MD5, 183

HMAC-SHA, 183

hop count, 79
   infinity, 81
   RIP, configuring, 130
   threshold, 128

hosts
   DHCP, relay agents, 109
   multicast forwarding, 76
   routing, 69–70
   silent (RIP), 87

I

IAS (Internet Authentication Service),
6–8, 229
   authentication, 231-232
   backup servers, exporting data to, 241
   configuring, 238-239
   console, launching, 237
   deploying
      large-scale, 242-243
      logging strategy, 235-236
      performance issues, 233
      security issues, 234-235
      small-scale, 242
   functionality, 230
   installation, 236, 239-241
   physical security, 235
   realms, configuring, 238
   starting/stopping, 237
   testing, 241

ICANN (Internet Corporation for
Assigned Names and Numbers), 105

ICMP (Internet Control Message
Protocol), 108
   router discovery, configuring, 127

icons, Connection Manager, 225

ICS (Internet Connection
Sharing), 270
   affect on network services, 272
   configuring, 270-272
   connection sharing, enabling, 271
   internal interface, 272

identifying red/black LANs, IP
addresses, 193

identity attacks, 299

IEAK 5 (Internet Explorer
Administration Kit 5), 213

IETF (Internet Engineering Task
Force), NAT, 105
   disadvantages, 108
   editors, 107
   global addresses, 106
   local addresses, 106

IGMP (Internet Group Management
Protocol), 7, 68, 75
   configuring, 137
   proxy mode, 77, 193
   routers, 77
   troubleshooting, 322
   version 2, 137

igmp command (Netsh), routing
context, 164

IGPs (Interior Gateway Protocols), RIP
   administrative router shutdown, 80
   advertisements, 78
   convergence, 81
   Destination Unreachable messages, 79
   hop count, 79
   initialization, 80
   looping, 83
   metrics, 78
   routing tables, 79
   split horizon, 84
   timers, 80
   triggered updates, 84

IGRPs (interior gateway routing
protocols), 100

IKE (Internet Key Exchange), 300

implementing
CHAP, 28
IPSec, 300–301
MS-CHAP, 30

importing IPSec policies, 306–307

inbound connections, 265

inbound filters (IP), 308

incoming connections, configuring, 64

Incoming Connections properties sheet, 65

incoming packet protocol (RIP), selecting, 130

infinity numbers, 81

infrared serial access, 51

initialization
AppleTalk nodes, 112
RIP, 80

initiating demand-dial connections, 153

installing
CMAK, 220
computer certificates on RAS (smart cards), 24–25
Connection Manager, requirements, 220
CPS, 215
IAS, 236, 239–241
ISDN adapters, 55
matching certificates, L2TP over IPSec VPNs, 204
modems, 53–54
Phone Book Administrator, 215
smart cards, 58
X.25 cards, 55

inter-area routing, 100

interface command (Netsh), 160

interfaces, 71, 122
adding, 123
cost, assigning, 95
deleting, 123
demand-dial, 123, 146, 151
IGMP, configuring, 137
internal, 123
ICS, 272
NAT, configuring, 268

IP-in-IP tunnel interfaces, 123
LAN interfaces, 123
OSPF, configuring, 135-136
RIP, configuring, 129
RIP for IPX, configuring, 141
SAP for IPX, configuring, 142

internal routers, OSPF, 101

Internet, tunnels, 75

Internet Authentication Service. See IAS

Internet Connection Sharing Settings dialog box (ICS), 271

Internet Corporation for Assigned Names and Numbers. See ICANN

Internet Group Management Protocol. See IGMP

Internet interface (NAT)
configuring, 268
L2TP over IPSec filters, configuring, 195-197

Internet Key Exchange. See IKE

Internet Multicast Backbone, 75

Internet-based VPNs, 178

Internet-Intranet VPNs, 179

Internetwork Packet Exchange. See IPX

InterNIC, 105

interoperability, ATM versions, 258

Intranet-based VPNs, 179

IP Address field (RIP v1 messages), 86

IP addresses
APIPA, 17
CIDR, 87
identifying on red/black LANs, 193
IPSec, 309-310
multicast scopes, 74
NAT, 105
disadvantages, 108
editors, 107, 265
global addresses, 106
local addresses, 106
private addresses, 263

reuse, 106
RIP v2, subnetting, 91
router IDs, 95
static IP address assignment, 18
supernetting, 88
TCP/IP configuration, 17–18

ip command (Netsh)
interface context, 165
ras context, 162
routing context, 163

IP Filter List dialog box, 308

IP Filter Wizard, 309-310

IP routing, 125
DHCP relay agent, configuring, 128
General Properties sheet, 125
Configuration Tab, 127
General Tab, 126-127
Heartbeat tab, 128
Multicast Boundaries tab, 128
IGMP, configuring, 137
multicasting, 7, 137
boundaries, 137
troubleshooting, 322
OSPF
areas, 133-134
configuring, 133
external routing, 135
interfaces, 135-136
virtual interfaces, 134-135
packet filtering, 155, 308
RIP, 78
administrative router shutdown, 80
advanced options, 131-132
advertisements, 78
configuring, 129
convergence, 81
hop count, 79
initialization, 80
metrics, 78
neighbors, 131
security, 130
timers, 80
static routing, 128
IP routing protocols

IP subcontext, command combinations, 164

IP-in-IP tunnels, 123, 138

IPSec, 180, 297
attacks, 297-298
authentication, 307-308
checksums, 299
connection types, 308
default response rule, 302
ESP, 299
filters, 309-310
implementing, 300–301
policies
assigning to Group Policy object, 306
creating, 303-304
exporting, 306-307
importing, 306-307
managing, 302-303
predefined, 301
predefined filter actions, 302
Request Security policy, 301
Require Security policy, 302
Respond Only policy, 301
rules, 304
activating, 305
creating, 305
Security Rules Wizard, 305

IPX (Internetwork Packet Exchange), 8, 19, 52, 68, 109
general properties, configuring, 139
NetBIOS broadcasts, configuring, 139-140
packet filtering, 155
RIP for IPX
advertisements, 110
configuring, 140
link failover, 111
routing tables, 110
SAP for IPX, configuring, 142
static routes, configuring, 140
ticks, 110

ipx command (Netsh)
ras context, 162
routing context, 163
subcontext, command combinations, 165

IrDA, 51

ISAKMP (Internet Security Association Key Management Protocol), 300

ISDN (Integrated Services Digital Network), 255
   2B+D, 255
   access interfaces, 255
   adapters, installing, 55
   BRI, 248
   connections, troubleshooting, 317
   last mile, 255
   Web sites, 256

isolating internal network topologies (OSPF), 100

ISPs (Internet Service Providers)
   dial-up links, 178
   NSIPS, 48
   remote access services, 233
   roaming, 48
   security, 48
   selecting, 48

K

KDC (Key Distribution Center), 296

Kerberos, 295–296

key management, 311

keyboard shortcuts, creating, 225

keys
   MS-CHAP v2, 30
   PKI, 296

L

L2TP (Layer 2 Tunneling Protocol), 5, 175, 182
   authentication, 183
   encryption, 184
   remote access VPN configuration, 192-197
      Internet interface, 192
      Intranet interface, 193
      over IPSec filters, 195-196
      ports, 195
      remote access policies, 197
   router-to-router VPNs, configuring, 204-207
   without DES, 184

LANs
   black, reachability, 188-189
   dial-up clients, 187
   interfaces, 123
   NAT (Network Address Translation), 106
   persistent static routes, adding, 187
   point-to-LAN remote access connectivity, 11
   protocols, 52

large networks
   connectivity, designing, 282–284
   IAS deployment, 242-243

last mile, 255

launching
   CMAK Wizard, 221
   IAS console, 237
   Performance console, 253

leased lines, T-carriers, 256

license agreement, profiles, 225

line speeds
   ATM, 257
   Frame Relay, 258

link state advertisements. See LSAs

link state routing protocols, OSPF (Open Shortest Path First), 7
   ABRs, 100
   adjacencies, 95-97
   areas, 92, 100
   ASBRs, 101
   backbone routers, 100–101
   BDRs, 99
   Database Exchange Process, 96
   Dead Interval, 96
   DRs, 96–97
   external routes, 92, 103
   hierarchical structure, 100
   inter-area routing, 100
   LSDB, building, 94-95
   network types, 97
   partitioning, 100
   router prioritization, 98-99
   routing tables, building, 95
   scaling, 98
   simple password authentication, 92
   SPF tree, 95
   summarization, 92
   TOS (type-of-service) requests, 93

Link State Update packets, 96

links
demand-dial, 143–145, 149–151
failover, 80–81
RIP for IPX, 111
split horizon, 84
PPP, bundling, 248
WANs, telecommunications, 254–256

listing scheduled tasks, 171

local addresses, 106

Location properties sheet, General tab, 57

logging
affect on IAS deployment, 235–236
Event Viewer options, 137
file formats, 236
IPX, configuring, 139
start options, 236

logical circuits, Frame Relay, 258

logical interfaces, IP-in-IP tunnels, 138

logon process, smart card configuration, 25

looping
multipath networks, 84
RIP, 83
split-horizon, 84

LSAs (link state advertisements), 92
flooding, 94–95

LSDBs (link state databases), 92
Database Description Packets, 96
Database Exchange Process, 96
synchronization, 95

M

MAC-level broadcasting, 87

machine certificates (L2TP over IPSec VPNs), installing, 204

maintenance protocols, ICMP (Internet Control Message Protocol), 108

man-in-the-middle attacks, 299

managing
IPSec policies, 302–303
keys, 311
policies (IPSec), rules, 304
security associations, 300

manipulating task files, 170

mapping tables (NAT), 108

MBONE (multicast backbone), 75

MD4 hashing scheme, 29

medium-sized networks, designing connectivity, 279–281

member servers, authentication, 37

membership
AppleTalk zones, 113
multicast groups, 75
stub areas, 105

merging profiles, 221

messages
advertisements, SAP for IPX, 111
DHCPINFORM, 19
EAP, 22
EAP-Request, 23
General RIP Requests, 80
PAP, exchange process, 33
RIP v1, 86
RIP v2, 89–90

metric field (RIP v1 messages), 86

metrics, 71
RIP, 78
See also cost

Microsoft Management Console. See MMC

mixed-mode domain controllers, authentication, 37

MMC (Microsoft Management Console), 68

Modem Configuration dialog box, 60

modems
dialing parameters, configuring, 56
installing, 53–54
properties, copying, 55
selecting, 54

modes, Netsh, 161

monitoring
connections, 59
traffic usage patterns, 250–251

MPPE (Microsoft Point-to-Point Encryption), 29, 181

mrinfo command-line tool, 166

MS-CHAP, 29–30

MS-CHAP v2 , 30-31, 176
encryption keys, 181

MS-RAS, 21

MTU (maximum transmission unit), 136

Multicast Boundaries tab (IP Routing general properties sheet), 128

Multicast Scopes tab (IP routing General Properties sheet), 126

multicasting
announcements, RIP v2, 91
applications, 75
boundaries, 137
boundaries, 74
Class D addresses, 76
forwarding, comparing to multicast routing, 76
groups, 75
heartbeats, configuring, 138
IGMP, 77
MBONE, 75
routing protocols, 7, 74–77
scopes, 74
troubleshooting, 322
tunnels, 75

Multilink, 5, 50, 248

multipath networks, looping, 84

multitasking, accounting and authentication, 230

Must Be Zero field (RIP v1 messages), 86

mutual authentication, 176-177, 181

N

nailed-up connections, packet-switched services, 256

name resolution
applications, 269
NAT, configuring, 269
TCP/IP, 18, 52

naming conventions
phone books, 218
Service Names (Connection Manager), 221

NAS (Network Access Server), 230

NAT (Network Address Translation), 68, 105, 262-263
addressing component, 263
global addresses, 106
local addresses, 106
mapping tables, 108
private addresses, 263
configuring, 265-270
application, 265
default static routes, 267
demand-dial interfaces, 266
dial-up connections, 266
internal interface, 268
Internet interface, 268
name resolution, 269
network card, 265-266
permanent connections, 267
remote application access, 269
disadvantages, 108
editors, 107, 265
translation component, 263
troubleshooting, 325

nat command (Netsh), routing context, 164

NBMA (non-broadcast multiple access) networks
OSPF, 97, 136
Poll interval, 136
star configuration, 98

NDIS.sys, 13

NDISWAN.sys, 13

negotiation, PPP, 20

neighbors
adjacencies, 96–97
OSPF, configuring, 136
RIP, configuring, 131

NetBEUI, 20, 52, 74
NetBIOS gateway, 14

netbeui command (Netsh), ras context, 162

netbios command (Netsh), routing context, 165

NetBIOS
broadcasts, IPX configuration, 139–140
gateway, 14

netmask, 70

Netsh, 159
commands. optional parameters, 160
contexts, 160–62
global commands, 160–161
modes, 161

Network Address Translation. See NAT

network cards (NAT), configuring, 265–266

Network Monitor, 252

network number (AppleTalk), 112

Network Unreachable messages, 79

Networking tab, Dial-Up Connection Properties sheet, 62

networks
addresses, 70, 106
attacks, 298
autonomous, 78
connectivity, designing
large networks, 282, 284
medium-sized networks, 279-281
SOHO, 276-277, 279
convergence, 81
monitoring, 251
resources, authorization, 51
routes, 70
single path, loops, 84
sizing guide, 275

New Static Route dialog box, 267

Next Hop field (RIP v2 messages), 90

nodes (AppleTalk), 112–113

Novell Netware, IPX (Internetwork Packet Exchange), 8

NSIPS (Navy Standard Integrated Personal System), 48

NTLM (Windows NT LAN Manager), 38, 294

numbered connections, 117

O

Oakley key generation protocol, 300

objects (Windows 2000), granular control, 291–292

offline command (Netsh), 160–161

online command (Netsh), 160–161

Open Shortest Path First. See OSPF

operation mode (RIP), selecting, 129

operator assisted dialing, 63

optional parameters, Netsh commands, 160

options
General tab (IP routing General Properties sheet)
Enable fragmentation checking, 127
Enable IP router manager, 126
ICMP router discovery, 127
mrinfo command, 166

Options dialog box, 218

Options tab, Dial-Up Connection Properties sheet, 60-61

organizational units. See OUs

OSPF (Open Shortest Path First)
ABRs (area border routers), 100–101
adjacencies, 95
calculating, 97
forming, 96-97
areas, 92, 100
configuring, 133-134
topology, 100
AS (Autonomous Systems), stub areas, 104
ASBRs (AS boundary routers), 101, 133
backbone, 100–101

BDRs (backup designated routers), 99
configuring, 133
Database Exchange Process, 96
Dead Interval, 96
Dijkstra algorithm, URL, 95
DRs, 96–97
    election, 98
    fault tolerance, 99
event logging, 133
external routes, 92, 103–104, 135
Hello packets, 96
hierarchical structure, 100
inter-area routing, 100
interfaces, configuring, 135-136
LSAs, flooding, 94-95
LSDB (link state database)
    building, 94-95
    synchronization, 95
NBMA networks, star configuration, 98
network types, 97
out-of-service routers, 96
packets, 96
    Database Description Packets, 96
    Link State Update packets, 96
    structure, 93
partitioning, 100
prioritizing routers, 98-99
routing table, building, 95
scaling, 98
simple password authentication, 92
SPF tree, 95
static IP address assignment, 18
stub areas, 133
summarization, 92
TOS (type-of-service) routing, 93
transit area, 134
troubleshooting, 321
virtual interfaces, configuring, 134–135
virtual links, 102

OSPF Area Configuration dialog box, 133

ospf command (Netsh), routing context, 164

OUs (organizational units), 291

out-of-service routers (OSPF), 96

outbound filters (IP), 308

outgoing packet protocol (RIP), selecting, 129

P

packet-switched services, 256
ATM
    connections, 257
    features, 257
    switches, 258
    versions, interoperability, 258
Frame Relay, 258

packets
capturing, 252
filtering, 154-155
fragmentation, 127
OSPF
    Database Description Packets, 96
    headers, 93
    Hello, 96
    Link State Update packets, 96
See also cells

PAP (Password Authentication Protocol), 32-33

Parallel Technologies Web site, 51

parameters
at command, 171
dialing rules, configuring, 56
Netsh commands, 160

partitioning, 100

pass-through VPNs, 179

passive attacks, 297

passwords
authentication, 21
    CHAP, 27-28
    PAP, 32-33
    RIP, configuring, 130
    RIP v2, 90
plaintext, enabling for OSPF, 133
See also shared secrets

pathping, 167–169

PBS (Phone Book Service), 214

peer filtering, 85

performance, affect on IAS deployment, 233

Performance console, 253

periodic announcement interval (RIP), setting, 131

permanent connections (NAT), configuring, 267

permissions
delegating, 293
remote access, 43

persistent connections, 123, 205

persistent static routes, 187

Phone and Modem Options (Control Panel)
Dialing Rules tab, 56
modem installation, 53-54
See also dialing rules

Phone Book Administrator, installing, 215

phone books, 214
creating, 218
customizing, 224
naming, 218
publishing, 219
Release directory, specifying, 219

phone numbers, server-provided, 249

physical security, IAS servers, 235

Ping of Death, 127

PKI (Public Key Infrastructure), 296

Plain Old Telephone Service. See POTS

plaintext passwords (OSPF), enabling, 133

planning
IAS deployment
logging strategy, 235-236
performance issues, 233
security issues, 234-235
VPN design, 191-192

Plug and Play, 53

point-to-LAN remote access connectivity, 11

point-to-point delivery. See unicast routing

point-to-point networks
adjacencies, 97
OSPF, 97
remote access connectivity, 11

poisoned-reverse processing (RIP), 132

policies, 6
Active Directory, domain security, 292
exporting, 306-307
importing, 306-307
IPSec
default response rule, 302
Request Security, 301
Respond Only, 301
remote access, configuring, 197

policies (IPSec)
adding, 303-304
assigning to Group Policy object, 306
managing, 302-303
predefined, 301
properties sheeet, 304
Require Security, 302
rules, 304-305
updating, 303-304

Poll interval, 136

POP (point-of-presence), 174, 214

ports, 124, 258
demand-dial routing, 145, 151
L2TP servers, configuring, 195

Ports Properties sheet, 266

POTS (Plain Old Telephone Service), 50, 254

PPP (Point-to-Point Protocol), 3, 20, 49
demand-dial routing, 115-116
EAP, 22
EAP-MD5, 23
EAP-TLS, 23-24
smart cards, 24-26
links, bundling, 248

PPTP (Point-to-Point Tunneling Protocol), 5, 181
authentication, 181
remote access VPN configuration, 198-199
filters, 199-201
Internet interface, 198
Intranet interface, 198
policies, 201
ports, 199
requirements, 182
router-to-router VPN configuration, 208-211

predefined filter actions (IPSec), 302

predefined policies (IPSec), 301

Preference Levels tab (IP Routing General Properties sheet), 125

preferences, dial-up connections, 63–64

preshared keys, authentication, 308

preventing dictionary attacks, 234

PRI (Primary Rate Interface), 255

prioritizing routers, 98–99

private addressing (NAT), 105, 263
  disadvantages, 108
  editors, 107
  global addresses, 106
  local addresses, 106
  network IDs, 106

private network services, 256

profiles, 44–46
  advanced configuration, 226
  authentication types, 45
  Connection Manager, 214, 221, 226
  editing, 227
  license agreement, 225
  merging, 221

promiscuous mode, 252

properties
  dial-up connections, 59
  ISDN adapters, configuring, 55
  modems, copying, 55

properties sheet
  IAS, configuring, 238–239
  remote access policy profile, 44–45
  RRAS, editing, 15–16

protocols
  challenge-response authentication
    CHAP, 27-28
    MS-CHAP, 29-30
    MS-CHAP v2, 30-31
    PAP, 32-33
    SPAP, 32
  remote access
    MS-RAS, 21
    PPP, 20
  routing. See routing protocols
  tunneling. See tunneling

PSTN (public switched telephone network), 50
  See also POTS

public addressing (NAT), 105
  disadvantages, 108
  editors, 107
  global addresses, 106
  local addresses, 106

Public Key Infrastructure. See PKI

public-key protocols, 295

publishing phone books, 219

pushd command (Netsh), 160

Q–R

QoS (Quality of Service), 257

quit command (Netsh), 161

radio-based wireless access, 51

RADIUS (Remote Authentication Dial-In User Service), 39, 229
  fault tolerance, 230
  IAS
    authentication, 231-232
    configuring, 238-239
    deploying, 233-236
    functionality, 230
    installation, 236, 239-241
    realms, 238
    starting/stopping, 237
    testing, 241
  NAS, 230

ranges (AppleTalk), 112

ras command (Netsh), 161
  subcontexts, 162

RAS Idle Disconnect, 5

RAS server interface, 14

reachability, black LANs, 188–189

realms (Kerberos), 296
  replacement, configuring, 239

red LANs, 185
  IP addresses, identifying, 193

referencing profiles, 222

Registry
account lockout configuration, 234
DHCP server configuration, 17

rejecting external routes, 104

relay agents, DHCP, 109

relay command (Netsh), routing context, 164

Release directory, 219

remote access
permissions, 39
policies (demand-dial routing), configuring, 148, 152
protocols
MS-RAS, 21
PPP, 20
services, ISPs, 233
smart cards, 6

remote access VPNs, 192
client setup, 202
connections, troubleshooting, 317–318
L2TP server, 192–197
Internet interface, 192
Intranet interface, 193
over IPSec filters, 195-196
policies, configuring, 197
ports, configuring, 195
policies, configuring, 197
PPTP server, 198–199
filters, 199-201
Internet interface, 198
Intranet interface, 198
policies, 201
ports, configuring, 199
returning traffic, 318
troubleshooting, 317

remote control software, 12

remote gateway, 185

remote users, account lockout, 234

removing interfaces, 123

Request Security policy (IPSec), 301

requests
logging, 235
LSAs, 96

Require Security policy (IPSec), 302

requirements
CPS installation, 215
demand-dial routing, 113–114
PPTP, 182
software rollout, 251
VPNs
connections, 177
design, 191-192

requirements gathering, 250–251

reset command (Netsh)
interface context, 165
routing context, 163–164

resetting account lockout, 235

resources
accessing on dial-up networks, 316
security, 298

Respond Only policy (IPsec), 301

responses, LSAs, 96

retransmit interval, 134

reusing IP addresses, 106

RFC 1256, router discovery and advertising, 127

RFC 158, OSPF (Open Shortest Path First), 92

RFC 1990, Multilink Protocol, 248

RIP (Routing Information Protocol), 7, 68, 78, 85
administrative router shutdown, 80
advertisements, 78
bandwidth consumption, 87
configuring, 129
advanced options, 131-132
authentication, 130
convergence, 81
count-to-infinity, 81
Destination Unreachable messages, 79
for IPX, 8, 110
configuring, 140
interfaces, configuring, 141
troubleshooting, 322-323
for SAP, troubleshooting, 322–323
hop count, 79
incoming packet protocol, selecting, 130
initialization, 80

links, failover, 80-81
looping, 83
MAC-level broadcasting, 87
messages, 86
metrics, 78
mixed version environment, 91
neighbors, configuring, 131
outgoing packet protocol, selecting, 129
poison-reverse processing, 132
routing tables, 79, 132
security, 89, 130
silent hosts, 87
split-horizon processing, 132
subnetting, 88
timers, 80
triggered updates, 84, 132
troubleshooting, 89, 320
Windows 2000 features, 85
See also RIP v2

rip command (Netsh), routing context, 164-165

RIP v2, 89–90

roaming, 48

rollout, software requirements, 251

route add command, 187

route filtering, 85

route print command, 187

Route Tag field (RIP v2 messages), 89

router ID, 95

router routing, 69

router-to-router VPNs, 202-203
calling router, configuring, 207
connections, configuring, 203
L2TP, configuring, 204-207
PPTP, configuring, 208-211
troubleshooting, 318-319

routerdiscovery command (Netsh), router context, 164

routing
demand-dial routing, troubleshooting, 323-324
discovery, heartbeats, 138
dynamic routing, 72
failover, 80-81
metrics, 71

point-to-LAN, 14
static routing, 71
summarization, 92
tables, 69-70
triggered updates, 84
troubleshooting, 319-320
upstream, 77
VPNs, 185-186
See also routing protocols

routing command (Netsh), 161

Routing Information Protocol. See RIP

routing protocols, 75
AppleTalk, 111
   configuring, 153
   network number, 112
   nodes, 112
   routers, 112
   RTMP, 113
   zones, 113
IGMP, configuring, 137
IP routing, packet filtering, 155
IPX, 109, 139
   general properties, configuring, 139
   NetBIOS broadcasts, 139
   packet filtering, 155
   RIP for IPX, 110, 140
   SAP for IPX, 111, 142
   static routes, 140
multicasting, 74
OSPF, 7, 92
   ABRs, 100
   adjacencies, 95-97
   areas, 92, 100, 133-134
   ASBRs, 101
   backbone routers, 100–101
   BDRs, 99
   configuring, 133
   Database Exchange Process, 96
   Dead Interval, 96
   DRs, 96–97
   external routes, 92, 103, 135
   hierarchical structure, 100
   inter-area routing, 100
   interfaces, 135-136
   LSDB, building, 94-95
   network types, 97

partitioning, 100
router prioritization, 98-99
routing tables, building, 95
scaling, 98
simple password authentication, 92
SPF tree, 95
summarization, 92
TOS requests, 93
troubleshooting, 321
virtual interfaces, 134-135
RIP, 7, 79
  advanced options, 131-132
  configuring, 129
  convergence, 81
  expiration interval, 132
  for IPX, 8, 110, 322-323
  for SAP, 111, 322–323
  hop count, 79
  looping, 83
  mixed version environments, 91
  neighbors, 131
  security, 130
  silent hosts, 87
  split horizon, 84
  triggered updates, 84
  troubleshooting, 320
  Windows 2000 features, 85
unicast, 73

RTMP (Routing Table Maintenance Protocol), 113

rules
activating, 305
IPSec, 302–305
realm replacement, configuring, 239

running Performance console, 253

S

SACL (system access control list), 292

SAM (security accounts manager), 291

SAP (Service Advertisement Protocol), 8, 68
  IPX, configuring, 111, 142

sap command (Netsh), routing context, 165

SAs (security associations), 300

scaling OSPF, 98

scenarios
IAS deployment
  large-scale, 242-243
  small-scale, 242
network connectivity
  large networks, 282–284
  medium-sized networks, 279-281
  SOHO networks, 276-277, 279

Scheduled Tasks, 169-170

scheduling
auto-static updates, 117
tasks, at command, 170

scopes
boundaries, 137
TTL, 138

scripts, 316
auto-static updates, 166

security, 48
affect on IAS deployment, 234-235
authentication, 21
  account lockout, 234
  CHAP, 27-28
  cross-forest, 38
  DPA, 294
  EAP, 22-26
  IAS, 8, 229, 231-232
  key management, 311
  L2TP, 183
  member servers, 37
  MS-CHAP, 29-30
  MS-CHAP v2, 30-31
  mutual authentication, 176-177
  PAP, 32-33
  PPTP, 181
  RADIUS, 39
  realm names, 238
  RIP v2, 91
  SLIP, 49
  SPAP, 32
  standalone servers, 37
  Windows NT 4.0, 38
authorization, 21
  IAS, 233
  remote access policies, 41-46
  user accounts, configuring, 39-40
CA (certificate authority), 24

checksums, 299
data encryption, 5
direct access, 51
Distributed Security Features (Windows
  2000), 290-291
    Active Directory, 291-293
    authentication, 295
    multi-protocol support, 295
    PKI, 296
encryption
    clear text, 234
    L2TP, 184
    MPPE, 29
firewalls, VPN configuration, 189-190
IAS, 229
IP filters, 308–310
IPSec, 297
    attacks, 297-298
    authentication, 307-308
    connection types, 308
    default response rule, 302
    ESP, 299
    implementing, 300-301
    policy management, 302-303
    predefined filter actions, 302
    Request Security policy, 301
    Require Security policy, 302
    Respond Only policy, 301
    rules, 304
ISPs, 48
packet filtering, 154-155
policies, 6
remote access VPNs, L2TP servers, 194
RIP, 89
    configuring, 130
    version 2, authentication, 90
shared secrets, 234
simple password authentication, 92
smart cards, 6
unauthenticated access, 33
    ANI/CLI, 34-35
    DNIS, 34
    guest accounts, 35-36
See also attacks
security associations. See SAs
security parameters index. See SPI
Security Rules Wizard, 305

**Security tab, Dial-Up Connection
  Properties sheet, 61**
seed routers, 112–113
selecting
  best path, RIP, 79
  EAP types, 22
  ISPs, 48
  key exchange security methods, 311
  log data, 235
  modems, 54
  operation mode (RIP), 129
serial connections, 51
server placement, VPNs
  behind firewall, 190
  in front of firewall, 189
server-provided phone numbers, 249
servers
  member, authentication, 37
  POPs, phone books, 214, 218
  RADIUS
    authentication, 39
    fault tolerance, 230
  standalone, authentication, 37
  upgrading, 37-38
  Windows 2000 Professional, inbound
    connections, 64
**Service Advertisement Protocol.
  See SAP**
**service name (Connection Manager),
  naming conventions, 221**
service profiles, 220
services
  ATM, 258
  NAT
    configuring, 265-270
    editors, 265
  telecommunications, 254
    ISDN, 255-256
    packet-switched, 256
    POTS, 254
    T-carriers, 256
sessions, establishing, 14
set command (Netsh), 161
  interface context, 165
  ras context, 162

set/show authmode command (Netsh), ras context, 163

set/show command (Netsh), routing context, 165

set/show loglevel command (Netsh), routing context, 164

set/show tracing command (Netsh), ras context, 163

set/show user command (Netsh), ras context, 163

shared secrets, 234

shared services, clouds, 256

shared–secret protocol, 296

sharing connections, 6, 271

shortcuts, commands, 161

show activeservers command (Netsh), ras context, 163

show boundarystats command (Netsh), routing context, 164

show client command (Netsh), ras context, 163

show command (Netsh), 161
 interface context, 165
 ras context, 162
 routing context, 163

show helper command (Netsh), routing context, 164

show mfe command (Netsh), routing context, 164

show mfestats command (Netsh), routing context, 164

show protocol command (Netsh), routing context, 164

show route command (Netsh), routing context, 165

show service command (Netsh), routing context, 165

showrtmdestinations command (Netsh), routing context, 164

silent RIP, 87

Simple Network Management Protocol. See SNMP, 68

simple password authentication, 92

single path networks, loops, 84

sizing guide, networks, 275

SLIP (Serial-Line Interface Protocol), 49

small IAS deployment, 242

smart cards, 6, 24
 authentication, 182
 configuring, 24–26
 installing, 58

SMS (Systems Management Server), 252

sniffing, 298

SNMP (Simple Network Management Protocol), 68

software
 remote control, 12
 rollout, requirements, 251

SOHO (small office/home office)
 connectivity, network design, 276-277, 279
 NAT, 262–263
  addressing component, 263
  configuring, 265-270
  name-resolution component, 264
  translation component, 263

SPAP, 32

SPF (Shortest Path First), 92, 95

SPI (security parameters index), 300

split–horizon processing
 RIP, 132
 with poison reverse, 84

SSL (Secure Socket Layer), 295

stack command (Netsh), 160

standalone servers
 authentication, 37
 EAP-TLS, 182
 upgrading, 37–38

star configuration, NBMA, 98

start options, logging, 236

starting
 CMAK Wizard, 221
 IAS, 237
 performance console, 253
 RIP routers, 80
 Schedule service, 170

static IP addresses, assigning, 18

static NetBIOS names (IPX), configuring, 140

static routes, 71, 104
configuring, 128
demand-dial routing, 117
auto-static updating, 117
configuring, 147-148, 152
IPX, configuring, 140
viewing, 187

static service entries (IPX), configuring, 140

statistical multiplexing, 259

stopping IAS, 237

storing log files, 235

structure, OSPF packets, 93

stub areas, 104–105, 133

subcontexts, 160
IP, command combinations, 164
IPX, command combinations, 165
ras context, 162

Subnet Mask field (RIP v2 messages), 90

subnetting
AppleTalk, seed routers, 112
masking
advertisements, 92
NAT configuration, 266
ranges, 112
RIP v1, 88
RIP v2, 91

summarization, 92

supernetting, 88

supported protocols, 6
AppleTalk, 20
IPX, 19
NetBEUI, 20
TCP/IP, 16
assigning IP addresses, 17-18
name resolution, 18
unicast routing protocols, 73
Windows 2000, 295

switches, 258
pathping, 167, 169
ports, 258

synchronization
accounts, 292
LSDB, 95

syntax
mrinfo command, 166
pathping, 167, 169

System applet (Device Manager), 55

system requirements
Connection Manager, installing, 220
CPS, 215

Systems Management Server. See SMS

T

T-carriers, 256

tabs
Dial-up Connection Properties sheet, 59
General Properties sheet (IP routing), 125
Configuration tab, 127
General tab, 126-127
Heatbeat tab, 128
Multicast Boundaries tab, 128
IP routing General Properties sheet
Configuration tab, 127
General tab, 126-127
Heartbeat tab, 128
Multicast Boundaries tab, 128

TAPI, 13

tasks
listing, 171
scheduling, 170

TCP/IP (Transmission Control Protocol/Internet Protocol), 16, 52
IP addresses
assigning, 17-18
name resolution, 18
NAT configuration, 265-266

telecommunications services, 254
ISDN, 255-256
packet-switched services, 256
ATM, 257
Frame Relay, 258
POTS, 254
T-carriers, 256

telephone numbers, server-provided, 249

template files, CMAK, 227

testing IAS, 241

throughput, domain controllers, 234

tickets, 296

ticks (IPX), 110

timers, RIP, 80

TLS (Transport Layer Security), 23-24

tools
  mrinfo, 166
  Netsh, 159
  pathping, 167, 169
  Scheduled Tasks, 169-170

topologies
  looping, multipath networks, 84
  OSPF, isolating, 100
  RIP
    advertisements, 78
    convergence, 81
  split horizon, 84

TOS (type-of-service) routing, 93

totally stubby areas, 104

traffic
  bursty, 256
  capturing, 252
  filtering, 154-155
    firewalls, 190
    IP, 308-310
  WANs
    analyzing, 250
    links, usage, 251

transit areas, 102, 134

translating private addresses to public addresses, 106

triggered updates, 84, 132

Triple DES, 184

troubleshooting
  count-to-infinity, 84
  demand-dial routing, 323-324
  DHCP relay agent, 322
  dial-up networking
    access to resources, 316
    connections, 314-316

  IP multicasting, 322
  ISDN connections, 317
  loops, multipath networks, 84
  NAT, 325
  OSPF, 321
  remote access VPNs, 317
    connections, 317-318
    returning traffic, 318
  RIP, 89
  router-to-router VPNs, 318-319
  routing protocols, 319-320
    RIP for IP, 320
    RIP for IPX, 322-323
    RIP for SAP, 322-323
  utilities
    mrinfo, 166
    Netsh, 159-162
    pathping, 167-169

trust relationships (domains), 293

TTL scoping, configuring, 138

tunneling, 75
  IP-in-IP, 138
  IPSec, 180
  L2TP, 182
    authentication, 183
    encryption, 184
    remote access VPN configuration, 192-197
    router-to-router VPNs, 204-207
  PPTP, 5, 181
    remote access VPN configuration, 198-201
    requirements, 182
    router-to-router VPNs, 208-211
  VPNs, 230

two-way demand-dial routing connections
  configuring, 143-145, 149-150
  interfaces, configuring, 146, 151
  ports, configuring, 145, 151

U

UBR (unspecified bit rate), 258

unalias command (Netsh), 161-163

unauthenticated access, 33

ANI/CLI, 34–35
brute force attacks, 36
DNIS, 34

uncontrolled adjacencies, 98

unicast routing, 73

unitless measurements, 95

unnumbered connections, 118

unreachable destinations, 81

unspecified bit rate. See UBR

unused connections, disconnecting, 249

update command (Netsh), routing context, 164–165

updates (routing)
auto-static, 117
demand-dial, 117
peer filtering, 85
split horizon, 84
triggered, 84

updating IPSec policies, 303–304

upgrading servers, 37–38

upstream routers, 77

URLs (Universal Resource Locators), Dijkstra's algorithm, 95

usage patterns (traffic)
monitoring, 250
WAN links, 251

user accounts
callback options, 40
caller ID verification, 40
configuring, 39
creating, 36
remote access permission, 39, 43
remote access policies, 41
   conditions, 43
   creating, 42
   profiles, 44–46
static IP address assignment, 40

user directory (Windows 2000), objects, 291

user services, enabling over shared connections, 272

usernames, demand-dial routing, 116

utilities
mrinfo, 166
Netsh, 159
   contexts, 162
   global commands, 160–161
pathping, 167, 169
Scheduled Tasks, 169–170

V

VBR (Variable Bit Rate), 258

vector, 78

verifying Caller ID, 40

Version field (RIP v1 messages), 86

versions, interoperability
ATM, 258
RIP, 78, 91

viewing
scheduled tasks, 171
static routes, 187

virtual interfaces (OSPF), configuring, 134–135

virtual links, 102

Virtual Path Identifier/Virtual Channel Identifier. See VPI/VCI

Virtual Private Networks. See VPNs

VPI/VCI (Virtual Path Identifier/Virtual Channel Identifier), 257

VPNs (Virtual Private Networks), 9
configuring, 191
connections, 174, 176
designing, 191–192
dial-up clients, 186, 188
firewalls, 189
incoming connections, configuring, 65
Internet-based, 178
Internet-Intranet, 179
Intranet-based, 179
remote access, 192
   client setup, 202
   L2TP server, 192–197
   PPTP server, 198–201
   troubleshooting, 317–318
remote gateway, 185

router-to-router, 202-203
calling router, configuring, 207
connections, 203
L2TP, 204-207
PPTP, 208-211
troubleshooting, 318-319
routing, 185-186
server configuration
behind firewall, 190
in front of firewall, 189
support configuration, 223
tunneling protocols, 230
IPSec, 180
L2TP, 182-184
PPTP, 181

W

WANs (wide-area networks)
demand-dial routing, 4
miniport drivers, 13
requirements, 250-251
telecommunication services, 254
ISDN, 255-256
packet-switched, 256
POTS, 254
T-carriers, 256
traffic
analyzing, 250
usage, 251

Web sites
ATM, 257
Dijkstra algorithm, 95
Frame Relay, 259
ICANN (Internet Corporation for
Assigned Names and Numbers), 105
InterNIC, 105
ISDN, 256
Parallel Technologies, 51
T-1, 256

Windows 2000
authentication, 36
cross-forest authentication, 38
IGMP proxy, 77
member servers, authentication, 37
standalone servers
authentication, 37
upgrading, 37-38

Windows 95, MS-CHAP v2, 31

Windows Components Wizard, 25, 237
CPS installation, 215

Windows NT 4.0
Service Pack 3, 38
Service Pack 4, 38

wins command (Netsh), 161

WINS servers, assigning, 19

wireless access, IrDA, 51

Wizards, 5
CMAK, starting, 221
Delegation of Control, 293
Demand Dial, 267
IP Filter Wizard, 309-310
Scheduled Task Wizard, 170
Security Rules Wizard (IPSec), 305
Windows Component Wizard, 25,
215, 237

X-Z

X.25, 51
card installation, 55
dialup connections, configuring, 61

X.509 certificates, 296

zones, 113

Windows 2000 Answers

This is the updated edition of New Riders' best-selling *Inside Windows NT Server 4*. Taking the author-driven, no-nonsense approach that we pioneered with our *Landmark* books, New Riders proudly offers something unique for Windows 2000 administrators—an interesting and discriminating book on Windows 2000 Server, written by someone in the trenches who can anticipate your situation and provide answers you can trust.

INSIDE
Windows 2000
Server

William Boswell

ISBN: 1-56205-929-7

Windows 2000
ESSENTIAL
REFERENCE

Steven Tate, et al.

ISBN: 0-7357-0869-X

Architected to be the most navigable, useful, and value-packed reference for Windows 2000, this book uses a creative "telescoping" design that you can adapt to your style of learning. It's a concise, focused, and quick reference for Windows 2000, providing the kind of practical advice, tips, procedures, and additional resources that every administrator will need.

Windows 2000 Active Directory is just one of several new Windows 2000 titles from New Riders' acclaimed *Landmark* series. Perfect for network architects and administrators, this book describes the intricacies of Active Directory while keeping real-world systems and constraints in mind. It's a detailed, solution-oriented book which addresses the need for a single work to planning, deploying, and managing Active Directory in an enterprise setting.

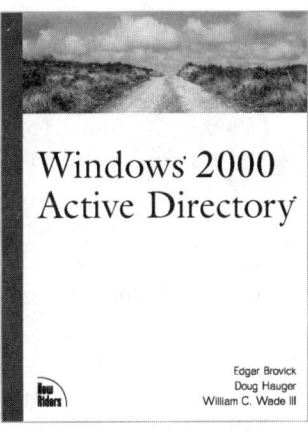

Windows 2000
Active Directory

Edgar Brovick
Doug Hauger
William C. Wade III

ISBN: 0-7357-0870-3

Advanced Information on Networking Technologies

New Riders Books Offer Advice and Experience

LANDMARK

Rethinking Computer Books

We know how important it is to have access to detailed, solution-oriented information on core technologies. *Landmark* books contain the essential information you need to solve technical problems. Written by experts and subjected to rigorous peer and technical reviews, our *Landmark* books are hard-core resources for practitioners like you.

ESSENTIAL REFERENCE

Smart, Like You

The *Essential Reference* series from New Riders provides answers when you know what you want to do but need to know how to do it. Each title skips extraneous material and assumes a strong base of knowledge. These are indispensable books for the practitioner who wants to find specific features of a technology quickly and efficiently. Avoiding fluff and basic material, these books present solutions in an innovative, clean format—and at a great value.

MCSE CERTIFICATION

Engineered for Test Success

New Riders offers a complete line of test preparation materials to help you achieve your certification. With books like the *MCSE Training Guide*, and software like the acclaimed *MCSE Complete* and the revolutionary *ExamGear*, New Riders offers comprehensive products built by experienced professionals who have passed the exams and instructed hundreds of candidates.

Books for Networking Professionals

Windows NT Titles

Windows NT TCP/IP
By Karanjit S. Siyan, Ph.D.
1st Edition
460 pages, $29.99
ISBN: 1-56205-887-8

If you're still looking for good documentation on Microsoft TCP/IP, look no further—this is your book. *Windows NT TCP/IP* cuts through the complexities to provide the most informative and complete reference on Windows-based TCP/IP. Concepts essential to TCP/IP administration are related to the practical use of Microsoft TCP/IP in a real-world networking environment. The book begins by covering TCP/IP architecture and advanced installation and configuration issues. Then it moves on to routing with TCP/IP, DHCP Management, and WINS/DNS Name Resolution.

Windows NT DNS
By Michael Masterson, Herman Knief, Scott Vinick, and Eric Roul
1st Edition
340 pages, $29.99
ISBN: 1-56205-943-2

Have you ever opened a Windows NT book looking for detailed information about DNS only to discover that it doesn't even begin to scratch the surface? DNS is probably one of the most complicated subjects for NT administrators, and there are few books on the market that address it in detail. This book answers your most complex DNS questions, focusing on the implementation of the Domain Name System within Windows NT. Written from the viewpoints of experienced Windows NT professionals, this book covers the details of how DNS functions within NT and then explores specific interactions with critical network components. Proven procedures to design and set up DNS are demonstrated. You'll also find coverage of related topics, such as maintenance, security, and troubleshooting.

Windows NT Registry:
A Settings Reference
By Sandra Osborne
1st Edition
550 pages, $29.99
ISBN: 1-56205-941-6

The NT Registry can be a very powerful tool for those capable of using it wisely. Unfortunately, there is little information regarding the NT Registry due to Microsoft's insistence that their source code be kept secret. This book covers critical issues and settings used for configuring network protocols, including NWLink, PTP, TCP/IP, and DHCP. It discusses the problems related to a particular component and then discusses settings, which are the actual changes necessary for implementing robust solutions.

Windows NT Performance:
Monitoring, Benchmarking, and Tuning
By Mark T. Edmead
and Paul Hinsberg
1st Edition
288 pages, $29.99
ISBN: 1-56205-942-4

Performance monitoring is a little like pre-ventive medicine for the administrator: No one enjoys a checkup, but it's a good thing to do on a regular basis. This book helps you focus on the critical aspects of improving the performance of your NT system by showing you how to monitor the system, implement benchmarking, and tune your network. The book is organized by resource components, which makes it easy to use as a reference tool.

Windows NT Terminal Server and Citrix MetaFrame
By Ted Harwood
1st Edition
400 pages, $29.99
ISBN: 1-56205-944-0

It's no surprise that most administration headaches revolve around integration with other networks and clients. This book addresses these types of real-world issues on a case-by-case basis, giving tools and advice for solving each problem. The author also offers the real nuts and bolts of thin client administration on multiple systems, covering relevant issues, such as installation, configuration, network connection, management, and application distribution.

Windows NT Power Toolkit
By Stu Sjouwerman and Ed Tittel
1st Edition
800 pages, $49.99
ISBN: 0-7357-0922-X

This book covers the analysis, tuning, optimization, automation, enhancement, maintenance, and troubleshooting of Windows NT Server 4.0 and Windows NT Workstation 4.0. In most cases, the two operating systems overlap completely and are discussed together. Where the two systems diverge, each platform is covered separately. This advanced title comprises a task-oriented treatment of the Windows NT 4 environment. By concen-trating on the use of operating system tools and utilities, Resource Kit elements, and selected third-party tuning, analysis, optimization, and productivity tools, this book will show its readers how to carry out everyday and advanced tasks.

Windows NT Network Management
Reducing Total Cost of Ownership
By Anil Desai
1st Edition
450 pages, $34.99
ISBN: 1-56205-946-7

Administering a Windows NT network is kind of like trying to herd cats—an impossible task characterized by constant motion, exhausting labor, and lots of hairballs. Author Anil Desai knows all about it; he's a consulting engineer for Sprint Paranet, which specializes in Windows NT implementation, integra-tion, and management. So, we asked him to put together a concise manual of the best practices—a book of tools and ideas that other administrators can turn to again and again in managing their own NT networks.

Planning for Windows 2000

By Eric K. Cone, Jon Boggs, and Sergio Perez
1st Edition
400 pages, $29.99
ISBN: 0-7357-0048-6

Windows 2000 is poised to be one of the largest and most important software releases of the next decade, and you are charged with planning, testing, and deploying it in your enterprise. Are you ready? With this book, you will be. *Planning for Windows 2000* lets you know what the upgrade hurdles will be, informs you how to clear them, guides you through effective Active Directory design, and presents you with detailed rollout procedures. Eric K. Cone, Jon Boggs, and Sergio Perez give you the benefit of their extensive experiences as Windows 2000 Rapid Deployment Program members by sharing problems and solutions they've encountered on the job.

Inside Windows 2000 Server

By William Boswell
1st Edition
1533 pages, $49.99
ISBN: 1-56205-929-7

Finally, a totally new edition of New Riders' best-selling *Inside Windows NT Server 4.* Taking the author-driven, no-nonsense approach we pioneered with our *Landmark* books, New Riders proudly offers something unique for Windows 2000 administrators—an interesting, discriminating book on Windows 2000 Server written by someone who can anticipate your situation and give you workarounds that won't leave a system unstable or sluggish.

BackOffice Titles

Implementing Exchange Server

By Doug Hauger, Marywynne Leon, and William C. Wade III
1st Edition
400 pages, $29.99
ISBN: 1-56205-931-9

If you're interested in connectivity and maintenance issues for Exchange Server, this book is for you. Exchange's power lies in its capability to be connected to multiple email subsystems to create a "universal email backbone." It's not unusual to have several different and complex systems all connected via email gateways, including Lotus Notes or cc:Mail, Microsoft Mail, legacy mainframe systems, and Internet mail. This book covers all of the problems and issues associated with getting an integrated system running smoothly, and it addresses troubleshooting and diagnosis of email problems with an eye toward prevention and best practices.

Exchange System Administration

By Janice Rice Howd
1st Edition
300 pages, $34.99
ISBN: 0-7357-0081-8

Okay, you've got your Exchange Server installed and connected; now what? Email administration is one of the most critical networking jobs, and Exchange can be particularly troublesome in large, heterogeneous environments. Janice Howd, a noted consultant and teacher with over a decade of email administration experience, has put together this advanced, concise handbook for daily, periodic, and emergency administration. With in-depth coverage of topics like managing disk resources, replication, and disaster recovery, this is the one reference every Exchange administrator needs.

SQL Server System Administration

By Sean Baird, Chris Miller, et al.
1st Edition
352 pages, $29.99
ISBN: 1-56205-955-6

How often does your SQL Server go down during the day when everyone wants to access the data? Do you spend most of your time being a "report monkey" for your coworkers and bosses? *SQL Server System Administration* helps you keep data consistently available to your users. This book omits introductory information. The authors don't spend time explaining queries and how they work. Instead, they focus on the information you can't get anywhere else, like how to choose the correct replication topology and achieve high availability of information.

Internet Information Services Administration

By Kelli Adam
1st Edition,
200 pages, $29.99
ISBN: 0-7357-0022-2

Are the new Internet technologies in Internet Information Services giving you headaches? Does protecting security on the Web take up all of your time? Then this is the book for you. With hands-on configuration training, advanced study of the new protocols the most recent version of IIS, and detailed instructions on authenticating users with the new Certificate Server and implementing and

managing the new e-commerce features, *Internet Information Services Administration* gives you the real-life solutions you need. This definitive resource prepares you for the release of Windows 2000 by giving you detailed advice on working with Microsoft Management Console, which was first used by IIS.

SMS 2 Administration

By Michael Lubanski and Darshan Doshi
1st Edition
350 pages, $39.99
ISBN: 0-7357-0082-6

Microsoft's new version of its Systems Management Server (SMS) is starting to turn heads. Although complex, it allows administrators to lower their total cost of ownership and more efficiently manage clients, applications, and support operations. So if your organization is using or implementing SMS, you'll need some expert advice. Darshan Doshi and Michael Lubanski can help you get the most bang for your buck with insight, expert tips, and real-world examples. Darshan and Michael are consultants specializing in SMS and have worked with Microsoft on one of the most complex SMS rollouts in the world, involving 32 countries, 15 languages, and thousands of clients.

UNIX/Linux Titles

Solaris Essential Reference
By John P. Mulligan
1st Edition,
300 pages, $24.95
ISBN: 0-7357-0023-0

Looking for the fastest, easiest way to find the Solaris command you need? Need a few pointers on shell scripting? How about advanced administration tips and sound, practical expertise on security issues? Are you looking for trustworthy information about available third-party software packages that will enhance your operating system? Author John Mulligan—creator of the popular "Unofficial Guide to The Solaris™ Operating Environment" Web site (sun.icsnet.com)—delivers all that and more in one attractive, easy-to-use reference book. With clear and concise instructions on how to perform important administration and management tasks and key information on powerful commands and advanced topics, *Solaris Essential Reference* is the book you need when you know what you want to do and only need to know how.

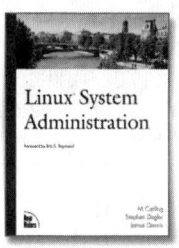

Linux System Administration
By M Carling,
Stephen Degler,
and James Dennis
1st Edition
450 pages, $29.99
ISBN: 1-56205-934-3

As an administrator, you probably feel that most of your time and energy is spent in endless firefighting. If your network has become a fragile quilt of temporary patches and work-arounds, this book is for you. Have you had trouble sending or receiving email lately? Are you looking for a way to keep your network running smoothly with enhanced performance? Are your users always hankering for more storage, services, and speed? *Linux System Administration* advises you on the many intricacies of maintaining a secure, stable system. In this definitive work, the authors address all the issues related to system administration, from adding users and managing file permissions, to Internet services and Web hosting, to recovery planning and security. This book fulfills the need for expert advice that will ensure a trouble-free Linux environment.

GTK+/Gnome Application Development
By Havoc Pennington
1st Edition
492 pages, $39.99
ISBN: 0-7357-0078-8

This title is for the reader who is conversant with the C programming language and UNIX/Linux development. It provides detailed and solution-oriented information designed to meet the needs of programmers and application developers using the GTK+/Gnome libraries. Coverage complements existing GTK+/Gnome documentation, going into more depth on pivotal issues, such as uncovering the GTK+ object system, working with the event loop, managing the Gdk substrate, writing custom widgets, and mastering GnomeCanvas.

Developing Linux Applications with GTK+ and GDK
By Eric Harlow
1st Edition
490 pages, $34.99
ISBN: 0-7357-0021-4

We all know that Linux is one of the most powerful and solid operating systems in existence. And as the success of Linux grows, there is an increasing interest in developing applications with graphical user interfaces that take advantage of the power of Linux. In this book, software developer Eric Harlow gives you an indispensable development handbook focusing on the GTK+ toolkit. More than an overview of the elements of application or GUI design, this is a hands-on book that delves deeply into the technology. With in-depth material on the various GUI programming tools and loads of examples, this book's unique focus will give you the information you need to design and launch professional-quality applications.

Linux Essential Reference
By Ed Petron
1st Edition
350 pages, $24.95
ISBN: 0-7357-0852-5

This book is all about getting things done as quickly and efficiently as possible by providing a structured organization for the plethora of available Linux information. We can sum it up in one word—value. This book has it all: concise instructions

on how to perform key administration tasks, advanced information on configuration, shell scripting, hardware management, systems management, data tasks, automation, and tons of other useful information. All of this coupled with an unique navigational structure and a great price. This book truly provides groundbreaking information for the growing community of advanced Linux professionals.

Lotus Notes and Domino Titles

Domino System Administration
By Rob Kirkland, CLP, CLI
1st Edition
850 pages, $49.99
ISBN: 1-56205-948-3

Your boss has just announced that you will be upgrading to the newest version of Notes and Domino when it ships. How are you supposed to get this new system installed, configured, and rolled out to all your end users? You understand how Lotus Notes works—you've been administering it for years. What you need is a concise, practical explanation of the new features and how to make some of the advanced stuff work smoothly by someone like you, who has worked with the product for years and understands what you need to know. *Domino System Administration* is the answer—the first book on Domino that attacks the technology at the professional level with practical, hands-on assistance to get Domino running in your organization.

Lotus Notes & Domino Essential Reference
By Tim Bankes, CLP
and Dave Hatter, CLP, MCP
1st Edition
650 pages, $45.00
ISBN: 0-7357-0007-9

You're in a bind because you've been asked to design and program a new database in Notes for an important client who will keep track of and itemize a myriad of inventory and shipping data. The client wants a user-friendly interface that won't sacrifice speed or functionality. You are experienced (and could develop this application in your sleep) but feel you need something to facilitate your creative and technical abilities—something to perfect your programming skills. The answer is waiting for you: *Lotus Notes & Domino Essential Reference*. It's compact and simply designed. It's loaded with information. All of the objects, classes, functions, and methods are listed. It shows you the object hierarchy and the relationship between each one. It's perfect for you. Problem solved.

Networking Titles

Cisco Router Configuration & Troubleshooting
By Mark Tripod
1st Edition
300 pages, $34.99
ISBN: 0-7357-0024-9

Want the real story on making your Cisco routers run like a dream? Why not pick up a copy of *Cisco Router Configuration & Troubleshooting* and see what Mark Tripod of Exodus Communications has to say? They're the folks responsible for making some of the largest sites on the Net scream, like Amazon.com, Hotmail, USAToday, Geocities, and Sony. In this book, they provide advanced configuration issues, sprinkled with advice and preferred practices. You won't see a general overview on TCP/IP. This book addresses more meaty issues, like security, monitoring, traffic management, and more. In the troubleshooting section, the author provides a unique methodology and lots of sample problems to illustrate. By providing real-world insight and examples instead of rehashing Cisco's documentation, Mark gives network administrators information they can start using today.

Network Intrusion Detection: An Analyst's Handbook
By Stephen Northcutt
1st Edition
267 pages, $39.99
ISBN: 0-7357-0868-1

Get answers and solutions from someone who has been in the trenches. The author, Stephen Northcutt, original developer of the Shadow intrusion detection system and former Director of the United States Navy's Information System Security Office at the Naval Security Warfare Center, gives his expertise to intrusion detection specialists, security analysts, and consultants responsible for setting up and maintaining an effective defense against network security attacks.

Understanding Data Communications, Sixth Edition

By Gilbert Held
6th Edition
600 pages, $39.99
ISBN: 0-7357-0036-2

Updated from the highly successful Fifth
Edition, this book explains how data
communications systems and their various
hardware and software components work.
More than an entry-level book, it
approaches the material in textbook
format, addressing the complex issues
involved in internetworking today. A great
reference book for the experienced networking professional that is written by the
noted networking authority, Gilbert Held.

Other Books By New Riders

Windows Technologies

Internet Information Services
Administration
0-7357-0022-2

SMS 2 Administration
0-7357-0082-6

Planning for Windows 2000
0-7357-0048-6

Windows NT Network Management:
Reducing Total Cost of Ownership
1-56205-946-7

Windows NT DNS
1-56205-943-2

Windows NT Performance Monitoring, Benchmarking, and Tuning
1-56205-942-4

Windows NT Power Toolkit
0-7357-0922-X

Windows NT Registry: A Settings
Reference
1-56205-941-6

Windows NT TCP/IP
1-56205-887-8

Windows NT Terminal Server and
Citrix MetaFrame
1-56205-944-0

Implementing Exchange Server
1-56205-931-9

Inside Window 2000 Server
1-56205-929-7

Exchange Server Administration
0-7357-0081-8

SQL Server System Administration
1-56205-955-6

Windows 2000 Active Directory
0-7357-0870-3

Networking

Understanding Directory Services
0-7357-0910-6

Understanding the Network
0-7357-0977-7

Domino System Administration
1-56205-948-3

Cisco Router Configuration and
Troubleshooting
0-7357-0024-9

Understanding Data
Communications, Sixth Edition
0-7357-0036-2

Network Intrusion Detection: An
Analyst's Handbook
0-7357-0868-1

Certification

A+ Certification TestPrep
1-56205-892-4

A+ Certification Training Guide, 2E
0-7357-0907-6

A+ Fast Track
0-7357-0028-1

MCSD Fast Track: Visual Basic 6,
Exam 70-176
0-7357-0019-2

MCSE Fast Track: Internet
Information Server 4
1-56205-936-X

MCSE Fast Track: Networking
Essentials
1-56205-939-4

MCSE Fast Track: TCP/IP
1-56205-937-8

MCSD Fast Track: VB 6, Exam 70-175
0-7357-0018-4

MCSE Fast Track: Windows 98
0-7357-0016-8

MCSE Fast Track: Windows NT
Server 4
1-56205-935-1

MCSE Fast Track: Windows NT
Server 4 Enterprise
1-56205-940-8

MCSE Fast Track: Windows NT
Workstation 4
1-56205-938-6

MCSE Simulation Guide: Windows
NT Server 4 Enterprise
1-56205-914-9

MCSE Simulation Guide: Windows
NT Workstation 4
1-56205-925-4

MCSE TestPrep: Networking
Essentials, Second Edition
0-7357-0010-9

MCSE TestPrep: TCP/IP, Second
Edition
0-7357-0025-7

MCSE TestPrep: Windows 98
1-56205-922-X

MCSE TestPrep: Windows NT
Server 4 Enterprise, Second Edition
0-7357-0009-5

MCSE TestPrep: Windows NT
Server 4, Second Edition
0-7357-0012-5

MCSE TestPrep: Windows NT
Workstation 4, Second Edition
0-7357-0008-7

MCSD TestPrep: VB 6 Exams
0-7357-0032-X

MCSE Training Guide: Networking
Essentials, Second Edition
1-56205-919-X

MCSE Training Guide: TCP/IP,
Second Edition
1-56205-920-3

MCSE Training Guide: Windows 98
1-56205-890-8

MCSE Training Guide: Windows
NT Server 4, Second Edition
1-56205-916-5

MCSE Training Guide: Windows
NT Server Enterprise, Second
Edition
1-56205-917-3

MCSE Training Guide: Windows
NT Workstation 4, Second Edition
1-56205-918-1

MCSD Training Guide: VB 6 Exams
0-7357-0002-8

Graphics

Inside 3D Studio MAX 2, Volume I
1-56205-857-6

Inside 3D Studio MAX 2, Volume
II: Modeling and Materials
1-56205-864-9

Inside 3D Studio MAX 2, Volume
III: Animation
1-56205-865-7

Inside 3D Studio MAX 2 Resource
Kit
1-56205-953-X

Inside AutoCAD 14, Limited
Edition
1-56205-898-3

Inside Softimage 3D
1-56205-885-1

HTML Web Magic, Second Edition
1-56830-475-7

Dynamic HTML Web Magic
1-56830-421-8

Designing Web Graphics.3
1-56205-949-1

Illustrator 8 Magic
1-56205-952-1

Inside trueSpace 4
1-56205-957-2

Inside Adobe Photoshop 5
1-56205-884-3

Inside Adobe Photoshop 5, Limited
Edition
1-56205-951-3

Photoshop 5 Artistry
1-56205-895-9

Photoshop 5 Type Magic
1-56830-465-X

Photoshop 5 Web Magic
1-56205-913-0

We Want to Know What You Think

To better serve you, we would like your opinion on the content and quality of this book. Please complete this card, and mail it to us or fax it to 317-581-4663.

Name _____

Address _____

City_____State_____Zip _____

Phone _____

Email Address _____

Occupation _____

Operating system(s) that you use _____

What influenced your purchase of this book?
- ❑ Recommendation
- ❑ Cover Design
- ❑ Table of Contents
- ❑ Index
- ❑ Magazine Review
- ❑ Advertisement
- ❑ New Riders' Reputation
- ❑ Author Name

How would you rate the contents of this book?
- ❑ Excellent
- ❑ Very Good
- ❑ Good
- ❑ Fair
- ❑ Below Average
- ❑ Poor

How do you plan to use this book?
- ❑ Quick Reference
- ❑ Self-Training
- ❑ Classroom
- ❑ Other

What do you like most about this book?
Check all that apply.
- ❑ Content
- ❑ Writing Style
- ❑ Accuracy
- ❑ Examples
- ❑ Listings
- ❑ Design
- ❑ Index
- ❑ Page Count
- ❑ Price
- ❑ Illustrations

What do you like least about this book?
Check all that apply.
- ❑ Content
- ❑ Writing Style
- ❑ Accuracy
- ❑ Examples
- ❑ Listings
- ❑ Design
- ❑ Index
- ❑ Page Count
- ❑ Price
- ❑ Illustrations

What would be a useful follow-up book for you? _____

Where did you purchase this book?_____
_____

Can you name a similar book that you like better than this one, or one that is as good? Why?
_____
_____

How many New Riders books do you own? _____

What are your favorite computer books?_____
_____

What other titles would you like to see us develop? _____
_____

Any comments for us? _____
_____
_____
_____

Windows 2000 Routing and Remote Access Service:
0-7357-0951-3

www.newriders.com   •   Fax   317-581-4663

Fold here and tape to mail

- -

New Riders Publishing
201 W. 103rd St.
Indianapolis, IN 46290

 # How to Contact Us

Visit Our Web Site

www.newriders.com

On our Web site you'll find information about our other books, authors, tables of contents, indexes, and book errata.

Email Us

Contact us at this address:

nrfeedback@newriders.com

- If you have comments or questions about this book
- To report errors that you have found in this book
- If you have a book proposal to submit or are interested in writing for New Riders
- If you would like to have an author kit sent to you
- If you are an expert in a computer topic or technology and are interested in being a technical editor who reviews manuscripts for technical accuracy

nrfeedback@newriders.com

- To find a distributor in your area, please contact our international department at this address.

nrmedia@newriders.com

- For instructors from educational institutions who want to preview New Riders books for classroom use. Email should include your name, title, school, department, address, phone number, office days/hours, text in use, and enrollment, along with your request for desk/examination copies and/or additional information.
- For members of the media who are interested in reviewing copies of New Riders books. Send your name, mailing address, and email address, along with the name of the publication or Web site you work for.

Write to Us

New Riders Publishing

201 W. 103rd St.

Indianapolis, IN 46290-1097

Call Us

Toll-free (800) 571-5840 + 9 + 4511

If outside U.S. (317) 581-3500. Ask for New Riders.

Fax Us

(317) 581-4663